THE LIFE AND DEATH OF A NEWSPAPER

BOOKS BY THE AUTHOR

THE DAY BEFORE YESTERDAY. (Methuen, 21s.)
'Enchanting.'—*New Statesman.* 'Delightful.'—*Observer.* 'Fresh and vivid.'—*Spectator.*
'A rich feast, the very essence of a vanished epoch.'—*Literary Guide.* 'Revealing.'—
Manchester Guardian. 'Arresting, engrossing.'—*Daily Telegraph.* 'More than the
autobiography of a Grand Old Man. A titbit on every page.'—*Edinburgh Evening News*

*THE STORY OF THE 'PALL MALL GAZETTE', OF ITS FIRST EDITOR,
FREDERICK GREENWOOD, AND OF ITS FOUNDER, GEORGE MURRAY
SMITH.* (Oxford University Press, 21s.)
'Engrossing and rewarding. New sidelights on the men, institutions and events of the
19th century.'—*New Statesman*
'Will be read for its wide range of literary anecdotage.'—*Manchester Guardian*
'An irresistible appeal.'—*Publisher's Circular*
'Altogether admirable.'—*Literary Guide*

THE FOUNDATIONS OF JAPAN, 6000 *MILES IN ITS RURAL DISTRICTS
AS A BASIS FOR A BETTER UNDERSTANDING OF THE JAPANESE
PEOPLE.*—(Murray, 24s.)
'Scholarly, exhaustive and delightfully readable, of great and lasting value, fearlessly and
impartially true.'—*Observer*
'Very readable and candid; the work of an honest observer.'—*Spectator*
'Only an unusual visitor could have done it.'—*London Mercury*

ENGLAND'S GREEN AND PLEASANT LAND. (Cape, two editions, 6s. Penguin,
two editions extended, 1s. 6d.)
'The vision of the end of an age, of permanent historical value. The author is of the great
legend and tradition. One cannot refrain from admiration at the extraordinary truth,
sincerity and appeal, his almost scientific accuracy, combining insight and humour, and
his passionate and fierce desire for the welfare of the people among whom he lives,
proclaimed almost in the spirit of the Hebrew prophets.'—*The Rt. Hon. Charles
Masterman in the New Statesman and Nation*
'Speaks straightly of things that Miss Mitford hides and greater realists foolishly slur
and cloak.'—*Observer*
'Disturbing and salutary; strongly to be recommended to the complacent and self-
satisfied.'—*Spectator*
'Seeks and finds the deeper meanings.'—*The Times Literary Supplement*
'What Cobbett did for an earlier generation, if not more effectively.'—*Publishers'
Circular*

FAITH AND WORKS IN FLEET STREET. (Hodder and Stoughton, 6s.)
'It has his characteristic virtue, we never know what he is going to say next.'—*The Times
Literary Supplement*
'Very wise essays, salutary reading.'—*Manchester Guardian*

THE COUNTRYMAN BOOK. (Odhams, 10s. 6d.)
'An ideal bedside book.'—*The Times Literary Supplement*
'Very attractive.'—*Sunday Times*

*THE COUNTRYMAN'S BREAKFAST POSER AND TOWNSMAN'S RURAL
REMEMBRANCER.* (Oxford University Press, 8s. 6d.)
'The perfect present.'—*Countryman*

OUT OF PRINT. 'The People of China', 'A Free Farmer in a Free State (Holland)',
'The Land Problem', 'The Small Farm', 'Country Cottages', 'Poultry Farming,
Some Facts and Some Conclusions', 'The Case for the Goat', 'The Townsman's
Farm', 'Sugar Beet, Some Facts and Some Illusions', 'A Study in Rural Therapeutics',
'The Story of the Women's Institute Movement', 'The Dying Peasant and the Future
of his Sons', 'Japan, Great Britain and the World', 'A Little Lesson in the English
Character', 'The Ignoble Warrior', 'The Country Citizen', &c.

JOHN, VISCOUNT MORLEY

From the portrait by A. Stuart, 1925, in the possession of Mr.
Guy Morley

THE LIFE AND DEATH
OF A NEWSPAPER

An Account of the Temperaments, Perturbations
and Achievements of

JOHN MORLEY, W. T. STEAD, E. T. COOK,

HARRY CUST, J. L. GARVIN

and three other Editors of the *Pall Mall Gazette*

How one of them went to gaol, one became a Viscount, two were knighted,
one gained a marble monument, one edited Ruskin in thirty-nine volumes,
another the *Encyclopædia Britannica*; the engaging conversations they had in
high places and with authors, and the entertaining letters they got; with their
animated relations with their proprietors, Henry Yates Thompson, William
Waldorf Astor (first Viscount Astor) and 'Mr. Newnes of *Tit-Bits*'

by

J. W. ROBERTSON SCOTT
C.H., HON. M.A. (OXON)

With 12 Plates and 47 Illustrations in the text

'He descended so low as to become the editor of a newspaper'—*Told of Dr. Dodd, Dr. Johnson's acquaintance who was
hanged*

METHUEN & CO. LTD.
36 Essex Street, Strand, London, W.C.2

First published in 1952

CATALOGUE NO. 5413/U

PRINTED IN GREAT BRITAIN BY
THE CAMELOT PRESS LTD., LONDON AND SOUTHAMPTON

To
the Memory of
The Bewildered Proprietors
whose Story
is as interesting as
their Editors'

CONTENTS

CONTENTS

The Pall Mall Gazette *Goes Gay*
HARRY CUST

The Bearers at the Funeral
SIR DOUGLAS STRAIGHT, J. L. GARVIN, F. J. HIGGINBOTTOM AND DONALD M. SUTHERLAND

ILLUSTRATIONS

PLATES

IN THE TEXT

THE STORY TO BE TOLD

EDITORS IN BONDS. Well-brought-up little boys are taught not to keep on saying 'I'. But there are men whom even 'I' does not content. Like Queen Victoria, they say 'We'. They are, of course, Editors. This book is about several daily paper Editors who were among the most distinguished of their time.

The fact that more newspapers are bought in Great Britain per head of the population than in any other country[1] gives our Press, even with the competition of fourteen million Wireless and Television sets, an enormous influence on political and social opinion. It is important, therefore, that more should be known not only about Editors, their training, skills and temperament and the conditions in which their work is done but about the personalities and resources of Newspaper Proprietors.

With the large capital now required to establish a daily newspaper,[2] it is rarer than it was for an Editor to be completely unfettered. The degree of freedom he possesses he owes to his force of character, his knowledge and the strength of his convictions. The man who provides or controls the money with which a paper is started or continued is a person with notions, a will and possibly ambitions of his own. So it comes about that some of an Editor's thought must be spared to accommodating himself to the commercial arrangement under which he discharges his duties. He may have an uneasy time of it. The rate at which Editors often succeed one another points to this.

In the following pages a painstaking effort is made to describe, on a basis of knowledge, the adventures of the Editors and Proprietors of a daily paper of a particular tradition, quality and size.[3] It was the *Pall Mall Gazette*, a London evening journal remarkable for the influence it exerted with a small circulation and no profits.

With three of the Editors I had the satisfaction of working. From another, John Morley (afterwards Viscount Morley), I had a gracious letter when, in youthful admiration of him, I unblushingly offered myself as his secretary.

[1] 'Newspaper circulations are smaller in the United States than in this country; the scale of distribution there is 354 copies a thousand of population, compared with 596 in this country'.—*The Times*, Feb. 5, 1952.
[2] 'It is not a happy thought that if some new movement in politics developed it would not be able to start a national daily paper.'—R. J. Cruikshank, Editor of the *News Chronicle*, May 10, 1952.
[3] A convenient 13½ inches high by about 10 inches wide. In the latter part of its life, the *Pall Mall Gazette* doubled the area of its pages.

In an autobiographical volume of mine which came out last year mention is made of how I was invited up to London by the most widely remembered of the *Pall Mall Gazette* Editors, W. T. Stead, to join its staff, and stayed with the paper (and its successor, the *Westminster Gazette*) for ten years.[1] As the last survivor but one of Stead's staff,[2] the duty seems to be laid upon me, even in what used to be regarded as old age—I am eighty-six—to do what I can to pass on an impression of the paper's remarkable character and achievement. Nothing of just its class and appeal remains in London.

THE QUALIFICATIONS OF EDITORS AND PROPRIETORS. The qualifications I offer for writing about the Editors and Proprietors whose characters, abilities, achievements and experiences are set forth in the following pages are that, one way or another, I have come to know a good deal about them and that, beyond my protracted Press career I happen to have founded and edited, in succession, a monthly review and a quarterly review, both of which gained some recognition. I edited the quarterly (as my own proprietor) for its first twenty years, and my old chiefs would be entertained to know that when I sold it to *Punch* it had a larger circulation than the daily on which we served ever reached.[3]

Many reasonably instructed people are curiously ill-informed about the relationship of Editors and Proprietors. How do these men come to be in their places of influence? What exactly are their qualifications for their positions? How in practice is the control they exert shared? This book, in its endeavour to answer these questions, must be not only a story of newspapers but a story of human nature, Editorial and Proprietorial. My hope is that what I have remembered and have been gathering together for many years may not only be of interest and service to newspaper readers but of substantial use to young men and women who are minded to enter journalism or are making their way in it.

*

THE FOUNDATION OF THE *PALL MALL GAZETTE*. In a book of the year before last I told the story of the gallant first Editor of the *Pall Mall Gazette*, Frederick Greenwood, and of George Murray Smith, his Proprietor, a narrative of outstanding journalism by one of them and of conscientious book production (for the honoured firm of Smith & Elder) by the other, in a frock-

[1] *The Day Before Yesterday* (Methuen, 1951).

[2] Of the Stead-Cook period in Northumberland Street there survives, as far as I can learn, only Hilaire Belloc, who gave some help to Stead for a short time while I was on the paper and, alas, has not been able to cheer us with anything for a long time.

[3] The bilingual *New East* in Tokyo and the half-crown *Countryman* in the Cotswolds, which has a sale of close on 80,000 copies.

coated, oil- and gas-lighted world without telephones, typewriters, wireless or aeroplanes, the United States a fortnight away, Emperors and Kings all over Europe, and Queen Victoria, Empress of India, defending the faith in quite a lot of mundane things we now smile at.[1]

When in 1865,[2] a year before I was born, the *Pall Mall Gazette* was established, it surprised people. This was because it named itself after a mythical paper, 'written by gentlemen for gentlemen', in Thackeray's *Pendennis*. The owner and name-giver of the actual journal won distinction in other fields than journalism. In one of them he made a million out of a mineral water. Then he laid out £150,000 of it in launching the *Dictionary of National Biography* and dropped £70,000. He also started the *Cornhill Magazine*.

The idea of an evening paper on the lines on which the *Pall Mall Gazette* was to be edited, with high intelligence, complete integrity, steadfast patriotism and, by present standards, small sales, was Greenwood's. A legend in the office in my time was that, in the early days, a message would sometimes come down a speaking-tube from the manager to the printers instructing them to 'work off another quire' (that is, print another two dozen copies!).

Among the things Greenwood did was to secure for Great Britain the Suez Canal shares (which, at a cost of four millions, have brought seventy to our Chancellors of the Exchequer). He never mentioned his service to the nation in his paper but let *The Times* have the news! (The limited claim of Beaconsfield to the honour of the transaction was disposed of in two chapters of my book. They appeared without correction from any reader in the *Quarterly Review*.)[3]

GEORGE MURRAY SMITH. The *Pall Mall Gazette* never recouped the outlay upon it, but Greenwood and his Proprietor had an honourable part in moulding the character of the journalism of their time and in setting a standard for the future. Smith was politically an easy-going Liberal, as were so many good fellows of his day. Greenwood himself had always been that ingenious combination, a Liberal-Conservative or Conservative-Liberal; he called himself an Independent Conservative. Many Conservatives groaned over the pointed criticisms and political waywardness of

---

[1] *The Story of the 'Pall Mall Gazette', of its first Editor, Frederick Greenwood, and of its Founder, George Murray Smith* (Oxford University Press, 1950).

[2] The year of the assassination of Lincoln and associated with Mendel's discovery and the introduction of antiseptic surgery. It was before the first Ministries of Disraeli and Gladstone and before the Franco-Prussian War, Marx's *Das Kapital*, the establishment of Girton, the opening of the Suez Canal, and Huxley's invention of the word 'agnostic'.

[3] He fully persuaded the Queen. See her latest biographer's quotation from a letter, 'It is *entirely* the doing of Mr. Disraeli' (italics Her Majesty's).—*Queen Victoria*, Roger Fulford (Collins, 1951).

B

his leading articles. The bee buzzing in the bonnet of Liberal editors of his day was 'Dizzy'. Greenwood warred with them as an unrelenting Anti-Gladstonian. In his view there were no limits to the machinations and political sinfulness of that 'Grand Old Man' at Hawarden. Smith's Liberal sentiments cannot be said to have been aglow, and, after fifteen years of the *Pall Mall*, he got tired of its *idée fixe*. What had become, in Leslie Stephen's words, 'the most thoroughgoing of Jingo newspapers' brought him no dividends, he received no knighthood, much less a peerage, and he had many business irons in the fire. So he gave the stormy petrel of Northumberland Street to a son-in-law.[1]

*

HENRY YATES THOMPSON AND JOHN MORLEY. Of this heir to trouble, Henry Yates Thompson, a man out of the common in many ways, fortunate in his education, his opportunities, his wife and his financial circumstances, little has been known. Something about his complex character, his praiseworthy connection with the early movement for a better Anglo-American understanding, and certain public benefactions of illuminated MSS. of high value is told in this book by the kindness of Sir Sydney Cockerell and Sir Christopher Chancellor, general manager of Reuters, and Lady Chancellor.

Yates Thompson was, for a time at any rate, more of a Liberal than Smith, and the *Pall Mall* was now 'in the hands of the Liberals'. Greenwood resigned and within a fortnight started the second of the *Gazettes*, the completely Conservative *St. James's*.[2] In his place as Editor of the *Pall Mall* Yates Thompson had the wit to appoint John Morley. This was the first *volte face* of a newspaper which was, to start with, of Greenwood's special politics, then Liberal, then Conservative again.

Greenwood, besides his pen of distinction, had judgment in the choice of contributors and a quality of character and temperament which attached them to him. He printed in the *Pall Mall* the work of the chief authors of his day and they were glad to be in his columns. The paper was now to be edited by one of these eminent writers. 'A cautious Whig by temperament, a sound Liberal by

---

[1] In passing along the Strand from Charing Cross Station to Trafalgar Square it is the narrow street on the left, next the Grand Hotel. 'Northumberland Street' came to be synonymous with the *Pall Mall Gazette*, as is Printing House Square with *The Times*. In Northumberland Street the offices were on the Strand side of the Northumberland Arms. Where the *Pall Mall* was once able to give the Clubs something to think about of an afternoon, there now stand the lodgings of the Junior Constitutional Club staff. See also page 47.

[2] The third was the *Westminster Gazette*, the story of which, with, more briefly, that of the *St James's Gazette*, will be among the contents of a later autobiographical book. So little is known of Greenwood that a leading review this year called him 'Sir'.

training and a thorough Radical by observation and experience' is what Morley called himself. I bring together what I have read, heard and discovered about a man who, remarkable to his generation, yet speaketh in his writing and in a life lived at a high level of mental cultivation and personal discipline.

I am glad that, in relation to a tragic incident, the secret of which one of his intimates has written 'can never be told', it is now possible, for the first time, to publish the honourable details, for nothing in Morley's life became him so well as what he did in so searching a trial.

Mr. F. W. Hirst's *Early Life and Letters of John Morley* and Brigadier-General Morgan's *John, Viscount Morley*, are both out of print and only accessible in libraries, and I am under obligation to their authors not only for quotations but also for the letters they have written to me. I have also had the advantage of reading several unpublished Morley letters, and Mr. Guy Morley, his uncle's literary legatee, has kindly made me free of all the writing under his control. A letter on pages 36 and 37 is printed for the first time.

*

WILLIAM THOMAS STEAD. 'That great journalist and earnest Puritan', as Mr. E. C. Bentley justly calls Stead, the acknowledged inventor of the New Journalism in its worthiest form,[1] as I wrote in two earlier books, did many memorable things. He sent General Gordon of the Sudan back to the Sudan, and the Khartoum Expedition followed—and Gordon's death. By urging 'two keels to one' in the *Pall Mall Gazette* 'Truth about the Navy' he was acknowledged by the puissant Admiral Fisher to have added substantially to our naval strength.[2] He sacrificed legateeship to the millionaire Cecil Rhodes in order to fight what he considered to be his misconceived policies. He was the courageous author of 'The Maiden Tribute of Modern Babylon', the most sensational and one of the most serviceable feats in newspaper history, for it raised the 'age of consent' from a pitiful thirteen to sixteen years. Over a technical slip, for which nobody of repute ever thought of blaming him, he went to gaol and, as an honoured first-class misdemeanant, edited the *Pall Mall Gazette* from his cell. 'For a season', as John Morley writes, he was 'the most powerful journalist in the island'. Beyond all his arresting daily journalism, he started in his *Review of Reviews* a periodical which initiated a useful development of the Press, at the head of which stands my friends the de Witt Wallaces' *Reader's Digest*, with its 15,500,000 circulation.

[1] See page 237.
[2] J. L. Garvin attributed to Stead a 'renaissance in sea power'. Mr. W. L. Langer, of the American Bureau of International Research, in *The Diplomacy of Imperialism*, calls him 'the father of modern Naval Programmes'.

He was born in a manse and arrived at John Morley's *Pall Mall Gazette* a healthy, bushy-bearded, blue-eyed, ill-dressed Boanerges or minor prophet with odds and ends of education—'why is he not more beautiful to look at?' asked Madame Novikoff—after an untutored but powerful editing of the ha'penny *Northern Echo*,[1] an amalgam (if it be conceivable) of the *Tribune* at its most Nye Bevan-ish but of Liberal sentiments, the *Christian World* and *John o' London's Weekly*. He conducted at home every day family worship, with hymns, possessed unending self-confidence and pluck and an impassioned urge towards close fighting in political and social discussion, was equipped with an amazing facility of the pen, and was stayed, like Cromwell and Gladstone, by his confidence in a God who directed every single thing he wanted to do.

When he got into the *Pall Mall Gazette* editorial chair he acclimatised the American interview, and the way he had with celebrities, aided by his remarkable memory, his gift for rapid writing and his wide sympathies, made him supreme in the use of a searching journalistic device which, at its best, is of real service. He developed the special article and signed contribution and, in the daily press, was a pioneer of illustrations and in the discussion of subjects of interest and importance which had been considered below the dignity of the upper journalism. As for his industry, he repeatedly wrote in an issue of the *Pall Mall Gazette* the leading article, half-a-dozen Occasional Notes, a special article or an interview, and some paragraphs of exclusive information. Innumerable confidential talks with what a Tory Solicitor General once called 'the great, wise and eminent', and hard reading of blue-books and Consular reports were the basis of his information. 'Get to know your facts' was his principle, continually harped on and effectively used. 'The great Delane himself'—and it is Delane's biographer who says so—'was not acquainted with more important personages, and his range of curiosity was far wider.' 'If the history of modern English journalism should ever be adequately written', writes E. T. Cook, assistant editor of the *Pall Mall Gazette* under Stead and afterwards his successor, 'he will figure, I am confident, as the most creative and invigorating force in it.' A man of wide experience told Cook that 'in sheer intellectual ability he had never met anyone who surpassed Stead'.

THE COMPLEXITIES OF HIS CHARACTER. 'This is an estimate which would be endorsed by many who knew the remarkable man in his prime', Cook continues. 'Not only in intellectual energy and quickness but also in strength of will, in driving power and in

---

[1] A morning paper started two years after the London Evening *Echo* on the coming into force of Forster's Education Act. 'The far seeing Radicals who brought it into being', Mr. Reginald Gray, the present Editor, tells me, 'did so in the belief that in a few years there would arise, as indeed there did, a new literate democracy'.

force of personality he had few equals among his contemporaries. He had the touch of genius which must have achieved distinction in whatever walk of life his lot had been cast. In one only of the qualities which make for practical success was he sometimes deficient; had his judgment been equal to his other faculties, there is no measure of success which he might not in any calling have attained.'[1]

Stead was one of the strangest mixtures of a man I have ever met. He was bound to be hardly judged. He gave himself away all the time and recked nothing of it. The facts about him which I have known or ascertained I state plainly. Particularly towards the end of the book, some readers may meet with surprises. But I am going to do, as well as I can, exactly what I am perfectly certain Stead would have wished me to do, print everything I believe to be true which helps a full presentation of his character. His shortcomings will be shown as well as his strength. His failures will be recorded with his triumphs. Stead was much given to talking with himself at length on foolscap, and stacks of this self-revealing writing I have before me.

I am printing these private communings because nobody could fully reckon up Stead but Stead. He has now the opportunity of answering all our questions. He approved of candour and confession, he craved understanding, and he believed in the virtue of the printed word for every situation. His diaries are no offhanded pieces of work. They are, in his own words, his 'soul's looking-glass' and he adds, 'in shameless nudity'. I am letting Stead speak in every detail for himself.

THE ATTEMPTS AT A BIOGRAPHY. There is a life of Stead in two volumes by the late Frederic Whyte to which I contributed, at Whyte's request, eight pages of recollections. Stead's last son to survive, Professor John Stead, of the Royal Naval College, Greenwich, who died a few years ago, wrote to me: 'I was profoundly disappointed with the book; adequate justice has not yet been done to my father.' Whyte, although a kind-hearted man of some literary skill and experience, had never met Stead, he was a Roman Catholic dealing with a fervent Evangelical, and he was dilatory. His book did not come out until thirteen years after Stead's death, and it was priced at the then high figure of thirty-six shillings.

In the following pages, beyond my own memories, I have based myself on the recollections of Stead's family and his surviving friends, on contemporary references and, as I have said, on Stead's plentiful MSS. and typescripts and other papers, all that exist—in weight not much less than a hundredweight!—placed at my

[1] *Contemporary Review.*

disposal by the goodness of Professor Stead and the continuous kindness of Miss Stead.[1] E. H. Stout, manager of the *Review of Reviews*, before that a member of the *Pall Mall Gazette* staff in Stead's time and associated with him in all for twenty-one years, added to the pile by handing over to me shortly before his own death all the letters and memoranda in his possession. I have also, of course, the letters which Stead wrote to me.

I remember, after Stead went down in the *Titanic*, being summoned from the country to London by one of his sons. Would I undertake a 'Popular Life' of his father, to be published at the earliest possible date? I knew the materials were vast. For years, when on the *Pall Mall Gazette*, I had often to visit an office in the next street where Stead had a staff assiduously collating letters, clipping newspapers and magazines, extracting from books and storing typescript; and the work went on during the *Review of Reviews* period. He never talked with a man or woman of consequence without dictating or writing down an account of what he had been told. Further, no journalist kept a letter-book more scrupulously. Henry Stead took me into a room full of Tate sugar-boxes, packed with carefully arranged papers, almost every sheet of which had, no doubt, the making of 'copy' of some sort. With such unparalleled stores—Gladstone left more, but how much of it was 'copy'?—I promptly characterised the notion of a 'Popular Life' as absurd. E. T. Cook should, I said, be got to work at once on two volumes. A cheap edition might come later. Cook, however, was deep in one of his admirable biographies. So, in view of the long intimacy of her husband with Lord Esher (*fidus Achates* of King Edward VII),[2] Mrs. Stead wisely invited him to undertake the Life. Had not Esher written that 'nothing has happened to the country since 1880 that has not been influenced by the personality of Stead', and that the *Pall Mall Gazette*, the confidant and backer of Pro-Consuls, 'came nearer to ruling the Empire than any living man'? (And had not the *Spectator* declared that 'Esher knew more about the Commonwealth and talked more sense than most rulers'?) But Lord Esher felt that Stead had too many aspects for him to cope with satisfactorily. J. L. Garvin, after being much attracted by the task, abandoned it on being asked to undertake the Life of Joseph Chamberlain. J. A. Spender wrote to me asking if I thought Mrs. Stead would like him to step into the breach. I told her of his great skill, integrity and efficiency and his considerable acquaintance with Stead, but made it clear that he was not fully in sympathy with her husband and would lack understanding

---

[1] Professor Stead wrote to me, 'If you would care to write to anyone asking for letters on behalf of the family we should be very pleased for you to do so'.
[2] Father of the present Lord Esher. See his *Cloud Capp'd Towers* (Murray).

of some of his work. So it came about that nothing was published except Miss Stead's loving, careful and telling *My Father*[1] (1913), a short book much of which, as a spiritualist, she devotes, as does Miss Edith K. Harper in *Stead, the Man*[2] (1918), to the later stages of Stead's life, after he had left the *Pall Mall Gazette*, when a great interest of his was in what he called 'spooks'. During the years I was in the Far East, plums from the sugar-boxes were being plundered for a failing *Review of Reviews*. Then Whyte stepped in, took a long time over his work and did not get out his volumes until 1925.[3] It was pitiful neglect of the man who, when someone of importance had to be written about, had never spared himself. Whyte pronounces Stead to have been 'amazingly, almost incredibly, good and lovable, the bravest and the most brilliant man ever seen in Fleet Street'. But he might have done more for him. The delay in the appearance of Whyte's in many ways excellent book kept a generation which had not known Stead in his prime from having a realising sense of his finest work. No wonder that in one book on journalism there is only a passing sniff at Stead. No wonder that many women, to the cause of whose emancipation he gave such valiant pioneering help, are unacquainted with it or have hardly heard of him. No wonder that, even among public men and journalists, there are those who know little more than the name of the man who, by his physical and moral courage, the purity of his character, his national spirit and unceasing activity, won the regard and indulgence of some of the truest men and women of his time. More than once I have heard Stead confounded with my friend and neighbour, the eminent publicist Wickham Steed, former correspondent in Berlin and Rome of *The Times* and one of its former Editors. In the *Dictionary of National Biography* Stead has but two columns and a half in comparison with pages given to men whose names are writ in water.[4] He now rightly claims the largest space in what shall be, as far as I can make it, a faithful account of the *Pall Mall Gazette*.

STEAD'S SUCCESSOR. Edward Tyas Cook, afterwards Sir Edward, was one of the most honest, able, urbane, modest, assiduous and highly instructed men who have had the direction of a newspaper. After his career at the *Pall Mall Gazette* he conducted the *Westminster Gazette* and then the *Daily News*, edited, as already noted, the thirty-nine-volume *Works of Ruskin*, wrote a life of him, of Delane of *The Times* (which a well-known daily paper editor has pronounced to be the best biography of a journalist), and of his doughty colleague and mine, Edmund Garrett, besides two volumes

---

[1] Heinemann.   [2] Rider.   [3] *The Life of W. T. Stead* (Cape).
[4] The Rev. A. H. Stanton, the man immediately preceding Stead, of whom few have heard, has two columns.

on Florence Nightingale which would alone hold him in remembrance.

A niece of Sir Edward Cook, Lady Hartley, the recipient from him of daily letters when he ceased to write a diary, has been good enough to entrust me with three hundred of them. They throw a light on his mettle, his goodness, his literary ability and his friendships. To this help she has added the writing for me of a Chapter of engaging recollections. Sir Harold Hartley had also a number of letters for me and has spared no effort to put me in touch with surviving members of the family and to provide me with all sorts of information in response to my profuse requests. To a nephew of Cook, Mr. D. G. Duff, I am under particular obligation. He has generously allowed me to make extracts from no fewer than eight volumes of diaries, which he has not yet been able to edit. Both Mr. A. H. M. Wedderburn, son of Cook's fellow worker on the monumental *Ruskin*, and Mr. A. F. Wise, a son of one of Cook's sisters, have been good enough to come to see me. So has Mr. Laurence Irving, a son of Dorothea Baird ('Trilby'), a sister -in-law of Cook. He is author of the much praised life of Sir Henry Irving.

*

HENRY COCKAYNE CUST. The fourth Editor of the *Pall Mall Gazette* could hardly have been more different than he was from Greenwood, Morley, Stead, Cook and Garvin. But, if one may imagine the six Editors gathered together in the Elysian Fields, and opening their minds and hearts in comradeship, they would find in one another rare endowments, high purpose and a common satisfaction in the privilege of public expression and public guidance. 'There are diversities of gifts, but the same spirit; and there are diversities of operations.'

Mrs. Cust and Harry Cust's nephew, Sir Ronald Storrs, whose *Orientations* was a memorable piece of autobiography, have responded to my desire to let a public which did not know Cust learn accurately of a man of fine parts and somewhat tragic life, who, though his career in newspaperdom was short, made his mark in it.

Viscount Astor could not have been kinder in reply to many enquiries about his father's ownership of the *Pall Mall Gazette* in the post-Yates Thompson stage and the Cust and J. L. Garvin terms; and Mr. J. E. Berridge, manager and director of the *Observer*, has been most helpful. I am also indebted for information about Garvin to Mr. Gordon Brett and Mr. Harold Gale.

*

In addition to helpers already mentioned, or to be mentioned in the text, I have specially to thank, for permission to use copyright letters or for other assistance kindly and promptly rendered, the

Trustees of the British Museum and Mr. H. R. Aldridge, the Public
Trustee and the Society of Authors, the Prime Minister, the
Marquess of Salisbury, the Earl of Rosebery, Viscount Astor, the
Earl of Balfour, the Viscountess Milner, Lord Elton, Lord Esher,
Lord Layton, the Hon. Anthony Asquith, the Hon. Maynard
Greville, Sir Osbert Sitwell, Sir Frank Newnes, Sir Frederick
Hamilton, Sir Francis Mitchell, Sir Alfred Watson, Sir Francis
Wylie, Messrs. George Allen and Unwin and the Ruskin Literary
Trustees, Mr. J. B. Atkins, Mr. Vernon Bartlett, Mr. G. H. Baxter,
Miss G. M. Briggs, Mr. H. N. Brailsford, Miss E. Nesbit Brown,
Mrs. James Carruthers, C.H., Mr. M. Bonham Carter, Mr. W. F.
Casey, Messrs. Constable & Co., Mr. John Connell, Mrs. W. L.
Courtney, Miss Gabrielle Curry, Mr. A. M. Conan Doyle, the
Eastern Province, Guardian, Loan and Investment Company
which looks after the affairs of Olive Schreiner, the Executors of
H. G. Wells, Miss Viola Garvin, Mr. Charles A. Gladstone, Mrs.
Katharine Gordon, Mr. N. Carruthers Gould, Mr. W. W. Hadley,
to whose own recollections we are looking forward, Mr. G. W.
Hudson, Mr. Edward Hulton, Mr. Gordon Leach, Messrs. Leman,
Harrison and Flegg, Miss Ebba Low, Mr. David Low, Messrs.
Macmillan & Co., Mr. Kingsley Martin, Mr. C. D. Medley, Mr.
Stanley Morison, Miss Birnie Philip, Mr. S. K. Ratcliffe, Mrs.
Gordon Selfridge, Mr. Andrew Stewart and the Press Club, Miss D.
Sutherland, Mr. H. M. and Mr. Philip Tomlinson, the University
Press, Cambridge, Messrs. A. P. Watt & Son, Mr. A. E. Watson,
and several other people whom I should like to thank if I could only
discover their addresses—and my wife, who has read every page
and many pages more than once. Bernard Shaw, with his historio-
grapher, Dr. Lowenstein, were also most obliging. So were the late
Lord Snell and Sir Peter Chalmers Mitchell.

Finally, Mr. Eric Parker, my oldest and most intimate journalist
friend, who has himself written as many as fifty books, has most
kindly looked through the whole of the proofs. I cannot thank him
too warmly.

Considerations of space compel me to leave over to a partly
written autobiographical volume, which will include an account
of experiences in founding and editing the *New East* in Tokyo and
the *Countryman* in the Cotswolds, my recollections of the life, work
and quality of four *Pall Mall Gazette* colleagues, the rarely gifted
Edmund Garrett, the able and always cheerful Charles Morley,
the famous cartoonist F. C. G., and a distinguished editor, J. A.
Spender, who later conducted the *Westminster Gazette*. I also want to
say something of Ernest Parke, my earliest journalistic friend
outside Northumberland Street, who was associated successively
with the *Star*, the *Morning Leader* and the *News Chronicle*.

Because I feel that my Editors deserve a chronicler who had at least the qualification of knowing several of them well, and that general readers and journalists will not only value but profit by their close acquaintance, I have gladly spent on this book a great deal of time and labour and, necessarily, much more money than I can ever receive from its sales. Apart from the countless enquiries and journeys and the number of newspaper columns and books consulted, I have read several thousand letters and a dozen MS. diaries.

In some ways, no doubt, the book takes a way of its own. It does so deliberately and at my time of life I may perhaps be allowed the liberty! I am protected by the ample form of G. K. Chesterton. Did he not say, so very truly, that there are in every newspaper far too many things suitable to the paper? One should not fail to print, whether in newspapers or books, things that really interest oneself, for they are bound to interest a number of other ordinary people. In following this plan I have not feared being now and then, it may be, a little discursive when I got on the track of out-of-the-way elucidatory incidents. But whatever my malpractices, I may modestly claim, at the end of my exertions, that a book which encounters not only Editors but a wide range of statesmen, travellers, scientific men, authors and miscellaneous men and women, does, in its anecdotage and obiter dicta of the famous, bring together illustrations of the psychology of political life and facts of interest in the public, social and artistic history of its period.

May I say again how grateful I am for the privilege of doing a modest service for a profession which, from the time I entered it in my teens, I have never for one moment thought of quitting? But I have realised the truth of what the *Manchester Guardian* once said, 'It is harder to write the history of a newspaper than of any institution'.

J. W. ROBERTSON SCOTT

IDBURY MANOR,
   KINGHAM, OXFORD
   Summer, 1952.

The Old and the New Journalism
JOHN MORLEY

CHAPTER I

THE *SATURDAY REVIEW*, G. H. LEWES, JOHN STUART MILL, GEORGE ELIOT AND SWINBURNE

'SATYR, RUFFIAN AND WILD BEAST.' In making up people's minds for them in the second half of the nineteenth century the part played by John Morley before he came to the *Pall Mall Gazette*, not only in his books but in his lettered, individual, courageous journalism, is less understood and less honoured than it ought to be. The careers of few men are more illuminating and refreshing for the citizen of a studious, reforming turn than that of the publicist and statesmen who, twenty-nine years ago, passed from the scene at the age of eighty-four. As Mr. F. W. Hirst says with confidence in his two-volume *Early Life and Letters of John Morley*,[1] 'his fame will endure'. He left behind him, writes Mr. Algernon Cecil,[2] 'a life so consistent that any man might be proud of it'. He had, like Burke, this writer justly says, 'the sacred gift of inspiring men to use a grave diligence in caring for high things and in making their lives at once grave and austere'.

Morley was a Blackburn doctor's son and was born, 'half Yorkshireman, half Northumbrian', on Christmas Eve 1838, a year after Queen Victoria came to the throne. Out of an average hundred inhabitants of Blackburn when he was six, only thirty-nine men and eleven women could write their names! He went to Oxford, where 'the star of Newman had set and the sun of Mill had risen', to rooms at Lincoln which were once Wesley's.[3] Morley arrived in the year in which the power to require from the winners of University scholarships membership of the Church of England was given up.[4] But evidence enough remained there of a former state

[1] Macmillan, 1927.

[2] *Six Oxford Thinkers* (Murray, 1909).

[3] The collector of coincidences notes that the Rector who nominated Wesley for a Fellowship was a John Morley, unrelated to the newcomer. There was a John Morley who in 1768 published *An Essay on the Nature and Cure of the King's Evil*.

[4] Two bishops voted in favour of the enabling Act and twenty-two against. Other tests were abolished in 1871.

of mental and physical sloth. The Rector of Lincoln—elected, Morley was to write, by 'a terribly degraded body' of Fellows—was Mark Pattison's 'satyr, ruffian and wild beast'!

The youth's first success was the winning of a prize open to the whole University, 'offered by a local bookseller', to whose trade Morley was to supply so many volumes of quality and significance. Or perhaps his first success was gaining the friendship of the Senior Commoner, Cotter Morison. 'Scholar and athlete', Morison was, in Meredith's phrase, 'a fountain of our sweetest, quick to spring, in fellowship abounding, ready to look at anything seriously presented to him'. The reading of Cotter Morison's *Service of Man, an Essay towards the Religion of the Future*, although but 'the rash attempt of failing days', and his moving, scholarly and sufficiently sceptical *St. Bernard*, praised by such different judges as Matthew Arnold, Cardinal Manning and Mark Pattison, was a memorable experience for many of us.

Honest, intrepid, earnest, vital, humorous were among the adjectives applied to Morley as an undergraduate. He had 'moral and intellectual' interests, but none in games. At the Union he moved that 'the intellectual, social and literary influence of Mr. Carlyle has been most important and beneficial', and supported a resolution which approved the beheading of Charles I.

'ON AN EMPTY PAUNCH' IN LONDON. When Morley turned away from a prospect of the Church, of which his father, originally a Methodist, was a firm adherent, funds from home were cut off. As an agnostic with a pass degree, the young man faced the problem of getting a living in London. 'I have scribbled many a day on an empty paunch', he wrote. He seems to have done some tutoring, and, in potboiling writing, even to have helped a friend with a history of the Archbishops of Canterbury. But there is mention of 'amateur acting and a course of musketry'.

He had some association with G. H. Lewes's *Leader*, which died in its tenth year after being merged in a publication with the alluring name of the *Saturday Analyst*. Herbert Spencer and Kinglake, as well as George Eliot, were contributors to it. Morley spoke of the 'vivacious intelligence' of Lewes, and said he was 'a source of incessant and varied stimulation'. But Morley had no liking for him. For one thing, because Lewes used to make vivisection experiments—on the ground floor of his house, 'while George Eliot was at her novel upstairs', said Morley, who 'was horrified at meeting in the hall or on the stairs some animal limping about in a mutilated state'.

Mark Pattison speaks of Morley 'developing so remarkably after leaving Oxford'. In his private life Morley seems to have stood out successfully against what he describes as 'the temptations lurking in irregularities, for men of defective quality, to ill-starred Bohemian ways, that waste priceless time, impoverish character, and as often as not spread long trails of overhanging cloud through life'.

When he was called to the bar (1873) it was to his 'long enduring regret' that, without connexions as he was, he was unable to practise in a profession 'with immense opportunities, honourable prizes, and fine gymnastic in combined common sense, accurate expression and strong thought'.

ON JOURNALISM AND THE JOURNALIST. He felt the lure, the drawbacks and the merits of journalism, and throughout his career often returned to them. 'Journalism', he says in his *Recollections* written when he was nearly eighty,[1] 'is precarious in a sense that does not affect the lawyer, the schoolmaster, the doctor, the clerk in holy orders, the soldier or the sailor. For the writer routine does nothing; the more it does for him, to be sure, the worse for his writing.' Though it 'may well kill a man, it quickens his life while it lasts. Of all the professions it is the least likely to degenerate into a life of somnolent routine or indifference to affairs. With intelligence and well-principled industry, and the faith that his private soldier's knapsack contains the baton of the field-marshal, he will do well enough for himself and his public.' But the journalist has to 'cultivate variety, freshness, originality, or give up the race. If his knack, whatever it amounts to, should cease to please he starves; if his little capital of ideas wears out he is despatched as monotonous or tiresome; if the journal to which he is attached changes hands or changes principles or expires, he too, may expire'.[2]

EDITOR OF THE *LITERARY GAZETTE*. Becoming known for his brains and for the 'thoroughness and care' with which he did his writing, Frederick Arnold, who had helped Morley to the Archbishops, got him the editorship of a weekly which described itself as 'A Journal of Literature, Science and Art and a Record of University, Ecclesiastical, Educational, Social and General Information', the *Literary Gazette*. During the short life of the *Gazette* as many as five different editors served it. The first was Shirley Brooks, who was to be editor of *Punch*. Morley was the last but one.

GEORGE MEREDITH. During Morley's term he wrote reviews of substance, some—such was journalism in those days—'extending over two or three numbers'. A 'fascinating work' called *Evan Harrington* (1861) secured, when George Meredith was little known, 'nearly four and a quarter columns'. It may seem an odd way of praising that book to say that it is 'entitled to a place on the same

[1] *Recollections*. By John Morley (Macmillan, 2 vols., 1917).
[2] *Recollections*.

shelf as *The Woman in White*'; but, as Hirst writes,[1] 'Wilkie Collins's masterpiece was then not only a best seller but the delight of so fine a critic as Edward Fitzgerald'. 'I did not go to the play last night', wrote Gladstone in the autumn of 1860, 'from finding *The Woman in White* so very interesting. It is far better sustained than *Adam Bede*.'[2] Morley seems to suggest that his close friendship with Meredith followed the review. He is known to have taken a turn at Meredith's task work for the *Ipswich Journal*. He once interpreted Meredith as follows: 'Live with the world. No cloister. No languor. Play your part. Fill the day. Ponder well and loiter not. Let laughter brace you. Exist in everyday communion with Nature. Nature bids you take all, only be sure you learn to do without'.

AN EDITOR AND A PROPRIETOR. From as early as 1863 Morley is supposed to have been writing for the *Saturday Review*. It was Tory 'with a dark suspicion of partnership with Dr. Pusey'. Bagehot describes it as 'the almost perfect embodiment of the corrective scepticism of a sleepy intellect'. John Bright gave it the name of the *Saturday Reviler*, and his reference to 'the praise of all good men and the hatred of the *Saturday Review*' is familiar. The editor was John Douglas Cook, 'the details of whose career, as narrated by himself', writes Leslie Stephen, 'were supposed to owe something to his creative imagination'. A 'stout, bull-necked, red-faced man' with a temper, Mrs. Lynn Linton of *The Girl of the Period* reports, and says he swore at her. He 'seemed to know little of literature outside the newspapers', but was a shrewd and successful editor. The bulky proprietor, Beresford Hope, M.P., who had failed with the *Morning Chronicle*, survives in Disraeli's allusion to his 'Batavian graces', after Beresford Hope, who had Dutch blood, had called him 'the Asian Mystery'.

MORLEY'S ARTICLES AND FIRST BOOKS. Morley did 'miles and miles of "middles"', he told St. Loe Strachey, while Lord Robert Cecil, the future Prime Minister, was writing party articles. The two men sat in 'the writing room together on Tuesdays', but Morley said that 'he, too, had a talent for silence'. Morley was once sent by his editor, in prospect of 'copy', to one of the Baroness Burdett Coutts's donkey shows. He is stated to have made 'a safe income of £400' from the *Saturday*; another report says that it

[1] In his *The Early Life and Letters of John Morley* (Macmillan, 1927). The two honest, workmanlike volumes have not a few of the excellent qualities of Morley's own *Recollections*, and are read for their informed account not only of Morley but of the political currents of his time. Happily the material gathered concerning Morley's later years is not to be lost to us through the author's regrettable ill-health. A book is announced under the editorship of Sir Edward Boyle, M.P.

[2] *Life of Gladstone.* By John Morley (Macmillan, 1905).

rose to £700. It was in the *Saturday* that Morley, in a three-column review of an indifferent translation of Hugo's *Toilers of the Sea*, noted that in the original there was *bugpipe* for bagpipe and *le premier de la quatrième* for Firth of Forth. In later years he visited the novelist. Among Morley's colleagues were Cotter Morison, the two Stephens (Leslie and Sir Fitzjames), Vernon Harcourt (afterwards Sir William), Goldwin Smith, and Maine (later Sir Henry), who had suggested the paper's name. Harcourt speaks of the *Saturday* 'doing so well that the proprietors have constituted five of us into a regular staff with a good salary'. Freeman, the historian, wrote for it seven hundred articles, among others those in which he assaulted Froude. J. R. Green, another kind of historian, whose work has worn so well, was also a frequent contributor.

FIRST BOOK. Morley's first book was a series of papers from the *Saturday*, called *Modern Characteristics* (1861). It did not bear his name and did not attract notice, and he once told H. J. Laski, who had come on a copy of the rarity, that he was ashamed of it. Nobody, he said, should be responsible for opinions written before forty. In the modest preface he states that his essays have at least 'the quality of suggestiveness'. 'Social Salamanders', 'False Steps', 'Clever Men's Wives', 'Thrift' and 'Literary Industry' are the kind of thing, and he undoubtedly knew something about the last two subjects. The time he spent in Wesley's rooms at Lincoln must have sent him to the career of the evangelist for in one 'middle' he quoted the preacher's letter of exasperation to his wife: 'Suspect me no more, asperse me no more, provoke me no more. Of what importance is your character to mankind? If you was buried just now, what loss would you be to mankind?' And some years afterwards he complained of the omission of Wesley from his friend Harrison's *Calendar of Great Men*.

It was a *Saturday* article[1] which brought Morley into relations of affection with John Stuart Mill, whom he honoured to the end of that stalwart's days. 'A strong pure light is gone out, the radiance of a clear vision and a beneficent purpose' is a sentence from his piece on 'The Death of Mill', which he judged to be 'the most stately and moving thing' he ever did.

'STYLE IS THE RESULT OF THINKING.' 'Some Notes on George Eliot' in *Macmillan's Magazine* (1866), left out of his *Miscellanies*, initiated a friendship with the novelist. It is in

---

[1] In it is that serviceable specimen of the 'commonsense view'—'second-rate wisdom which will not examine a new idea until very old': Canals 'would cause a serious falling off in the breed of the draught-horse. They would entail the sinking of enormous sums, and by diminishing the circulating capital, would cripple trade. They would be the means of withdrawing a great deal of land from cultivation. They would cause the natural navigation of rivers to be neglected. They would affect the coasting trade, and so the supply of seamen for the navy would be impaired'.

reference to her work that he has the wise remark that 'style is not
the result of reading but of thinking, the cultivation of the intellect
and feelings; style comes of brooding over ideas, not over words'.

In a review in the *Saturday* of Swinburne's *Poems and Ballads* in
the summer of 1866 Morley termed Swinburne 'the libidinous
laureate of a pack of satyrs', 'an unclean fiery imp from the pit'
who had revealed 'a mind aflame with the feverish carnality of a
schoolboy'. He also accused the poet of 'tuning his lyre in a sty'.

As early as 1867 Morley became a reader to Macmillan's in
order to gain 'freedom from journalistic urgencies'. His report on
The Poor Man and the Lady by Hardy was that 'if the man is young
he has stuff and purpose in him'. Housman believed that he voted
against *A Shropshire Lad*.

CHAPTER II

EDITOR OF THE *FORTNIGHTLY REVIEW* AND THE *MORNING STAR*

A N 'ORGAN OF OPEN ENQUIRY.' The *Fortnightly Review* had been begun with £8,000 in 1865, the year of the foundation of the *Pall Mall Gazette*. The proprietor, Cotter Morison, was a well-to-do man, but Trollope and Lewes, with Chapman the publisher, also contributed funds. It was to be a non-party periodical of 'freedom of speech combined with personal responsibility; let any man who has a thing to say, and knows how to say it, speak freely'. The words are Trollope's. He was chairman of the board, which was to meet fortnightly. Lewes was editor. But 'the theory of eclecticism', Trollope owns, with his customary candour and practical view, 'was altogether impracticable'. 'It was as though a gentleman should go into the House of Commons determined to serve no Party. Such gentlemen have gone into the House but they have not served their country very much. Liberalism, free-thinking and open enquiry will never object to appear in company with their opposites because they have the conceit to think they can quell those opposites; but the opposites will not appear in conjunction with liberalism, free-thinking and open enquiry. As a natural consequence, our new publication became an organ of liberalism, free-thinking and open enquiry and has asserted for itself a position in our periodical literature which is well understood and highly respected.'

EDITOR AT TWENTY-NINE. 'It had been decided by the board, somewhat in opposition to my own ideas', Trollope says, 'that the *Fortnightly* should always contain a novel', and in the first volume he wrote *The Belton Estate*, which few of us have read. But Meredith's *Beauchamp's Career* was among later fiction. Fellow contributors were George Eliot, Herbert Spencer and Frederic Harrison. When Lewes had had enough of what seemed likely to be a losing concern, or as Trollope writes, 'the work pressed too severely on his moderate health', he was followed, in 1867, through Cotter Morison's influence, by Morley. Not quite twenty-nine, he was to edit the review for fifteen years. The owners, after laying out £9,000, had been glad to make over their publication to Chapman. Morley became editor 'in a sort of partnership' with him.

SIGNED OR UNSIGNED ARTICLES. The *Fortnightly* had ceased

c

to be fortnightly. Trollope acknowledged that the name was 'a fault' for which he 'alone was responsible'. The idea of fortnightly publication had been taken from a Paris bi-monthly. The unfortunate title did not prevent the starting of another review that also dated itself, the *Nineteenth Century*. When the time came, Sir James Knowles had to add *And After*, and in our day, leaving A.D. 2000 to be faced when the time comes, the name has become the *Twentieth Century*.

The *Fortnightly* took a course of its own in many directions. One was with signed articles. 'The immeasurably momentous task of forming national opinion should not be in the hands of men who did not put their names at the end of what they wrote.' The signing of articles, Morley was persuaded, and so was Trollope, 'would contribute to the improvement of journalism and the diffusion of sound views'. With the unsigned system, 'journalists were tempted to a weak pliancy'. Under the influence of 'the Tone and Spirit of a journal'—Morley indulges in his rare capital letters— writers, 'not deliberately dishonest', he acknowledges, 'instead of thinking out questions independently and exercising their own judgment, find themselves consulting this demigod of an abstraction, reflecting moods, almost phrases they might suppose it using'. And 'writing year after year upon instructions can hardly be good for the mental health', he says; 'I have in mind more than one contemporary with first rate literary talent whom the check upon initiative reduced to rather second-rate work and name.' Nevertheless in later life he acknowledged, and was probably thinking of the *Pall Mall Gazette*, that 'the goodness or badness of a newspaper' may depend 'far more on the character of its owner and editor than upon whether the articles are signed or not'.

'READERS SHAN'T HAVE SKIM MILK.' On how to write for the *Fortnightly* he once expressed himself as follows to a warm friend and skilful controversialist, Frederic Harrison, who was doing 'Foreign Affairs': 'Light judicial philosophic politics in easy undress; a mixture of the jaunty and severe. Above all things direct, not allusive; no esoteric smirks for this party or that; but a manly downright sort of stroke, taking all things seriously but not solemnly, putting events in their place and due proportion. An artistic whole certainly ought to be aimed at.' Which puts a great deal in a paragraph. A reference by Morley to someone's article he had returned is: 'It was like a good schoolboy coming to politics, and too much in the style of a divine addressing a Sunday School on the rudiments. *F.R.* readers shan't have skim milk foisted on them.'

EDITORIAL DEALING WITH MSS. The nice phrasing of a letter which shall be sufficiently persuasive to secure a contribution—one thinks of a letter from Thackeray when editor of *Cornhill* to Mrs. Browning[1]—while intimating a right to reject if it does not prove to be up to the mark, is a precious editorial gift. Morley tells his sister that his room has 'a small mountain of MSS neatly packed up on the cabinet, with pleasant billets-doux to match, "regrets", "cannot avail", "kind enough to send" and all the rest of it'. With a fellow townsman at Blackburn he managed matters as follows: 'I like your subject very much. I cannot guarantee to accept an article until I have seen it, but I think such an article would be certain to suit me if you like to write it subject to the small risk thus implied.' On another occasion he ejaculates, 'What an impossible thing it is for an editor to keep friends with people who write books, and at the same time keep friends with his own poor conscience!'

Hirst, with his own editorial experience, notes that Morley 'not only knew what he wanted but acquired wonderful skill in restraining prolixity and in keeping bores at a distance'. Morley writes that he gave 'chilly welcome to promiscuous persons'—there are more of them than ever to-day—'who will offer you now a remark on the Sistine Madonna, now an opinion on Bonapartism, now an observation on the steam engine, seldom anything absolutely stupid but more seldom still anything shrewdly to the point'. To the Blackburn contributor on conditions in that town he gives this guidance about his article: '1. It ought not to exceed 16 or 18 of our pp. 2. Be sure to select salient points only, and not to attempt to exhaust the matter. 3. No figures and statistics. 4. Expound their *ideas*, manners, aspirations, above all their feelings about religion, property, their masters, etc. 5. The ordinary career of an average artisan.' As for length of articles, Morley once asked Frederic Harrison to get his contribution into twenty pages and on another occasion into twenty-seven, allotments of space the like of which survive only in the *Quarterly Review*. The good terms on which Morley and Harrison were with one another is illustrated in the following correspondence quoted by Mrs. Knickerbocker:[2]

Morley to Harrison. I don't see why faith should not be kept with a wretched editor, just as it is with a wretched solicitor, or anybody else. You vowed by Humanity, the Grand Etre, the Supreme Mother, and all the other capital letters of your faith that you would lead off in January. 'Tis indispensable. I must have it. You must write it. You have three whole weeks. You might beat the Psalms of David in that time. *Harrison to Morley.* I am the vilest of men and you are the most considerate and encouraging of editors. What a task you must have if you have to bottle-hold all your contributors and keep up their peckers as you do mine.

---

[1] *The Story of the 'Pall Mall Gazette'*, page 78 (Oxford University Press, 1950).
[2] *Free Minds*, Frances W. Knickerbocker (Oxford University Press, 1943).

Before typewriting, what a *corvée* for editors the reading of MSS must have been! And handwriting was often bad. 'I shall be able to tell your biographer', Morley wrote to Lord Houghton, 'that, whereas the printers only demand half-a-crown a sheet extra for Dean Stanley, for you they will have nothing less than 50 per cent.'[1]

'A CRITIC ALWAYS BUT A CYNIC NEVER.' Morley was only thirty-five when Harrison notes that, 'with unanimity and regularity, the whole Press of every shade prints the *Fortnightly* first among the reviews!' At that time the dailies noticed the reviews at length. Even when, up to the outbreak of the Boer War, I did them for the *Daily Chronicle* every month, I had three columns or more!

The kind of man Morley was is partly reflected in the counsel he gave, in what H. M. Hyndman, Marxist contributor to the *Fortnightly*, called his 'fine, superior, practical manner', to young writers. 'Be a critic always if you like, but a cynic never', and 'Suppose yourself with a company of friends in your room, and you are telling them an event in your life; affectation would fill you with horror; sublime words and sonorous antithesis dare not intrude.'

FIRST RATE CONTRIBUTIONS AT LOW FEES. What is a successful editor? 'We may mean', says Hirst, who was once editor of the *Economist*, 'that he has made a newspaper or a periodical pay by increasing its circulation, or advertisement revenue, or both; we may mean that he has won a reputation for himself and for his organ. In both these respects Morley succeeded. Within three or four years he had gained for it a position of acknowledged influence; he increased its circulation and made out of a derelict venture a profitable concern.' Describing its position in 1872 to a friend who had expressed a fear that its opinions were 'too unpopular to pay', Morley said with modest pride: 'When I began in 1867 the circulation was 1400. To-day (1873) it is 2500 and quietly rising every month', with, he added, 'say 30,000 readers'. He had offered Chapman three times the price Chapman had paid for it, and the offer had been refused. 'The increase of influence, very slow, very impalpable, very easy to sneer at, very hard to define, but still influence', Morley wrote: 'that's what I mean by success'. The list of Morley's contributors is remarkable. They included:

Matthew Arnold	G. H. Lewes
Walter Bagehot	Robert Lowe
Arthur Balfour	Sir John Lubbock
Professor Beesley	Alfred Marshall
Dr. J. H. Bridges	Mazzini

[1] *Monckton Milnes, Lord Houghton*, by Wemyss Reid (Cassell, 1890).

Joseph Chamberlain
W. K. Clifford
Edward Dicey
Sir Charles Dilke
Sir M. Grant Duff
George Eliot
E. A. Freeman
Sir Robert Giffen
W. E. Gladstone (he signed 'Judex')
Frederic Harrison
W. Holt Hutton
T. H. Huxley
H. M. Hyndman

Whyte Melville
George Meredith
F. W. H. Myers
Walter Pater
Mark Pattison
Dante Gabriel Rossetti
Henry Sidgwick
Herbert Spencer
Leslie Stephen
Algernon Swinburne
J. A. Symonds
Professor Tyndall
Anthony Trollope

How was such an array of talent obtained for moderate payment, or, as in the case of Mill's early articles, for nothing at all? Morley's explanation is that 'if the publisher's cheque was small, the editor's letter enclosing it often mollified the ruffled feelings of a good contributor'. One contributor said, 'Though the pay of the *Fortnightly* is not as much as I can earn in the *Saturday* or *Cornhill*, I value the chance of writing because a thing that appears in the *F.R.* is somehow or other talked about.' 'I am always very glad to have anything of mine in the *Fortnightly*', Huxley told Morley, 'as it is sure to be in good company.' How varied the review was and how good the editing is illustrated in a number which contained articles by Robert Lowe, Alfred Russell Wallace, Leslie Stephen, Dr. J. Guinness Rogers, J. Addington Symonds, the Hon. Lionel Tollemache and Sir Henry Cotton. When Meredith looked after the interests of the review in Morley's absence in the United States he explained to Swinburne, who was dissatisfied with his cheque, that the *Fortnightly* had passed from a philanthropic company to an unphilanthropic publisher who 'tries to diminish the expenses as much as he can, the editor being the chief sufferer' and 'from the sum he gets it's scarcely possible for him to pay more without doing so out of his own pocket'.

It may be that some contributors were glad to see anonymity banned and to have their names at the end of their articles. At that time, also, people of eminence were not so often asked for articles as they are now. Appearance in the *Fortnightly* soon became something of a distinction. An eighteen page article by W. K. Clifford on *The Unseen Universe* was done 'at a sitting which lasted from a quarter to ten in the evening till nine o'clock the following morning'. Trollope, who, as he said, was out of sympathy with many views expressed by contributors to the *Fortnightly*, acknowledged the review to be of all the monthlies 'the most serious, the most earnest, the least devoted to amusement, the least flippant, the least jocose'. Lord Craigmyle alludes to Morley's own 'exquisite and daring papers'. Mrs. Humphry Ward notes the 'frank and uncompromising agnosticism'.

THE HUNTING MAN AND THE HISTORIAN. As a hunting man, Trollope had particularly objected to an article by the historian Freeman against the pursuit of foxes. Morley allowed Trollope an answer but withstood him when he asked to be allowed to reply to Freeman's rejoinder. As the Lewes note has shown, Morley was tender-hearted to animals. In a well-known photograph he has his dog with him, he used to walk with his horse uphill, and when he had to vacate his house, offered to leave the animal to a tenant of 'strictly Freemanian views on cruelty to animals'. He speaks of 'the spirit of compassion, justice, understanding more steadily extending to those dumb friends and oppressed servitors of ours who have such strange resemblances to us in form, faculty and feeling'. 'I have never killed an animal in my life', he said towards the end of his career, 'and if I ever write anything more I think it will be a tract against field sports.'

AN EDITOR'S METHODS. Mr. Arthur Waugh knew a member of the staff of Chapman & Hall who could picture Morley as editor of the *Fortnightly*, 'firm, erect, and meditative, calling for his letters, standing at a high desk to slit them open, running an eagle eye over the contents, and as often as not slipping a shilling into the young assistant's hand.[1] When I mentioned to Hirst that once as a youth, in an access of enthusiasm for Morley, as I have already explained, I had had the assurance to offer myself as his secretary, he wrote to me: 'It must be some consolation to you to know that he never had a private secretary, and hardly ever dictated a letter except to his sister-in-law and nephew, apart from his assistants in office'. He can only have got through all his writing by studious industry and wise organisation of time. His table at home, Hirst tells me, 'was always clear and free from papers, which he kept in drawers'. It is characteristic that he liked to sit down to write 'in clean linen'. He had always more than one journalistic iron in the fire, always in hand his own books or other people's (for Macmillan). In a letter in 1878 to his sister he says: 'I am simply overwhelmed. (1) All my books are going through the press for a new and cheap edition and I have to revise the proofs—five sets coming in by every post. (2) The Series ('English Men of Letters') is beginning—MSS, proofs, etc. (3) Completion of *Diderot*. (4) *F.R.* doing well. (5) MSS for Macmillan. (6) Refusing invitation to dinner.' When he asks Harrison to do an article on the death of Carlyle he says, 'My own poor "Vale" was flung off in half an hour amid the clatter of the office and the ceaseless interruptions

[1] *A Hundred Years of Publishing* (Chapman & Hall, 1930).

of printer's devils'. In 1877 he thinks of closing with Macmillan for a book to be done in three months. The publisher believes that it will sell in large numbers.

SOME BOOKS. In the year in which he went to the *Fortnightly*, 1867, his *Edmund Burke* ('by John Morley, B.A. Oxon') came out. It was followed by *Condorcet*, 1870 (which Frederic Harrison regarded as 'an absolutely model biography'), *Turgot* (in the same authority's view 'an admirable piece of biography') and the *Miscellanies* (which Morley's friend declared put him 'at the top of the critics'). The date of *Voltaire* ('our best modern biography,'[1] Harrison was certain) was 1872, of *Rousseau* 1873 ('a consummate piece of biography', Harrison felt,[2] and wanted to review it in the *Fortnightly* but Morley's 'conscience' would not allow him to do so), of *On Compromise*, 1874,[3] of *Diderot and the Encyclopaedists*, 1878, of *Burke* in the English Men of Letters, 1879,[4] with *Cobden* to come out in 1881 and *Gladstone* in 1903. Morley's reference to Cobden, with which he took such pains, had been 'Will not be at all wearing like *Diderot*—one year'. He was compensated for his labour by the great reception the work got.

Mention has been made of Morley's visit to the United States. He spent time with Emerson, Oliver Wendell Holmes, Nathaniel Hawthorne, and Gordon Bennett of the *New York Herald*, and saw Northern generals and Sumner. An amusing newspaper comment on a speech of his was, 'Demosthenes and Cicero are all very well, Mr. Pitt and Mr. Fox were good speakers, but no orator, in any country in any age, ever addressed so much wealth as Mr. Morley!'

STAR AND PALL MALL GAZETTE. His eyes, when he came back, were turned towards the House of Commons. But in 1869 he added to his labours for the *Fortnightly* the editorship of the *Morning Star*. His predecessor had been a future leader of the Irish party, Justin McCarthy, whose *History of Our Own Times* we have

[1] Voltaire, Morley acknowledges—his book (Macmillan) was soon in a third edition—'had no ear for the finer vibrations of the human voice', but 'the Christianity which he assailed was as little touched as Voltairism itself with that spirit of holiness which poured itself round the lives and words of the two founders, the great master and the great apostle'. One recalls that in speaking of Voltaire's humanity he says, and it is an example of Morley's style, 'This is not humanity in the pale shape of kindly sentiment and bland pity, but humanity strong, aggressive, and alert stalking the land like heroes to slay monsters'.

[2] H. J. Laski related that Morley, on finding him reading *Rousseau*, said: 'I am wondering whether it would not have been better for the world if Rousseau had never been born. When people put emotion in the place of reason they lead the world to the devil'.

[3] I still remember the effect *On Compromise* had on me in my youthful reading, and in the month in which I am writing I have twice recommended the book. I am interested to find Viscount Samuel saying in the paper quoted on a later page, 'It went far to shape my ideas in my formative years'.

[4] There were three *Burkes*. The final presentation is dated 1879.

all found serviceable. The paper had been started by Cobden and Bright, and had been politely welcomed by Morley's old weekly, the *Saturday*, for its avoidance of 'the vulgarity of the *Daily News* and the imbecility of the *Morning Herald*'. The circulation at the time Morley became editor was no more than 5,000, and funds were short. Within four months he had to write the journal's obituary notice. Its readers were advised to try the *Daily News*, with which it amalgamated. Morley's last leader was in favour of better education for women.

He had the wisdom not to be drawn to the deathbed of the *Examiner*. Two years later he was writing in the *Pall Mall Gazette* for Greenwood. In a review of Darwin he offered a correction which that modest great man accepted.

Chapman gave him £500 for *Rousseau*. Morley tells Harrison that he lives up to his income 'save for an insurance of £3,000'. 'Not under £2,000', was the price he got for his *Cobden*. He used himself to pay 'the modest amount of £100' for a book in his Men of Letters series, '110 pages of the *Fortnightly*'.

CARLYLE AND FREDERIC HARRISON. Morley's relations with Harrison were so close that the belligerent expounder of Comte has been described as 'co-editor' of the *Fortnightly*. To him Morley wrote many pithy letters. On a visit Morley had made to 'the old Prophet' Carlyle in Chelsea he speaks of 'the poor, soured, wise old genius coiling himself up in his own virtue where one might expect to find one's washerwoman'. Going farther back among gospellers, he notes that 'Peter, Matthew, Mark, Luke and John did not belong to the tail-coat class'. Harrison is allowed in the *Fortnightly* to speak of the British 'aristocratic republic with a democratic machinery and a hereditary grand master of ceremonies'. It is of interest to find Morley writing on the 'bustling ponderosity of the man who is killing the *P. Mall Gazette*' (*sic*).[1] As we shall see, it took a good deal of killing. He tells Harrison his editorial troubles. A new number in 1870, for which distinguished writers had not got their articles done, 'looks like chopped straw'. Three years later he is confiding to his crony that his dream is not of editing but to be general manager of the London and North Western Railway. He makes no reference to the blessing of income tax at 2d. in the £.

[1] Greenwood.

CHAPTER III

AN EDITOR'S MEDITATIONS

THE 'NEST OF COCKATRICES'. Someone said of the *Fortnightly* that it had 'become a trumpet'. It valiantly led the way in all forward thinking on science, religion, ethics, politics and literature, dared to say (on Gladstonian views on Church schools) that 'a poorer sophism was never coined in that busy mint of logical counterfeits', was down upon Disraeli, 'worked out the Radical programme and prepared the way for Home Rule'. 'Wha-at a na-est of cockatreeces!' cried Carlyle. On another occasion, however, the message from Chelsea was that 'whatever that man Morley writes is worth having'. Hirst, who measures his words, considers Morley's journalistic rank 'comparable, in the influence exerted on public opinion, with that of Defoe, Jeffrey, Cobbett, Delane and Bagehot'.

But an editor who had had the *nous* to include both Whyte Melville and Meredith in his first number saw to it that all his writers were not manifestly pulpiteering. Few editors have assembled more of what editors call 'good stuff'. Few editors have themselves written for their publications more pages of distinction. There were not only his studies of de Maistre, Condorcet and Turgot and his writing on Carlyle and other eminent Britons, but noble deliverances on political topics. Morley's book *National Education* was published in 1873. Much of what was to be his *Burke* and *On Compromise* was given to *Fortnightly* readers. The review was always humane, as witness Morley's fiery article on 'the iniquity' of twelve months' imprisonment given to five gas stokers; he had been 'so much cut up' by that business that he 'lay awake at nights'. His contributors brought him sound writing which in the editor's excellent phrase, 'came from the heart by way of the head'.

LITERATURE AS 'A WEAPON'. In his *Recollections*[1] Morley does not say a word about his *Literary Gazette* and the *Morning Star* connexion, and makes only two references to his articles in the *Saturday*. But he unbends a little concerning his term at the *Fortnightly*. His service there concluded in 1882 with what he dismisses as 'a pretty lively quarrel' with Chapman & Hall, one of several rows between editors and proprietors to be chronicled in these pages. Mr. Hirst says Morley had 'what was known in the family

[1] Macmillan, 1917.

as the "Morley temper" and was very sensitive'. But more on his character later on. Much that he printed during his editorship touched the roots of his beliefs and feelings. Further, he was in the *Fortnightly* something of a statesman, something of an historian, biographer and critic, a man of letters to whom literature was 'a weapon and an arm, not merely a liberal art, letters in terms of life and in relation to life'. The *Fortnightly* 'saw his character formed and his philosophy of life and government developed'. The Review —I am quoting Morley himself—had 'a marked place in the diffusion and encouragement of rationalistic standards in things spiritual and temporal'. There was a particular half-year in which 'nearly every number contained an attack by some powerful writer, either on theology as a whole or on some generally accepted article of theological belief'. The stir caused by such an article as Huxley's 'On the Physical Basis of Life' (1869) is almost inconceivable in our day. 'Evolution', says Morley, 'was passed on from the study to the parlour'. It was a time which badly needed the constant reminder, in Archbishop Whately's immortal sentence, which was the motto of *On Compromise* (1874), that 'it makes all the difference whether we put truth in the first or the second place'. ('A friend whose happy fortune it had been to know many leading men of his time', said Morley, 'assured me that he did not think he could count more than five as really unsparing lovers of truth.') Equally necessary was Jowett's remark on Voltaire that 'he has done more good than all the Fathers of the Church put together'.

BURNING THE *FORTNIGHTLY*. Harrison's powerful defence of trade unions 'caused the review to be regarded as an incendiary publication', and 'papers of every view on national education were thought to indicate a deliberate plot for suppressing the Scriptures'. Did not Goschen at a political meeting call Morley 'the St. Just of the Revolution'? When the editor of the *Fortnightly* 'hinted at Welsh Disestablishment or the modest principle of one-man-one-vote' it was charged against him that 'in his secret heart he looked for his models in the Reign of Terror'. 'When I was seventeen', writes the author of *New Lamps and Ancient Lights*,[1] 'a copy of the *Fortnightly*, bought second-hand for a few pence, was discovered in my bedroom by an orthodox relative. Taking it in a pair of tongs and holding it high above his head, he marched downstairs and placed it at the back of the kitchen fire, with an awestruck household looking on'.

In the October issue of 1882, Morley took leave of the review.[2]

[1] By J. A. Spender (Cassell, 1940).
[2] THE W. L. COURTNEY RÉGIME. An informed and vigorous account of the *Fortnightly* under its various editorships is given by Mrs. W. L. Courtney in her attractive book on her husband, who edited the review for fifteen years (*The Making of an Editor*, Macmillan, 1930). She notes that no one before Morley

The *Fortnightly*, its departing editor wrote, had been 'confided to me fifteen years ago, *grande mortalis ævi spatium*, enough to bring a man from youth to middle age, to test the working value of convictions, to measure the advance of principles and beliefs'. It was 'hardly possible', he admitted, 'that a review should have been conducted for so considerable a time without the commission of some mistakes, articles admitted which might as well have been left out, opinions expressed which have a crudish look in the mellow light of years, phrases dropped in the heat or hurry of the moment which one would fain obliterate'.

The chief experiment which had been made by the review, as has been noted, was to print signed articles. This practice, a quarterly, to which heed was still given, had pronounced as 'senseless' as to have a magazine 'open to both sides of the question'. Morley wrote with satisfaction—but at what period might not a similar remark be made?—that 'principles and aims are coming into prominence which would hardly have found a hearing twenty years ago'. (Harrison had thought Morley's election to the Athenæum Club 'very significant'.) Also 'a certain number of people have been persuaded to share opinions that fifteen years ago were more unpopular than they are now'. 'A certain resistance' had been offered by the review 'to the stubborn influence of prejudice and use and wont', and 'whatever gives freedom of thought and earnestness to men's interest in the world must contribute to a good end'. It has been happily said that Morley was one of those who, as he himself wrote of Gladstone, 'helped to keep the soul alive in England'.

'THE DIFFICULT ART OF WRITING'. Morley, who speaks of 'the great, the noble and the difficult art of writing', quoted Lewes for the view that 'the first condition must be sincerity', and from

thought of indexing the articles! She quotes Morley's statement about the *Fortnightly* that it offered 'Rationalism without chill' and adds to Frederic Harrison's praises of Morley, his assertion that 'no other politician has been a great writer, and no other writer has directed great affairs'. Thomas Hay Sweet Escott, Morley's successor, was, Mrs. Courtney says, 'a surprise choice, in no sense a man of mark'. See page 123. 'The immediate result of the new editorship was an incursion of Conservative contributors'. After three years of Escott, whose later days were those of mental enfeeblement, Frank Harris had his fling, 1886–1894. Courtney followed 1895–1900. With the death of Frederic Chapman in 1895 he became, first, a director and then chairman of Chapman & Hall. Mrs. Courtney, who was his highly competent assistant, records that one of Mr. Courtney's instructions, with three underlinings, to the *Fortnightly* 'readers' was, 'Do not correct Mr. Henry James's style'. Her close association with the direction of the review is evidenced by the fact that when Courtney was dying his last words to her were, 'Do you think you can carry on?' Courtney's successor was a Canadian named Hammond, who had bought the review for a large sum. He was titular editor, and was succeeded by W. Horsfall Carter. In 1939 John Armitage, the present editor, sat metaphorically in John Morley's chair, metaphorically because, he tells me, his great predecessor seems to have done his work not at an office at his publisher's, but at home, and neither he nor Chapman & Hall have memorials or records of any kind.

Mill: 'It is qualities of mind rather than doctrine that make the inspiring teacher; though seriousness must be the *fond* of all charac- ters worth thinking about, a certain infusion of the laughing philosopher is a prodigious help towards bearing the evils of life.'

As for literature, 'are we not apt to make too much of it?' Morley asked. 'Literature is great and splendid, but it is only a part of life'. 'I really don't know', he went on, 'but would you rather have passed Mr. Gladstone's Irish Land Act, which brought a certain amount of concrete happiness to a great number of men, women and children, or would you rather have written Locke's *Human Understanding*? Which, the Act? I almost think so. Of course, literature inspires and stimulates actions, but how many books have had any profound influence on the world? Professor Bury said six in three hundred years. No, literature and politics ought to go together. The author has duties outside his study. He is a citizen, he is a man.' When Morley was asked why he preferred to write a biography of Cromwell rather than of Milton, he told Hirst that 'Cromwell was a statesman and a man of action, whereas Milton was a poet and a student, a man of letters first'. One thinks of the remark of Morley's recorded by Austin Harrison, that he went into politics 'to try to lead men' because he knew the futility of an attempt 'to reform them through books'.

RELIGION AND 'THE SMILE OF THIS WORLD'. Like Glad- stone, Morley was, as we have seen, a hard and methodical worker— the G.O.M. spoke of what he owed to using odd ten minutes—a man who tried to employ all his time. That was one of the bonds between Gladstone and his biographer. They did not speak on religion. Yet Gladstone in his later years expressed a desire to live in 'ever closer sympathy and communion with John Morley'. 'On the whole', Gladstone wrote on another occasion, 'the best stay I have.' What succoured Morley on his own journey was his conviction that 'the world grows better, that man is happier in doing good than in doing evil, and that life—even as we know it— is good'. Even as we know it—'Have you ever thought', he asked, 'that the mass of the world is always hungry? Hunger and fear are the familiars of the great majority of men and women and little children.'

It was 'certainly not less possible to disbelieve religiously than to believe religiously', he said to a former tenant of mine in Essex, Harold Begbie. Morley told him the old story of the priest who was too ill to preach, and, when the Devil appeared in the sacristy, prevailed on that versatile personage to go into the pulpit and harangue the congregation. Satan preached a masterly sermon and the priest condoled with him on having well nigh ruined himself. 'O dear no', said the Devil; 'no harm done; there was no unction in it.' Morley urged that there was 'little unction in my poor books, and there ought to be; it ought not to be all preaching'. But who among his readers is not content with the moralist's books as they are? I will allow myself a favourite passage for a quarter of a century, from *On Compromise*, a title which prompted the well-known witticism that no sign of compromise could be found in it except on the title page. Augustine Birrell acknowledged that the reading of the book was a landmark in his life:

And what is this smile of the world, to win which we are bidden to sacrifice our moral manhood; this frown of the world, whose terrors are more awful than the withering up of truth and the slow going out of light within the souls of us? Consider the triviality of life and conversation and purpose in the bulk of those whose approval is held out for our prize and the mark of our high calling. Measure, if you can, the empire over them of prejudice unadulterated by a single element of rationality, and weigh, if you can, the huge burden of custom, unrelieved by a single leavening particle of fresh thought. Ponder the share which selfishness and love of ease have in the vitality and the maintenance of the opinions that we are forbidden to dispute. Then how pitiful a thing seems the approval or disapproval of these creatures of the conventions of the hour, as one figures the merciless vastness of the universe of matter[1] sweeping us headlong through viewless space; as one hears the wail of misery that is for ever ascending to the deaf gods; as one counts the little tale of the years that separate us from eternal silence. In the light of these things, a man should surely dare to live his small span of life with little heed of the common speech upon him or his life, only caring that his days may be full of reality, and his conversation of truth-speaking and wholeness.[2]

And here is a quotation in moving terms, in appreciation of Morley, from Hirst's rich store:

The convictions slowly gained by hard reading, reflection, discussion, and controversy were always tenaciously held, nor ever discarded or disowned in hours of trial and discomfiture. Beneath a fine tolerance and affability in the society of friends from whom he differed, lay a stern fidelity to unfashionable principles, a grim loyalty to desperate causes, which more than once outweighed all other claims and interests. The blood of the martyr was in his veins. Politics, with all its second bests and compromises, was for him a religion when great moral issues had to be faced. In those times he did not flinch, but was ready and willing to testify. His articles of faith were few and simple—trust in reason and in the reasonableness of mankind, a profound love of peace, a sturdy belief in personal liberty, in the virtue of self-government, in public economy, in free trade. Even those who reject them all can esteem his sincerity.

[1] Universes now.
[2] Morley's books were published—on the pleasant page and in the good type of the period—by Macmillan. I am sorry to learn that, except *Burke*, all of them, even *Cobden* and *Gladstone*, are out of print. This also applies to Hirst's *Early Life and Letters of John Morley* which is no longer published by Macmillan in co-operation with Mr. Hirst. *On Compromise* is however in the 1s. 6d. 'Thrift Library' (Watts).

A MORLEY ANTHOLOGY. It is strange that the collectors of aphorisms of quality, of pithy phrases and discerning judgments have never made a selection from Morley. No modern's pages draw more pencillings down their margins. 'A slack-minded, wool-gathering, sluttish piece of work', he says of one author. 'A limp intelligence straining itself into mock force' is what he thinks about another. He described an ex-Premier and former Derby winner as 'a dark horse in a loose box' and called political rhetoricians 'wordsters'.

Without conning the twelve volumes in the *Collected Works*, what a haul one can have merely in turning over some pages of the *Recollections*, now out of print! Mr. Guy Morley kindly allows me to quote freely:

Mill compared with Carlyle. 'All the grand sources of human suffering, Mill was convinced, are remediable more or less by human effort. The process is slow; many generations perish in the breach; every mind intelligent enough and generous enough to bear a part, however small, will draw an enjoyment in the contest which he would not for any bribe in selfish indulgence consent to be without. After an hour with Carlyle you walked away stirred to the depths by a torrent of humour. But of direction, of any sign-post or way out, not a trace. It was a healthy restorative in passing homeward along the Embankment to fling oneself into the arms of any statistician, politician, political economist, sanitary authority, poor-law reformer, drainage enthusiast, or other practical friend of improvement whom genial accident might throw in one's way. Things may be only a bad second-best, but energy and action, not general ruination, is the moral. *On Liberty* belongs to the rare books that, after hostile criticism has done its best, are still found to have somehow added to man's stature.'

'A daylight mood'. 'If it found you in a daylight mood, it acted as a stirring rebuke to loitering quietism of brain and all cowardice of soul.'

Meredith. 'It was his buoyant energy, his sincerity of vision, his spaciousness of mind and outlook, his brave faith in good, in the rise of good standards, in the triumphs of good—these it was that made him a rare moral and intellectual force, the teacher of a sane and wholesome lesson, among those who had the happiness to be his friends, long years before the world found out the fire and strength and richness in his genius.'[1]

The day of Herbert Spencer's funeral. 'Pondering upon an indefatigable intellect, an iron love of truth, a pure and scrupulous conscience, a spirit of loyal and beneficent intention, a noble passion for knowledge and systematic thought, as the instruments of man's elevation.'

In justification of Parliamentary Government. 'I hinted delicately and respectfully [to Taine] that when you have inspected all the vices and shortcomings of parliamentary government through the strongest magnifying glass

---

[1] The only person Meredith asked to his wife's funeral was Morley, 'to support him on his forlorn march of dust'. From a letter to Morley: 'I do not see you, but I live much with you.' There is a sonnet 'To J.M.' to be found in Meredith's *Poems and Lyrics*.

that any critic or doctrinaire can construct, parliamentary government is
still better for a Western society than the best despot that ever was known.
If so, what is the use, and what is the manliness, of shivering about
democracy?

Wise statesmen. 'Great economic and social forces flow with tidal sweep
over communities only half conscious of that which is befalling them.'

Leslie Stephen. 'It is a comfort to think of you as having undergone your
full share of varied experiences of life, and yet remaining so kind, serene,
genial, penetrating, ripe.' Soon after he died, 'Patient, open-minded,
unselfish, firm, unshaken to the end'.

After a successful speech. 'Felt not exactly deficient but pleasantly intrepid. It was *me*, and 'tis the *me* that makes the fleeting fortune of a
speech.'

The 'rough unhewn substance of English character.' 'A very good substance,
too, if well treated, and capable of very effective polish if lucky enough to
get a chance of it.'

The coast of the Western Highlands. 'The weather perfect, lovely films of
vapour, great sweeping bursts of sunshine, dark iron mountains, gleaming
slopes of verdure, glistening crags, strange evanescent veils of cloud and
luminous curtains of rain, the fresh tumbling sea. The gulls, with their
hoarse cries, wheeling in great flocks; the little puffins; the strange pairs
of guillemots battling with the water, ducking and diving—the hand of
man or history counting for nothing in the scene.'

'Agitator' and 'Philanthropist'. It is a life-long way of mine not to be
afraid of either word. Most of what is decently good in our curious world
has been done by these two much-abused sets of folk.'

The Commonplace. 'I am always finding the commonplace is the true
essential.'

Plaindealer and Thinker. 'I persistently admire the Plaindealer, while
ready to own that the Plaindealer is not necessarily the clear thinker.'

Non-party people. 'Mostly we may safely assume that they are passably
good Tories.'

Workaday truth. 'People of good temper are not always kind people.'

Low spirits. 'Love of truth is often a true name for temper. Our opinions
are not more important than the spirit and temper with which they possess
us. Though I am commonly a man of good though pretty serious spirits,
low spirits are what we call the mood in which we see things as they are.'

Decision. 'I may delude the House of Commons, or constituents, or a
public meeting into thinking me somebody quite different from what I
really am. But your office has you at close quarters; every hour of the day
it is testing your temper, judgment, tact, industry, insight, foresight,
firmness, will, commonsense.'

Loitering. 'With Hobbes's warning at heart that we should either work or
play but never loiter, I stayed in my library.'

A full life. 'Too often a euphemism for a rather empty one.'

The sacred service. 'An incident that does the sacred service of making
hearts feel the warmer for mankind.'

The End. 'Unmanly repinings or garrulous self-pity which not seldom,
even in the case of men who have done good work in their noontide, rob

the close of life of its divinity and fortitude. There is no solace obtainable except that of an energetic fortitude.'

The Anchor. 'In common lines of human thought and act, as in the business of the elements, winds shift, tides ebb and flow, the boat swings. Only let the anchor hold.'

Difficulties. 'It is difficult, but we are all of us engaged in surmounting difficulties.'

The Future. 'Though the obstructionists in the Church and State may have their little day we others have the future.'

CHAPTER IV

POLITICIAN, PUBLICIST AND FRIEND

M.P. AND MINISTER. Morley was backing Gladstone's attitude in the Russo-Turkish war when I, as a boy of eleven, seemed to be the only supporter of Russia at my grammar school. He sought a better understanding with Russia and was an early admirer of Sir D. Mackenzie Wallace's great work, the reading of which marked for some of us an advance in our knowledge of that vast land—'one of the stoutest and most honest pieces of work produced in our time' was his just encomium. About Ireland he had, as he once said, read, thought and written all his life. Two years after he became editor of the *Fortnightly* he spoke at the first meeting in London in support of votes for women. He had been drawn into politics, H. A. L. Fisher says, 'by the spectacle of poverty seen from his windows in Lincoln's Inn'. When he stood unsuccessfully for Blackburn in 1869, in, of course, pre-ballot days, he was one of four candidates who addressed a difficult audience from the hustings. The only Liberal who ever got in for the town, Philip Snowden said, owed his success to the fact that his dog had just won the Waterloo Cup. It was not until 1880 that Morley became at Newcastle-on-Tyne the colleague of the robustious Radical Imperialist, Joe Cowen, of the rude but not a little serviceable Newcastle *Chronicle* which I often read in my boyhood in the North.[1] There Morley was 'honest John' who 'hated a hugger mugger of truth or a smoothing out of facts, and would not subscribe perfunctorily to church or chapel or to any sporting enterprise'. 'Unbeliever' though he was, he held the confidence of a largely Nonconformist constituency through six elections. Finally, in 1895, through imperfect 'nursing' and the growing demand for an eight hours' day, with which he was not in sympathy, he lost the seat. He had then the satisfaction of being returned for the constituency which had sent Joseph Hume to St. Stephens, Montrose Burghs, and represented it acceptably—he dedicated his *Gladstone* to the electors—until he received his Viscountcy in 1908.

He had been Chief Secretary at Dublin Castle, helper with the

---

[1] There is a good account of this curious character in Aaron Watson's *Newspaper Man's Memories* (Hutchinson).

57. Elm Park Gardens,
South Kensington.
S.W.

Oct. 16. 97.

My dear C.B.—

AMUSING LETTER FROM JOHN MORLEY TO

CAMPBELL-BANNERMAN WHEN PRIME MINISTER

Home Rule Bill, as a son to Gladstone in his old age (see Laurence
Housman's 'Gladstone's Comforter'), and, after the Liberal leader's
death, his masterly biographer (1903). He was a resolute preacher
of common sense about South Africa on the eve of the Boer War
(1899) and, with John Burns, retired from the Asquith Government
on national policy before the War of 1914. On a second visit to
the United States he stayed with President Theodore Roosevelt.
The patience, enlightenment and tact which he exercised in the
office of Secretary of State for India are reflected in his friendly
letters to the Viceroy, Lord Minto, in the *Recollections*, and in the
Life by Syed Sirdar Ali Khan, who says he 'introduced a new era
in Indian life' and 'widened the horizon of her peoples'. In a large
collection of letters between Morley and Campbell-Bannerman
during C-B's Prime Ministership, preserved in the British Museum,
Morley reports in reference to the trouble between Curzon and
Kitchener, that he had told the King that he was 'trying to build
a bridge of gold for the angry creatures.'

'PRISCILLA' AND CAMPBELL–BANNERMAN. The letters
incidentally illuminate the relationship of Morley and Campbell-
Bannerman, who is known to have called him Priscilla. One letter
suggests the O.M. for James Bryce. Another, on Cabinet reconstruc-
tion, is marked 'Secretissimus'. A third recounts an incident of a
visit to the Prime Minister's home: 'An elderly gent did indeed by
inadvertence pull the bath string, but when the douche came down
he gave a sharp howl, huddled on his dressing gown and was back
in his bed in a trice. That's me'. A common signature is 'Ever
Yours'. One letter ends 'With sentiments of the highest and most
unalterable consideration'. Another adds 'A Biscuit for Bordeaux',
evidently a dog; one letter sends greetings to Zulu.

If ever in the course of his political career he saw himself leading
the Liberal Party and being Prime Minister—and Spender says
that 'at one time they were very serious ambitions'—his dreams
had closed when Gladstone's mantle was thrown on the shoulders
of Campbell-Bannerman. Towards the end of that volume of
correspondence in the British Museum I came on this letter (Feb.
28, 1907): 'As the King is to be absent for a long time you might
think it well to mention to him the possibility (the bare possibility)
of its being convenient to you to banish one of your colleagues to
the House of Lords, and so discover what view H.M. would take
of the matter. Pray hint to him that a Dukedom and the Garter
would be cheap at the price. Of course don't answer this whimsical
and superfluous note'. Morley received his Viscountcy from Asquith
after the death of Campbell-Bannerman. He told an American
correspondent that, having done for the cause of Indian reform all
he could as a Commoner, it was necessary for him to enter the

House of Lords in order to finish the task.[1] He once expressed a
wish to 'walk along the House of Lords with Aristotle on one arm
and Machiavelli on the other'. He did not take the oath of allegiance
but affirmed, and an observer reported that he 'blushed like a
girl'. He once spoke of 'we middle class people disguised as peers'.
A rhymester recalled Morley's make-them-or-end-them and declared
that the King

> Improves the peers by ten per cent
> In making John a Viscount.

One of the best appreciations of Morley as a politician is H. W.
Massingham's obituary article in the *Fortnightly*: 'He was the last
of the great, the true Liberals. With him there retires from politics
the Liberalism that men knew as a definite thing, a scheme of
thought different from Conservatism or Socialism but with a
meaning and principles of its own; a temper and habit of mind
peculiar to the great thinkers and moralists of the eighteenth and
nineteenth centuries; and a conception of government consonant
with much peace and happiness to mankind.'

THE BIOGRAPHIES. The success of his *Life of Richard Cobden*,
Morley told Chamberlain, amazed him. 'Long, prompt and
uniformly laudatory reviews in all quarters. 1,500 exhausted in
four days: they are going to press with another 1,500 at once.
Gladstone wrote me seven pages, very civil and friendly. Altogether,
I'm astonished.' To meet the expenses involved in the writing,
Chamberlain had made a loan to Morley, 'punctiliously repaid'
when the task was done. 'Dear Chamberlain', he wrote to his
friend, 'you know how grateful I am to you and shall remain all
my days.' The wide sale—of the popular edition more than 30,000
copies were bought—explains something of Morley's hold on
Liberal opinion before the publication of his monumental *Life of
Gladstone* (1903). Of that second task he says that it 'occupied four
years of pretty vigorous exertion'. The papers at Hawarden num-
bered 300,000![2]

---

[1] *John Morley and other Essays*, G. McLean Harper. Published by the Princeton
University Press, which also published *The Liberal Mind of John Morley* by Warren
Staefler.

[2] The severity of the task which Morley and his assistants faced may be imagined
when it is learnt, as stated in an article in *The Times*, that, when the Hawarden
papers were finished with, two large vans were needed to take them to the British
Museum. The Museum kept about a quarter of a million. They now occupy
750 indexed volumes. As many as 3,000 of Gladstone's correspondents are in the
Dictionary of National Biography. Gladstone had kept the notes of 'my maiden speech'
at the debating society at Eton. He had also 200 sermons which he had delivered
to his family in the course of thirty years. Morley speaks of the 'willing and
valuable help' of Hirst, 'afterwards so well known as a political economist'. For
the second half of the *Life*, Morley mentions, his assistant was W. T. Stead's son
William, 'too soon taken from his friends, admirably trained by his wonderful father
in all those arts of close attention and minute accuracy required by such a work.'

Morley's own *Recollections* (1917) were written, as he acknowledged, when he felt that he could not always fully recall or keenly interest himself in some of the events in which he had played his part. The personage who is a hero to his literary aide, working day by day with him in conditions of some strain, must be of no ordinary clay, and it may well be noted that Hirst, after the searching Hawarden experience, and after seeing Morley 'in ordinary times in London at least once a week', regards him as 'the greatest man I have ever met, most inspiring of politicians, most fascinating of talkers', a great man 'even when he failed, as I sometimes thought, in political action—cautious, responsible, slow'—did he not in his dedication of his *Cobden* to Bright speak of his devotion to 'sedate government'?

It was Morley's view that 'biography in the hands of a man of the requisite capacity and sensibility is perhaps the very highest form of prose writing'. He was thoroughly English, too, in holding that the lives of good men and true should be a means of edification.

To Morley's biographical and autobiographical works of his *Fortnightly* period there are to be added his *Walpole* in his *Twelve English Statesmen* (1889), and his *Cromwell*, a work of which he himself thought well and his old colleague at the *Saturday Review*, Lord Salisbury, praised (1900), *Notes on Politics and History* (1913), four volumes of *Miscellanies*, *Indian Speeches* and *Memorandum on Resignation* which was published after his death (1928). The 'Men of Letters' series which he edited has never been bettered in ability and concision; in his *Twelve English Statesmen* there were some noteworthy books including Rosebery's *Pitt*, Harrison's *Cromwell* and *Chatham*, and his own *Walpole*. In 1883 he wrote a considerable introduction to some volumes of Emerson. He 'reluctantly' declined an invitation to write the life of Disraeli.

RECOLLECTIONS AND LORD ACTON'S LIBRARY. In the two volumes of *Recollections* the experiences of a full life are related with dignity, liveliness and exactitude. I for one have valued the work enough to buy it once in this country and, in order to read it again, once more in Japan. The work is a staying thing, for it has not only thought and matter but charm, not only history but a close view of the making of it. Besides the intrinsic value of what is written, there are, as we have seen, the fit phrases—and what writer has a greater wealth of apposite words? Until Winston Churchill, the writing of no modern statesman has been at so high a literary level in so many volumes. In Morley there was also a discernment of and a devotion to the best things in life, passion for the welfare of mankind, joy in its moral and intellectual advance and firm faith in its future which give freshness to his oldest work.

The Scots-American millionaire Andrew Carnegie, of Pittsburgh and the British provincial free libraries, gave Morley Lord Acton's great library. Most of it the recipient passed on to Cambridge—not his own university. 'I toyed with the fancy of retaining it for my own use and delectation, but I am not covetous of splendid possessions, and life is short'. Morley's library of his own 'genial, instructive and fortifying comrades' was, Lord Esher tells us, forty feet square: 'I found J.M. in that charming library of his, tacked on to a Wimbledon commonplace villa, surrounded by 11,000 books, reading a volume of Calvin. Two servant maids, and a plain old wrinkled wife. Memories of Lancashire hovered about him still. The virtue of the books he has read has passed into him and helps to give this frail middle-class library student moral and intellectual fibre.'[1]

Mrs. Asquith mentions[2] that 'the most fastidious and fascinating of men suggested seriously that, when we went out of office (which might happen any day), he and I should write a novel together. He said that if I would write the story and do the female characters, he would manage the men and politics'.

'THE AIR OF OLYMPUS'. Of the career of Morley in the House of Commons—the Speaker's secretary assured Lord Morley that he was 'the most popular man' there—an impression is given by J. A. Spender, who had frequent access to him. Morley had asked Spender to read 'mercifully' his studies of Voltaire, Rousseau, Turgot and Condorcet, remembering 'the volume of water which has flowed under the bridges since they were written'. On which Spender makes a pointed comment in reference to Morley's Parliamentary life:

These studies of the great Frenchmen to whom nineteenth century Liberalism traced back many of its leading ideas earned him the reputation, which he never quite shook off, of being a doctrinaire in practical affairs. The large discursive generalisations which gave profundity to his writings were not easily reduced to the scale of party politics. He was recognised as a most distinguished ornament of the party, and it was agreed that everything in the world should be done to give him pleasure and show him respect, but the dyed-in-the-wool Parliamentarians were clear that he was not one of them and that he would not do to lead them. The literary man, the late-comer into Parliament should go thus far and no farther. This is what chiefly weighed upon him, when to Asquith's great astonishment in 1908 he announced his decision to quit the Commons for the Lords.[3]

'An unfulfilled wish of Morley's was to be Secretary for Foreign Affairs; his style was exactly suited to the great occasions in international affairs'. He once took the place of Lord Grey for a fortnight in order to give him a holiday, and the Foreign Secretary

[1] *Journals* (Nicholson & Watson, 1934).
[2] *The Autobiography of Margot Asquith* (Penguin edition).
[3] *Life, Journalism and Politics*, J. A. Spender (Cassell, 1927).

afterwards wrote: 'From what I heard from officials at the Foreign Office, he enjoyed it almost as much as I enjoyed the holiday'.[1]

Spender, who had good sources of information, wrote that in the posts Morley had filled as a Secretary of State he was 'first class'. 'Unlike most literary men he was both methodical and industrious; whether at home or in the office you could seldom ask for a paper or a reference without his instantly being able to find it, and he brought the same conscientious care to the small things as to the great.' Dr. Gilbert Murray kindly tells me that Morley once said to him that 'at journalism or writing he was tired out at the end of a seven hours day, but as Chief Secretary for Ireland he could work thirteen hours without trouble, because the work had all been done by his office, and he had for the most part only to read files and confirm decisions'. Indeed, as Hirst says, 'the air of Olympus agreed with him. He enjoyed the pomps and ceremonies and privileges of high office.'

MORLEY'S TEMPERAMENT. Morley told Spender that on his becoming Secretary of State for India (1905), when the Curzon-Brodrick-Kitchener quarrel was still simmering, the first thing he did was 'to issue a warning to all and sundry that if any of them threatened to resign, his resignation would be instantly accepted.'[2] Yet within a few weeks he himself was telling the Prime Minister that if he did not get his way on what seemed to be some relatively unimportant point there would be a 'vacant stool in Whitehall'. 'The threat of the "vacant stool" was a constant worry to Campbell-Bannerman and Asquith. Asquith told me that he had at least twenty letters of resignation from Morley before he accepted the resignation of 1910.' Another member of the Government put the number at precisely twenty-three. Rosebery said that in office Morley could be 'extraordinarily irritable', and that 'he would not put up with the thorns; he was 'very trying'. When someone said to Rosebery that Morley was 'such a perfect gentleman' he replied, 'Such a perfect lady'. Guy Morley once told me that Augustine Birrell used to say he always pictured Morley as sitting back in his armchair and saying 'No, no, no'. Sir Newman Flower states in his history of Cassell's that Asquith, in a moment of exasperation, once called Morley a 'skunk'. It seems incredible but Sir Newman assured a friend of mine that it was true.

On his resignation with John Burns, Lord Grey said, 'We felt sure the eve-of-the-War resignations were based on deep and sincere conviction, not on any pusillanimity or opportunism and respected the two men accordingly'.[3] Lord Esher notes Morley having spoken to him on 'the insanity of all forms of war'.

[1] *Twenty-five Years*, Lord Grey of Fallodon (Hodder & Stoughton), 1925.
[2] *Twenty-five Years*.   [3] *Twenty-five Years*.

AS A SPEAKER. Lord Haldane writing of Morley said 'there was a good deal of the Conservative element in him'. One remembers his, 'Be reformers but be slow reformers'. Bernard Shaw spoke of Morley's 'eighteenth-century Rip-van-winkleism'. As for ambition, to which allusion will be made later on, Haldane says: 'He was not ambitious in any commonplace sense, but he was in reality ambitious. I have always believed that his real desire was to be Prime Minister. But for such a position he was wholly unsuited by his nature, physical as well as mental. I am not sure that he did not know this. He had courage in drawing conclusions, but he had not much physical courage. I have seen him shrink from an encounter with a strong personality when he need not. As a speaker, when he had time to prepare closely and polish his phrases, he was very effective. His speeches on the platform were among the best of the time. But for the House of Commons he was lacking in individual force. He was not good at the lightning-like decisions which debate there often requires. Looking back, I think his was the most interesting personality I ever knew.'[1] Lord Esher has a note of having counselled Lord Kitchener 'not to threaten John Morley as he is a stubborn, proud and obstinate man'.

Mr. Hadley once wrote to me: 'Morley was a "nervy" speaker. The first time I heard him, at an open-air meeting in 1886, he broke down and begged that no report should be sent to *The Times*. But, at his best, he was remarkably impressive; there was no one in the Liberal Party then, except of course Gladstone, who so profoundly moved a great audience. Later, throat trouble made him "nervy" again; I remember one occasion when, as a big provincial meeting was due to begin, he was seized with funk and for a time refused to leave his hotel. Yet the speech he made that night was described to me by a distinguished Parliamentarian as "one of Morley's very best".' Mr. Ratcliffe tells me that 'by the time Morley was Secretary for India his speaking was ragged; his big platform orations were written'.

THE FRIENDSHIPS OF POLITICAL OPPONENTS. Like Chamberlain, Balfour had uttered many a sharp criticism of Morley, but that Conservative Prime Minister wrote: 'Morley and I were made to get on together, if only we had not fundamentally differed on every question of political or religious interest. This unfortunate fact left our friendship essentially unchanged, but hampered its manifestations.'[2] Balfour once said he liked Morley better when he was writing history than when he was making it. They were seen at concerts together—a phrase of Morley's sticks in one's mind, 'a piece of ineffable, heartsearching melody by Beethoven or Handel'.

[1] *Journals and Letters of Reginald Brett, Viscount Esher* (Nicholson & Watson, 1934).
[2] *Chapters of Autobiography*, Lord Balfour (Cassell, 1930).

'Balfour and Morley', in Spender's view, 'had more in common in their mental make-up than any other two men in public life. Had Balfour been required to earn his living as a young man, he too would surely have started as a writer. Throughout his life he has spoken as the writer speaks, delicately picking his words, amending and erasing as he goes along, never hesitating to keep his audience waiting while visibly in their presence he searches for the perfect mode of expression. Morley had actually more of the rhetorical in his composition than Balfour, and on the full-dress occasions of which he had received adequate notice, he could deliver stately and highly-polished orations beyond Balfour's compass.'[1]

Sir William Harcourt and Morley had flung gibes at one another. But it is to Morley that one finds Harcourt writing in support of an invitation to stay with him, 'Before you leave you shall be taught to milk a cow, make butter, set a hen, and all things which an educated man should know.'[2] Lord Rosebery said to Sir Edward Cook of Morley, 'He sincerely opposes me on foreign policy, but he would never thwart me; he's about my closest political friend'. Of Morley's letters Mrs. Humphry Ward has written, 'Nothing could have been kinder; at the same time there was scarcely one of them that did not convey some hint, some touch of the critical goad'. Morley was, she said, 'a great man to whom I owed much, a singular personal power combined with a moral atmosphere which had in it both the bracing and the charm that, physically, are the gift of the highest.' The same friend applies to Morley a sentence of Darmesteter's about Renan, 'So pliant in appearance, so courteous in manner, he became a bar of iron as soon as one sought to wrest from him an act or word contrary to the intimate sense of his conscience'. Florence Nightingale distributed several copies of that address of Morley's on 'Popular Culture' to be found in the *Miscellanies*.

THE SOCIAL SIDE. A glimpse at Morley's social side is afforded by a paragraph in a letter to his sister in 1884 mentioning that half a dozen friends to whom he gave dinner at the Reform Club included Chamberlain, Trevelyan, Lord Justice Bowen ('Conscious as we are of each other's shortcomings'), Delane of *The Times* and Meredith Townsend of the *Spectator*. One day he had Cobden's daughter to lunch, Mrs. T. H. Huxley to tea and Chamberlain to dinner. His long friendship with Chamberlain, in spite of their differing politics—they went to the theatre and the Continent together—was a credit to both men. After their political separation Chamberlain still sent Morley a gift of oysters at Christmas. Chamberlain, he said, had 'a genius for friendship'.

[1] *Life, Journalism and Politics*, J. A. Spender (Cassell, 1927).
[2] *Life of Sir William Harcourt*, A. G. Gardiner (Constable, 1923).

Miss Haldane speaks of discussing with Morley a subject always congenial to him, 'which one would rather have been, a great politician, a great preacher or a great legal orator. Morley fell heavily for the second, and quoted Savonarola as his ideal. In the pulpit, he said, you have the widest aims and the widest scope.'[1] 'He began to read at 5 a.m.' 'Morley had a gift rare in the eminent, he was an admirable, even a creative listener', says Mrs. M. A. Hamilton.[2] 'He started interesting topics and made everybody else talk better than they ever did before by virtue of some vivifying quality in his attention to and interpretation of what they said.'

'Personal association with Morley in any capacity', to quote Spender again, 'was delightful. His voice was fascinating; his manner exquisitely polite; he treated the "striplings", as he called us younger men, as if we were his equals in age and authority. Early in the day he peremptorily told me to drop the "Mister" either in writing or talk. Yet there were long periods in which the *Westminster* and its editor were a chronic irritant to him, and though he was always friendly to my face, he spoke and wrote his mind freely to other people, some of whom were obliging enough to pass on his observations and even his letters to me. These were more medicinal than flattering, but knowing the vehemence and transience in his moods, and the provocation I had offered, I could not take offence.'

Lord Grey, an old colleague with whom Morley had been at issue, spent two nights and a Sunday at Wimbledon and reports that 'it was very good to be with a mind which has voyaged so far and long through seas of thought'.[3] 'On the last evening of our visit, as Gilbert Murray and I were taking our leave', writes H. A. L. Fisher, 'Morley said, "I will send you away with a text", and kneeling on the floor, read out by the light of a candle, from a well-worn little copy of Bain's life of Mill, the master's prescription for a happy life, that we should never expect from life more than life can give, and that the happy life should be three parts practical'.[4]

Leslie Stephen told an American correspondent that he had 'no friend on this side of the water whom it gives me such pleasure to meet as Morley'. Meredith addressed him as 'Dearest St. B' (St. Bernard) and 'Dearest of Friends'. In his message to Morley when he went to the United States he said 'My thoughts and feelings will be the same as your wife's'.

'A STRONG INNER LIFE'. Once when I was talking with Lord Samuel he spoke with appreciation of Morley and happened to mention that he had contributed some memories of him to a

B.B.C. Overseas Service. I begged him to let me see a copy of his talk. Here are a few extracts: 'I was a young man, not long down from Oxford, and he was nearing sixty. He received me in his library—a bright room with large windows, lined with books in white painted book-cases; a man of slight build, not tall; with keen twinkling eyes; the nose strong, the chin somewhat receding; he had a voice that was clear and friendly, his manner was kindly and gentle. He came downstairs to see me out, patting me on the shoulder and saying "Bless you", as I was leaving.'

Continuing Lord Samuel said: 'There was a certain aloofness about him and he was aware of this. In his book of memoirs he quotes an article about himself which had mentioned among his characteristics "a certain austerity, as of a man who had fixed his face in many a solitary place against the wind and open sky". He was indeed a man with a strong inner life, resolute, self-reliant. His principles, purposes and actions, his writings and his speeches, were all the outcome of careful reflection, leading to firm conclusions. A keen intellect was incessantly at work, guided by a sensitive conscience and inspired by a fundamental humanity and goodwill.'

Lord Samuel recalled that at the meetings of the Asquith Cabinet, Morley, by virtue of seniority, used to sit next to the Prime Minister, 'Except when the matters under discussion directly concerned his own Department, he seldom intervened, and then briefly. A sensitive man, with strong convictions and not easily persuadable, I imagine that Prime Ministers must sometimes have found him an uncomfortable colleague.'

Lord Samuel concluded that when Morley died at eighty-four 'he had lived a full life. He brought to the public service a character of high integrity, and an acute mind, steeped in the broadest culture. And those gifts he had used abundantly to help to advance the welfare of mankind.'

CHAPTER V

'A GREAT ROMANCE'

AN UNPUBLISHED PORTRAIT. When I went to the *Pall Mall* I frequently worked at a deal desk-top made for Morley by the carpenter down the street.[1] I often asked what one of the most famous editors of the paper looked like. I could never get a satisfying picture. I am glad, therefore, to have been allowed to photograph the painting in the possession of Guy Morley, which, on the basis of years of association with his uncle, he believes to be the most successful representation of him. In print the best description of Morley, beyond what I have just reproduced from Lord Samuel, is to be found in a book to which I am indebted, *John, Viscount Morley* by Brigadier-General John H. Morgan.[2] 'To look at Morley's features in old age', he writes, 'was to read the story of a life of singular purity, in which the desires of the flesh had played little part—a life chaste, meditative and almost ascetic in its pursuit of Truth. He was small in stature and even frail in physique, but nature had given him a noble head. The face was long, narrow at the base, wide at the brow, with that fullness at the temples which is always the mark of intellectual distinction. The nose was large and slightly aquiline, the lips thin to severity, but capable of a most engaging smile, the eyes deep-set and of a bluish-grey like cooling steel as though hidden fires lurked within them. The eyebrows could be eloquent. In earlier years his face had a combative, almost disputatious expression, completely masking his innate kindness of heart, but

---

[1] Northumberland Street, referred to on page 4, contained, beyond this man's shop, only the office of the paper and a public house next door, both opposite the back premises of the Grand Hotel. The street is described in my *Story of the 'Pall Mall Gazette'* in relation to the unfortunate Richard Savage and to the outrage 'than which,' Thackeray said, 'Eugene Sue never invented anything more tremendous'. In view of the fact that the *Pall Mall* was to be so often accused of sensationalism and that in *A Newspaper Man's Memories* (Hutchinson) Aaron Watson, who was closely connected with the paper in the Morley-Stead days, recounts several sensational investigations conducted by Stead under the cold eye of Morley, it is of interest that Watson believed that the Thackeray outrage took place in the very building in which the *Pall Mall* was published. Mr. C. F. Osborn, archivist at the City of Westminster, refers me to mention of the pulling down in 1761 of Hartshorn Alley, which preceded Northumberland Street.

[2] Murray, 1924. This well-known authority on constitutional law, whose book is most attractive altogether apart from the excellent Morley matter, was a valuable functionary in uniform as a Deputy Adjutant General and Brigadier General. He is Emeritus Professor of Constitutional Law in London University.

as he grew older, Time, the most cunning of all sculptors, refined upon the original, the harsh traits were effaced, a certain suavity of line appeared, and the result was one of the most finely-chiselled faces of his age and generation.'

'AN INTELLECTUAL DISCIPLINE'. Morgan continuing says that to know Morley was 'an intellectual discipline'. 'It was not merely that he had read widely in all literature, ancient and modern, pagan and divine, but that he had thought deeply and had trained his mind as an athlete trains his muscles until he seemed to be always in the pink of intellectual condition.' He had not only 'a passion for literature' but 'an instinct for life'. John Buchan, Lord Tweedsmuir, once said that there ought to be a book called *The Three Saints of Rationalism*,[1] the three being Mill, Spencer and Morley. To understand Morley's 'intellectual ruthlessness'—Morgan has particularly in mind *On Compromise*, which I seem to be always mentioning—'one must remember that it was the work of a rationalist who had been all his life under arms against dogmatic theology, of a Liberal who had been fighting the battle of Nonconformity, of an educationist who had been the advocate of secular education, of a secularist who had joined issue over the abolition of University tests, of a Utilitarian who had attacked a philosophy which taught people to take certain things on trust instead of examining them for themselves. He was a disciple of Mill, "the wisest and most virtuous man I have ever known or am likely to know".' Morley, as Morgan says, was 'always everywhere a moralist'; 'Morley represents to me', Lord Esher told Stead, 'the moral element in our Party.' The estimate in *John, Viscount Morley* closes with the words applied to Cromwell, 'a larger soul hath seldom dwelt in a house of clay'.

Morgan's excellence is manifested in the candour with which he recognises the shortcomings of the man at whom Disraeli girded as a 'political finishing governess'—'he would not have been so intensely human if he had had them not'. He says that 'it is the supple opportunist, not the lofty moralist who is at home in politics; Gladstone is only an exception because he was a casuist'. Morley 'became less and less sure of anything as he grew old; to the end of his public days a man of letters in the custody of a politician'.

Morley tried Asquith sorely, so it is of interest to read Asquith's view of him as given to Spender:[2] 'There was nothing Morley disliked more than the suggestion that he was the literary man who had strayed into politics. He had high political ambitions, and protested that his writing was part of his politics. The claim was well founded, but the pen and the tongue have essentially different

---

[1] 'The Saint of Rationalism' was applied to Mill by Gladstone.
[2] *Life, Journalism and Politics* (Cassell, 1927).

techniques. To take his career as the test of the literary man in politics would be a serious mistake. He was Morley—a fascinating, gifted, exceptional man, as unlike other literary men as he was unlike most politicians. He was in fact less a literary man than a moralist with the pen.'

'WITH MY COLOURS FLYING'. I never heard Morley speak, but when I saw him from the gallery of the House of Commons I was struck by his moderate stature. But 'Nature had set upon him her own hall-mark of distinction'. Morgan says of his speaking to a North-country audience of miners and railwaymen that 'there was an unstudied downrightness of speech which was strangely moving'. It was 'emphasised rather than attenuated by the awkward gestures, the husky voice, the ragged sentence—in strange contrast with the polish of his literary style, for he was an orator *malgré lui* —all leaving on the mind of the hearer the impression that he was wrestling with his very soul, as perhaps indeed he was. Morley was a great platform force because his audience recognised in him the moral earnestness of the man'.

As has been noted, he lost his seat for Newcastle-on-Tyne by his downright opposition to the Eight Hours' Bill. A North-country-man, Angus Watson, writes: 'I heard him speak when he fully explained his attitude, finishing up his address with the statement: "Gentlemen, I desire to represent you to the best of my ability, but I will not endeavour to secure your vote on false pretences, and if to-morrow my ship goes down, at least it will sink with my colours flying." That it did.'[1] 'I believe that, agnostic though he be', wrote Canon MacColl to Lord Salisbury, 'he has more influence in the country than any Liberal leader, because of his moral earnestness and conscientious fidelity to his convictions regardless of personal consequences.' Lord Randolph Churchill thought that Morley was the best Liberal speaker of his day. Hirst says that he had 'the utmost contempt for the art of studying appearances and for the tricks by which public men catch the limelight'. 'He was the soul of sincerity, almost naïve; if he wanted high office he said so.' He applauded Hardy for having what Thucydides called 'the simplicity of all noble natures'.

In reviewing the fifteen volumes of Morley's *Collected Works* Morgan declares that their author 'was always more concerned to understand men than to condemn them'. Did he not say that 'there is a marvellous element in the human soul'? He had no sympathy with biographers who could not 'conceive of conduct excepting as either right or wrong'. 'What interests the world in Mr. Gladstone', he said in his great biography, 'is more what he was than what he did'.

[1] *My Life*, Angus Watson (Nicholson & Watson, 1937).

'PROFOUNDLY AMBITIOUS'. What was the explanation in Morley, Morgan asks, of 'those moods of estrangement from politicians and politics'? He answers that he had 'undoubtedly an abnormally thin skin' and he was 'profoundly ambitious'. 'Despite the glittering prizes he won, and winning, greatly enjoyed', he was out of his element in the heat and dust of politics. Balfour said of Morley that 'his fault in politics is being too negative. Morley's own assertion was that politics was 'a dodge, one long second best'—Rosebery said 'a poor business, aren't they?' E. T. Cook records in one of his diaries Morley having said to him in his library: 'Why should I leave this sunny room for that bench in the House of Commons with Harcourt bellowing into one ear and some bore into the other? I've twice discussed with Mr. G whether I may not fairly consider myself Emeritus. I've fought eleven fights. I've done what I could to hold up Mr. G's hands, and he said to me, "I can't deny you have earned Emeritus".'

As for the charge against Morley of ambition, he owned that 'it is always most difficult to draw a line between arrogant egoism and the identification of a man's personal elevation with the success of his public cause'. Morgan says there were 'few high offices of State to which he did not at one time or another aspire. He had great abilities, and, like most men, was conscious of them without being conscious of his limitations'. One finds Esher saying the same as another observer who has been quoted, he 'would like to be Prime Minister'. 'Failing that', he adds, 'he would go to the House of Lords.' His 'patrician moods', Morgan admits, 'were not rare; he loved power and enjoyed its exercise'. Hirst came to the same conclusion. 'Over-emphasis is the mark of self-distrust', Morgan goes on; 'no more autocratic Secretary for India ever reigned in Whitehall, none ever consulted his Council less, and assuredly ever admonished a Viceroy more'. Which is what we have heard already. Hirst explains, 'It was as though he was trying to live down a reputation as a doctrinaire.'

The suggestion has been made more than once that Morley had the feminine side, common in some measure to us all, science says, more developed than ordinary. In his *Recollections* Morley uses over and over again the word 'manly'. If these memories give us anything like a true presentation of the man—and, having regard to his firm rectitude, they cannot be far out—he himself was, in some ways indeed, a 'manly' fellow. His firm admirer, Morgan is driven to say, in a letter to me, that 'his great weakness was vanity'. But has it been noticed how many autobiographers of equal rank have omitted, as Morley does, a portrait from their memoirs? The readers of the *Recollections* receive the impression that he did not over-estimate himself. What he did do, as Morgan has said, was to under-estimate his qualifications for some kinds of work. His political career, Morgan thinks, was 'a triumph of character rather than of achievement'.

Stead, who at the *Pall Mall* had three years of the closest association with Morley, put the matter thus: 'There is one strange incongruity in his character. With idealism and all the elements, which, as he said, fitted him for the post of a religious teacher, there was mingled a strange seam of what an enemy might call self-seeking and personal ambition. He never lost himself in his cause, nor was he ever willing to be trodden under-foot if thereby the cause might prosper. At the beginning of the Irish business I was very much struck by the consciousness which he always had of himself and of his record. This rather grew upon him than otherwise. And when he got into Parliament it was more so than ever.'

In another place Stead recurs to Morley having said to him, that it was a mistake to have entered politics. 'His mood of mind harmonises more than mine with the truly religious ideal.' Morgan recalls the fact that Morley said to him, 'All the most important steps in my life, and the most successful, I've taken against advice'.

'SOMETHING REAL'. The judgment of most of the readers of the *Recollections* must be, I feel, that Morley was a man of high character, of deep and tried convictions, of uncommon powers, of unremitting industry—see the work he did on Guicciardini—and, for all those upright collars of his and for all the stiffness in his handwriting, a considerate, companionable man. No one ever presented me with a more vivid aspect of Morley than a journalist who had a fine gift, a gentle spirit and a clean heart, but had to write more than he ought to have done, Harold Begbie. He had paid a visit to Morley at his home, and a few weeks later he recorded in an article in the long-since-dead *Pall Mall Magazine* the impressions he gave me. He found Morley a 'blithe' soul, 'joyful and gentle, glad and kind, merry and merciful'. There was 'something real about the man, something noble, something charming, something very human.' Morley said to Begbie: 'I am very fond of books. But I like, with all my heart, good talk, talk that interests and amuses and perhaps stimulates. One's mind is stirred; one's heart is drawn.'

THE CHARGE OF VANITY. What is the very worst imputed to Morley? Some years ago I felt jarred by two passages in a well-written book of great interest, *My Fill of Days* by Sir Peter Chalmers Mitchell.[1] On Morley he cited the views of two friends of his, William Minto, his old instructor at Aberdeen University,[2] and

[1] Faber & Faber, 1937.
[2] Author of *A Manual of English Prose Literature* and *Characteristics of English Poets from Chaucer to Shirley*.

E

Professor Ray Lankester. Minto was once editor of the *Examiner*
and had a wide acquaintance which included Meredith, Browning,
Tennyson, George Eliot and Lewes. He disliked Morley; but
Minto had, Sir Peter admits, occasionally his 'east-windy atmosphere'. Lankester had 'a violent distaste' based on what he took
to be Morley's active share in his troubles with the British Museum
Trustees, of whom Morley was one. 'Lankester was with William
Heinemann and myself in the South Cevennes, and on the top of
the Causse Noir gave us a vivid representation of how Lord Morley
would appear hanged by the neck until he was dead, with his head
on one side and his tongue lolling out.' I have myself only a hazy
recollection of Lankester but I recall the fact that, although a
scientist of unquestionable distinction, he was an easily ruffled
and by no means judicious person. Sir Peter in a letter to me
conceded that what he wrote fifteen years ago was 'not a criticism
of Morley but of a superior benevolence which I thought was
irrelevant to the harsh struggles into which the world was plunging;
the plunge was made and my criticism seems more just than ever.
Morley was a queer mixture, but then so we all are'. And he said
that it was of interest to collect, as I was doing, 'reflections from
Morley's facets'.

Going back to the charge of vanity, is it not possible, in Burns's
phrase, to 'propone defences'? Everyone dislikes vanity. But vanity
is not always overweening. Is it fair usage to humanity to judge
severely a man's honest self-recognition of the value of painstakingly
cultivated talent and toiled-at performance? 'I am not a fool, my
intelligence is far above average', Mr. Nehru was moved last year
to say in a speech. The remarkable man standing out among his
contemporaries who was Morley was the man he had himself made.
His intellectual achievement was the fruit of long-sustained effort
and self-discipline. His writing of distinction was the fruit of a
life-time of unslackened labour. His statesmanlike outlook was
gained by protracted study at high levels, by openness of mind and
warm feelings, and by a disposition towards justice and charity.

LADY MORLEY. Many readers of both Morgan and Hirst
must think of the motto cut on the mantelpiece of Morley's
library, 'The nobler a soul is the more objects of compassion it
hath'. I have spoken of the fine feelings of the owner of that library
towards dumb creatures. In a well known photograph he has the
devotion of his snuggling terrier. But there are people who have
dogs or cats and make much of them who are not conspicuously
humane in their relations with human beings. On the domestic
side, Morley was unknown to the public. Lady Morley went nowhere. I do not remember any photograph of them together.
I know no photograph of her alone. So I am going to say something

about Morley's domestic relations, for a conspicuous test of a man's character is his relationship with women.

Lord Esher has been quoted as referring, towards the end of Morley's life, to his 'plain wrinkled wife'. Marriage, Morley wrote, is 'dependent on elements too delicate to be capable of being fully divulged or fairly seized'. His sister said, 'I am not surprised that he married her'. She lived only a few weeks after his death. Meredith refers to her name, Rose: 'As for the rose of Patterdale, her coronet has been too long withheld; she won it on the Westmorland-Cumberland hills and fells'. Hirst says: 'She was a good walker' —as Morley was; he once said that he was 'made of iron and catgut'—'and afterwards an ardent cyclist, fond of the country, of trees and plants and birds'.[1] Lady Morley 'never cared much for politics, books or society; seldom visited or dined out', Hirst says; 'but she proved a loyal and devoted wife'. In a note to me he is good enough to add, 'She was simple and nice and we were on most affectionate terms'. She helped him greatly in giving him traits in her husband's character. 'J.M. was not the first eminent man', Hirst suggests, 'who did not want to have an intellectual wife'. When the Morleys were living at Pitfield Down, Morley, in a letter to Harrison, recounted that on Mill's visiting them, his 'simplicity and soft amiable way put Rose at ease and all through lunch they chattered most sociably and gaily of wild flowers and birds and weasels, in which he takes as keen an interest as she does'.

In another letter to Harrison there is a paragraph about Morley's 'day after day of laborious reading and still more laborious writing'. (The 'stoical obsession' of his table 'drives my sister so mad, out of its sheer monotony, that she fleeth to the noisy home of a surgical brother.) My wife, kindest of souls, sometimes wonders whether it would not be better to live in the carter's cottage whose farthing dip glimmers at this minute in the bottom of the valley at our feet, and earn a subsistence, I at the head of the team and she picking hops and pulling turnips and binding sheaves'.

'IF THAT STORY WERE EVER TOLD'. I have taken a good deal from Morgan's *John, Viscount Morley*, but has not its author genially written—caring only that the qualities of his friend should be known—'there are worse things than having one's stories cribbed'? I shall copy out from him the fine passage in which he takes leave of Morley: 'There never was a man more honest in his private life, and there can have been few more magnanimous; if that story were ever told, which it will never be,

[1] Morley himself once wrote: 'Country life, in spite of a certain danger of smallness and narrowness, is best for everybody. Of that I am, and have long been, convinced'. On another occasion his words were, 'I find Nature and the green earth the great composer; a quarter of an hour in my garden or on the heath puts the feverish battle of the day into the last century'.

it would be a tale of singular devotion, a tale of one whose whole
life was a noble comment on "Bear ye one another's burdens",
and who, living, fulfilled the law of Christianity. His ear was
strangely sensitive to the plaintive murmur of that river of human
tears "falling always in the shadow of the world". No man knew
better how to feel for human frailty and error. Hence a sympathy
with his kind, almost feminine in its delicacy and more than
masculine in its strength; to many a wounded spirit did he bring
words of assuagement and of peace. Of that "best portion of a
good man's life":

> His little, nameless, unremembered acts
> Of kindness and of love,

his share was large. No kinder heart nor one more sensitive ever
sweetened the intercourse of life. If I had to choose any one word
to express the quality of his soul, I should say it was his loving-
kindness'.

Morgan, restricting himself to two sentences, writes: 'There
had been a great romance. If the story were ever told, which
it will never be.' But it is close on half a century since Morley died.
He has entered into history.[1] His books, his writing in hundreds
of articles, his conversation, were marked by a solicitude for truth,
the whole truth. It may be said of biography, as Morley said
of autobiography, that it cannot be written if it 'cannot conscien-
tiously invite the world in general to come and be edified'. The
memorial which has been raised to Morley by Hirst and
Morgan, to which I am making my humble addition, cannot now be flecked by the relation of any fact. The echoes of
sly talk may still be heard now and then. The time has come to
dispose of it. Here is the story that has never been in print before.
It came to me several years ago.

'NEVER PREJUDICED HIS CAREER'. 'When a young man,
Morley became friends with a young married woman whom he
afterwards married. It was, as one would expect, a strictly honourable and very respectable friendship and nothing in the nature of
a liaison. One dark winter night she knocked at the door of his
rooms and in great distress told him she could stand no more of
her husband's brutality (he *was* a brute), had fled from the house
and had nowhere to go as she was penniless. Morley had only two
rooms—he told her to sleep in his bedroom and spent an uncomfortable night on the sofa in his sitting-room. The next day he said:
"I have compromised you; the only thing to do is for me to write
to your husband and invite him to divorce you and then I will

---

[1] 'What can it matter when we are both dead? Who can be hurt? We shall not
feel'.—*Havelock Ellis*, on his wife who lived apart from him.

marry you". The husband refused to divorce her, with the result that she and Morley lived together for many years until her husband died, whereupon Morley married her. She had several young children by her first husband—she and Morley never had any of their own—and Morley had them educated. "Everyone" knew of this long cohabitation before marriage and it says much for Morley's high reputation as a man of strict integrity that it never prejudiced his social and political career. But she "never went anywhere" with him socially and led a life almost of a recluse, and this had become such a habit with her that, even when they were eventually married, she rarely went out to social functions with him.

'I recall that I met him often at Lord Oxford and Asquith's but she *never* accompanied him. I met her myself often in Morley's own home where I was a constant visitor. I remember being struck, the first time I saw her, and before I knew anything of her unhappy married life, by the appearance of her face; it was the face of a woman who had evidently once been beautiful but whose features were *ravaged* by tragedy.' So much for the 'wrinkled' wife.

THE CRIMINAL PROCEEDINGS. The story goes on: 'By that time another tragedy had occurred in her life. A son of hers, that is Morley's stepson, got ten years' penal servitude for forgery in Scotland. He had gone round Edinburgh interesting wealthy Liberals and saying that Morley wanted them to finance a new Liberal daily paper for Edinburgh, holding out as a bribe a prospect of knighthoods for those who put up the money. He produced letters to this effect in Morley's handwriting—which he had forged. He received large sums of money. Then came his trial and conviction. Morley was "so upset" that he wanted to retire from public life but Asquith persuaded him not to. Morley took charge of this criminal stepson's children, who were I think many in number, and brought them up. It was a further distressing experience for Morley when a step-daughter joined the Roman Catholic Church and became a nun.'

In his *Life of Gladstone* Morley tells how the distinguished subject of his biography emerged with honour from what he terms 'a painful incident'. 'It cannot', Morley said, 'be wholly passed over.'[1] This wise decision has guided me in dealing with the matter which so much distressed Morley. X, employed by the well-known firm of publishers and printers, Messrs. T. & A. Constable, of Edinburgh, was a J.P. There were five charges of forgery for, in sum, the large amount of £13,350. As he pleaded guilty, Morley was not called upon to give evidence.

[1] It was a foul canard which had its basis in the fact that Gladstone had been seen speaking to a prostitute. He took her to his wife and it was afterwards explained that the Gladstones had long worked together to rescue women from the streets.

Two pathetic notes from Morley to Campbell-Bannerman I lighted on in the correspondence in the British Museum. One of them runs: 'Tomorrow is a mournful domestic occasion here, for sentence is to be passed. I must be with my two stricken women. So you will not mind my absence from the Cabinet'. Two days later Morley writes: 'There is a great deal of distress here as you will well believe, so I have again most unwillingly to absent myself from the Cabinet. Pray forgive me.'

A passage of Morley's in his *Cobden* comes to mind, 'It is one of the privileges of strength to add to its own the burdens of the weak'.

CHAPTER VI

EDITOR OF THE *PALL MALL GAZETTE*

A T THE HEIGHT OF HIS REPUTATION. On May 8, 1880, at the time of the formation of a new Liberal Government by Gladstone,[1] Morley sent this scrap to Chamberlain: 'Such strong pressure was brought upon me about the *P.M.G.* that today at four o'clock I agreed to become editor-in-chief'. He adds—in a curious phrase for him—'God knows what will become of it'.[2]

Viewed from the world of journalism Morley was among the leading intellects. He was constant, honest and pungent. He had ability, information and authority. He was 'a statesman among journalists'. As Sir Edward Cook, a later editor of the *Pall Mall*, was to write (in an historical article in the *Manchester Guardian*, of which Mr. A. P. Wadsworth has kindly discovered the authorship) Morley was 'a political influence of first-rate importance'. His accession to the editorship of the *Pall Mall* was 'a great gain to the Liberal Party'. Hyndman, the leader of the Social Democratic League, says in his *Record of an Adventurous Life*,[3] 'Morley was at the height of his reputation and the most important writer on the advanced side'.

WHAT IS AN EDITOR? But, as hopeful capitalists of newspapers and magazines have so often discovered, a man may be a public personage, a writer of marked skill, experience and devotion, and have high ideals of the mission of his journal or periodical,

---

[1] Gladstone's leading Ministers included Chamberlain, Lord Hartington, Lord Granville, Lord Derby, Lord Kimberley, Lord Spencer and Lord Selborne—so many peers were not to appear again in a Government until Mr. Churchill's Cabinet of 1940.

[2] Readers may refresh their recollection of the circumstances in which the editorship of the *Pall Mall Gazette* became vacant by turning back to page 4. Whether Morley was Yates Thompson's first choice I do not know. W. T. Stead had an impression that consideration was given to 'Scott of Manchester', that is, the famous C. P. Scott of the *Manchester Guardian*. Mr. A. P. Wadsworth tells me that he spoke on the matter on my behalf to a contributor, the late Dr. J. L. Hammond (of *The Village Labourer* and *The Town Labourer*) who, as the biographer of Scott, went through all the Scott papers. 'He had no recollection of anything connecting Scott with the *P.M.G.*' 'I should think, however', Mr. Wadsworth added, 'that it was quite possibly C. P. He would then have been in Manchester ten years'. It is indeed one of the 'ifs' of political, social and newspaper history if a pen so different from that of Morley and Stead had swayed the *Pall Mall* and there had not been the long and fruitful C.P.S. period at the *Manchester Guardian*! The note to Chamberlain is in J. L. Garvin's *Joseph Chamberlain* (Macmillan, 1932–3–4).

[3] Macmillan, 1911.

and lack that curious and, in truth, rather rare endowment that makes the born editor. His interest may be almost exclusively in what he and his friends write. He may not be the active editor of all his publication. He may not grasp the fact that it must be of wide interest as well as hortatory, that politics, literature and art are only some of the subjects for which the world cares. He may have no faculty or experience for the elementary duty of keeping in healthy existence the vehicle of which he is in charge. He may have no real appetite for current events. Frederick Greenwood, an editor who made history but lost several editorial chairs, confessed that he never looked at the news side of his paper, an evening paper, until the last edition was out !

H. W. Massingham, editor of the *Daily Chronicle* and then of the *Nation*, wrote sardonically: 'Mr. Morley had doubtless some of the gifts which go to make a journalist, but a passionate zeal for his profession, the journalist's *flair* for news—a coming crisis, an interesting personality, a picturesque event—he never had. The *Pall Mall* became the medium of an honourable, severe, able, but limited school of political Radicalism. Mr. Morley's essay-like leaders, written with less warmth of colour than his best literary work but models of pure and nervous English, were read, but his paper was not'. This although its price was reduced from two-pence to a penny.

Journalism, Morley's friend Carlyle had said, 'is juist ditch-watter'.[1] He himself had called it 'a huge engine for keeping discussion at a low level'. 'The avowed principle', even of *The Times*, he had averred, 'has always been to keep very close to the political opinion of the day in its unregenerate state'. Meredith declared that Morley's conception of a newspaper was 'a medium for circulating leading articles'.

'A DIFFICULT TASK'. Whatever his conception was—he did once tell Newcastle working men to give more attention to news than to leading articles—he faced a difficult task at the *Pall Mall*. Leslie Stephen, describing the *Pall Mall* as 'the incarnation of Greenwood', said 'the experiment will be a very ticklish one; it must clearly involve the loss of a great many of the old audience'. That audience was not large enough to permit of many desertions. Stephen acknowledges that Morley 'gives distinction' to the paper, but it is 'a pretty hard fight', for there is also in the field the *St. James's Gazette* 'with the old commander'. 'The *P.M.* and *St. James's* run a race which I guess is unprofitable to both'. A time came, however, when there were to be not two *Gazettes* but three.

Lord Houghton was also timorous. But Meredith was soon writing to a friend, 'How wonderfully well Morley is driving the

[1] Yet he saluted 'the Able Editor'.

THE *P.M.G.* OFFICES, NORTHUMBERLAND STREET

From the 'Review of Reviews'

Pall Mall. We may say he is too good for that, but he is a priceless editor. On the other hand the *St. James's* is an astonishing collapse of ability. It is nothing but incessant barking.' And he broke into rhyme:

> The day is going, now 'tis noon,
> Greenwood 'gins bay the Gladstone moon,
> While temperate Morley with assuaging voice
> Bids England in her bigger G. rejoice.

We hear of Mrs. Humphry Ward's and Sydney Colvin's 'Occ. Notes'. 'Colvin's collaboration on my small paper'—the date is May 14, 1880—'will be most welcome. We are in urgent need. Can you not send one from 8 to 15 lines now and then, while we wait to arrange for more serious matters. Pray help me, if you can. The shortest Note will be useful. Avoid the beaten track, as you would naturally do. Anything literary, social, educational, academic'. On another occasion he refers to 'my little paper'; the phrase had also been Greenwood's. A year later Morley says to Colvin: 'I wish Comyns Carr would write a bit harder for me. Why does a taste for the fine arts make men so tardy with their copy?' As to Occ. Notes, we come on one off 'the beaten track' which observes that 'it is not a happy omen that the consent of the Ecclesiastical Commissioners is required before the well-fed donkey who disports himself in the Lambeth Palace Grounds can be joined by the ill-fed, ragged urchins who now have no playground but the streets'.[1]

At the beginning of Morley's editorship—he was getting £2,000 a year, I believe—it would seem that the proprietor, Yates Thompson, took some share in the work of the paper. He had been applied to by W. E. Henley who wanted to do dramatic criticism. The future editor of the *National Observer* was told 'that there were one or two at it already; if I wished to get it I was to best them out of the field'. E. V. Lucas notes in *The Colvins and their Friends*[2] that, though Henley had both the *P.M.G.* and *St. James's* open to him, he did not seem to be 'able to adapt his very idiosyncratic style to the complete satisfaction of either'. Indeed there is a Colvin letter, a page long, to Henley, on that style, lecturing him on 'a tendency to a quaintness which is rather slangy than quaint and to a use of eccentric forms and dubious constructions not at all really serving to improve the colour and life of your writing'. Henley, in a letter to Colvin, fears he will find Morley's 'finger thicker than Greenwood's loins'. 'He cut my "Whole Duty", he has suppressed my Swinburne altogether and my Blackmore as well'.

---

[1] *Bygones Worth Remembering*, George Jacob Holyoake (Fisher Unwin, 1905).
[2] Methuen, 1928.

GETTING RID OF FORSTER. I shall not burden the reader with extracts from Morley's leading articles. But a few opinions he expressed may be noted. As he said, 'there was one thing that the public could be sure about the *Pall Mall Gazette*; they could be certain that we knew our own minds'. During the Arabi Pasha and bombardment of Alexandria period his view, of interest today, was that 'until a system is devised which fulfils the programme not only of "Egypt for the Egyptians" but "Egypt by the Egyptians", we shall find ourselves plunging deeper into entanglements'.

He opposed a Channel Tunnel and went back on his early devotion to women's suffrage. He stood out against coercion in Ireland—Parnell and others were in Kilmainham Gaol—and demanded what the Chief Secretary, W. E. Forster, called 'my dismissal or resignation', though it was 'painful to say a word that sounds like disparagement of one of the most honest, devoted and well-intentioned men that ever entered the public service'. But Forster was 'not versatile, flexible' or quick of apprehension. 'The *Pall Mall Gazette* is right in one thing', the victim owned, 'this is no time for personal considerations', and placed his resignation in Gladstone's hands. Mrs. Humphry Ward calls the attacks on her uncle 'brilliant, pitiless'.

Morley, in the course of making an end of Forster, did his friend Chamberlain an ill turn by naming him as Forster's successor. 'Forster's friends insinuated', writes Garvin, 'that these articles were instigated by Chamberlain's ambitions and intrigues. No surmise could be more natural and none more baseless. The articles causing the untoward commotion were written on the editor's initiative to Chamberlain's discomfort. Morley, at first not amenable, was soon vexed with himself and regretful—but the mischief was done'.[1]

When Sir William Harcourt's Prevention of Crime Bill followed on the murder of Lord Frederick Cavendish and T. H. Burke in Phoenix Park, Morley criticised it. 'I am one of the best abused men in Pall Mall', he wrote. (Within a week of his own appointment as Chief Secretary, in 1886, he was to suspend the Crimes Act, and, in his own words, 'lift coercion off the back of Ireland'.) Sir Edward Grey, as he then was, 'chose the Home Rule side, less, he tells us, on the authority of Gladstone than by convictions derived from Morley's articles in the *Pall Mall*'.[2]

FROM 'AN ARTICLE A DAY, PLUS' TO THE CABINET. During his early days at the *Pall Mall* Morley reports, he 'came through the strain pretty well; an article a day for a month, plus 11 pages of the *F.R.*, and all my other work as well'. As a result

[1] *Life of Joseph Chamberlain*, J. L. Garvin (Macmillan, 1932, 1933, 1934, 1951).
[2] *Grey of Fallodon*, G. M. Trevelyan (Longman's, 1937).

of his break with Chapman & Hall his relations with the congenial Macmillans became closer. From May 1883 to the summer of 1885 he edited their magazine, which at once acquired something of the flavour of the *Fortnightly*. Huxley and Bryce were in his first number, and Mrs. Humphry Ward was among his contributors. When he gave up the magazine it ceased to be political.

A brief glimpse of the domestic side of the *Pall Mall* is afforded in an allusion to Morley's attendance at the annual *P.M.G.* dinner at the Crystal Palace, 'a horrid affair with speeches, glees, etc.' Morley has a reference to a visit to the Highlands. 'The quiet, and the distance from *Pall Mall* render it worth while to traverse all those scores of miles'.

In 1883 Meredith makes this May Day announcement to Admiral Maxse: 'Morley throws up the *Pall Mall*. It will be good for him, though he may miss the assistance it gave. But it bled him too constantly. His withdrawal is likely to be the death of the paper, which will meander to extinction through the flats of tepid Liberalism.'[1] Meredith forgot Stead—see next Chapter. Room must be found for the remark of Lord Northcliffe's henchman, Kennedy Jones, to Morley, 'You left journalism a profession; we have made it a branch of commerce'.

MORLEY ON FREDERICK GREENWOOD. In a letter which I had from Morgan in response to a request of mine for anything Morley might have said to him about the *Pall Mall* and his editorship of it, he wrote: 'I am almost certain, as I kept a full record of all his conversations with me, that he never once mentioned the subject. As you know, he liked people to think of him as a statesman and as a man of letters rather than as a journalist. There is certainly nothing in my diaries. Nor did he ever mention Greenwood or Stead to me.' Yet as the author of *John, Viscount Morley* says, 'One of the first questions he would put to a traveller from a foreign country was as to the position of the Press. What was its influence on political life? What talents did it attract? What part did the leading article play in its economy'?

On April 8, 1905, Morley stepped forward as a journalist of memorable experience when he took the chair at the dinner which leading editors of the day (and night), and a variety of literary men, in all a hundred and fifty, gave to Greenwood, his predecessor at the *Pall Mall*. Stead and Cook and two successors of theirs were among the editors. The writers of books included Hardy, Meredith, Barrie, Sir Edmund Gosse and Andrew Lang (as committee), and Sir Max Beerbohm, Augustine Birrell, E. V. Lucas and Maurice Hewlett. With Sir James Knowles (of the *Nineteenth Century*) were the cartoonists, F. C. Gould and E. T. Reed. By the kindness of

---

[1] *Letters of George Meredith* (Constable, 1912).

Mrs. Alice Watts, I have before me the brochure *Honouring Frederick Greenwood* which was circulated by Clement Shorter, the irrepressible, goodhearted and variously informed editor of the *Sphere.*

Morley spoke of the 'little family of *Gazettes*' (*P.M.G., St. James's* and *W.G.*) which owed their being to Greenwood's initiative, When Greenwood was at the *Pall Mall,* Morley said—and his tribute enables this generation to realise what a person of note Greenwood was—he had round him 'a phalanx of men in intellectual training and in power of mind unsurpassed by any Englishmen of their generation. He assimilated from each one of them. He sank his own shafts deeper. He scaled eminences of survey upon the affairs of the nation and other nations. He added a flavour of his own, his own play of mind, his own versatility and other qualities of a really sparkling mind. He welcomed all newcomers, all younger men with fresh gifts. He showed an extraordinary aptitude for public affairs in their widest, highest sense. He also showed extraordinary gifts as a pugilistic controversialist. The *Pall Mall* started rather as a sort of serious pleasure yacht. Then we found that, very far from being a pleasure yacht, when the decks were cleared it was an armed cruiser; there were guns of very heavy metal indeed, and there was a captain on the bridge of a gallantry and martial quality never surpassed in the history of English journalism.' He quoted Meredith's judgment that 'Greenwood is not only a great journalist, he has a statesman's head'. He added that he often heard Gladstone say that 'no Minister ever had a more effective supporter than Lord Beaconsfield had in Mr. Greenwood—he gave him an ardent support from day to day'. Nor did Morley forget to pay his tribute to Greenwood's 'intrepidity and foresight' over the Suez Canal shares, and 'his disinterestedness, splendid and unstained'. Morley added that he spoke of Greenwood after having 'worked with him and under him and against him', and concluded with the testimony that he had 'fought the battle of public life as honourably and uprightly as that battle can be fought'. Morley's encomium was the more impressive because he also testified to the high merits of Hutton and Townsend of the *Spectator* and Leonard Courtney of *The Times,* 'the one man whom Delane could trust to put a leading article to press without his having seen it'.

As might be expected, Greenwood was moved by what Morley said and by the way a remarkable audience applauded his words. He was 'unused to public praise'; 'the Suez shares, that really was doing something'—but what he said is reported fully in my *Story of the 'Pall Mall Gazette'.*[1] Greenwood did not fail

[1] Oxford University Press, 1950.

to allude to Morley as one of his *P.M.G.'s* 'choicest contributors'.[1]

Mr. Augustine Birrell expressed the opinion that Morley's 'contact with politics has greatly improved his literature, has improved his style, enriched his wisdom, and enables him, when dealing with great topics, to employ a wealth of illustrations, a happiness of feeling and a depth of philosophy which he would not have been capable of exhibiting had he not had that experience which is born of public affairs.' This, Birrell said, was seen in his books written after experience of public life.

THE GAINS OF LITERATURE AND JOURNALISM. Some readers may wonder how Morley's journalistic, literary and political life answered from a monetary point of view. He started with nothing, and his early struggles taught him to be careful in his expenditures and to give solvency a high place among the virtues. Although he no doubt got the best journalistic pay of his time, it was not remarkable in amount considering the pains he took. He went into the House of Commons (at 45) before payment for members, but he was in office for twelve years. A piece of good fortune was a legacy of £2,000 a year from Carnegie. Morley left about £50,000. Most of it he bequeathed, after making provision for his family, to his adopted nephew and helper, Guy Morley. There was a gift of £100 each to Frederick (afterwards Sir Frederick) Macmillan and to Hirst. A number of his books, beyond those Guy Morley wished to keep, went to Manchester. Morley had done reasonably well over his *Cobden* and, in respect of his *Gladstone*, the G.O.M.'s family arranged that he should have £10,000 and an additional three or four thousand later when the work was so prodigious a success. In view of the prices at which books have necessarily to be sold today, it is of interest that the three volumes were priced at 42s. the set; for the well-bound popular edition of 1974 pages in two volumes the charge was 5s. each.

As I have noted, Morley was careful in money matters. He kept his accounts rigidly, chortled over an investment of £5,000 which brought him in £8,500, and was interested in public finance. So he might not have been such a bad Chancellor of the Exchequer after all.

With regard to his method of writing, his 'copy' was what printers call 'clean'. He was one of the fortunates who do not need

---

[1] In his correspondence with J. H. Blackwood, of the famous firm of Blackwood & Sons, which the firm kindly let me use in *The Story of the 'Pall Mall Gazette'*, Greenwood is unsparing about his supplanter in the opposite political camp. 'Morley was never a politician—hadn't in him the making of a statesman; even as a writer is great more by study and industry than by judgment. His judgment is exceptionally good in no field: though he has all the graces and a great garner of reading'. But in the same letter he was equally down on the author of one of the best biographies in the language, G. O. Trevelyan.

to correct MS. heavily. He sat up to his writing in a stiff-backed chair—I have used two chairs in which he worked—and, like some others of us, he was not averse to a cat reposing on his desk.

It is a pity that Guy Morley, who as a young man lived with his uncle, has not recorded some of his memories of him and his friends. One of his recollections is of Augustine Birrell declaring that when Arthur Henderson spoke of 'Labour' it was as if he were elevating the Host.

Morley, in his last years, it must be owned, grew more conservative, and sometimes perhaps a little difficult. During these years— and the period, alas, was not a short one, for he lived to be eighty-four—he cannot be said to have been either physically or psychologically at his best.

CHAPTER VII

AN EDITOR AS HIS ASSISTANT EDITOR SAW HIM

'A NOBLE SHAMELESSNESS.' In the previous chapter mention has been made of W. T. Stead who came to the *Pall Mall* soon after Morley's acceptance of the editorship. I cannot close this account without his impression. The *Review of Reviews* character sketch also tells us something about Stead, whose career we are next to consider.

Stead felt that he must counter the view of Morley as 'an austere, stern, unsympathetic person, the genius of political righteousness'. He was 'very human, anything but a dry stick'. There was about him, however, as he had himself said about Burke, 'a certain inborn stateliness of nature'. 'He has'—Morley was still alive—'a great deal of the poetic temperament, while deep within him burns that central fire of passion without which poetry is but as the tinkling cymbal. He exercises a stern restraint on himself which is so habitual that few but his intimates suspect how much "fire he has got in his belly", the Carlylean phrase which was constantly in use at the *Pall Mall* when he was there. But, although he is one of the most genial of hosts and most cordial and delightful of companions, he has no amusements. He revels in long walks across the hills or solitary meditations in country lanes. Give him a book and a familiar garden seat and he has all that can most minister to his pleasurable content.'

'Mill in philosophy, Burke in politics and Wordsworth in poetry—he wrote an introduction to an edition—are his spiritual pastors and masters, and "much and very much", he once told me, did he "owe to the wise and stimulating friendship of George Meredith in the impressionable time". He used to stay with him and in the evening Meredith would read over the chapter or the poem he had written in the day. "The important thing", Mr. Morley said, is that "personality itself should be as little as possible broken, incoherent and fragmentary; that reasoned and consistent opinions should back a firm will, and independent convictions inspire intellectual self-respect and strenuous self-possession.'

'Mr. Gladstone is always demonstrating his consistency: Mr. Morley does not regard consistency as a virtue. What does a change of opinion show except a readiness to admit that you may be wiser and better informed today than yesterday? There has always been about him a noble shamelessness in avowing that he has changed his mind. When he asked me to come up to London and work with him, I diligently read up the old *Fortnightlies* to see whether we were likely to agree. I told him that I thought we agreed very well, with one important exception. "You mean religion?" said he. "No", I replied, "I think we should agree there whenever the subject became practical. The subject on which we disagree is the Contagious Diseases Acts. You have written strongly in their favour; I am dead against them." "Oh", said Mr. Morley, "that article was written many years ago. It was a mistake. I have changed my mind. I am entirely with you".'

As for Morley the editor, 'no power on earth could command his interest in three-fourths of the matters that interest the British tomfool, as the general reader used sometimes to be designated when considerations of management clashed with editorial aspirations. He had no eye for news. To him a newspaper was simply a pulpit. During his stay at the *Pall Mall* he did many things fairly well, but the only subject on which he left his mark was Ireland.'

'NO DITHYRAMBS.' 'When I was writing the chronique for the *Fortnightly* there was this sentence in his instruction, "It is so easy to denounce; let us gravely and responsibly face the difficulties". At the *Pall Mall* he was very often a chilly frost on my more youthful enthusiasms. "No dithyrambs, *s'il vous plaît*", he would remark drily as he returned me my article with all the most telling passages struck out. He was a great stickler for severity of style, and restraint and sobriety of expression. He was always down on my besetting temptation to bawl when a word in an ordinary tone would be sufficient. But there was never any trouble. He believed in authority and I believed in obedience. No-one took liberties with Mr. Morley. Everyone went more or less in awe of him. When the thunder-cloud gathered in his eyes or the gout was prowling about his extremities we minded our p's and q's. But we all liked him. I must have been an unusual trial to him with my exuberance and my fads and what he considered my superstition.' He quotes Morley as saying, 'I like drab men best'.

From old Morley letters Stead makes a few excerpts—here further reduced—which he thinks are models of editorial kindliness and authority:

July 22, 1881. You ought not to write anything tonight—nor on other nights. The whole policy is a mistake and will break you down. You ought to have a list of men; to distribute topics. I must make a bargain with you on this point.

August 6. The *Pall Mall* of Friday is infinitely too stiff and crammed with politics. Only on the hardest compunction should there be a word of politics after pages 5 or 6. [So perhaps Morley had wider human interests as an editor than I have given him credit for.]

F

August 8. By all my divinities I beseech you not to let D. [Dicey] or anyone else talk about 'their lordships'. If it is irony it is very poor; if it's serious it's very vulgar. And what's the fun about 'the gilded chamber'?

August 11. You must not take my little criticisms too much to heart. The paper looks very well. Take care of yourself. Don't trouble to write me.

August 21. I am concerned at the washy ending of the article on coercion. Please not to allow any halting.

Sept. 24. I do not like your note on the Russian ukase at all. For one thing it is against our rule to go out of one's way to quarrel with the *Daily News.* Better leave Russia alone until my return. When I resume my ferule let Tsars tremble!

Sept. 26. You should have let a sleeping dog lie.

A note a little later had a sentence, 'Your article tonight turned my hair grey'. 'I believe', says Stead, 'that it contained the expression of a hope that England and America would some day be united by a supreme tribunal. It was one about which Lowell wrote me, "It is a beautiful dream. But it is none the worse for that. Many of the best things we have began by being dreams". Mr. Morley had small tolerance, however, for dreams in editorial columns.'

Most heartily your friend

J. R. Lowell

JAMES RUSSELL LOWELL TO STEAD

Nov. 20. Don't scarify Harcourt and Cowen[1] but live generally in Christian amity and peace.

August 18, 1882. Say what you think best (this is in the *Fortnightly*), only remember this, the *F.R.* is a very grave and dull organ. Let me beseech you, not merely in the interests of yourself but of the *Pall Mall*, not to write two leaders a day. No man can do it well, and they will become words, only words, if you persist. Take the monition of a friend and editor.

Sept. 3. I take the liberty of hinting that the language about X. grates terrifically on my ears. It strikes me as downright unseemly. The accident that he and his wife are my friends does not make it pleasanter. Apart from that, I fancy disapproval is none the less effective for being courteously worded. You have had some capital articles otherwise. But don't be so strenuous, *s.v.p.* You'll tear yourself asunder.

Sept. 12. Your leader tonight takes my breath away. On the whole, I think I may as well take command tomorrow. If you have a leader ready, all the better.

[1] The Radical who was the *Newcastle Chronicle.*

'GOD'. On Morley's having written—not in the *Pall Mall*—'God' with a little 'g'[1] the evangelical Stead says: 'I sometimes wish he had gone on using it. The disuse of the capital letter was an act of faith. It was dropped in deference to the larger expediences of human intercourse. The man, however, who felt driven to such irreverence to the conventionalities had in him the same sturdy faith that led the Quakers to keep on their hats in a court of justice. The Quakers personified their Invisible, Mr. Morley idealised it. But both recognised the Categorical Imperative. It may seem strange to those who have no eye but for the surface of things, no ear but for the familiar jingle of the European substitutes for the praying mills of Tibet, to speak of Mr. Morley as one of the great religious teachers of our time.[2] But those who know him and his writings have long recognised him as one of the potent influences for religion and righteousness. He is a puritan pulpiteer born in the 19th century, when our hot gospellers betake themselves to the Press instead of to the Pulpit. Cardinal Manning fully recognised that; Morley, even in the most advanced of his writings, had not attacked Christianity so much as the corrupt, governmental forms of it. When we used to talk of these things Mr. Morley was wont to refer familiarly to the human race as cheese mites. He wrote: "The manifold experiences of humanity are daily opening out to us vaster and, at the same time, more ordered proportions. Religion, whatever destinies may be in store for it, is at least for the present, no longer an organic power. But if the religious spirit leads to a worthy and beautiful life, if it shows itself in cheerfulness, in pity, in charity, and tolerance, in forgiveness, in a sense of largeness and the mystery of things, in lifting up the soul in gratitude and awe to some power and sovereign force, then whatever drawback there may be in the way of superstitious dogma, still such a spirit is on the whole a good thing".' Sirdar Ali Khan in his *Life* of Morley[3] recounts as an illustration of a liberal disposition that, when staying with the Aberdeens in Scotland, Morley insisted on joining in family prayers 'to renew his own sense of littleness among the mysteries of life and to begin the day with a feeling of fellowship in service with the humblest member of the household'. On Sunday evenings he 'stood at the piano singing hymns heartily'.

Morley's 'Psalm of Life', he once told Stead, was Goethe's 'Das Gottliche', which concludes—the translation is Miss Grey's—

---

[1] When Morley first stood for Newcastle the editor of the local *Express* reminded the electors that Newcastle had just been made a bishopric, and called on them to reject the 'atheist' who 'seeks to decapitate the head of our faith'.

[2] 'Cut him open and you will find a clergyman inside.'—Meredith on Morley.

[3] Pitman, 1923.

>'Tis the glory of man
>To be helpful and good.
>Unwearied procuring
>The useful, the right:
>A prototype so
>Of the gods we grope after.

In 1891 a French journalist visited Morley in the home to which he betook himself, with his wife, in that 'broad quiet street in South Kensington with long drawn out perspective of houses all exactly alike, four stories high, with steps and porticoes and rows of three front windows'.[1] In 'Mr. Morley's home', wrote the Frenchman, 'you are struck by the sense of seclusion. There are no children's voices. The house is silent. In the drawing room the whole of one side is filled by a bookcase. There are no nick-nacks, no trace of affectation or exceptionality. There is a severity which hovers between banality and eloquence. The furniture is vaguely modern. The master of the house must love a discreet, grey-toned, restful whiteness'.

MORLEY AND STEAD. Stead examined Morley's record and character not only in the notes I have quoted from the *Review of Reviews* but in a *Pall Mall* 'Extra', published after Morley's departure from the paper, *John Morley: The Irish Record of the New Chief Secretary*. An earlier 'Extra', got out during Morley's editorship, was *Fifty Years of the House of Lords*. Morley once said to Stead that abolishing the House of Lords was 'a large order'. Meantime he adjured him, abuse was going 'the wrong track; a gentle irony is the best weapon'. Nor did Morley care for Stead's continual references to 'the people'.[2] As for Ireland, he made the remark to someone that after keeping Stead in order for three years he didn't see why he shouldn't be able to govern the Irish. Morley and Stead continually disagreed but they maintained their regard and respect for one another; Carlyle's phrase 'except in opinion, not disagreeing' fits their relationship. Only once did Stead threaten resignation. It was over an article by Sir James Fitzjames Stephen which Stead thought would identify the *Pall Mall* with atheism. Morley gave way.

In a private memorandum Stead is more plainspoken than in his other writing: 'Morley has a high opinion of himself, and he succeeds in communicating some share of it to all who surround him. The awe of him lies upon all his relatives and acquaintances, especially among those of his own household. Yet Gladstone told Madame Novikoff that "We like M. he is such a humble man"!

[1] Elm Park Gardens.
[2] This was a not infrequent phrase of Gladstone's. The most popular weekly in Scotland a generation or two ago was the *People's Friend*. A new paper would not make just that appeal in its title today.

Humility is not exactly M's forte. He is kindly, candid, dignified and even austere. Sometimes, but rarely, he is cruel and if he gave full swing to his impulse would be even savage. He is fond of good living, very genial after dinner, and excepting when gouty or "put out" is always pleasant.' Stead speaks once of having been 'in the shade' for a month, 'ever since I approved of Ministerial appointments of which he disapproved'. 'He nearly boiled over with rage, paced the room in wrath and passed his hand through his hair, declaring that the Government deserved to be turned out. He has been more or less distant with me. But he is a good fellow and I am very much attached to him.'

When in the early days of Morley's editorship he was absent from the office labouring at *Cobden*, the vigour and loyalty with which Stead took charge 'touched me to the core', he said; it was 'so unlike the ways of the world'. He told Stead that 'when Perfect Wisdom comes to the account between us it is I who shall be left heavily the debtor'. He said he should retain 'an affectionate memory' of their association. Morley was ten years older than Stead.

From Manse to Babylon
W. T. STEAD

CHAPTER VIII

AN ASSISTANT EDITOR AS HIS EDITOR SAW HIM

If a prophet is wholly successful and his teaching is absorbed it may afterwards hardly be understood how anyone might ever have believed otherwise. It is the prophet's aim thus to be abolished in absorption, to be lost by diffusion.—W. R. LETHABY.

INVITATION TO LONDON. Morley came to the *Pall Mall* with both *Cobden* and his *English Men of Letters* series on his hands. There was also his life as a politician, although he had not yet got into the House. 'That golden rule for men with heavy tasks, *nulla dies sine linea*', he writes, 'stood me in good stead'; but it was plain that he could not write a daily leader for the *Pall Mall*, and that sometimes he must be absent from the office. He required right away an assistant editor of skill, readiness and conviction.[1] I have heard that the name of Stead was suggested to Morley by Gladstone, but Morley could not have helped knowing of such an ardent, belligerent and intelligent Liberal as the editor of the *Northern Echo*. I remember him in my later school days in Cumberland, as valued by the forward-looking forces of the North and by Gladstone himself, and as given to printing political catechisms. I recall in one of them: '*Q*. What is Afghanistan? *A*. The Switzerland of Asia, the political Naboth's vineyard'.

'OUR MASTER.' Morley pressed Stead in the public interest to come to London, and Yates Thompson, the *Pall Mall* proprietor, had been to see him at Darlington. 'Thompson', Morley explained, 'would be very acquiescent, on the whole, if he saw the thing [i.e. the paper] alive and moving'—the 'on the whole' was typical of the careful Morley. 'He is not a very high-minded man but he is good-natured and very energetic'. 'With Voules, the manager'— later of *Truth*—he went on, 'I do not think you would find many difficulties'. 'It will make all the difference', Morley said, 'to have

[1] He was not, of course, to be 'sub-editor', as Hyndman says, but assistant editor. For the novice it may be explained that, in English journalism—there is a different usage in the United States—the assistant editor helps the editor on the editorial, that is the political and literary side of the paper, and edits in the editor's absence. The sub-editor and his colleagues have to do with the news. When I first became a sub-editor in the *Pall Mall* office there were days when we never saw even as active and alert an editor as Stead.

someone with whom I can discuss every day the line of the paper. My official friends are too busy; besides my notion is'—and here spoke the 'Able Editor'—'that we should inspire them, rather than they us.' Meantime Stead was sending Occasional Notes. 'Thompson', wrote Morley again, 'is very anxious that you should come, and I wish you were here now, for I bear the burden without competent aids and it is rather much for me'. When Stead came, Morley's phrase was, 'We were lucky enough to induce him to join us'.

EXTRACT FROM A LETTER FROM YATES THOMPSON

Stead was not quite sure of Yates Thompson, and 'Thompy' as we knew him, a man to be somewhat tried in patience in the time to come, had his ways. Morley felt it desirable to explain that 'our master is really a most considerate and friendly man'. 'As soon as ever you have got your hand in', he went on, 'I shall retire to the background to finish my *Cobden*'.

'COALING.' Writing a few days later, Morley wisely says: 'You will not be hurt if I say that one consideration present to my mind is that you ought to have leisure for "coaling", i.e. leisure for reading and meditating. We all need more of that than we get.' I recall the judicious remark of an exceedingly productive editor I was acquainted with, Sir William Robertson Nicoll (of the *British Weekly* and the *Bookman*, a man who had books in his house wherever he could find any place for them), that the journalist whose 'exports exceed his imports is soon bankrupt'. A Morley letter from the Athenaeum in October, 1880, gives a hint on dealing in Notes with the Turks, based on a chat with Gladstone—whom 'I saw this morning': 'Don't put too much steam on'. And 'when you come up, pray stay quietly at my house for a couple of days'. The next year, when Stead is established at the office, there is a message to say 'I cannot screw a leader out of myself'. But 'don't write more than two or three Notes'—he is trying to abate Stead's ardour a bit; 'you must spare yourself more than you do or the crack will come'.

'TWO BLACK EYES.' Morley finds himself by no means sharing Stead's Russian sympathies. A Note of Stead's 'did not contribute to my Sabbatical calm. You will not be surprised if I go to work pretty steadily to scrape off the Slavophil label'. A later letter opens with the measured sentence, 'I have read your two Notes with the same satisfaction with which a man receives two black eyes'. He had been preparing 'by early rising' and 'hard pressure' a political address, and he had returned home from his meeting 'not without a certain poor complacency'. Then 'I read your two Notes. My complacency withered up and the proof went in shreds into the basket. However, you have the satisfaction of your yap at Jupiter's heels—and that's something. And I feel wholesomely rebuked for my egotism—and that's good too. Pray don't trouble to answer. There's no more to be said.' He continues, rather inconsequently it would seem: 'Mind, you give it well to the *Saturday*, *Spectator*, *Daily News* and our other contemporaries on Saturday: bloody noses all round.' Yet he says in another letter: 'Please remember, my dear Stead, not to shout when talking will do'. The next month the editor thinks he 'may be in a better mood for *P.M.* conversation this day week than I am to-day. Leave Ireland alone and don't worry other papers. Otherwise follow your instinct'.

Morley is now 'Ever yours'. But at no time in his relations with Stead as his adjutant or, later, as friend, does he write—such was the starchiness of the period—less formally than 'Dear Mr. Stead'! Yet he likes him well. Stead's return from a holiday gives him 'a feeling of comfort, as if someone had left me a legacy'. He is 'with most cordial greetings, yours most sincerely'.

STEAD, EDITOR. In 1883, on Morley at last getting into Parliament, after three failures, Stead became editor of the *Pall Mall*. Three years later, on Christmas Eve, and here I get ahead of our narrative, but it is convenient to have all the Morley correspondence with Stead in one Chapter—his old chief wrote: 'In the hurry I do not think that I gave my good wishes with as much cordiality as I feel. Pray believe that I hope every good thing will fall to you and yours at this season and every other. You sometimes make me blaspheme a little, but that does not go below the skin—and I hope that our friendship is stable'.

The correspondence continues not only during Stead's editorship, but when his *Review of Reviews* is started. On Lord Iddesleigh's tragically sudden death Morley expresses the hope that 'we shall all of us go out so simply'. In 1891, in allusion to a *Review of Reviews* character sketch of Albert Edward, Prince of Wales, by Stead, which attracted, I remember, a good deal of notice, Morley's comment is: 'Your promise or prospect of a career for the Heir Apparent is a very forlorn hope indeed. If that be so—if there is no possible duty for an Heir Apparent—what a danger for the Monarchy!' In other letters he is asking for a reference to the *ipsissima verba* of some declaration by Lord Salisbury or telling Stead that he had better 'come and have half a day's talk with me', with a bed, from Saturday to Monday, 'before you make your final selection' for some particular public post, or he is helping with the names of the right books for Cecil Rhodes—who at this time was making Stead his sole legatee.

A year later Morley proposes a second visit to Mowbray House (the office of the *Review of Reviews*) though 'when you are in that humour and I am in the humour in which I now find myself, it's dangerous to meet, for then I am apt to be expansive'. In August he had a letter from Stead to which he replied: 'I am in a fine heroic humour, determined to fight as hard as ever I can against the powers of darkness. If they beat us, I shall have plenty of other work for the rest of my days, and I promise my friends they shall not be ashamed of me'.

In 1898 Morley is writing at some length on 'those competitive and ever-swelling armaments which load the taxpayer, dislocate industry, waste capital, scourge the family and the home, and swallow up resources that ought to go to the elevation and content-ment of the people'. (What does his ghost make of our present defence expenditure?) The following year he says of a Dean of the time that he is 'abominable, almost incredible', and sends thanks to Stead for 'your excellent tract' on the Boer War.

A pleasing extract from a birthday letter of 1911 runs: 'You have said hundreds of things from which it has been my ill fortune pretty violently to dissent, but this matters little in view of the thousands of things said by you that needed saying. I rejoice to think that your rare vivacity of mind and pen is unimpaired. Your *Review of Reviews* is marked, as not all public instructors are, by diligent exploration of fact, and it conveys a human voice— from a bold and sincere worker. I wish you good luck and hope to remain what I have been for a generation past, your friend, Morley of B', for he had become a Viscount. In 1912, in the final letter of my collection, Stead is bidden to 'lunch with me among Generals and Admirals at the United Services Club' of which Morley was an honorary member.

CHAPTER IX

THE MAN AND HIS WORK

THE CLOSER VIEW. Twenty-eight years ago, with the advantage of being that much nearer Stead and his work than we are today, I set down an account of my association with him, my feelings about him as a man and my convictions regarding his achievement. A year afterwards I took some pains with a long review, to which the *Nation and Athenaeum* gave prominence, of Frederic Whyte's *Life of W. T. Stead*. I also contributed two articles to the *Manchester Guardian*. Edwin H. Stout, who had in many ways a fuller knowledge of Stead as an editor than anyone then alive, was good enough to read carefully through all this matter and to say that he was 'well satisfied'. I have come to the conclusion, therefore, that I shall best serve my readers, and Stead's memory, if in this chapter, an introductory survey of his life, I follow what I wrote; and then, in later chapters, record the ampler particulars drawn from a mass of material chiefly brought together when I planned to write, after my retirement from the *Countryman*, a book concerned with Stead alone. I abandoned the idea of a biography because I felt that a book in which Stead took his place in the history of the *Pall Mall Gazette* had the prospect of doing fuller justice to him and of being of greater service.

MY FIRST INTERVIEW WITH STEAD. 'If a new *Pall Mall* and an old *Pall Mall* met in the street', said a wag when Stead succeeded Morley, 'they would assuredly cut one another'. As a youth I came into touch with Stead by confessing my discipleship in a re-writing I set about—he saw a proof[1]—of his 'Gospel of Journalism' in the *Contemporary Review*; and by my exceptional good fortune, for an obscure young provincial, in getting into the *Pall Mall* a variety of 'followers'[2] with a Steadian approach and, in their headlines, a Steadian flavour at a time when headlines were less conspicuous in the London Press than they are today.[3]

[1] In *Sell's Dictionary of the World's Press* for 1899, a volume of 1,942 pages.

[2] Articles following the leader which, with theatre advertisements, occupied the first page of the *Pall Mall*.

[3] 'The theory of *The Times* was that, as every reader found everything in the paper indispensable to him, he worked his way through the entire print, from the first page to the last; and, dominated by *The Times*, the morning newspaper Press continued to print its news and headlines in a uniform tone. But the *Pall Mall Gazette*, under Stead, set a new fashion with its bold headings and liberal use of "cross-heads". The title to leaders did not appear until 1907'.—Mr. Stanley Morison in an address at Cambridge as Sanders Reader in Bibliography.

To Roberton Scott

Companion of my Rosary

From W. T. Stead

Christmas 1897

STEAD'S HANDWRITING IN A COPY OF HIS
LETTERS FROM JULIA

I heard afterwards that Stead amused the office by his account of the first interview I had with him. I had pulled out a large note-book, bought for the occasion, which contained a long list of possible articles and had worked through the lot with poised pencil, gravely ticking off the titles of those he 'ordered'. He was equally amused by the way in which I had straitly interrogated him on his personal feelings towards Madame Novikoff,[1] Joseph Chamberlain and the Prince of Wales. This interview took place in the days when contributors were paid by the *Pall Mall* in cheques on thick paper of abnormal area and when the *Quarterly Review's* cheques were made out, for privacy, not to names but to numbers.

STEAD'S EYES. My recollections of this meeting are of Stead's piercing blue eyes, of his friendliness, of his urging me to become perfect in French and German, of his talking a little through his nose, and, sometimes with his feet on the mantelpiece and some-times, as he stalked about, of beating his legs with a long-handled clothes-brush. I must make a special reference to his eyes. John Buchan spoke of the eyes of Augustus being 'so penetrating, so intense in their regard that those on whom he bent them had to avert their gaze.[2] 'Don't pierce me with thy eyes, keep thy eyes off me', someone said to George Fox. J. L. Garvin wrote to me: 'Sidney Whitman, who had seen much and known many, told me that when Stead met great personages (Pope, Tsar, Empress, Chancellor, Prime Minister) he looked quite steadily right into their eyes, and that it was an almost daunting expression of "nerve force".'[3]

'TOMORROW!' Lord Northcliffe has described the conven-tionalities of the daily press when the *Daily Mail* burst upon Fleet Street, but Stead was before him. The conservatism and rigidity of the Press in the earlier *Pall Mall* period is fully credible only to those who turn up daily paper files at Colindale. Stead's conception of the journalist as the 'Sandalphon[4] of humanity' kindled a fire in the hearts of a few young men (and a smaller company of women with, at that time, limited access to education and no votes) who, if they lacked the endowments of the *Pall Mall* editor, had some of his fervour and convictions, flow and strenuousness. They were minded to enter Journalism as some entered the Church. When Stead wrote to ask me how soon I could come up to London to join the staff I telegraphed 'Tomorrow'![5]

[1] See page 107.

[2] *Geminas cui tempora flammas lacta vomunt.* Verg. Aen., VIII, 680.

[3] Sir Walter Scott, whose own eyes were 'the most penetrating' Haydon ever saw, described Burns's eyes as 'living coals'. Furnivall said Ruskin's 'frank blue eyes looked through you and drew you to him'. Leigh Hunt was struck by Carlyle's.

[4] One of the angels who, in Longfellow's poem, receive the prayers of the Israelites.

[5] *The Day before Yesterday*, J. W. Robertson Scott (Methuen, 1951).

NORTHUMBERLAND STREET. There may have been less convenient, darker and grubbier daily paper offices in London than
our old building in Northumberland Street but I never heard of
them. Some of the printers had memories of the Thames water
that invaded the machine room before the building of the Embankment. I do not think we possessed more than two tape machines
(including the 'City' one)[1] and I cannot remember a telephone,
though I suppose we must have had one somewhere. Many editions
were late if Stead was in the office. I remember his delaying us
during the Dock Strike—for a total of 6d. an hour!—with an
account he had written of a John Burns speech at Tower Hill.
'I see', he reported Burns declaiming, 'I see rising above the
horizon the full round orb of the docker's tanner'. But the *Pall
Mall*, in spite of coming out late, and in spite of its worn type and
antiquated machines, was read by an appreciative public and was
quoted by its contemporaries and in speeches in and out of Parliament. The business side was a meagre minor department somewhere
upstairs, from which now and then moderate protest was heard
over the trains we missed.

SOME CHARACTERISTICS OF STEAD. Something of the man
Stead was may be seen not only in the eyes in his portraits, but in
his extraordinarily characteristic handwriting. There is such grip,
vigour and industry in it that his nibs had a short life. He was one
of the first users of a fountain pen. In his handwriting is exhibited
his inartistic side as well as his vigour and mental animation.
His insensitiveness was illustrated in the cover of the *Review of
Reviews*, which succeeded his *Pall Mall* period, in the format of his
still later *Daily Paper*, in the get-up of all his publications indeed,
and in his clothes—I have seen him in the office wearing for a shirt
an undergarment tied with a tassel at the neck. Some of his following
were no doubt blind on that side too, and a man is judged a little
by the following he attracts.

Sir Arthur Quiller-Couch would have found in Stead's articles
some of the jargon against which he warred. But 'Q' would have
been the first to repudiate the notion that no man may write who
is slipshod about 'in the case of' and indifferent to literature which
may 'glad a few high souls once in a century'. Stead's strength of
conviction, his fervour, his sense of effectual calling, his consciousness

---

[1] We had, I think, in addition to Reuter, the Exchange Telegraph, Central
News and Press Association flimsy services, supply of flimsies from police court
reporters, some of them interesting characters. Flimsies are the tissue paper
sheets by means of which the reporters multiplied with carbons the number of
their reports so that they could serve the newspapers simultaneously. The Exchange Telegraph Company kindly informs me that their first tape machine was
installed at the *P.M.G.* in 1885—it was for sporting news—and two years later
a machine was put in carrying home and foreign news and financial intelligence.
The *P.M.G.*, I am told, appears in the P.O. telephone directory of 1884.

THE
PALL MALL GAZETT

An Evening Newspaper and Review.

No. 6621.—Vol. XLIII.   *SATURDAY, JUNE* 5, 1886.   *Price One Pen*

A VOTE OF "NO CONFIDENCE."

Mr. GLADSTONE can do most things, but he could never have written the latter half of the Decalogue. The terse peremptoriness of the Commandments would in his hands have disappeared, to give place to long-winded periphrasis and a multitude of saving clauses. Even to say "Thou shalt not kill" or "Thou shalt not commit adultery," would have been beyond him, for his mind, ingeniously sophistical, would have added a dozen saving clauses and explanations as to exceptions and qualifications beneath which the plain word for the plain man would have altogether disappeared. Bearing this constitutional incapacity in mind, Mr. GLADSTONE has done fairly well in his letter to Mr. MOULTON to make it clear to Liberal doubters that they may vote for the second reading with a clear conscience even if they altogether disapprove of every proposal in the Bill save the establishment of an Irish Parliament to deal with Irish affairs. Mr. MOULTON wrote to Mr. GLADSTONE to say that the interpretation which he personally had given to the expressions of the Government was as follows:—

That in voting for the second reading of the present Bill, one is affirming only the principle of the establishment in Ireland of a legislative body for the conduct of Irish as distinguished from Imperial affairs.

To this Mr. GLADSTONE replies in "brief but explicit terms":—

I hold this to be indispensable, and, indeed, elementary.

That is not bad. "Indispensable" is rather an odd word to employ, but "elementary" is clear and explicit. It is a declaration that Mr. GLADSTONE will accept a vote on the second reading simply and solely as an affirmation of the principle of Home Rule, or, as we would put it, as the recognition of the principle that the local affairs of Ireland should be directed and controlled by the representatives of Ireland. We need not concern ourselves with the second head of Mr. GLADSTONE'S reply to Mr. MOULTON. Ministers are, of course, bound to consider any amendments and free to accept any proposals for improving their Bill during the recess. If they carry the second reading by a majority of six, there need be little fear but that they will not only consider, but accept, amendments at which some time ago they would have refused even to look. What they have to do now is to carry the second reading, and, as they can only carry it by reducing the Bill to the position of a resolution shaped as a "draft for discussion," it is only natural that Mr. GLADSTONE should regard such reduction as "indispensable, and indeed elementary." We are utterly at a loss to see how any Radical who accepts the principle of Home Rule can refuse to vote for the second reading now that Mr. GLADSTONE has, in Mr. CHAMBERLAIN'S phrase, offered them the principle without the details. Even if we were against one central Parliament at Dublin, and approved of establishing two or four provincial Legislatures, we would still vote for the Bill, and distinctly affirm before we voted that we did so solely as a recognition of the principle of leaving the conduct of Irish affairs in Irish hands. Mr. GLADSTONE will repeat his assurances in the House on Monday night, and great will be the responsibility of any Liberal member who, with such assurances before him, deals a fatal blow at the Bill at the Government, and at the organization of the party. It will not be forgiven him. We are not among those who maintain a doctrine of subservience. We upheld the cause of political independence against Mr. CHAMBERLAIN when Mr. CHAMBERLAIN ran the machine. We have nothing but commendation for those who, like Mr. BRIGHT and Lord HARTINGTON, give effect to their conscientious objection to the principle of Home Rule by voting against the second reading. But we cannot understand the attitude of those men who proclaim their devotion to Home Rule in the same breath in which they pledge themselves to vote against the acceptance of the principle of Home Rule by the House of Commons. And our difficulty will be the difficulty of the Liberal electors.

Of course if Mr. CHAMBERLAIN and his friends cannot trust Mr. GLADSTONE even on his oath, that is another matter. A statesman who will deceive, is a statesman who should be turned out. If they give a hostile vote on that ground, it will not be so much a vote of opposition to the Home Rule but a vote of no confidence in its author. We do not envy the [?] who has to justify before his constituents a vote which has w[?] the Government and the party, given because he b[?] that Mr. GLADSTONE is a sayer of falsehoods. For is what it will come to. When Mr. GLADSTONE declares, believe he will declare, unmistakeably on the floor of the of Commons on Monday next that the only question on whi[?] vote will be taken is as to whether the conduct of Irish should be placed in Irish hands, and that no one who votes will be held thereby committed in the least degree to any proposals of the Bill, it will only be possible for Mr. CHAMBE[?] and his friends to vote against the second reading on the g[?] that Mr. GLADSTONE'S word is not to be trusted ; th[?] plain English, he lies. Mr. CHAMBERLAIN has done many [?] in his time which make his friends mourn, but this is beyond him. Hence we repeat once more our belief t[?] spite of all the gloomy forebodings and faintheartedness of terialists and their newspapers, the Bill will get through necessary majority of six.

"TRUTH" ON THE SITUATION.
AN INTERVIEW WITH MR. LABOUCHERE.

A member of our staff called yesterday upon Mr. Labouchere and him whether he would mind answering a few questions. Mr. Lab[?] replied, "Ask them."

"Did you read Mr. Caine's account of the political position that a[?] in the *Pall Mall* of yesterday?"—I did.

In your opinion is it correct?

Mr. L. : Quite the reverse. Mr. Caine says that there a[?] "stalwarts," by which he means men who have absolutely determined against the bill. Seventy would be nearer the mark. I believe t[?] maximum estimate is 72. You may take this as the present s[?] things. There are 316 members who, it is known, will vote for t[?] and the same number who will vote against it. The rest are either or have not definitely made up their minds what they will do. T[?] therefore, as things now stand, is neither won nor lost. A considerable [?] of this residuum are already convinced that they have been tricked : oth[?] as Mr. Bannerman would phrase it, hesitating on the brink of salvati[?]

You say "tricked," will you please explain?

Mr. L. : Lord Hartington has about sixty adherents who agree wi[?] in his view that a domestic Legislature ought in no case to be gra[?] Ireland. Mr. Chamberlain has about six personal followers, whose vo[?] consciences he owns. These together were not enough to def[?] bill ; every effort has therefore been made to increase the flock. few have been gained over by playing upon their conviction th[?] country ought to have the benefit of their administrative wisdo[?] will secure it in the event of a Hartington Administration ; oth[?] being assured that if they vote against the bill the Conservatives [?] oppose them at a general election ; the rest have been hustled and [?] and they are now told that they have given pledges, and are in honour to fulfil them. The tactical skill with which the[?] been captured is great, the morality doubtful. Every redundant wo[?] by Mr. Gladstone has been turned against him, while Mr. Chamberlain at one of the "cave" meetings that the spirit as well as the letter Gladstone's concessions must be taken into consideration, and the "[?] has been used against him, wherever the words were satisfactory. I[?] have been far more simple to have said, "Distrust him, and do not one word that he utters."

But Mr. Caine has said that he did his best to induce Liberals to from voting?

Mr. L. : His intention may have been this, but his mo[?] giving effect to it was curious. He excluded from the Cham[?] meeting on Monday almost all who had been at previous[?] ings and who were inclined to accept Mr. Gladstone's conce[?] and he himself voted against abstention. If thirty could have got to abstain, he told your interviewer, abstention would have be proper course ; but because only twelve voted for it, therefore it w[?] wrong course. This looks to me rather a matter of tactics than of pr[?] His heart, he says, is broken. This is pathetic, if not exactly correct broken heart is certainly *corpore sano* ; and he bears up against this breakage with such singular fortitude that no one to see him suppose that he is suffering like a love-lorn maiden from a broken[?] Why he should talk this nonsense I do not know, for he can hardly any one to swallow it. No Midsterialist ever supposed that he was in [?]

of ability in his profession, his untiring industry[1] and curiosity, his faculty for enlisting all his powers, and his drilling in the Bible, Bunyan, Milton and Lowell gave him an effectiveness as a writer for the day which eclipsed all faults of style and some errors of taste. His quiet, cultivated assistant editor, of Winchester and Oxford, E. T. Cook, must have suffered many things because of him. I have the Bible that Stead used at the *Pall Mall*. It has one or two holes in its pages where the scissors of an editor 'with no feeling for books' have pounced into it in a hurry for a favourite text for that leader which was always being written against time. Stead's godlier following would have been aghast had they had a sight of the mutilated Scriptures, but Stead, though he had a rare acquaintance with the Bible and valued it intensely, revolted at the sanctimonious. As I have noted, he was on as easy terms as Cromwell with both his Bible and his God. The religious folk who followed Carlyle's 'good man Stead' got shocks. But not more shocks than were received by the ungodly who came along with him because he was a political force and found themselves in the company of one who cared as little for the *convenances* as Ezekiel.

The *Pall Mall*, in spite of the endeavours of Cook and Edmund Garrett—on whom a word later—was often, as I say, a scorn to literary persons. But Stead had some niceties of his own. Within the first few weeks of my novitiate in the office he opened the shutter in the wall which divided his writing den from the room in which I worked and demanded to know what I meant by writing 'the *P.M.G.* man' in a few lines of chat I had had with a celebrity.

Ruskin was not the only master of letters who overlooked Stead's literary infelicities in appreciation of his purposes. Ruskin was indeed a frequent correspondent for publication or for private counsel. On one occasion he sent to the office a copy of the paper—a copy now, alas, lost—with almost every item in it re-headed or marked to be cut down, or omitted, or to occupy greater space or a more prominent position.

MORAL AND PHYSICAL COURAGE. I have never known a man who united moral and physical courage in a greater degree than Stead. To him the trite 'He feared no foe' might be applied accurately. The sturdiness with which he risked his reputation successively over 'The Maiden Tribute of Modern Babylon', by his stand at considerable financial sacrifice in resistance to Rhodes and the Boer War, by his active sympathy with Russia when Russia

---

[1] Asked for an account of the system on which he worked, Stead said it was 'just to do the first thing first and let the rest slide'.

had few interpreters, by his deference to the Salvation Army at a time when good men spoke rudely of the Booths, by his parleyings with 'spooks', by his championing of Mrs. Crawford and Mrs. Langworthy,[1] must be held in grateful remembrance by every worthy journalist. As for Stead's physical courage, we have Admiral Lord Fisher's fine story about what he did on H.M.S. *Indomitable*.[2] Stead confidently expected that, in support of some cause, he would come to a violent end and had never a qualm about it. Miss Dixon, once a member of his staff, reminds me how 'on each anniversary of his going to prison—in order that the Parliamentary success achieved against wrong should not be forgotten—he used to come up in the train from Wimbledon and over Waterloo Bridge clad in his prison garb, a remarkable figure in the streets'. Some of his friends have photographs of him in the *Pall Mall* office wearing his prison clothes.

That a man had abused the editor of the *Pall Mall* in speech or print would not in the least prevent Stead from going to see him and hearing what he had to say for himself, or offering him an opportunity to state his views. It is not easy to credit how gross were the attacks on Stead after 'The Maiden Tribute'. He had stirred ugly depths in more than one part of London life. At the starting of the *Review of Reviews* it was pleasantly suggested that Stead had got capital out of the headquarters fund of the Salvation Army. I heard him reply to the suggestion that in this instance he should bring a libel action 'I would not take legal proceedings if it were stated that I had killed my grandmother and eaten her'.

Stead was big. He would have welcomed to his sanctum, with equal vivacity and the office cup of tea, Gabriel and Judas and, on the departure of each of them, would at once have dictated one of those marvellously accurate interviews of his, for, as there is no end of testimony, his memory was—one is tempted to write the ill-used word—phenomenal.

[1] Mrs. Crawford was the respondent in the divorce suit brought by a Scottish M.P. in which Sir Charles Dilke, the Duke of Marlborough and Shaw, Captain of the London Fire Brigade, were co-respondents. One of Stead's *Pall Mall Gazette* Extras, *The Langworthy Marriage, or a Millionaire's Shame*, told the extraordinary Langworthy story. The offender had drawn the daughter of an Irish landlord into a marriage which was no marriage and had ill-used her and afterwards deserted her and her child. The case in one aspect or another was known to half a dozen judges but redress had not been obtained. In the result, by Stead's exertions, a verdict for £20,000 with £1,500 costs was obtained. The sensations did not end there. Later in her life Mrs. Langworthy received a message from Langworthy saying he was ill in Paris and asking to see her. She went to see him and dined with him. The same night Mrs. Langworthy suddenly died and was buried without a *post mortem* examination. The next day Langworthy committed suicide! Another of the many cases in which the *Pall Mall* did good service was that of Miss Cass, a victim of vicious police evidence. Not only was she acquitted; the magistrate was reprimanded by the Lord Chancellor and the Home Secretary.

[2] See page 234.

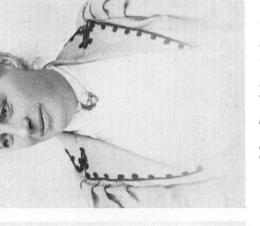

On the anniversary of his conviction Stead used to wear his gaol suit (1885)

Mrs. Stead in 1896

Stead in his Hayling Island garden. He was an intrepid boatman (1896)

W. T. STEAD AND HIS WIFE

AN AGE OF HUSH-HUSH. It was urged that Stead pursued
Dilke and Parnell with bitterness. Dilke was in Stead's view a
guilty public man pretending he was not,[1] Parnell a trusted Irish

*I am anxious to
see you for ten minutes*

W. H. O'Shea

CAPTAIN O'SHEA TO STEAD

leader who, after letting his country down by his relations with
Mrs. O'Shea, suggested that his scandalous behaviour did not
matter. Stead's crusades, like his 'Maiden Tribute', may be fairly
judged by those only who are able sufficiently to reconstitute his
era. (Has not Goethe urged that if you would understand a man
you must understand his age?) I remember having myself to call
one morning at Scotland Yard to make inquiries regarding two
M.P.s who, within a few days, had fled the country on charges of
immorality of one type or another. I also recall the death in a
brothel of a Judge of the High Court. Stead's was a day in which
a hypocritical opposition to Bradlaugh taking his seat in Parliament,
a mirthful attitude towards the elementary rights of women and
girls, patronage or becalling of the United States, a ghastly Sublime
Porte policy, the densest ignorance of the Colonies (as we called
them) and of Asia—some of the chickens have come home to roost—
and much stodginess and complacency in the Press and public life
disturbed most of the educated electorate very little. Not irony,
not literary rapier fighting but prophetic plainspeaking and a
pen tipped with flame were found to be the equipment for a struggle
with ignorance, thick heads, dull hearts and entrenched power.

But Stead could do a good turn to what he took to be deserving
objects, like the Pope and the Tsar. There were functions of his
Holiness which appealed to him—the *Review of Reviews*' telegraphic
address was 'Vatican'—and his Imperial Majesty, poor fellow,
would do so much better if he had new and better prisons in place
of his out-of-date, over-populated ones.

In judging some of Stead's attitudes it must be borne in mind
that, although no contemporary editor worked harder to instruct
himself, knew more persons of mark, more persistently sought sound

[1] See page 180.

G

information in his own country and on the Continent, or did more, on a basis of knowledge, to modify opinion in Home and European politics or to instruct the public regarding Britain overseas, his upbringing and early adult life had been in some respects narrow. It was not until some years after he left Northumberland Street that he paid his first visit to a theatre. He knew a great deal of Spenser, but a whole world of fancy was closed to him. No one fully acquainted with the volume, the range and the verve of the work that Stead did can doubt that he was a man of unusual force and ardour, great gifts and personal goodness; but he was not, in the ordinary sense, an intellectual man. He knew nothing of music, pictures were little more to him than illustrations, and with many phases of life he had no contact. But he was a good man, a generous man, a man of merit in a dozen ways in which merit may be rightly reckoned. A maker of footpaths, a breaker of many bonds, an unsparing toiler, a laborious citizen and faithful friend, a patriot, a man rooted in integrity, one of the ablest journalists the world has seen, a joyous colleague, an unselfish lover, he was of those who are remembered with affection after their death by men and women of many creeds, parties and ranks, remembered not only for their kindnesses and their character but for their helpful life in that, being in Ephesus, they diligently and gallantly sought out the lions to destroy them.

'THE VERY HALLMARK OF GENIUS.' At no point are biographers so futile, a friend of mine, Havelock Ellis, says with his usual sagacity, 'as in toning down, glozing over or altogether ignoring weaknesses, defects and failures which are the very hallmark of genius'. Stead's extravagances and credulities, crudities and, if you like, trumperies; his vain attempts to combine the exhorter and expositor with the business man will be forgotten. It is easy to write that and it is true. But I would rather write that, in estimating Stead, his weaknesses should not be forgotten. What is remembered of him—just to him and of help to those who come after him—is that, bound up though his nature was with weakness, he ran his course courageously It is not stated that the good and faithful servant who received his 'well done!' and entered into joy was faultless.

Stead had all the virtues credited to him, along with warmth, accessibility and self-criticism, but little humour. Think of trying to sell the public the truth about South Africa in a brochure called *Shall I Slay My Brother Boer?* (Is it surprising that there was a skit, 'Shall I Kick My Brother Stead?') He got on the nerves of people who were as concerned, or almost as much concerned, as he was about objects he had in view. Many men and women with only a public impression of him or without sympathy for his aims detested

I never spoke to Stead in my life, nor even saw him except once at a public meeting, where he behaved so outrageously that I walked out in disgust. I was a contributor to the Pall Mall under his editorship; but as my department was literature and art, and he was an utter Philistine, no contacts between us were possible. Outside political journalism such as can be picked up in a newspaper office he was a complete ignoramus. I wrote him a few letters about politics which he acknowledged very sensibly as "intended for his instruction"; but he was unteachable except by himself.

We backed him up over The Maiden Tribute only to discover that the Eliza Armstrong case was a put-up job of his. After that, it was clear that he was a man who could not work with anybody; and nobody would work with him. When he was set up years after as editor of a new London daily he had learnt nothing and forgotten nothing, being so hopelessly out of date journalistically that the paper collapsed almost at once. He wanted me to review for it on the old P.M.G. terms though I had become a Big Noise in the interval.

G. Bernard Shaw

A POSTCARD TO THE AUTHOR FROM G.B.S. See page 128

him. Some people had no doubt that he was mad. There was at the time, in large sections of the public, much prudery, widespread unwillingness to have truths blurted out, not a little contentment with things, on the whole, as they were, and amazing ignorance.

SHOWMAN? No doubt Stead liked appreciation as other people do; but he had also a relish for abuse. Did it not show that what he was writing was hitting the mark? A common criticism of him was that he was a good showman. 'Barnum' was flung at him. Certainly he saw no good in hiding his light under a bushel or in keeping back what he thought it was for the good of the public that it should buy and read. He was a downright speaker at a public meeting because he knew it was no good addressing people if they did not listen. There was no knowing, of course, what he might not say—or do. He was in dead earnest. Bernard Shaw told me that he had to leave some political demonstration 'because Stead turned it into a prayer meeting'. Hadley thinks this may be misleading. 'I never knew Stead attend a party political meeting. More than once I heard him preface his own speech with a very short prayer. It was his common practice to say a few words of prayer before addressing his Peace Crusade meetings.'

Allowances had to be made, and were made by thousands, for Stead. For the work he had to do for his time it is not easy to see that he could have been very different from what he was. His methods were not what his critics would have chosen. These methods seemed the only possible ones to him. He was a little turbulent, spectacular, melodramatic, but how few of us have left adolescence completely behind? Stead puts in our minds Francis Thompson's aspirations:

> Oh for the flushed excitement of keen strife!
> For mountains, gulfs and torrents in my way,
> With perils, anguish, fear and strugglings rife!
> For friends and foes, for love and hate in fray—
> And not this lone, flat, torpid life.

Stead lacked the poise, balance and judgment often possessed by persons of mediocre achievement. He divided his strength. He used up his energies not only in the pursuit of great ideals but fidgeted and frayed by idle, vain and selfish people and by some crude and trifling efforts made in association with them. He had moments of defeat and abasement; but, when account is taken of all, he did experience the joy of life which, as Shaw has told us, is 'being a force, being thoroughly worn out before you are thrown on the scrap heap'.

Something should be added concerning Stead's extraordinary tenacity of purpose in union with an uncommon willingness to turn

right about when he found on enquiry that the facts were against
him. Only a few of his intimates understood this. 'Get to
know your facts' was, as I keep saying, his workaday motto. It
was in a search for facts, a spiritual search that he was persuaded
must be successful, that he was led into some morasses. Of the
sincerity of his telepathic beliefs no one who knew him could doubt
for an instant. One day I wired to him that I should come
in the evening to see him at Wimbledon. 'My dear Robertson
Scott', he said on my arrival, 'why did you take the trouble to
wire? You know that you could have made me aware of your
coming'.

WOMEN'S DEBT. Stead's name is remembered with gratitude
by many women. It might well be cherished by more. The other
day I met a woman of education and public spirit, in a circle
usually supposed to be well-informed, who had never heard of
'The Maiden Tribute'. To pose Stead as a plaster saint for the
women's movement would be, of course, ignorant and absurd.
Sincere Congregationalist he was to the last, a 'twicer', like Gladstone, at his Sunday religious exercises; but no man was less 'tied
up wi' godly laces'. He was not 'sicklied o'er' with his religion.
He was a religious and honest man. A Galahad, no man of his
time can have been more exposed to 'temptation'. Stead, like so
many big natures, had a saving vein of Rabelaisianism, but his
life was lived at a high level of morality.

Clever women with sparks of ability but often stranded, undiscip-
lined and unfit, women to whom no other editor than Stead would
have given any hearing at all, were often to be met with ascending
or descending his stairs or lying in wait for his kind word, his
recommendation or his charity. A young woman once said to me,
'He talked to me as if I were his equal'. I remember, too, one of
Stead's meetings. There was a good and famous woman on the
platform beside him who, as she came forward to speak, attracted
the attention of the reporters, for her bonnet seemed to slide to a
sharper angle, a piece of stuff in the penetralia of her skirts ripped
and a hairpin dropped beside her. A rather superior representative
of *The Times* attending his first 'purity' meeting muttered to me as
he gazed, 'Gad, I could trust that woman anywhere!'

THE GOSPEL ACCORDING TO *THE PALL MALL GAZETTE*.
When a final judgment on Stead's career comes to be passed it may
well be asked just what our journalism would have been without
him. The roots of some of the better things which were cropped by
Northcliffe are to be found, as Northcliffe agreed with me more than
once, in the pioneering and vision of Stead. It would have been a
worthy exercise if, when his circle began to narrow and his light
to fail a little, more of those who with advantage walked in daily

and periodical journalism in his footsteps had owned their indebtedness to Northumberland Street and Mowbray House. Not only at home but all over the world the 'gospel' according to the *Pall Mall*, as Stead taught it, came to be practised. Some will have in mind the service of the American and Australasian *Review of Reviews*. Nor will readers of Sir Edward Cook's *Edmund Garrett* (Arnold), in which one of Stead's men writes of a colleague, fail to see how much of the *Pall Mall* there was, in a time of Imperial crisis, in the *Cape Times*, how much of Stead was its Editor-Assemblyman in that public work which is part of the history of South Africa and is proudly acknowledged in Capetown Cathedral. Nothing touched me more during my publication in wartime of a monthly review in Tokyo (*The New East*) than a message from Havelock Ellis in which he said: 'It is clear that you have been largely inspired by Stead and in this, I think, you have been wise'.

And that emboldens me to tell something of Stead which is more personal. Because, no doubt, I was bred among Cumberland fells farmers, learnt out of *Rob Roy* some wisdom regarding the North-West Frontier of India and had for a close friend from my 'teens the doyen of the press of the Netherlands, I early gained some understanding of those difficult but mostly genuine enough Boers. Years before there were any 'pro-Boers' and years before the Raid, I used to try to get Stead to take a fairer view of the uncouth, 'ill tae deal wi'' and sometimes not too scrupulous Transvaalers; but I made no headway. When the Boer War came and Britain threw away in South Africa two hundred millions sterling—a vast sum at that time—many thousands of lives and some of her good name and influence and Stead was early among the 'pro-Boers', he owned to me, with a kindness and bigness all his own, how far he had been wrong for years past. (In the War, of course, military lessons were learnt which were valuable against Germany.)

Stead was happy in the time of his death, for his work was done. Even the place of his passing, halfway between England and America, was enviable for one of the most loyal, open-minded and far-sighted citizens of the English-speaking world.

OUT OF ONE GENERATION INTO ANOTHER. When the life and work of Stead are judged by a generation which has benefited by wider opportunities than he had, a generation to which he has been a faded name, let it be remembered, as I am not the first to write, that no man may be censured for not having been always in advance of the times in which he strove.

The story of Stead's life is worthy to be known because of the balm it may bring to weary fighting men and women. We pass our years in a different world from that through which Stead fought—it has visibly moved on—and those who come after us will live in a world rid of many of our bugaboos. Finally, this book—may I humbly say?—sets our minds inwardly. When the sober and successful contemplate the hurry-scurry and vociferousness, the constant nudging of the Almighty and of everybody else which was some—not all—of Stead's life, they say that he was a little 'un-balanced'. But, judging from the strange attitudes of some of us *sub specie aeternitatis,* just how sane are we?

Kelvin

Signature of the famous physicist. One of the autographs from Stead's correspondence which are dropped in at the end of Chapters IX to XIX. Fairly familiar signatures like those of Gladstone, Salisbury and Balfour are not included. For autographs from cordial letters from some interesting men like Lombroso and Flammarion it was feared there would not be space.

CHAPTER X

STEAD'S EARLY LOVES AND
JOURNALISTIC INITIATION

THE DIMITY APRON. In some notes I have by Stead about his childhood, dated April 15, 1893, he says: 'In 1850 we left Embleton, near Alnwick, where I was born (1849), for North Shields, whence we came to Howden, about five miles from Newcastle, on the north bank of the Tyne, where my father was Congregational minister until he died. I remember the Russian War, and how sorry I used to be for the horses that were killed. Somehow, I have been very sorry for horses, women and birds, but men have not touched me. When I was a child, and stories used to be told of carriage accidents and so forth, I never manifested the slightest interest in the fate of the people in the carriage, but I would cry bitterly if the horses broke their legs or got hurt.

'Before 1864 I fell in love—with Queen Elizabeth. I remember distinctly feeling about her exactly what you would feel about a woman you are in love with; i.e. you are greatly interested to hear everything about her that you can, you believe that she is the peerless ideal of all women, and you regard all her enemies as your enemies. To this day I have never been able to get over the feeling of exultation that Mary, Queen of Scots, had her head cut off. I could not deny that Mary was better looking than Elizabeth, although I did occasionally deny even that in those days.

'I think I was about eight when I first fell in love with a girl. I do not know anything about her except that they called her Lizzie, and that she wore a dimity apron, which was rather stiff. I remember the apron, because the first time I kissed her I had a battle for it. My sister, who valiantly assisted me, held her on one side, while I succeeded, in spite of vigorous scratches, on the other.

'My first real serious love affair was when I was between ten and eleven, when I fell in love with a girl called Lydia, who had long golden curls, bright blue eyes and a beautiful white and red complexion. She was the belle of the village, and all the boys were crazy over her. Alas, she was two years older than I was, and when you are eleven, two years are a lot. I never dared to breathe my affection. In the wintertime I used to walk at a distance behind her, and put my feet into the footprints she had made in the snow, and feel inexpressibly happy. It was about this girl that the fight occurred to which Benjamin Waugh alludes,[1] but, like most historians, he ignores that very vital consideration, precise truth, in order to make it appear that my battle was on behalf of her modesty or from general devotion to ideal virtue, whereas it was really inspired by a very devoted love for the girl herself.

SCHOOLING. 'Up to 1861, my sister and I got all our teaching from my father, who taught us Latin and to read French, although he did not know it at all as a spoken language. In 1861, I went to school at Silcoates, near Wakefield.[2] It was a school for Congregational ministers' sons, and I had not been there for two months before a remarkable revival of religion broke out in the school, and nearly all the boys, excepting half-a-dozen, professed to be converted. Some twenty, I think, joined the chapel, myself among the number. I had previous to that time had an occasional but very intense sense of my sinfulness, and I remember at one time sobbing so bitterly after I had gone to bed at the thought of my lost condition, that my mother had to come up, and I had to have a great deal of comforting before I could get to sleep. I was a little more than twelve when I joined the Congregational Church and I have remained a member of that Church ever since. The Congregationalists, as the heirs of Cromwell, Milton and the Pilgrim Fathers, and the representatives of extreme democracy, which knows neither male nor female, and makes the votes of the whole church the supreme and only authority in the Church, have always attracted me.

'When I was at school I became an enthusiastic devotee of cricket, and also learnt the principles of self-government, for the boys were left very much to themselves.

'I left school in 1863, and was apprenticed as office boy in the counting house of a merchant on the Quayside, Newcastle [who, and this proved to be of some importance, was the Russian Vice-Consul]. We had an hour for dinner, during which I got in a good deal of reading. Then I competed for prizes in a boys' paper. I got a prize for an essay on Oliver Cromwell. That essay was decisive for me, but I was obliged to cease reading as I feared I was going blind.

THE YOUNG SOCIAL REFORMER. 'Then occurred what I always regard as my second conversion. From that time to 1869 I was intensely ambitious with a personal ambition that made me

---

[1] *William T. Stead.* By the Rev. Benjamin Waugh (Vickers). A correspondent of *The Times* has explained, Dec. 24, 1951, how Waugh by his energy and eloquence made the National Society for the Prevention of Cruelty to Children.

[2] The school also attended by Sir George Newnes, a future proprietor of the *Pall Mall Gazette.*

wish to make a name for myself.[1] I wanted to write the history of
the Puritan movement between where Froude left off and Macaulay
began. That was the dream of my life for some years. When my
eyes went bad, and I had the whole of Cromwell's life, letters,
and speeches fermenting in my head, it grew upon me that this
dream of ambition was unworthy and un-Christian. I attempted
to make out that I did not want to write this history so much to
make a name for myself as to do justice to Cromwell, etc., which
was largely true, but I gradually woke up to the conviction that
all that was wrong and that I must put away all idea of ever writing
the book, or of making a name for myself and simply set to work to
labour for those who were around me. I set to work to organise
social and religious agencies in the village, becoming a kind of lay
curate to my father. My class of lads in the Sunday School was the
social microcosm where I studied human nature and the organisation of society. I sometimes think that I have hardly gained a
single idea since I left school. I have learned a great many more
facts, and to know a great many more people, but my standpoint
or outlook upon life, my conception of what is possible and of what
ought to be done, in other words, my ideal and objective were
fixed by the time I was twenty. I am today what I was in 1869.

FIRST JOURNALISM. 'I had in 1865 and 1868 written two
leading articles, one on the assassination of President Lincoln,
the other upon the disestablishment of the Irish Church. The former
was published in a little Jarrow weekly paper, the other in the
Sheffield Independent, but after that I did not write any more until
1870. My eyes got better, for the dimness of sight was caused simply
by nervous exhaustion,[2] but I never contemplated the possibility
of depending for my living on my pen. My mother, whose shaping
influence upon me was constant and abiding, had developed, I
think from reading Johnson's *Lives of the Poets*, a terror of any
human being ever depending for the necessities of life upon literary
work. When I built my castles in the air in this period, what I
dreamt of was to be in a situation where I should get away from
the office as early as possible and have my nights to myself. The
position of a bank clerk, with £150 a year, and free to leave the
bank between 4 and 5, seemed to me to come near the zenith of
human felicity. When I was out of my apprenticeship I was engaged
as junior clerk at £60 per annum in the office where I served my time.

'A LITTLE DAFT.' 'The love affairs I had between 1861 and
1871 were numerous. But I should mention two things: one was
that I fell in love with my present wife when I was about thirteen,

---

[1] Gladstone as a young man asked himself whether he would 'best serve God as
Archbishop of Canterbury or Prime Minister'.

[2] This is interesting in view of the facts mentioned on page 78.

in a romantic, distant kind of way, and that when I fell in love with her again I was about seventeen. As, however, she was of my own age I did not make much progress. School girls of seventeen are very difficult to get on with. One of the most useful love affairs that I ever had was when I was about eighteen. The sister of the village doctor came to stay with him. She was about twenty-eight or twenty-nine, and, finding the village rather dull, took a great deal of notice of me. She was the first woman outside my own family who ever said a civil word to me. My devotion to the other girls was one-sided.

'I was a somewhat eccentric youth, who had an objection to wearing gloves, and always preferred to run, weekdays and Sundays, rather than to walk. The spectacle could be seen of the minister's eldest son running home as soon as chapel was out, through the streets, which were thick with people leaving their respective places of worship, at as hard a gallop as his legs would carry him. It was thought in the village that I was a little daft, and the girls did not care to receive the attentions of a suitor who was more or less looked down upon and ridiculed by local public opinion. However, I did not care. I liked the lift that comes from running as hard as you can and like it to this day.

'I remember very well telling Morley when I came to London that if I felt cold any day I would not hesitate at running as hard as I could from one end of Pall Mall to the other, and noting with some amusement the expression that came over his face. It all recurred to me vividly yesterday, when after having had a rather exciting conversation with a friend whom I left at the corner of the Athenaeum Club, I ran up part of Regent Street full tilt, pretty much for the same reason as I suppose a mainspring uncoils when it has been wound too tight.

A WAY TO LEARN TO WRITE. 'The doctor's sister played and sang Scotch airs. I fell deeply in love with her. She was the first woman to whom I ever said the word "love". I remember the occasion as well as if it were yesterday. It was between 11 and 12 o'clock. We were setting home. The stars were shining.

'Up to that time it had always been more or less of an effort to me to write letters. I could write essays but I always preferred to talk than to write. After some months of very delicious experience, during which I was allowed to make love to her, she accepted the calf love of the hobbledehoy as a kind of pleasant homage which in no way interfered with her attachment to the naval officer to whom she was expecting to be married. She left our village for Edinburgh. I felt as if the sun had gone down in mid-heaven. Out of the misery of the parting I wrote her immense letters three times a week, and the exercise and the straining always to write my best did me more good than anything else. I often advise young people, who ask me what would be the best school in which to learn to write well, to fall in love with a clever woman a dozen years older than themselves, who lives at a distance from them, and can only be communicated with by writing. It is love that makes difficult things easy, and constrains you to do things that otherwise you would never attempt.

A LEADER WRITER. 'About 1870 I had very much laid upon my heart the misery of the vagrant class. I helped a very clever scoundrel. I gave him what I could, wrapped him up in an old coat, gave him an old bible, and was very friendly and brotherly to him. When he ascertained that he had got as much out of me as I had to give he vanished, carrying off with him all the portable property of his fellow lodgers in the lodging house where I had maintained him, but leaving behind him, as a souvenir, my poor little bible.

'Thinking over this, I came to the conclusion that nothing could be done except by organisation, and, reading at that time some chance paragraph as to the way in which the Blackheath Mendicity Society had attempted to grapple with the evil, I wrote a letter to the *Northern Daily Express* advocating the formation of a Charity Organisation or Mendicity Society in Newcastle. The editor inserted it, and I sent round marked copies to leading people. Someone wrote a letter replying to mine. I replied, writing a longer letter which, to my great delight, the editor put in as a leading article. We got up a town's meeting. My employer undertook to act as secretary on the understanding that I wrote his speeches for him, and the Charity Organisation Society of Newcastle came into being. I believe it is still in existence. I became consumed by a great zeal to establish Charity Organisation Societies everywhere.

'About that time the *Northern Echo* of Darlington, a new halfpenny paper, had just appeared or was about to appear. I sent a leader to the editor which he put in and wrote a letter thanking me for my contribution. He inserted various sentences of his own from which I dissented, and I wrote to tell him so. This brought about a correspondence and he asked me to write more. That marks my initiation into journalism. I wrote occasional notes and leaders and a series of articles upon America and the Americans. The contribution that attracted most attention was about Christianity and Democracy, and the proprietor of the paper was much struck by it, and made inquiries as to the writer.

'I was not paid for any of these contributions. After having written for about nine months I modestly ventured to suggest that, as I was writing about three leaders a week and half a dozen occasional notes, the labourer might be worthy of his hire. The editor replied saying that he was very sorry but that there was no fund available to pay for outside contributions, and that if I insisted on payment he would simply have to fall back upon his own unaided pen. He sent me a book by Miss Yonge with a shorthand inscription which I subsequently learnt was "May your soul be bound up in the bundle of life."

EDITOR ON 'STRICT CONDITIONS'. 'I still had no intention of becoming a journalist, but one day I was much astonished by a visit of a stranger who turned out to be Mr. Hyslop Bell of the *Northern Echo*. After a few preliminary words, he offered me the editorship of the *Echo* at a salary of £150 a year.[1] I asked if the editor was leaving. He said that he was going to go, and that his place had to be filled. I said I would take no further step until I had communicated with him, as he was my friend. Mr. Bell demurred a little but ultimately gave way. I wrote to the editor and told him of the offer that had been made and said that if it would in any way help him for me to refuse to entertain the idea, I would refuse. He said that it would not make any difference: that he was going anyway. Then came negotiations, in the course of which I once or twice refused to accept the proposal, but finally agreed under strict conditions. I was to have a fortnight's holiday. I was not to be required to write anything that was opposed to my convictions. I was never to be required to do any Sunday work, and I was never to be expected to work later than 9 o'clock. But that arrangement didn't last. I became editor of the *Northern Echo* in July 1871 and remained there until 1880, when I became assistant editor of the *Pall Mall Gazette* under Morley.

'QUITE MAD.' 'In 1873 I married my wife, whom I had fallen in love with for the third time, and we have six children. When I was editing the *Northern Echo* I was a thoroughgoing Gladstonian of the very stalwart fighting kind, with the conviction that the Tories were children of the devil, and that the supreme duty of a Liberal journalist was to win as many seats as possible for the Liberal Party. In the *Northern Echo* I preached just the same as I preach now, advocating Industrial Arbitration and Imperial

---

[1] J. Hyslop Bell, who came to be overshadowed by Stead, was a noteworthy man. A Methodist minister turned daily newspaper conductor whose writing was commended by Archbishop Temple, he gave the *Northern Echo* character before Stead's editorship. He owned a weekly paper, the *South Durham and Cleveland Mercury*, before the Pease family invited him to start the *Echo* on which he gave the youthful Stead his chance. During Stead's association with the *Echo* Bell was thrice threatened with libel actions. Bell's daughter Mrs. Jackson, tells me that two or three years ago she was thrilled to notice in a film, 'Fame is the Spur', a group of working men who were awaiting an election result picking out the news in the *Northern Echo*. Lord Rosebery and Sir Joseph Pease initiated a testimonial to Bell in recognition of his services to Liberalism as journalist and speaker.

extension, much to the horror of the good Quakers who, I believe, found the money with which the *Echo* was established. I also was a heretic on the subject of capital punishment, and was always a very strong opponent of Sir Wilfrid Lawson's Permissive Bill. On the other hand I was from the first a vehement supporter of Mrs. Josephine Butler in her crusade against the Contagious Diseases Acts. I remember very well how, before I went into journalism at all, my mother used to go canvassing our village for signatures against those Acts. It was one of the subjects upon which I have always been quite mad. I am ready to allow anybody to discuss anything in any newspaper that I edit: they may deny the existence of God, or of the soul, they may blaspheme the angels and all the saints, they may maintain that I am the latest authentic incarnation of the devil; but the thing I have never allowed them to do was to say a word in favour of the C.D. Acts, or of any extension of the system which makes a woman the chattel and slave of the administration for the purpose of ministering to the passions of men.

'SHUT DOWN TO MY HALFPENNY PAPER.' 'It was curious that I failed to obtain extraneous literary employment all the time I was on the *Northern Echo*. I was shut down, and kept down, to my halfpenny paper. My efforts to get literary work or external engagements were total failures, and a very good thing it was for me too. What made me was the Bulgarian Atrocities, in the setting forth of which I took a leading part in the north of England. I was tremendously excited about it. I did not approach the Eastern Question with any of the Russophobia which affects so many minds. One of the first articles I wrote for the *Echo* was in favour of more reasonable relations with Russia. The part which I took in getting up public meetings and generally rousing the North against Lord Beaconsfield brought me in contact with Mr. Gladstone, Mr. Bright, and Mr. Forster, and afterwards with Madame Novikoff.[1] For nearly three years I hardly published an issue in which I did not solemnly commit Lord Beaconsfield to the devil. I loathed Jingoism. The *Electors' Guide* which I got out just before the Election had a great vogue and I am rather proud of it to this day as a sample of journalistic pemmican. I have never done anything so good in that way since.' A fly in his ointment at the *Northern Echo* was that his proprietor expected him to wear a silk hat.

A GRATEFUL SON TO HIS FATHER. The following are quotations from two of Stead's remarkable letters to his father. They may seem a little bombastic, but Stead in extolling himself was

[1] There can be no doubt that Stead's articles and his letters to Gladstone encouraged him in the course he took. I have before me a letter of Stead's to Gladstone (March 28, 1878) saying plainly 'We shall want more vigorous leadership than we have had yet'.

really paying tribute to his father. The first letter, written in 1881, that is some time after the preceding notes, runs:

This thirty-second anniversary of my birthday reminds me once more of the great debt of gratitude and love which I owe to you, to whom I owe everything I am or have.

Life has perhaps been a somewhat stormy ocean for me as for others, but the storms have blown the ship faster through the waves and I stand now astonished and amazed at the rapidity with which the small infant of Embleton has been hurried upwards and onwards to be one of the handful of men to whom in his mysterious providence the Almighty has entrusted the government of the Empire.

To your fundamental virtues and capacities transmitted to your first-born son, to your education and example, to your encouragement and inspiration, I owe under God and my mother all that I have, all that I can do.

And I have so much, too much sometimes I think. Health, strength, an energy which never flags except from absolute exhaustion of the body, a charming house in the loveliest part of England, a darling wife, lovely children, ample means, intercourse with the leading minds of the age, opportunity and demand for literary work far beyond my utmost ability to turn it out, the love and confidence of my father, sisters and brothers, the sense of perpetually increasing usefulness, the consciousness that I am constantly and clearly guided by the invisible hand of God. What more could I have? What more has any mortal had?

And for all that, and perhaps still more for the spirit which enables me to enjoy all that without feeling exalted or puffed up, and which keeps me ever ready to admit mistakes, confess shortcomings and receive correction even from the humblest,—no small addition to the sum of human comfort— I owe you endless thanks and the constant service of grateful love.

'SOME STIR IN THE WORLD.' A second letter of three years later, when his father was dying, is as follows:

I have been very busy of late setting the world and its affairs in order, as you used to say in your tender, loving way when you would ask me not to forget that God had still left to Himself some share in the government of the Universe.

The interview with General Gordon and the subsequent appointment of that brave and pious man were great achievements for your harum-scarum son to be instrumental in bringing about. I always knew that with God's help I was destined to make some stir in the world, but I never ventured to hope that the time would come so soon. Here am I not yet thirty-five, and already almost the most influential man in England! Dear father, when good souls like Mrs. Butler write saying how it does their heart good to see at last a great London newspaper edited in Christian fashion, I think of the dear old home, where at your feet and on your knee and in the dear old chapel where I heard so many excellent discourses, I imbibed those principles of religion and of duty which thank God I can now repeat in the hearing of the whole world. God bless you, dearest father, for all you have been to me!

CHAPTER XI

STEAD'S CONFESSIONS TO STEAD

CACOETHES SCRIBENDI. It is difficult to believe that even Dr. Johnson talked more than Stead did. But with this gift or habit of speech went the practice of communing with himself on paper. These exchanges of Stead with Stead, for which throughout his life he always managed to find time, had voluminous results for three reasons. First, he had uncommon facility in a clear penmanship which in his young days must have been nearly copperplate. Secondly, he liked writing. If any man ever had *cacoethes scribendi* it was he. The words poured from his pen. Thirdly, he was intent and in earnest and always a preacher. He wrote because he had something to say pressingly. In the piles of his closely-written ruled foolscap, often twenty words to the line, in close lines, there are rarely any emendations, for he wrote, unlike many writing men, almost without corrections.

These pages tell us the truth about Stead. He was writing for Stead only, the man who knew all there was to know about him, who was patient with him when many were impatient, who would always be with him. In my extracts I shall condense greatly, of course, merely to avoid repetition. The last thing Stead is thinking of is literary excellence. All he is eager about is getting on paper quickly, for himself, some note of what has been said to him, of what has happened to him or of what he is thinking. I shall make no expurgatory omissions. Stead would not have wanted them. He is dead and his wife is dead, and only two understanding daughters remain. Moreover, intimate though much of what is set down may be, he had it indexed by his secretary, and a young man at that.

'THE SENIOR PARTNER.' The writing is often naïve. Sometimes it may be thought crude, inflated, unpleasing (Matthew Arnold's word), pious, in a way in which piety is not so often heard expressing itself today. In course of time Stead was to get away from some of his early taboos and notions, but only from some of them. No man can cut off his roots. From the beginning of his life to the end, as I have noted, the God of his era was above him directing his every step, putting in his mind and heart, without exception, every plan and project he had, leading him to the future and to the duties for which he was destined. Often the way might be hard, its end hidden, the discipline bitter, but it was not his way but Another's.

W. T. STEAD AFTER THE FAILURE OF THE *DAILY PAPER* (1904)

Stead's whole daily task, he felt, was to walk in the way. He had to be worthy, as worthy as an erring mortal could be, of the work set for him, and at any hour, in any place, the Senior Partner of his life—his constant phrase—was there to sustain him, to guide him, and ultimately to reward him with such measure of success in his labours and such happiness as was good for him and good for the world.

These notes of Stead's (the abbreviations and punctuation of which I sometimes leave as in the MSS.) begin during his editorship of the *Northern Echo*. I have cut out a little more than half. The narrative or confession rambles and is, at the start, youthful stuff. Yet it loses crudity and gets grip as it goes on, and is, now and then, almost amusing in view of the development of opinion and character that was to take place.

The patient reader will be rewarded. There can be few franker personal records. They have the quality of a sincerely written novel. The plainness with which Stead expresses himself on how he fell short in his relations with his wife, the candour with which he describes his love for Madame Novikoff, the openness with which he records his notions of himself, his journalistic powers and God-assigned duties and their vast range, combine to make a picture which no one could paint so well as himself. It is egoism, but such frank egoism that one is continually finding explanations and excuses for it.

'ON THE PLATFORM OF THE WORLD.' '*Bowness-on-Winder-mere, July 5, 1874, Sunday.* I have employed these 25 years how? Our first-born refuses to be still on the sofa. He cried so long that I had to postpone writing. I have now a little time to collect my thoughts and indulge in the luxury of a birthday, the right to look back and to look forward with the consciousness that such retrospect and prospect are surveyed as a duty as well as a pleasure. Twenty-five years have given me a position upon the platform of the world, in the vineyard of the world with a reaping hook in my hand, and I recognise in the responsibility of the position a call to labour. By the lapse of another quarter of a century my lifework must be achieved. After fifty there is not much for a man to do, save as a statesman. Then his life may be said almost to begin. I wished when I was 15 to die at 30 because after 30, said I, men begin to grow old, the dreams and the splendid illusions of youth vanish. Yet I am not growing old. I am in a state of semi-torpor, as it were, from which I shall hereafter issue with new faiths, new ideals. At present I am so highly favoured by the Most High that I am almost unable to dream of any blessing which I have not got in abundance.

'EVERYTHING THAT HEART CAN DESIRE.' 'In everything

H

worldly, behold me surrounded with everything that heart can desire. A house in the country, a horse, a little farm with livestock, goat, rabbits, bees, liquid manure in a tank, flowers, birds' nests, shrubs, everything I ever dreamed of as a boy. My wife, the girl upon whom even at school I had poured out my love, my son, healthy, vigorous and promising much. Never could I have believed that I would have found such peace, such content, such tranquillity. It is not an inward peace arising from religion. It is an outward peace more complete than religion has ever afforded me. My religion hitherto has not been so much of a peace as of unrest. It has given me fiery, restless impulse. It made me uneasy unless I was working with the last pound of steam on. Only in that vehement labour could I find the semblance of rest. I have a dread that this complete satisfaction of every want may render me oblivious to the call of duty, to the ideal of faith, to the aspirations after a nobler and better future, that I may sink into a hulk rotting in port instead of being a God-sent messenger to the age in which I live.

'STUPEFACTION OF CONTENT AND ITS CAUSES.' 'The causes of this stupefaction of content are due to several things. First, the complete abandonment of all directly religious work. Secondly, the physical results of marriage. Thirdly, the gratification of almost every desire. Fourthly, the consciousness of my ability to do my work. Fifthly, the absorbing nature of that work, leaving me no time for reading anything beyond the requirements of the day. Sixthly, the placid temperament of my wife. Seventhly, the delightful calm of country life. These are good, but my fear is that they may lead to a clouding of the fair ideal of life. I think sometimes that I may trust God to call me out in time, but none the less ought I scrupulously to guard against that canker of the heart which a self-centred life is almost certain to engender. It costs me hardly any trouble to be good in the ordinary sense. There is no difficulty in preserving good temper and cheerfulness. Yet I am not always cheerful. This year I have to save £120 of an income of £300!¹

'LESS OF A PROPHET'; MODIFIED OPINIONS. 'As editor, how easily a man may fall! Here am I only 3 years Editor, fresh and untrammelled by professionalism, already regarding the daily sermon to 10,000 persons as if it were a literary exercise, the chief point its creditable performance from a professional point of view. I am less of a prophet and more of a journalist than in 1871. It is

¹ Stead's modest way of living is reflected in the letter he wrote about lodgings in or near Darlington when first appointed to the *Echo*. 'One room with gas and a prospect' were his requirements. 'A blossoming orchard has a most powerful effect on my temperament.'

as if Elijah thought more of his girdle's polish than of his message to Ahab, or as if Jonah, instead of being filled with awe at the message to Nineveh, were chiefly concerned with its declamation, his rhetoric or his dramatic skill. O for me!

'What is my message? That is what troubles me. I have not got a message. I am not by any means so ardent a Radical or as ardent in anything as I was. I have read so many newspapers on both sides that my old views have become so greatly modified that I no longer feel certain of anything. That is too strong, but it is true to a certain extent. Facts and existing circumstances prevent me being so enthusiastic as some are about remodelling the Universe. Even the disestablishment of the State Church, for instance, which I still believe in, seems no longer to me so clear as once it did. Then as to Republicanism and Democracy, I used once to chant hymns of joy over the advance. Now Democracy, altho' inevitable, altho' on the whole better than autocracy or monarchy, is no emancipator, no regenerator of the people. My faith in "the people" in general and in the Parisian people in particular was severely shaken by the Commune, and the faith which was tottering was not steadied by the result of the appeal to the people which marked the dictatorship of Castelar. I see more of good in my opponents, and the consciousness that I am naturally biassed in the old direction causes me to feel a species of doubt as to the certainty of many political and social problems which I before thought to be indisputable. The zeal which formerly distinguished me on behalf of the poor is now almost imperceptible. As for the emancipation of England resulting from any modification of the land laws, I doubt it. I doubt the degenerating influence of property in the soil. I doubt any solution of the social problem which is not based upon the regulation of the increase of the human race by law or by custom. I have hankerings after cumulative votes. I have a distrust of uneducated majorities. I used to believe in international arbitration as a substitute for War. I have been compelled to admit that it is hopeless. I advocated disarmament, but in the present state of Europe what can be done?

'BUNCOMBE.' 'At present almost the only fixed principle which I possess, almost the only message which I have to deliver is the duty of England as a civilising power among the weaker, more degraded nations of the earth. The Anglo-Saxon idea has gained possession of my brain. I believe in education for all, but I have lost faith in the regenerative powers of education, of legislation, of almost everything save God's spirit. I have laboured myself with educating, with evangelising, with civilising the ignorant masses, and I recoil almost in despair from the masses of vice, indifference, ignorance and brutishness which surround me. I do not despair.

I simply don't think about them. If I think about them it makes me ill, weak, tired, unfit for work.

'I have now written over 1000 leading articles, nine-tenths of them fired off by events, written about because they had to be written about. I have, in 3,000 Notes, expressed opinions more or less hasty, more or less dogmatically, and so far I have a pretty clear conscience. Occasionally I have indulged in buncombe and sometimes I have written more like a partisan than I should have done. As for my so-called personal attacks upon Tory candidates, etc., my only qualms are felt because Liberal noodles were not equally pulled to pieces, but this is not to be done in a Liberal paper.

'There should be more method in my work. To secure system would involve: 9 to 9.30, breakfast; 9.30 to 10, worship; 10 to 10.30, look round livestock, horse, baby, etc., and see that all is in order; 10.30 to 11, read bluebooks; 11 to 2, papers and write; 2 to 2.30, dinner; 2.30 to 3, with Emma [Mrs. Stead] for French and German or for other things; 3 to 5, papers, cut out and stick in, write letters, etc.; 5 to 6, garden; 6 to 6.30, tea; 6.30 to 7.30, worship and questions; 7.30 to 9, read and write; 9 to 9.30, to office; 9.30 to 11, proofs, letters, etc.; 11.30, home; 11.30 to 12, supper; 12 bed. To get office righted up should be the first step to this reform.

'TEMPTATIONS OF SUICIDE AND FEARFUL DESPONDENCY.' '*July 4, 1875.* Twenty-six years old tomorrow. Only three years more and I shall be in my thirtieth year! I am getting old. The calm, passionless content I noted as possessed by me last year has been slightly impaired, chiefly by ill-health occasioned by too much work and too little sleep, ill-health which brought on a dreadful nervousness, a dread horror of great darkness with temptations of suicide and fearful despondency. I am better now, thank God, but I am not far from the border of the precipice. Wealth is less than nothing to health. Sleep I need. I am bound over to sleep on penalty of death.

'Since last year much has changed. The ties that bind me to Howdon have been relaxed by the conduct of the village lads. My work with them is done for good or for bad. They are beyond my control. Already outside our own dear family circle, I have next to no person at Howdon essential to me. A new world is coming into existence at Howdon that does not know me, and for the first time in my life I can note the operation of this natural and inevitable law without bursting into a flood of passionate tears. Trying to keep up the old interest in Howdon is as if a tree were trying to grow its branches as well as its roots in the earth.

TO LONDON OR FARM WORK? 'Last year I did not know but

that at any moment I might be summoned to another paper or to London. I have tried to get engagements elsewhere and have failed. I had one offer to go to Cornwall at £250. I have been to London and have no wish to go again. If the Lord wishes me to go He will have to drive me thither with whips. I am ever so much more of a man now that I am familiar with farm work. I wish I could plough. A healthier spot could not be found. For children it is admirable and I myself need strong health to do my work. As to the paper, I am better satisfied with it than ever. It has the first position in the district. We now reach 13,000; we may reach 20,000. To address 20,000 people as the sole preacher is better than to be a tenth part of the preaching power on a journal with 200,000 circulation. There is no paper now in existence which can be to me what the *Echo* is. I have given it its character, its existence, its circulation. It is myself. Other papers could not bear my image and superscription so distinctly. I have more power and more influence here than on almost any other paper, for I work according to my inclinations and bias. In money of course it is not much, but it is enough to keep me comfortable, and Bell has promised me a share in profit hereafter. I think I shall stop here. All signs are for it.

'A SENSE OF PROPHETHOOD.' 'The great event of this year has been the rekindling of the ideal which since my marriage burnt dim. In reading Victor Hugo's *Man Who Laughs* a sense of my prophethood returned. I felt once more the sacredness of the power placed in my hands, to be used on behalf of the poor, the outcast and the oppressed. It was a gift of renewed faith, aided by *Joshua Davidson*. I clearly and decidedly grasped the idea that everything is given to one to be employed on behalf of him that has nothing, and that only by the patient laborious unselfish labour of the good can the bad be extinguished, and that my mission was to labour unceasingly, by all methods and in every season, to help on the social regeneration of the people of the world. Politics fade except as means to an end. I am less a Radical if Radicalism is adherence to Radical watchwords. I am doubtful about extension of the suffrage. I fear that we shall yet suffer evil results from the extension of the franchise to ignorant men.

'*Dec. 26, 1875.* I must compel myself, after months of shrinking from the duty, to record my mother's dying words: "(1) Don't domineer over Emma. (2) Don't overtax your strength by doing extra and avoidable work. (3) Submit your will in *all* things to God. 'Nervousness' arose in great part from not doing so. "I have tried both", said she, "and you have no idea of the difference between absolute submission and rebellion". And she added, "Don't grieve over what you have done or not done to me. I know you always meant well and loved me dearly." I said I would try. "No", said she, "that won't do. You must promise me absolutely you will not." And I did.'

'IN AN AGONY OF TEARS.' '*Jan. 14, 1877*. I am apparently more useful than ever. The Bulgarian atrocity agitation was in a great measure my work. I have received the highest compliments from Gladstone, Freeman [the historian], W. E. Forster, John Bright and Lord Hartington. I have been praised beyond my utmost expectation. I believe that in God's hands I have been instrumental in doing much to prevent a great national crime, a war with Russia on the side of the Turks. New possibilities of usefulness open out. Life is once more brilliant as in the heroic days. Our time is as capable of Divine service as Puritan times. The agitation of this Recess has rekindled my faith in my countrymen, renewed my faith in Liberalism, strengthened my trust in God. For the Bulgarian agitation was due to a Divine voice. I felt the clear call of God's voice, "Arouse the nation or be damned". If I did not do *all* I could, I would deserve damnation.

'I had a terrible afternoon. It was like a Divine possession that shook me almost to pieces, wrung me and left me shuddering and weak in an agony of tears. I went out determined to do this and nothing else until such time as my mission was revoked. I knew not how it would be taken. Bell fortunately was away in Switzerland and I threw myself heart and soul, and the paper heart and soul, into the movement. I knew I might perish by overstrained excitement. I felt that like Jacob I had met the angel of God and I did not know but that I might have a lifelong limp in consequence of the meeting. There were minor considerations. It was with fear and trembling that I went to the first meeting at Darlington, but it was a great success. Others followed and, when Mr. Gladstone published his pamphlet, I felt that my work was crowned and assumed by other hands, more able than mine. I had written to Mr. Gladstone on the night of the meeting expressing my hope that he would justify the confidence reposed in him by all of us. I felt his pamphlet to be an answer to my letter. I am inclined to attribute some of Mr. Gladstone's evident desire to please me to his consciousness that I was the first to sound in his ears the summons which God had already spoken to his soul. I look back with unfeigned joy to the strain and exertion of that exciting time. I wrote dozens of letters a day, appealing, exhorting, entreating and at last I roused the North. I felt that I was called to preach a new crusade. Not against Islam, which I reverenced, but against the Turks who disgraced Humanity. I realised the feelings of Peter the Hermit. God was with me.

'AT A RISK OF LOSING MY PLACE.' 'But after a time came

a lull, and once more we were threatened with a war for the Turks. This time I was hindered by Bell from doing my duty. But after Dizzy's speech, I wrote in defiance of Bell's views and got into a great row over it. It was a case of speaking out at a risk of losing my place. I was so near the latter that I wrote letters asking for a situation or hints as to how to get one. But I postponed sending them. In the meantime Bell cooled and all went well. I had a terrible walk home on the 10th of Novem. in early morning after receiving Dizzy's speech. War once declared, all voices would be drowned in the war spirit.

'I remember the images of wife and children rising up before me, destitute, widow and orphans. I thought of myself in gaol pining to death. I saw myself mobbed, murdered; and, I thought, all this may be, nay probably will be if you determine to resist the war passion with whole-souled energy. And then I thought the welfare of untold generations depends upon this. Millions of fellow creatures may be saved if you do your duty. You may lose but, to what extent you can, you must do it or betray your Christ. And then I thought of "He that loveth father or mother more than Me is not worthy of Me". Shame was it that I ever had faltered. I chose death.

'I well remember how strange I felt as I went to bed and saw Emma and the baby and thought how soon they might be mourning me. I even thought of Emma's means of livelihood, how much the sale of things would bring, and then I thought of the Father of the fatherless and these poor noble Russian volunteers. I read a chapter out of one of the minor prophets and was consoled. I never before found myself so distinctly and deliberately called upon to leave all and follow Him if He chose to call. Briefly, the results are:

(1) More confidence in God. (2) More faith in my countrymen. (3) More distrust of the newspapers. (4) More brotherly feeling towards the Church clergy as elements of the moral forces of the nation. (5) More intolerance of all that weakens the moral force whether it be Liberal crotchets, high falutin' "patriotism", sectarian divisions, mean jealousies, etc. (6) More intense conviction of the supreme importance of religious education, not merely of children but of adults. The honour of Bulgarian virgins is in the custody of the English voter. And what is true of Bulgaria is true of larger things. (7) More intense desire to stimulate all religious men and women, to inspire children and neighbours with sense of supreme sovereignty of duty, of the right. The safety of our Empire—which keeps the peace of one-sixth human race—depends upon our Sunday schools. (8) Realised more vividly than ever the incalculable importance of the individual. (9) Conviction that the keen sense of female honour is a more potent force to arouse man to generous action than any mere massacre. Hence lowering of sense of chastity the direct road to that apathy and selfishness which tends to national, imperial and individual ruin. Hence

repeal C.D. Act and all that it implies a supreme duty, perhaps the most pressing duty of the time. (10) More earnest desire to make the profession of the Press the worthy leader of a regimented people. At present it does not lead, it follows, reluctantly. The higher element in the nation is badly represented in the Press.

'THE JOY OF FAME AND LOVE.' 'A truth forcibly taught me is that all the joy of fame is to tell it to those you love. Reputation is a bubble, beautiful no doubt but it does little or nothing for you. I don't suppose that I shall be more profoundly pleased with anything as with Mr. Gladstone's letters, and yet how little they are to Emma's love. I must devote more time to her and to my family. Methodise more. Make her more of a companion and spend more time on my bairns. I must not work so much out of doors. Losing hold of the Howdon lads is a bad sign. Win them back. Be more careful to make worship pleasant and instructive. And to relieve Emma of worry during pregnancy. Believe it would be better to have a lot of children. Breeding of good citizens is the first duty of a citizen. With God above I go forward, trusting in Him and fearing nothing excepting shame at times, a kind of lingering muffled, half-hidden dread lest something might happen to Emma. I could spare a child, I sometimes feel, but, oh God, not my wife! But in this as in all things, His Will be done and if He should see fit to lay that heavy cross upon me, altho' I feel as if it would crush me outright, I doubt not but that He will give me strength to bear it.'

'EXACTING TOIL AND FAMILY TROUBLE.' '*July 8, 1877.* My twenty-eighth birthday passed. I am too heavily pressed by work to live. Life is not healthy when it is consumed by a ceaseless round of exacting toil. Leisure is essential to life and I have no leisure. The hay, the garden, the expectancy of a third child, hope deferred day after day, week after week, Emma needing attention, myself losing sleep, and a useless girl downstairs, exhaust my vitality and leave me nothing at all but a treadmill round. I must change this at any cost. I must have leisure to train my children, to attend to my wife, to study. If I could have two hours a day more! The need of nine hours' sleep cuts my day short. Neither wife nor self good disciplinarians. Cannot dragoon a household into order. We sigh in vain for the ideal servant, intelligent, cultivated, hard-working. My social circle grows slowly. My Sundays are execrable. Worship is more and more of a form. I enjoy Sunday but it is only as a rest. I must stop that. Punctuality, precision, etc., are impossible while domestic routine is chaos. It is a terrible waste of a day waiting hour after hour for papers. The essential untrustworthiness of girls of all kinds to go four miles in less than two hours and even sometimes in three is painfully impressed upon my mind. I have had no holiday and need one.

'THE REPROACHES OF MY WIFE.' 'Jan. 5, 1879. The most memorable and most trying year through which I have lived, and without an entry, a year in which the nation hung by a thread over the abyss of Hell, and it depended upon you whether that thread should snap. Of course I was not the only one, but the responsibility was as great as if I had been. I marvel how I survived. God has given us another chance. We have not gone to Hell but we are being singed in Afghanistan, just to make us feel what it is like in order that we may avoid future Jingoism.

'And what a year also or rather what an eighteen months in my own individual history. It was just after writing the 1877 entry that I first heard of Madame Novikoff.[1] Since then how large a place she has occupied in my life. How my life has broadened, my views widened, and intensified. What friends have I not made, what work have I not done since then!

'It s a marvel that I am alive. What with agonies of remorse, the reproaches more often implied than spoken of my wife, the intense absorption in politics to the exclusion of family, social or any other life, the misery of knowing that the life which you hoped to make gloriously happy you have made wretchedly miserable. The consciousness of all this, plus the wearing, exhausting strain of being almost alone in sounding the alarm—in the Afghan war I was quite alone for some time—it is a wonder that I live. And yet I not only live but I work as hard as ever and contemplate writing my book, *History of the Nation in Revolt against Turkish Alliance*. But for the goodness of God I had utterly perished.'

MADAME NOVIKOFF AND 'A WRECKED HOME.' 'And yet looking at the misery I have occasioned my wife, it would seem blasphemous to attribute anything to the Lord, for it seems wicked almost to have permitted me to live. I have had some terrible moments, when death, but for the poor children, seemed the only solution. God help me. It is almost as frightful to see a wrecked home as to look at a lost soul. Sometimes, I felt as if I had done Emma a cruel wrong by persuading her to marry me. I have seen no woman who would have been acceptable as a wife but her, but she might have found many a more suitable husband. More like herself, I mean, living on the same plane, and not absorbed by work with a passion for seclusion. I have treated her cruelly, not wilfully, but because my whole soul was charged, to the exclusion of everything else, with political subjects with which she sympathised but languidly, and at the crisis of these three years I had not time nor patience nor strength to interest her.

[1] Russian patriot, not agent. Often opposed to her Government. Friend of Gladstone, Kinglake and Froude. See *M.P. for Russia*.

'So it came to pass that I met another soul as surcharged with kindred thoughts, and we met and our existences mingled. But I do not wish I had married O.K. I prefer and even in the height of the first excitement I never wavered in preferring Emma as a wife, the only possible wife to me on this planet and I have repaid her how? How dark the future looks. This new year must see a change. Either it restores my wife to me, or it consummates the shipwreck of what I had fondly, passionately hoped would be a Christian home.

'But my head is very bad and it is time to go to chapel, at least to get tea before going to chapel. Oh God, almighty yet loving God, help me to live without torturing those who love me'.

'I HAVE TO MOW FOR MY ANIMALS.' '*July 6, 1879.* Completed my thirtieth year yesterday and where do I stand now? Wife still, three boys still and another child expected. I no longer feel like a prophet without a message. Beaconsfield and his possible foreign policy have at least done that much for me. Never before the terrible ordeal of the last three years did I realise so intensely my mission, my power, my responsibility and the frightful issues which come of neglecting the Christian ideal of citizenship.

I still labour under my chronic trouble of want of time. With nine hours' sleep the remaining fifteen leave me barely room to turn round. Without nine hours I get languid, tired and unable to write with freedom or with ease. My only worry, family needs, looking up. I am awfully busy. I have a lad, but he cannot mow and I have to mow for my animals, but this will soon be over. I am neglecting my correspondents, even Madame Novikoff. Whether my book will ever be done or not I don't know. The Zulu War has thrown the Afghan crime into the shade, and a General Election looms.

IN THE HOUSE OF COMMONS? 'Last year I made my first public speeches at Manchester. Was well received and reported in *The Times, Daily News* and *Scotsman*. Believe I could speak effectively if occasion arose. Was somewhat elated at the ease with which I commanded the audience and spoke without exhaustion. Annand predicts jocularly that I will be in Parliament in six years. I have no ambition that way. If I can be more useful there than here I will be sent. I have been more useful, more powerful than half-a-dozen ordinary M.P.s, and a Parliamentary career offers few attractions compared with those of a journalist.

'The times are hard; Bell is very hard pinched. I have not had a rise since I was married, save £50 for the weekly and a £50 for the year now concluding, which I may never get. I have stuck exclusively to the *Echo*, having written nothing or rather had nothing accepted save Darlington for the *Encyclopaedia Brit.* I wrote

Henry Pease's life but the old man has got better. I am still as much or rather more bothered by want of space in the *Echo*.

'A FRIGHTFUL RESPONSIBILITY.' 'My political creed or rather the present phases of it may be summed up thuswise:

(1) English race, like Jews and Romans even more, has a world wide mission to civilise, colonise, Christianise, conquer, police the world and fill it with an English-speaking law-abiding Xian race. I am an Imperialist "within the limits of sanity and the ten Commandments", the phrase quoted by Forster. God has given us the most magnificent of missions, and it is impious to seek help from the devil to carry it out. We must never use the sword save as a policeman's baton. (2) From this primary conception of our providential position and mission many other doctrines are legitimately deduced. (*a*) In Europe our duty is to act as peacemakers, promote goodwill, remove misunderstandings and systematically crusade against the system of national war. (*b*) Promotion by every means of a hearty union between all branches of the English race. If we cannot have a Parliament of Man and a Federation of the World, we ought at least to have a Parliament of Anglo-Saxondom and the federation of the English-speaking and English-ruled realms. (*c*) The elevation and education, in every sense, of the English people. The gutter child of today may be the founder of a settlement tomorrow. (3) The great object of England in the counsels of the Continent should be the establishment of the United States of Europe. A European Senate may be among the realised ideals of this generation. This Senate must for European purposes dispose of European force. (4) The special duty of England is to cultivate friendly relations with the Power with which there is the most danger of collision, viz Russia. (5) We ought to use our taxes, etc., in developing the character of our own people, not in civilising others. Others, as in India, should pay their own charges. Missionary voluntary enterprise by all means, but it ought to be voluntary. Our subjugated realms ought not to be policed at the cost of the Durham miner and the Lancashire operative, except so far as that policing is done to maintain highways of commerce, necessary for disposing of British manufactured goods. (6) I am not very sanguine about the Land question. We are on the eve of a revolution in agriculture and I am among the foremost in helping the farmers to help themselves. It is possible that the aristocracy may emerge more powerful than ever from the crisis with which we are threatened. (7) A great deal needs to be done in developing and maintaining a high standard of political intelligence and public spirit. (8) The Established Church is an anomaly, an injustice and inconsistent with religious equality, out of place in a democratic State where its faith is repudiated by a large proportion of the people. But all these things weigh less with me than the fact that, judged by results, the Church lowers the standard of Xian citizenship. Its influence is always on the selfish side, in favour of high-handed wrong, against justice, against right. It is a great nursery for Jingoism. It has made itself a friend of the mammon of unrighteousness, it has joined itself unto Caesar and it approves of all that Caesar does except when he does an act of justice from which it suffers. (9) Theologically, I think self-sacrifice is the essence of Xianity, and as for Hell, there is too real a hell all around for any one to find much

consolation in thinking of another in the next world. Immortality dowered with endless Hell for the majority is no glad tidings but a terrible, horrible nightmare. It is a subject which always leaves me troubled. So goodbye. God loves us, Christ died for us and between them they will get us out of the fix somehow.'

'VERY BITTER MOMENTS.' '*Sunday, Jan. 11, 1880.* Sunday is my first at Darlington. The old year was a troubled one. Emma, who appears never to have been quite herself after the birth of Alfred, suffering from nervous depression and the like, became worse and at last she definitely refused to live any longer at Grainey Hill in winter. The change saddened the whole year, unsettling me more than might be imagined by those who did not understand how vitally were connected country life and employment in the realisation of an ideal home. It cost me many a wrench and some very bitter moments as I seemed to see the blighting of the aspirations of a life, the gradual widening of the rift, the shattered home and the devastated household. I feel as if the wife's indisposition to live in Grainey Hill is the first signal to move to another sphere of labour.

'About the direction in which God may lead me, my own secret premonition is that I shall be summoned to edit a London daily, possibly the London *Echo* or the *Daily Chronicle*. The great lack of the London Press is the absence of enthusiasm. If God needs an editor of enthusiasm in London I will serve His turn best. He will send for me and make it clear beyond all doubt that I must go. One of the signs should be giving me a free hand as I have here to control and to speak as seemeth good to my own conscience.

'IF EMMA HAD GONE ABOUT WITH TRACTS.' 'I am filled with grave misgivings when I look back upon my married life, chiefly on account of the absence of direct religious work for God and man. Emma, I feel instinctively, has grown cold from lack of Christian work. I also have lacked that evangelical fervour, that craving anxiety for the souls of others that ought to characterise all Xians. Emma would have felt less lonely if she had gone about with tracts, taught classes or in other ways gone about doing good. [With a string of babies and untrustworthy help and a rather trying husband!] Worship has again been a sad failure. We must sing, come what may of baby, and I must say a few words on the reading, come what may of my other work. Bible reading again has been a sad failure. This year I have more time, having a new sub-editor. Part of leisure should be devoted to Emma and the children and the Bible. I have begun on Sunday afternoons to tell them the story of Christ's life. They are good listeners. Dear little things. Emma is going to teach them and I must help her. She needs a helper, a stimulus, support, and I waste my strength so much on other things that I have none left. I must talk more, read more, and suggest more reading for her.

'A FORTNIGHT'S FLIRTATION.' 'I have also grieved my wife deeply this year by a fortnight's flirtation with [name given], a Scotch lassie who came over to spend the holidays with us. It was a passing folly. I liked the girl very much and like her still. She was a good listener, had good spirits, good complexion and told me her troubles. I kissed her a good deal more than was wise or right, but I was on my holidays and had better spirits and was more in the mood for any kind of fun than I had been for long. It was in driving about in the phaeton that it all happened and at a farewell visit to Keswick. But I had no idea my wife was so grieved about it till long after the girl had returned to Scotland and the baby was born. It was a mistake, and I am sorry for the girl, because my wife deprecates the continuance of the correspondence, and I cannot explain.

'I SIN NO MORE.' 'With regard to Madame Novikoff, I sin no more in relation to her. I am still deeply attached to her and would do anything for her, but I no longer love her with that sinful passion the memory of which covers me with loathing, remorse and humiliation. Poor body, she is much shattered, has aged much in the last two trying years and has no longer the self-control she had. She is now getting out her book[1]—almost every line of which I wrote in draft for her, copied with corrections, revisions and rewritings, and all of which I have repeatedly revised in proof from MSS. I think her book will be useful. She is passionately devoted to it. She suspects the change that has taken place in me and resents it. But as I am the same in all respects to her cause, all except the fever-blistering passion directed to her, I manage to scrape through without inflicting upon her the pain which I dread. I love her intensely, but no longer as a second wife. I am disgusted with myself for having to confess a change, which nevertheless is right. The wrong rises in the passion. And yet who could help? God pardon the weakness of his erring child. My hope that I might be the means of leading her to a trustful faith and hope in God and his Christ is dimmed by the damning memory of my own weakness in having so far succumbed to the temptation of the devil.[2]

'The Hallelujah Lasses have done me a great deal of good, renewed my faith in the simple gospel and in the power of the

---

[1] *M.P. for Russia* (Melrose).
[2] 'The worth of a man must be measured by his life, not by his failure under a single and peculiar trial. The Apostle, though forewarned, denied his Master on the first alarm of danger; yet the Master, who knew his nature with his strength and its infirmity, chose him for the rock on which He would build His Church.' So Herbert Paul. It was a provincial's first experience of the great world.

preached word. Propose in the New Year to write an article in the *Contemporary Review* on the Salvation Army, on the ideal Church, and on Russophobia. Review of O.K.'s book. Series of articles in the *Echo*, possibly lives of local M.P.s and possibly larger Political Catechism. Health remarkably good. Tempted to go revivalising. God has given me a dear little girl. She shall be taught to earn her living and get education like lads. God give me grace and keep me faithful to Christ. Amen.'

CHAPTER XII

AT THE *PALL MALL GAZETTE*

'WICKED TO DISCUSS A BUSINESS ENGAGEMENT ON SUNDAY.' '*My 31st birthday entry.* H. Yates Thompson, proprietor of the *Pall Mall Gazette*, wrote saying that he would like to know if there were any chance of enticing me to London. I replied saying I hated London, it was the grave of all earnestness, but that it was the centre of power and if he thought I would suit I would not feel justified in refusing. I told him also that I was a barbarian of the North, detesting conventionalities, and without other newspaper experience than that gained in 9 years' editorship of the *Northern Echo*. Thompson consulted with Morley, the editor, and suggested an interview. I declined, owing to Mr. Bell's absence and because I wanted to see father and Annand. Then they proposed Sunday (tonight). I declined "because Sunday was awkward for me to be from home" and suggested Friday or Monday. I objected to Sunday chiefly because I would have felt wicked going to discuss a business engagement on that day. I did not like to say so to Thompson by letter because it would have implied a censure upon him for proposing it. I thought I ought at least to try to avoid starting London life with a Sunday dinner party. If I see a fair chance I will tell him frankly that that was why. It was perfectly true it was awkward for me to be away over Sunday. Wife, nurse and children need me to drive them down twice a day to chapel, and in my absence they must stay at home if it is wet and tire themselves out if it is fine. Besides I had Monday's leader to do, and the Monday leader for the London *Echo*. [This is the first news of this connexion.] So it was arranged that I had to dine on Monday night.

THE LORD AND FINANCE. 'What will be the issue I do not know. It is in the hands of the Lord, and He knows better than I. Looked at from a human point of view, it seems a most desirable opening. Looked at from the standpoint of signs and leadings, it seems as if it were likely to be an effectual call. These are so numerous and so apparently conclusive, that I feel little doubt that in a few months I will be assistant editor of the *Pall Mall*. I shall not feel any chagrin should they deem me unsuitable. I know I am unfit for the work when I compare my slender attainments, reading, and experience, with what are presupposed in even a very low ideal as to what should be possessed by a newspaper editor. I feel that I am not fit to edit the *Northern Echo*, let alone be left in charge of the *Pall Mall*, for that is to be my lot during Mr. Morley's temporary absences. But it may be that I am the ablest assistant Morley can get. If there is a better man than I am I hope he may get the post. I am quite content here. I received (since July 17, 1880) £400 a year for editing the *Northern Echo*, £50 for only one leader a week for the *Darlington Herald*, and £60 per an. for liberty to say whatever I please one day a week in the London *Echo*. I have opportunity to contribute occasionally to the *Pall Mall*, and I have at last made an entry into magazine literature by writing in this month's *Fortnightly* an article on the coercion of the Turk for which I received £15. My prospective earnings therefore are at least £550 per an. As I have hitherto lived slightly within £350, the income secured me is one of affluence.

'DRIVING THE MACHINE OF STATE.' 'As lieutenant of a chief who will probably be often absent, I would have more power in driving the machine of State and of reaching the ears of those who with tongue or pen reach others. I will have to sacrifice something of liberty but will unquestionably gain in power. It is possible that Morley may not long remain there, or rather attenuate his editorship more and more to mere nominality, and if I am able to do the work, I may become more and more the *Pall Mall Gazette*, that is to say one of the half-dozen men in London whose advice is at least listened to by the rulers of the Empire on every subject that arises for settlement.

'When I see the devil so strong and his assailants so timorous and half-hearted I long to be in a place where I can have a full slap at him. If, after having all along trusted in the Lord to guide my steps, He guides me to accept it, I think I shall be equal to the place, so long of course as I am amenable to the Divine Will and do, however feebly, my utmost to carry out what are revealed to me as the Divine purposes. The suitable arrangements are (1) Liberty to teach all my faith, excepting when it differs from the proprietor or chief editor, when I must have the luxury of silence. (2) Liberty to live in the country, for my own health and for the sake of the children who must not be reared in Babylon. (3) Not less salary than £500, with liberty to write elsewhere. I am in some doubt as to Morley's irreligion. If the *P.M.G.* became an aggressive anti-Christian paper I could not remain on it.

'The Lord help me to come to a right decision. "Trust in the Lord with all thy heart, lean not on thine own understanding. In all thy ways acknowledge Him and He shall direct thy paths." Even so, Amen, O Lord. Direct Thou me in the paths wherein Thou wouldst have me to walk and give me grace and strength to

walk therein, as Thou hast done in the past, and make me useful
to help Thee in subduing the world with Thy Christ. Amen
and Amen.

'After thanking Morley most cordially for his confidence, sympathy and extraordinary kindness, proceeded to explain what I
meant by "prophetic" journalism: that any man who has to
guide the opinions of other men ought ever to have before
his eyes the fundamental fact that Right is Right and Wrong is
Wrong.'

DEAN CHURCH AND CANON LIDDON. *I am writing on Sunday
night, Aug. 15.* 'During my London visit I went to Dean Church.
He hoped I would see my way clear. I said I had no doubt
about that. When the time came I should see my way clear
before me as if a voice from Heaven said "This is the way, walk
ye in it". "What a happy man you are", he said, with a half-
incredulous, envious expression. I said I thought it was what I
had a right to expect and had always realised. Canon Liddon
agreed that if I came in deference to a divine call I might rely
upon the Divine Grace to keep me from demoralisation. I told
him I had always been trained to expect guidance and should feel
rather swindled if I did not get it.

'Forster[1] was most anxious that I should be chief editor of the
Daily Chronicle instead of second to Morley. Morley was doing the
P.M.G. very well and there was no great need for me there. I
could not tell him that Morley said that he would not go on
without me. Stansfeld was more prompt and decisive. "Go by all
means", he said; "Morley is a thoroughly good fellow". Forster
had summed up his advice by saying that I should be guided by
my feeling. I have no doubt I can work with Mr. Morley very well.
I like Morley. He is a straight good fellow. I don't like Thompson
but I do like his wife. I told Morley about my belief in guidance.
He said "You are not the first man of strong character who has
had the same belief." I said it was hardly a faith with me now so
much as a fact. It had been verified so often. In a multitude of
ways he agreed both in prejudices and in likings. I await with but
little curiosity how Thompson will take my letter informing him
that I will work with Morley and won't tolerate his interference.
I say this as delicately as possible but it must be said. I am full of
hope and confidence. If the Lord has thought fit to raise me to so
powerful a position, He will give me grace to fill it.

'I dream also of organising a home of plain living and high
thinking, a centre of usefulness and of thought, a place for social
experiments, and a meeting place of all the people who are doing

---

[1] Afterwards Secretary for Ireland. Evicted from office, as we have seen, largely
under the influence of Morley's leading articles.

good in the world. But if the whole thing fell through I should not be distressed. Thank God for that.'

THE UNOPENED LETTER. '*I am writing on Aug. 23.* Last week I received the formal offer of the assistant editorship from Yates Thompson. Morley's letter accompanying implied dissatisfaction with Thompson's terms and refused to undertake the responsibility of advising me to accept them. The terms were £400 salary and 10s. per column for contributions inserted, with the guarantee that the money should be made up to £700. I objected to £700 and I objected to be paid at a quarter of the ordinary *Pall Mall* tariff. The best arrangement, I wrote, was to pay it all as salary and to define the duties of assistant editor as including the supply of so many columns per week. T.'s reply came to hand on Sunday and I have not yet opened it. I wrote to Morley on Friday telling him I feared he would misjudge me, that I was not a mercenary humbug, but that I did not like Thompson and that, although I would have accepted at once without scruple or demur a salary of £700 from M., I did not feel inclined to do so with Thompson. I cannot exactly describe why, but the great danger is that Thompson and I may not get on, that Thompson's meddling may lead to a quarrel in which I should have to go. If T. is really in earnest he will not stick at a trifle about the mode of payment?

'THE MAIDEN TRIBUTE' FORESHADOWED. 'I have had a curious impulse in the direction of London by reading the memorial to the Foreign Office about the export of English girls for State-regulated prostitution in Brussels, a sense of the burden imposed upon me to write an *Uncle Tom's Cabin* on *The Slavery of Europe.* The burden is greater than I can bear. But, if it is ultimately to be laid on my back, God will strengthen me for it. If I have to write it I shall have to plunge into the depths of the social hell, and that is impossible outside a great city. May God guide me right in all things.'

Later. 'I had a straight guidance and a clear call. T. accepted my terms, came down to Darlington, offered £800, to be raised next year to £1,000. And, to crown all, got a house [at Wimbledon] with garden in a situation better than I could have dreamed of, the clenching sign of the call. I used to tell Morley that I should find a good house. It was waiting for me somewhere if I did right to come up.'

Mrs. Bell Jackson, daughter of Bell of the *Northern Echo*, writes to me that when Stead got his invitation to the *Pall Mall* he had just signed an agreement with her father for five years. But Bell said, 'No agreement can stand against this. Your future is made. I can only congratulate you.'

'HEBREW PROPHET, ROMAN TRIBUNE AND GREEK TEACHER.'
Here are a few remarkable paragraphs from one of my finds, a
thick journal begun by Stead on October 22, 1880, immediately
on his arrival at the *Pall Mall*. It is written with great confidence
and certainty. Only on two or three pages is there any kind of
correction. It begins:

'Ideal to be aimed at, "Thy Kingdom Come, Thy Will be done
on Earth as it is in Heaven". To be ever in the van, going ahead,
accepting the responsibilities and discharging the duties of leadership of our race in its upward striving, hearing new words of
command in every cry of the sorrowing, and goaded and spurred
on to fresh exertion by every spectacle of sin and misery. Every
man and woman who falls short of the perfect manhood of Christ
Jesus cries out for help to realise that manhood and womanhood,
which is their birthright in Christ, with earnestness and emphasis
proportioned to their remoteness from the ideal. Lowell's "A
Parable", last verse. Men make Christ's images into paupers and
prostitutes. To redeem the world every agency for good needed
and new agencies still. The great need: intelligent sympathy,
imagination, true catholicity, charity, all the rest included, and
their baser parts discouraged, more by favour to the good than
direct censure. To work on, to yearn on, in faith, Christ the best
remedy for pessimism and despair. He saw all the chances and,
seeing, chose as the better part the life of shame, sorrow and death.
The gain was worth the sacrifice. If it was so for Him it is not less
for us.'

Stead goes on—he was thirty-one—defining the objects of the
Pall Mall: 'To lead the leaders of public opinion, and to supply
briefs for the journalists of the country, and to defend in advance
every position the forward party is about to occupy. To enrich
the literature of the country by combining, as far as possible,
permanent literary value with good selling journalistic worth.
To promote good taste, good feeling and good working politics,
science and letters. To interpret the aspirations of dumb classes to
the vocal classes, to explain clearly to every reader the inner
thoughts of every thinker, the object of every reform, the nature
of every abuse. To combine the function of Hebrew prophet and
Roman tribune with that of Greek teacher. To inform the public
mind about everything that comes up, and to keep a distinct
object in view before every reader on every subject on which
improvement is needed, and yet at the same time to make the
paper lively, amusing and newsy.'

Then there is a list of 'Political Aims'. Among them:

'To promote a sense of unity among (1) English-speaking races and
(2) the nations of Europe. To promote universal Free Trade and especially

a British Zollverein. To dwell more on points of union than on differences. To insist that the control of native policy be directed by the Home Government. To watch vigilantly the Government of India. To resist all encroachments, not absolutely necessary, on the liberty of the subject. To abolish the *police des mœurs* in garrison towns and abroad. To advocate the organisation of emigration and transmigration. To advocate early marriages and limitation of families. To improve education all round. To nationalise the Church [No doubt he was thinking of some kind of union of the Churches]. To reform the landlords.

OFFICE IMPROVEMENTS. After that there come good resolutions, among which are: To compare closely the *Pall Mall* and *St. James's* every day and once a week every edition; to have speaking-tube between the editor's table, the printing office, the boy outside [in the lobby] and sub-editors; sub-editors, reporters, Morley and self to lunch together once a week; to keep files of *Journal des Débats, Nord, Koelnische Zeitung*.[1]

He regarded an epitome not only of the London papers but of the provincial papers as a matter of the first importance, directed it himself and was complimented on it by Gladstone and Bright. (A few years later I was to do this epitome.)

Occasional Notes are 'to cover the world if possible. They are not to exceed on the average twenty lines each and to be humorous when possible. Anniversaries to be noted in them and American papers to be scanned for interesting topics.'

He proposed a series of articles on 'Latter-day Prophets', also on 'High Priests of Modern Science'. 'Sunday in London' is also projected and he apparently aims at doing it himself. He has in mind a dozen articles on leading London and provincial papers. Another series is to be on 'European National Movements of the Century'. One more is on 'Modern Apostles' and yet another on 'Landmarks of Liberty'. He plans 'a column of gossip at a high level'. Reviews he proposes to have in advance of the *St. James's*, and his plan is 'often to give the gist of a book so that anyone reading it will be able to converse intelligently about it'. He was a pioneer in this and was good at it. He wishes to have some special feature for each day of the week. There are several pages of subjects for special articles, yet I see no women's column. Nor is there anything about the drama, but at this time Stead had never been to the

---

[1] EARLY ILLUSTRATIONS. Stead says nothing about the primitive illustrations he introduced. E. H. Stout described them in the *Newspaper World*: 'A rough outline pencil sketch, showing the positions of the garrisons in the Sudan, and the location of the fighting, if any, was sent up to the composing room where Mr. Hunt, one of the foremen, bent plain brass rules and dotted brass rules into the required shapes on a galley [a long narrow tray on which the composed type lies]. Names of the places were set up in type and put into position, filled in with plaster of Paris, and the whole was firmly tied up and introduced into the news page.'

theatre. He is particularly keen on the office having good maps. One thing he did not contemplate doing, joining a club or clubs. He never did this.

A TUSSLE WITH MORLEY. And now, on Dec. 31, come further notes: 'When Liddon preached on Darwin he provoked Morley and Fitzjames Stephen, who wrote an article against the sermon, laying down plump and plain the atheistic or at best agnostic creed. When the proof was given to me I remarked that it committed the paper to atheistic propaganda. "Yes", said M., "I have been silent too long. It is high time to speak out. It is time your Noncon. Radical friends had it rubbed into them." "Then", I said, "you mean to make this the point of a new departure". "Yes", said he, "new since I came to the *Pall Mall* but it is only a reversion to the old *Pall Mall* line". "Well", I said, "if the *Pall Mall* is to be an 'evening' edition of the *National Reformer* [Bradlaugh's paper] I cannot possibly remain on the staff. The article ought to be published as an expression of opinion on an important controversy." He said he would think of it. I remained in suspense a week and then the article was dissed [type distributed]. All that he said was, "If you won't let me have my atheism, you shan't have your religion". Since which time there has been no pulpit pencilling in the *Pall Mall* ['Sunday in London' series.] But the Nonconformist Radical rubbed his hands and silently smiled. How the issue confirmed all my convictions about divine leadings!

'THE MOST POWERFUL MAN IN ENGLAND.' 'I am the happiest man in England, I frequently say. My only grief is that I have too much joy. It seems so unjust that I should have so largely and the millions of the disinherited have so little. Yet I nearly lost my wife in the spring and Alfie is at this moment down with scarlet fever. Nevertheless I am not in trouble as other men. I have all things and abound. No one is so highly favoured as I. God grant that all this heaping up of mercies upon me may in the end make others, the great masses, happier also.'

What follows for the next page or so is of psychological interest. 'For the past two years I have been practically suppressed. My individuality has been absorbed. Morley has become more and more the editor instead of less and less and I have ceased to be more than a very secondary personage indeed. My period of chrysalis is now nearly ended. Then I shall blossom forth, I hope to some purpose. I have a curious presentiment that M. will be gone in April. It is possible that he may be in Parliament; in any case he will have left the *Pall Mall*. When he goes, Thompson becomes nominal editor and manager. I become autocrat. Voules goes at once or rather as soon as he can be removed without making him revengeful. [He makes some severe strictures on Voules.] I found him out first. But now all agree.

'I think I see my way now to make the paper a success. I shall not change its shape or its character for some months. Then I will revolutionise everything and sink or swim. I shall swim not sink. If my health keeps good, I shall in after years be the most powerful man in England. My great newspaper will seize me and I shall have a power for good which no one at present possesses.'

'IN WHAT MAY BE A FATAL FIELD.' 'I feel now, by comparing myself with my contemporaries and looking at my competitors, that the field of pre-eminent success in journalism is left absolutely at my disposal. There are no rivals, no competitor properly so called. There is no one who has seen the vision of the things which might be, the things which, with all humility and even with a certain dread, I feel I am called to accomplish.

'I say with dread, because of the sacrifices which it involves of the domesticities. Alas my poor children and my beloved wife! But if the lot is cast for the soldier to go forth to die, why should I shrink when I too am drafted off to a command in what may be a fatal field? No, if I am called I go. And next year at this time I shall have begun once more to assert my individuality, to exert my power, to see everything and to fear nothing. That is the ideal. To help all good causes, to smite with the thunderbolt of God all baseness, falsehoods, devilishness, to be the hope of every good man or woman working in every good cause, to be the dread of every evildoer, to reproduce in a paper the ideal of a God, the helper of those who have no helper, the hope of the oppressed, the fiery cloud by day, the cloudy pillar by night, the rescuer of the society of God, the director of the steps of His people, the centre of a beneficent influence flowing out over the whole world, the strengthener of all good tendencies, a tabernacle against encroaching wrong, the enlightener of all men as to the good in their neighbours, and as to the wrongs which remain unremoved, the great tribune of the poor, the conscience of the rich, the brooding influence which will quicken into activity all good aspirations and spin into unrest all lethargic souls, the constant presentation of a sublime ideal side by side with an intensely practical guidance as to every immediate step to be taken towards its attainment, a medium of intercommunication between all departments of human activity, a source of consolation and inspiration to all the better longings of the human heart. In short to make my paper like Longfellow's universal Church,

As lofty as the love of God
And wide as are the wants of man.

To that I am called. Who am I? Weak and of a stammering tongue like Moses. I am nothing, but in so far as God strengthens me and uses me, as his instrument.

'THE WHOLE IDEAL OF NEWSPAPERS MAY BE RAISED.' 'Who can hear the wail of misery that rises ceaselessly from the great aching heart of man, who can see the frightful seething gulf of wretchedness, the sulphurous hell in which whole generations welter, without wishing to multiply a thousandfold the agencies by which these fires can be quenched and their feet planted on the rock; that in short Thy kingdom may come on earth even as in heaven, without crying "Here am I Lord, send me." And I believe that God has called me and anointed me with this vision. And I shall be not only a centre of life and love and power in my paper, but the whole ideal of newspapers will be so raised that my own paper will be but as one among many. I am content if it be done by others. But I feel I am called, and to me as of old comes the word spoken by Joshua, "Be of a good courage, be not afraid, neither be thou dismayed, for the Lord thy God is with thee whithersoever thou goest." '

'DISTRUST IN MY LITERARY ABILITIES.' '*Later.* The chief effect of my nine months in London has been an increase of confidence, a consciousness of superiority in my own judgments and industry and a sense of hesitation and distrust in my literary abilities. My political judgment I feel more than ever exceptionally good, partly because it is based on more facts than that of others—few people taking the trouble to ascertain their facts—and partly because it is intuitively right as judged by experience. Where I have differed from Mr. Morley I think events showed I was right. Morley's political judgment is excellent when he has his facts. But especially on foreign affairs he has not his facts and he has his prejudices. It seems awfully conceited in my thus complacently reflecting on my own superiority. But Mr. Morley is so much superior to me in so many things that I can afford to admit my superiority to him in others without being unduly puffed up. I also think, altho in this I may be utterly mistaken, that I have more go, more drive, more journalistic capacity in fact than Mr. Morley, who is primarily a man of letters.

'But in regard to literature I feel rather depressed. I used to think I could write Occ. Notes if I could write anything. But Morley does not like my Occ. Notes. I thought he liked my middle articles, but he has dropped these. I think for a solid, forcible, telling leader I can beat most people. It is well I should learn my forte and stick to it. But I feel rather crestfallen at my evident incapacity to write light articles to please Morley's taste. But as yet I have not had my swing. When Morley is away I shall see how

I get along. The training along with Morley is invaluable, and I am grateful for it. I am more than ever painfully impressed with a sense of the enormous responsibility which rests upon me.

'There are not half a dozen men in England who combine the journalistic faculty with political acumen and propagandist fervour to the same extent; and even where these exist their possessors either, like Freeman, have not the faculty of getting on with people, or have not the opportunity, as yet, of reaching the ear of the world. Seen nearer, the leading men dwindle, except Gladstone. With how little wisdom the world is governed! In such a lazy world, there is no saying how far an industrious man may go. I feel ashamed of myself being so far up until I see those who are further up and then I am not surprised.'

CARNEGIE, MORLEY AND STEAD. I have had typed out no fewer than thirty-two sheets of Stead's notes for articles in the *Pall Mall*, but there is no space for even an abbreviated list. It is enough to record the energy, eagerness, confidence and conviction of divine guidance he brought first to his assistant editorship and then to his editorship. He gave a copy of 'The Gospel according to the *Pall Mall Gazette*', 'the things which are most surely received among us' to every member of the staff. Stead told Aaron Watson that when he arrived at the paper he aimed at 'doing in a day as much as six other men'. When he became editor and his leader was late, as it so often was, Stead (a contributor to the *World's Press News* wrote) was known to have 'called on the reporters to take minute turns in shorthand so that the leader was got out in about twelve minutes and in type in a quarter of an hour'.

'It appears that before the retirement of Morley from the *Pall Mall*', Stead writes, 'he had thought of continuing his connexion with the paper as Andrew Carnegie's man or proprietor, with me as editor. He told me he thought a Morley-Stead combination would be, in many respects, much more useful than a Stead sole. Because, he said, Stead sole is given to fads and is inclined to shrieking and shrewing Passmore Edwardishness.[1] Stead, however, without denying that the Morley element would have its advantage, naturally preferred Stead sole and was well satisfied when the Carnegie combination broke down and Morley burnt his ships.

STEAD'S HEALTH AND 'THOMPSON'S RÉGIME'. 'About my ability to write', Stead goes on, 'I think I need have no fear. I have written the first three chroniques for *Macmillan* and everywhere

---

[1] Passmore Edwards was the shrewd proprietor of the London *Echo* and gave away free libraries in London; but he had his limitations, as Ernest Parke, later of the *Star* and other members of his staff told me; and some readers found his paper at times, perhaps a little goody-goody.

the review has been acclaimed a brilliant specimen of Mr. Morley's best style! Charles, his nephew, thinks my leaders are best and I think they have more point. There is Egotism for you and no mistake. But Morley is now being left behind. He has embarked in a new sphere. [He had accepted a place in the Cabinet.] He may rise high, but he is complicated by all his allies; he may find that Chamberlain is a worse foe than ever he thought to find him a good friend.

'But a truce to Morley, more important to me is my health. This year my health has not been firstrate. My head ailed much in the early months. I am better now, but the strain will be enormous, and M. evidently thinks it will be too much for my constitution.

'I do not regard the *Pall Mall* as having yet assumed its final evolution. Thompson's régime will not last. It will pave the way. I shall before long have full swing. When I don't know. How I don't know. M. seemed to think some weeks since that I had lost my chance because Carnegie was inclined to back Chamberlain and Chamberlain's man was Escott. Escott, however, gets tipsy after dinner and disgusts Carnegie. Storey [with whom Carnegie had entered into a provincial newspaper association] is found out. M. is retiring. I am alone in possession of the field. God gives me health as he wills me to work, and if he withhold then His will is not that I should attain into the highest place. I may be wrecked in sight of port. But I scarcely think that He brought me all this way merely to spill me off the bar. At any rate, if He does, it is His will and it will be better to be wrecked outside than to founder inside, which may be the alternative.

THE *REVIEW OF REVIEWS* ANTICIPATED. 'I have not the heart to go into details of my plans for the new year in the paper. I think, however, that the Magazine of the Month, a twopenny monthly extra to the *Pall Mall*, might bring me half-profit sufficient to keep me easy about gold. I have some notion of taking up Church Reform in earnest.' Among series of articles he is thinking of are 'The Richest Men in the World' and 'The Great Newspapers of the World'. One cannot but suspect that his mind is working on his own great daily paper of the future.

'With regard to my family,' he goes on, 'everything continues to move smoothly, but I must, really *must* make time to superintend the children's studies more. I dream of half an hour with them from 6 to 6.30 for dumbbells, and $\frac{1}{4}$ hour worship, read some great event of the day, some verse, prayer, sing a little hymn. Then give them something to do till breakfast. Then to have them all at night for an hour. By this means I might keep them in hand. But alas, alas, time, time, where have I time, or even if I had time where have I strength? May God help me to carry out my good resolves and help my wife and me to make our home an ideal abode of virtue, liberty and love.'

A mightier voice than Death's speaks 'Peace be still'

Roger Casement.

The line has a particular interest as, it will be remembered, Casement was hanged for treason. Mrs. Sidney Webb says Bernard Shaw offered to write a dying speech for him that would 'thunder down the ages'

CHAPTER XIII

STEAD'S OWN STORY OF HIS CRIME AND CONVICTION

THE APPEAL MADE TO STEAD. The most momentous and significant of Stead's achievements—they have been summarised in the Introduction—was 'The Maiden Tribute of Modern Babylon' on which I have before me much of his own MS. account. 'It is not often', he says, 'that a man can look back upon his conviction and sentence as a criminal convict with pride and exultation. Every tenth day of November since then has been as a Red Letter Day in my life and will be so until I die.[1]

'In the spring of 1885 a venerable man, the Chamberlain of the City of London, came to me in great distress. He informed me that, owing to the unexpected defeat of Mr. Gladstone's Government and the confusion occasioned by the installation of his successor, a Bill for strengthening the laws for the protection of girls and young women, which had been introduced into the House of Commons by the outgoing Government, would be sacrificed. The Bill was based upon the report of a Select Committee of the House of Lords. Everyone admitted that juvenile prostitution had increased to a terrible extent. All agreed that the law as it stood was powerless to deal with the evil. The Bill amending the law had been twice passed through the House of Lords but it had always been held up by the House of Commons. "All our work," said the Chamberlain, "will be wasted unless you can rouse public opinion and compel the new Government to take up the Bill and pass it into law."

---

[1] 'THE TRUTH ABOUT THE NAVY.' Stead sometimes said that there was never a more remarkable success achieved by a series of articles in a paper than was gained by the *Pall Mall*'s 'Truth about the Navy'. 'In May Lord Northbrook said the Navy was so perfect that if he had another two millions thrust into his hands he would not know what to do with it. In November he declared that he must have an extra five millions to put the Navy into proper condition. Nothing had altered in the meantime but the publication of "The Truth about the Navy" articles.' Marie Belloc Lowndes, who was much about the *Pall Mall* offices in my time, wrote to me shortly before her death: 'You ought to make a point of the great work Stead did for the Navy. On two occasions a famous admiral spoke to me of what he had done, and of the great debt his country owed him.'

THE LANGWORTHY CASE. Apart from this, 'The Maiden Tribute' and what he had done to promote a better understanding with Russia, Stead recalled with satisfaction the triumph in the Langworthy case. 'The fact that Langworthy was hissed off a platform in the interior of the Argentine because of what we had published', he writes, 'abides with me as one of those permanent consolations with which a man can comfort himself in the days when he is depressed and disheartened'. Page 82.

The Bill was a comprehensive measure dealing not only with the corruption of minors but also with the white slave traffic, the export of English girls to purchasers in the vice markets abroad.

THE LAW AS IT WAS. 'The law as it stood declared that any child of thirteen was legally competent to consent to her seduction. It also refused to allow little girls under eight to give evidence against the monsters who had outraged them, on the ground that the victims were too young to understand the nature of an oath. The law against abduction was criminally lax. What the reformers wanted was to raise the age of consent from thirteen to sixteen, to allow children under eight to give evidence as to their assailants, and to stiffen the law against abduction and the traffic in vice. "I do not know if you can do it", said the old Chamberlain, "but if you cannot no one else will help us. You might be able to force the Bill through. Will you try?"

'I naturally wanted to try, but every instinct of prudence and self-preservation restrained me. The subject was tabooed by the Press.[1] The very horror of the crime was the chief secret of its persistence. The task was almost hopeless. No ordinary means could overcome the obstacles which were presented by the political situation. Through a personal friend who was a member of the new Cabinet I took soundings as to the chance of getting the Bill passed. The answer I received was decisive and emphatic. "The New Ministry will not attempt any legislation whatever. It is utterly impossible to make any exception in favour of this Bill. We are very sorry but nothing can be done this session." '

STEAD'S VISIT TO SCOTLAND YARD. Lord Snell, in his *Men, Movements, and Myself*,[2] describes a visit of Stead to Howard Vincent at the Metropolitan Criminal Investigation Department. 'Do you mean to tell me', said Stead, 'that actual violation, in the legal sense of the word, is constantly being perpetrated in London, on unwilling virgins, purveyed and procured to rich men at so much a head by brothel-keepers?' 'Certainly,' replied the chief of the department, 'there is no doubt of it'. 'Why', exclaimed Stead, 'the very thought is enough to raise hell'. 'It is true,' said the officer, 'and although it ought to raise hell it does not even rouse the neighbours.' 'Then *I* will raise hell,' said Stead, and set himself to arouse the nation. 'Be the results what they may,' he wrote, 'no nobler work could a man ever be privileged to take. Even a humble part in it is enough to make one grateful for the privilege of life'.

---

[1] An indication of the way in which convention kept some subjects out of the papers may be found in the fact that, long after 'The Maiden Tribute', we never printed the word syphilis in the *Pall Mall* itself. The word was also barred for years in *The Times*.

[2] Dent, 1936.

It was necessary to the end in view that the sale of a child should be clearly established and, with the knowledge and approval of the Bishop of London, the Cardinal Archbishop of Westminster, Archdeacon (later Dean) Farrar, Mrs. Josephine Butler, and the first General of the Salvation Army, William Booth, arrangements

From one of the letters from the founder of the Salvation Army to Stead

were made for the 'purchase' of a child, who when handed over was at once placed under the protection of reliable people'. The facts are similarly stated in the biography of Sir James Stansfeld.[1]

'THE MAIDEN TRIBUTE' PUBLISHED AND THE BILL CARRIED. 'With the aid of a few faithful friends', writes Stead, 'I went disguised into the lowest haunts of criminal vice and obtained only too ample proof of the reality and extent of the evils complained of. I then published in the *Pall Mall* the Report of the Secret Commission into the Criminal Vice of London, under the title of 'The Maiden Tribute of Modern Babylon', beginning on the 6th July and closing its publication on the 12th. The sensation which these articles produced was instantaneous and world-wide. They set London and the whole country in a blaze of indignation.[2]

'An influential Committee consisting of the Archbishop of Canterbury, the Bishop of London, Cardinal Manning, Mr. John Morley

[1] 'The Archbishop of Canterbury did his best to dissuade me', Stead writes. 'Cardinal Manning heartily encouraged me. Bishop Temple, in his brusque, businesslike way, promised to back me up.' Stead stated that the procuress was given £2 for obtaining the consent of the girl's mother to the transaction and that the mother had £3. Stansfeld's biography was written by the Hammonds. (Longmans, 1932).

[2] Lord Snell gives a vivid account: 'England was stripped naked and shamed before the world and she did not like it. Such things might happen on the wicked Continent but that anyone should say that these infamies occurred in Pimlico, under the very shadow of the home of "our dear Queen", was an indefensible and wanton outrage. Patriots and brothel-keepers gave a united shout of angry protest, and the accusation that girl children could be bought from their parents in London and sold to rich men for seduction was stoutly denied by an offended and injured public—until Stead proved it by facts which were conclusive. And then there was a savage cry of resentment against the man who had exposed the loathsome traffic. The music halls inflamed the tempers of their patrons with patriotic guff, accompanied with as much lubricity as could be safely introduced into rhyme and gesture.'

and Sir Robert Reid, Q.C. investigated the accuracy of my statements.[1] The Ministry capitulated to the storm. The Bill, abandoned
as hopeless, they revived and strengthened and passed into law
with the utmost celerity. It was undoubtedly one of the greatest
achievements which any journalist single-handed had ever accomplished in the coercion of an unwilling legislature and a reluctant
Ministry.

STEAD PROSECUTED. 'After the law had received the Royal
Assent it was discovered that in one of the first—nay the very first
experiment which I had made to verify at first-hand the truth of
the statement that some British mothers were willing to sell the
virginity of their girls for a five-pound note to the procurers of vice,
I had omitted to take the necessary precautions to prove the fact
legally. My only excuse was that I was utterly inexperienced, that
I had of necessity to rely upon the assistance of people whose
characters made them very bad witnesses, and that from the first
I had refused to do anything to incriminate individuals. I was an
investigator exposing a vast system of organised crime. I could
not bring myself to be a detective worming myself into the confidence
of criminals in order to betray their trust and to secure their
punishment. Be that as it may, the fact was that the first child of
thirteen procured for me in my disguise as an immoral man in
return for the usual payment to the procuress and to the mother
was handed to me without the consent of the father, and without
any written evidence as to the payment to the mother. The mother
of course, as soon as the hue and cry was raised, protested that she
only let her daughter go to be a servant girl. The father quite truly
swore that he never consented for her to go at all. The opportunity
was tempting. The opponents of the reform which the *Pall Mall*
had forced upon the Government and the House of Commons
exulted over the chance which this case afforded them of dealing
what they believed would be a fatal blow at the man who had
defeated them. So the very legal officer, the Attorney General,
who had been compelled by agitation to carry the amending Bill
through the House of Commons, prosecuted me and three or four

---

[1] I have had before me many pages of notes of conversations with 'unfortunates'
which Stead dictated to his secretary, Underhill. For example, there are three
sheets on what 'Carroty Kate' told him. She implicates and gives the addresses
of 'old gentlemen'—the Earl of Blank and some other men whose names were
known to the public. These persons were unquestionably in the habit of buying
little girls, who were taken for them to certain houses which, as Stead notes,
the Secretary of the Vigilance Association and various detectives watched. Stead
was not deceived by the stories that were told him but took the utmost pains to
have them investigated. There can be no doubt that Stead's character impressed
many of the women he interviewed under pledge of secrecy and that these poor
creatures sympathised with the efforts he was making. They felt that what grown
women were doing was their own affair, but that the ill-usage of children was
unpardonable.

of my comrades [one was Bramwell Booth, General Booth's son] on the charge of abducting the girl in question.

'The trial created almost as great a sensation as the original publication. We were several days in the police court, and then we were sent to the Old Bailey for trial. A public defence fund of £10,000 was raised. Sir Charles Russell, afterwards Lord Chief Justice, Mr. Henry Matthews, afterwards Home Secretary, and other leading counsel were retained for the defence of my comrades. I defended myself. The importance of the trial did not in the least consist in the verdict of the jury. What was necessary to prove was (1) that the inquiry which resulted in the strengthening of the law was a *bona fide* investigation, conducted by men of undisputed integrity under a supreme sense of public duty, and (2) that whatever might have been the failure to collect incriminating evidence in the first case, the existence of the system could be proved by facts which no one could question. Both these ends were secured. The trial placed in the full light of day the facts which the majority of newspapers had carefully shrouded into obscurity. On the main question our evidence was overwhelming. The Archbishop of Canterbury, the Bishop of London, Cardinal Manning, Mr. John Morley and Mr. Arthur Balfour (now Prime Minister) were among my witnesses subpoenaed to prove the purity of my motive.

AND TRIPPED UP. 'On the second point, the existence of the evil, its extent, the hopelessness of any reform, and the fact that almost singlehanded I had forced the legislature to pass the Bill, were not only proved but admitted to be true by the prosecution. It was admitted that the child had never been better cared for in her life. It was proved that the only reason why she had not been returned to her mother was the belief, which the police shared, that if she went back she would be sold in deadly earnest next time. But the consent of the father had never been obtained and the judge ruled that this was fatal to our defence and that the jury had no option but to return a verdict of guilty.

'If I had but persisted in asking one question this fatal fault would have been wiped out. I wanted to ask the mother for her marriage lines. Sir Charles Russell, who was leading on our side protested. "I will never be a party to such a license of cross-examination", he said. I gladly concurred, for I had frequently protested against the way in which women were insulted in the witness box by a cross-examining counsel. But months after I had served my sentence and had come out of gaol, it was discovered at Somerset House that the child had been born out of wedlock and that the nominal father had no legal right over the girl who bore his name. It was then too late and I have never ceased to be grateful that the fact was not discovered till afterwards. If I had asked that question

I should probably have been acquitted and so have lost that experience in prison which is one of the most valuable lessons of my life.

'GUILTY'. 'The Court was crowded and had been so from start to finish. Every morning and evening for more than a week the papers which had carefully boycotted the subject when the fate of the Bill was in danger, contained columns upon columns of reports of the trial which it was hoped would finish me for ever. The judge spent the whole day in summing up against us. His animus was undisguised. He constructed with such care a series of questions to which the jury would have to answer "Yes" or "No" that it was impossible for them to do other than return a verdict of guilty. But so signal had been the vindication of the motive and the method of the defendants that there were many who believed that the jury, despite the charge of the judge, would persist in returning a verdict of not guilty.

'I spent the whole day when the judge was summing up, writing letters. I wrote to Lord Salisbury and to Mr. Gladstone, to the Archbishop of Canterbury and to Cardinal Manning and at the same time I wrote with even greater pleasure and feeling to the humble helpers—some of them women of the town—bidding them goodbye for a season and thanking them for all that they had done in the good cause. The Old Bailey dock itself is an inspiration. Many of the men who have made history, from William Penn downwards, have faced hostile judges from that coign of vantage.

BRAMWELL BOOTH ACQUITTED. 'The jury were absent for a considerable time. I think that I was about the most unconcerned person in Court. In the dock with me were Bramwell Booth, Chief of the Staff of the Salvation Army, and another devoted member of the Army, Madame Combes, who had rendered yeoman service in the enquiry. With them, also, was an old war correspondent of Greek descent who had aided me in my excursions into regions with which he was familiar. The remaining occupants of the dock were a Frenchwoman of infamous repute, who was convicted and

---

CONFIDENCES TO MRS. FAWCETT. Miss Douie has kindly shown me a number of letters which Mrs. Fawcett had from Stead when he was in gaol. He wrote to her almost every other day. In one letter he says: 'My wife came, full of joy, brightness and love. When the door closed behind her I laid down and had a bitter cry, like a weak fool that I am and always will be. I tell you this because I cannot bear to think of your thinking I am heroic. I am chafing about my sad shortcomings and my regret that when I am trying to do good to all women I cannot always be a means of good to the one woman whom I love most on earth. If I could always make my wife happy without giving in on matters on which I know it would be wrong of me to yield a cloud would clear from my sky. But perhaps I have written too much.' He speaks of some men's lack of 'kindly warmth, and inability to make you cry, which I regard as a fatal defect in the highest type of man'. Once he writes, 'Men are exactly what they believe, not what they say they believe'.

Private

The Dock Old Bailey,
November 7 1885

Dear Mrs Fawcett

Will you pardon me who is all but a convicted criminal to say just one word of heartfelt gratitude and more, to you who have been so good & kind to one who has made such a mess of things his now going to gaol with a feeling of satisfaction born of a hope that my imprisonment may be some atonement for all my blunders & all the trouble I have brought upon so many good people. God bless you and keep you from ever again having to defend so poor a creature as . Yours in sincere humiliation

William T Stead

Kindly supplied by the London and National Society for Women's Service

A LETTER FROM THE DOCK

died in gaol, and a converted procuress who had aided me in exposing the traffic by which she had formerly made her livelihood.

'It was a verdict of "Not guilty" against Bramwell Booth and Madame Combes, of guilty against the Frenchwoman and the ex-procuress, guilty against the Greek war correspondent, and guilty against me. But in my case the jury added an extraordinary rider. They found me guilty of being deceived by my agents. They recommended me to mercy and they wished to put on record their high appreciation of the services I had rendered the nation by securing the passage of a much needed law.

'Some of my friends were very angry. But I could not for the life of me see how the jury could have done otherwise. The foreman of the jury called upon my wife and explained with tears in his eyes how utterly impossible he had found it to answer the judge's questions in any other way. "Tell him not to grieve", I wrote to my wife from gaol; "if I had been in his place I should have done as he did."[1]

IN GAOL. 'Next day was Lord Mayor's Day and I spent hours walking up and down the streets through the thousands who turned out to see London's annual pageant. I was going to be secluded from my fellow creatures for some months; I wanted to take my fill of the crowd before I returned to my cell.

'The following day the second charge springing out of the same incident was tried before a second jury. I took no part in the proceedings, and when the inevitable verdict came and we stood up for sentence, the Judge sentenced me to three months imprisonment. When I got into my cell I found that the sentence ran from the opening of the Sessions, and that the precise period of detention I had to undergo was two months and seven days. My dear wife, who had displayed the most splendid courage through it all, bade me good-bye, and then the gaoler led us down dark corridors into Newgate. The contrast between the hot crowded, excited court and the cold, silent cell was very great. Another hour passed and then we were packed into the prison van and driven through the streets of London to Coldbath in the Fields prison.'

PITIFUL INCIDENTS. A shocking thing was the way in which men of some literary eminence ranged themselves against Stead. Edmund Gosse wrote sanctimoniously to R. L. Stevenson of 'those spurious revelations' and that his 'bond with the *Pall Mall* was broken when it burst into the Romance of the Brothel'. W. E.

---

[1] Mr. E. S. Hole writes to me that he went once with Stead to a meeting on behalf of this foreman of the jury who was standing as a Liberal candidate. Stead addressed the audience in these words: 'I am pleased to have to ask your support for Mr. Branch. He is worthy of your support. He is a man of proven integrity. The last time we met I was in the dock at the Old Bailey and he was foreman of the jury which convicted me.'

Henley's fine pieces, his services to journalism and his courage do not excuse his references to 'Bed-Stead'.

Mrs. Jackson, who was one of Stead's secretaries, tells me of a pitiful incident. 'When he was touring the country awaiting his trial he was to address a meeting in Darlington. My mother who was thoroughly Victorian had told him that she would not allow me to go but he somehow persuaded her. She found him in his bedroom sobbing as only a man can. His wife had stood nobly by him, but in his absence from home some "friend" had suggested to her that no man who was faithful to his wife could engage in the work he was doing. She had written to him indicating that at least he had not been fair to her. It was a brief mistrust, but at the time a terrible addition to the burden he was carrying'.

THE INJUSTICE OF THE CONVICTION. It is hardly necessary to draw the attention of the reader to the glaring injustice of the trial. No real offence had been committed. The judge's summing-up was one-sided, and the prejudiced attitude of Sir Richard Webster did not escape criticism, either then or later in his career. Mr. C. H. Rolph has recently recounted in the *New Statesman* how the evidence of the Archbishop of Canterbury, that he had been privy to what Stead was doing, was not admitted. He also recalled the fact that the petitions to the Foreign Secretary before Stead came on the scene at all had said:[1]

There exists a system of abduction, to Brussels and elsewhere on the continent, of girls who are British subjects, for the purposes of prostitution. They are induced to go abroad under promise of marriage or employment. On arrival they are taken to the *Police des Mœurs* for registration as prostitutes. They are told that this place is the Custom House and that they are brought there to comply with the formalities required from travellers.

The girls are registered in false names, supported by copies of the birth certificates of other people over 21, because Belgian women could not be registered as prostitutes under 21.

CONSOLATION AND CONGRATULATION FROM CARDINAL MANNING. When Stead was on bail at the Old Bailey, Auberon Herbert wrote, 'I will most gladly go bail for £1,500'. Bramwell Booth, the second General of the Salvation Army, is 'Yours affectionately'. A remarkable woman, Catherine Booth, the wife of the first General, writes that she is 'Yours in the war'. There are, of course, many letters in the most grateful terms from women prominent in the women's cause. Josephine Butler begins 'My dear beloved friend' and subscribes herself 'Yours affectionately'. (A letter from Cardinal Manning to Mrs. Josephine Butler is also signed 'Yours affectionately'.) Writing to Mrs. Stead, Mrs. Henry

[1] Page 116.

I am reading your revelations with great honor, & will work with you with all my strength

Yours very truly

Henry. E.

From one of Cardinal Manning's many letters to Stead

Fawcett says her husband is 'the hero saint who in every age of the world's history has been picked out for misrepresentation'. On Christmas Eve, 1885, Spurgeon writes: 'I have often lifted up my heart in prayer for you. Your self-sacrificial spirit is thought of with glowing admiration. In your retirement you will be able to buckle on your armour with supreme and sacred vigil for the fray in the future.' Before the trial began Cardinal Manning asked Stead to get counsel to apply for him to sit, 'as I have always hitherto done', on the Bench; 'I will not fail you'. When Stead goes to gaol he writes: ' "All things work together for good to them that love God". You have served Him with a single eye. And the work has been done, as you wrote; no sentence can undo it. You have now the crown upon your work. I have so strongly felt this, and have so clearly seen through the animosities against you, that I believe what has now befallen will work out some unforeseen and greater good for your consolation. Whatever it may be in my power to do it shall be done. May God give you his peace'.

Stead writes on the back of his Christmas Card to the Cardinal from gaol: 'The Chaplain said in his sermon that no one could have a happy Christmas in gaol. I could have flung my Bible at his head. I have seldom had a happier time. People forget that it is sometimes a greater joy to be alone with the dead and ever-living than to remember the former and forget the latter amid a noisy festival'.

'THE HERETICAL USE OF THE WORD "CHRISTIAN".' Then comes a declaration by Stead to which he often returned: 'Today at the gaol service I had it borne in upon my mind that the time has come to discontinue as heretical the use of the word Christian. Would it not be much more real, vivid and stirring, to say to man and woman, not "Be a Christian" but "Be a Christ"?

And, after all, is that not the central truth of Christ's teaching, and does not the Church exist in order to multiply infinitely the Christ?' The Cardinal replies: 'The joy of Christmas springs from faith and clear conscience, and you have both. Moreover, you have the consciousness of having suffered in saving souls enough to make your Christmas joyful. Walls and bars cannot cramp or imprison our inward freedom in the Kingdom of God. What you say of Christians is true. St. Paul speaks of travailing "till Christ be formed in you", and also "With Christ I am nailed to the Cross. And I live, not now I, but Christ liveth in me". In the measure in which He reigns in us we are conformed to Him and are his Anointed, His image and representative, and the witness that is identified with Him. May every blessing be with you'.

The Cardinal saw Stead at least once in prison. Writing again in a few days he says: 'I am glad that your health keeps up; for your courage I have no fear or doubt. There can be no misgiving as to the work you have done or the work you have begun: or of the effect of trial, sentence and imprisonment. It will all stir greater resolution and add wisdom and caution to those who are working with you. And if it does not "stop the mouth of lions" it is only because nothing can; but it will pacify and disarm many good but feeble minds.'

Your ever admiring friend,

Björnstjerne Björnson

CHAPTER XIV

THE DAYS IN GAOL

A JOYFUL CONVICT. Before three days were over Stead, who had been put in broad-arrow-marked convict dress, had been cropped and had been made to pick coir fibre, was made a first-class misdemeanant at the instance of Lord Salisbury. He sent this letter to his family:

'If any of you imagine that I, being a prisoner, am needing consolation, and that you ought to address me at this Xmastide in accents of crape, don't! I am here in the pleasantest of little rooms imaginable, with a snug armchair and a blazing fire and the walls full of Christmas cheer[1] and, what is far more, my heart full of joy and peace and goodwill to all men, including Mr. Justice Lopes.

'It is true that now and then I have squirmed. The other day when we all had to sing in the gaol chapel, "Hark the herald angels sing" my eyes filled with tears, and through the tears I saw, not the close-cropped yellow-jacketed congregation but a yard full of people with fiddles and hymnbooks, and out of a bedroom window up above appeared faces that were curiously like yours and mine. Then the hot tears dropped heavy on the floor, and there I was, with my fellow-criminals, singing as best I could for the sobbing of my heart, "Glory to the Newborn King".

'This morning, too, when I woke at three and remembered it was father's birthday, there was a great stab as of pain. Dear man, how he was in all things "our father" to us, enabling us to understand what God is. Oh, my God, my God, it was almost more than I could bear. He was a good man. I am not, never was, and I fear never will be. I often feel as if I was far worse than any of the other convicts. For they had not such a home as ours, such a father, such a mother. And now I must wish you all a merry Xmas and a Happy and useful New Year. I have indeed had a very happy and joyous time. I sometimes get bothered about money. "My grace is sufficient for thee" I interpret too often except so far as cash is concerned, in which my faith gets weak. With that exception I have great serenity of soul.

'TO PLAY A GREAT PART AND THEN GET KILLED.'
'I spend my time in working. I have written all the leaders but one

---

[1] Some members of the *Pall Mall Gazette* staff sent him a muzzled imitation dog which barked.

since I came here and several of the reviews. I have written an article on "Government by Journalism" which will make fifty instead of fifteen pages of the *Contemporary Review* and now I have finished, very nearly, the first two chapters of my book. When I have my hour's walk, I perambulate the infirmary grounds, round and round, like a horse in a threshing machine, seeing Apocalyptic visions of a new earth in which the only thing quite distinct is that I am called to play a great part and then get killed at the end of it all. How, what, where, I don't know. I think I wrote to you, did I not?—about my idea of founding a secular Salvation Army that will consist of all who are willing to bestir themselves and take trouble for England's sake, with my newspaper as its *War Cry*, and myself as its General. It is a great idea. It links the Church idea on to the Journal and combines both for saving the world on its secular side. This is all written out fully in my "Government by Journalism".

'What I have to do when I come out I don't know. Thompson has effectively gagged the *P.M.G.* by taking contracts for advertisements on the understanding that there are to be "no more virgins" in the paper. It has to be like other papers.

'I have a feeling as if I could spend Sunday night in preaching as a kind of itinerant apostle of the New Faith, which, after all, is about the oldest there is.'

In his diary under date New Year's Eve, there is this long entry, headed '11 o'clock'—the side headings are mine—in which we get farther into the tender heart and developing religion of a remarkable man, remarkable when full account has been taken of what may be pronounced to be his extravagances and egoisms.

'A GREAT PASSION OF TEARS'. 'Praise God! Truly God is good. Indeed He is. Almost too good, at least to me, but I fear almost to complain of receiving more than my share. It seems ungrateful. But the other, the poor other, who have none of what I have. For I have everything and many have nothing. I remember once having a great passion of tears over it. It was when I was appointed to the *Pall Mall* at £800 per ann. And I thought of father working away so many years at £80. There is mixed with it a shuddering kind of dim, misty foreboding that I have all these things now but in compensation they will be taken away and Job's story will repeat itself with me. And yet why should I show such unbelief? For it is unbelief and it goes counter to all my experience. For my step has ever been upheld, and every year has brought me more and more into the very storehouse of all God's bounties. Up till now I have lost nothing. My parents have been taken to a better world, but they live in me. I have more than ever at this moment when I sit here holding a strangely joyous watchnight all by myself in Holloway Prison. I know no one who ever loved me who does not love me still. I know no one who was a friend who has turned out a foe. Some acquaintances, perhaps two or three, have been somewhat queer, but I cannot say that I have a personal enemy in the world. I don't feel like an enemy to any one. I am all compassed about and borne up and inspired with a love which is marvellous. When I think of many poor lone units, male and female, who have no kind soul to say "I love you", no one to sorrow for them if they die, to rejoice with them in their successes, what a millionaire monopolist of affection I must be. I must give it out more and more, ever more and more, so that, since it has pleased God to make me the centre where converges so great a mass of human loves, I must make Him make me not a stagnant reservoir of affection but a supply cistern constantly replenished because constantly drawn upon. Love, love, it is the want of the world, and I have so much!

'I realise more than ever the 1st chapter of Isaiah. I think God must be sick of being worshipped so much when men and women are left to perish, physically, morally and spiritually. I am sick of hearing my praises sung and of hearing petitions being signed by the hundred thousand for my release, and all the meetings, etc. It is very kind of the people no doubt, a fine impulse, hero worshipful and all the rest of it and, let me add, by no means distasteful to my poor vanity. But when you think of it all, when you think how little need there is for it, how comfortable I am, and how much need there is for some exertion for the great multitude of the uncomfortable, it seems a prodigious waste of human effort. If these people really appreciated the soul of good that was in my exploits they would not worry about me. And yet I don't know, I am getting censorious, and there is a false note somewhere.

'HIS CHURCH HIS GREATEST CROSS!' 'Jesus Christ must be very grieved at Christianity, and must feel as if His Church was His greatest Cross. I think if Christ came to this world now he would go to all the Churches and attend all the services. And he would see all heads bow at His name being mentioned in the Creed. And he would hear priests and preachers speak with reverent adoration of Him. And he would hear the singing and the praying and everything giving glory and honour and praise and dominion to Him. And He would find that this kind of thing was regarded as religion. And it was the only religion which most of those who attended His Churches practised. Outside he would go into the slums and He would walk down the Strand and He would go into the upper rooms where needlewomen worked, and he would see the men at the Dockgates clamouring for work. And He would see little children growing up like little wolves. And He would

find millions loveless and joyless, and He would wonder where
His followers were. A few here and there. One in a hundred perhaps
working, the others where were these? And He would go into the
Churches and He would find them all sitting there in their cushioned
pews, praying their prayers and saying their creeds, and worship-
ping Christ. And then Christ would stand up in the midst of the
whole congregation and He would say out quite loud in terrible
tones "Damn Christ!" Because they have made an idol of Christ
and debased his worship into a mere word-clicking and puppet-
jigging performance. And He would speak out. For the worship of
Christ has become Nehushtan, like the brazen serpent which once
healed all who looked to it when bitten by fiery serpents, but which,
having become a mere idol and thing of brass, was smitten into
powder by Hezekiah. It sounds bad that "Damn Christ!" I would
not put it into the mouth of anyone but Christ Himself. But if
Christ were Christ that is just what he would say.

'That is one thing borne in upon my mind by my own experience.
I am far off. But Christ has put some of His spirit in me. And if I
saw, as Christ sees, that a poor girl was being driven to the streets
by sheer ignorance and want of timely, friendly help, and the
people who could have given her that help had all left home to
attend a meeting to praise me, I should feel as if I ought to tell
them to go to the devil, because I should feel they were actually
making me an excuse for neglect which ruined a girl—making me,
at two removes, the ruiner of that girl. And I would not like to
stand that. But Christ has to stand it.

'This in brief I told John Morley. What he thought I don't know.

'EACH ONE IS THE CHURCH.' 'Another thing that impressed
me much and I talked over with Albert Grey and Milner[1] is that
each one ought to feel that He is the Church, the whole Church.
And set about in all things to fulfil the whole duty of the Church.
Wherever there is a human want unsatisfied the Church, and therefore the individual, ought to feel this is a distinct call to him or her
to supply that want. Is it light or food, water, recreation, education,
love, sympathy? Not until you have realised your responsibility are
you likely to know what you can do. The mere noting in your mind
of the existence of the want is a step towards its removal. First,
remove the first difficulty of every reformer, convincing others
that a reform is needed.

'I was writing a letter to a poor fallen girl who, while wishing
to do right and even proposing to join the Church, was finding
a life of virtue dull and was pining for the old friends. And I said:
"I am glad you are going to join the Church because that means

---

[1] Afterwards fourth Earl Grey and Alfred Milner, afterwards Viscount Milner,
formerly of the *Pall Mall*.

you are going to live like Christ, active, constant, sacrificing service for others. You will save others as He did. That is your life.''

'And then I went to the prison chapel. It was Christmas morning, and the confession had just been said when suddenly there flashed into my mind: the true formula is not "Be a Christian" but "Be a Christ!"'

'The clock is chiming midnight. The Old Year is going. Goodbye, old year! To me you have been a year of joy unspeakable and full of glory. I don't think I shall ever have more serene delight and joyous gratitude to God for his infinite goodness and tenderness to me and with higher hopes and confidence in the future than since I have been in gaol. Thank God!

'AND THEN THE MOB WILL CATCH ME AND KILL ME.' '"Be a Christ", said the Old Year, and "You have not been" says the New. Alas no! And I can never be unless Christ dwells in me and I am willing in the doing of His power. Make me a Christ, oh God. Make me willing to be abased for Thy sake, to suffer all things gladly, for I feel as if there were lying in reach for me trials and punishments compared with which all that has been is as nothing. But that again is want of faith. Why not trust God? He will see me through whatever has got to come! But did not even Christ pray, "If it be possible let this cup pass from me?" Oh God, You know best, but sometimes I feel rather timid. However, law courts and jails are no longer to me terrors. I have had a feeling that I shall be in gaol again and that I shall hail a prison as the only safe retreat from a mob thirsting for my blood. I remember feeling the door to see if in such a case the mob could get in. They won't get in. And their fury will pass. And I shall come out again and finish my work and then the mob will catch me and kill me. And my death will be like a halo round my memory, and more will believe in my life because of my death than ever would have believed by my mere living. Why does God give me this strange foreshadowing of coming events?

'CHRISTIANS CANNOT SAVE THE WORLD.' 'People don't believe in God because we have been Christians, not Christs. Christians cannot save the world. The Church exists to breed Christs. God the Father, the Church the Mother. It is a great formula. My mission is to cause Christian to cease to be used as a noun. It is an adjective. The substantive is Christ. "Be ye Christ." And you have to go bearing God in you, to men who have not God. Seeking, saving, teaching, helping, healing, and dying for men. Christs. Christian, it may take three centuries to dele[1] *i-a-n.* Each century destroying one letter. It is worth three centuries.

---

[1] Short for delete. The instruction marked on a printer's proof, to indicate deletion.

Christs. So far as a man does a Christlike act or thought, he is a Christ, God's messenger to man. And if he is not Christ he is an anti-Christ. Oh God, make us all Christs offering Thee the service of our daily work, knowing that if we do it unto the least of these thy brethren we do it unto Thee. That is my message. And I think it has the power of God in it.

'GOVERNMENT BY JOURNALISM.' 'And out of this springs another message. I have been thinking long and deeply about the ideal of Government by Journalism. I think that there also I have grasped a great idea. To organise a secular Church with a journal as preacher and all readers congregation and a select body of readers the ecclesia, the church. But how to get people to take the trouble to correspond, to interview, to interrogate and to report for nothing. The answer is that there must be a great revival, almost a new birth of Civic faith, of the religion of the State. The new great religious idea must be driven home to the heart and conscience of the community, that active self-sacrificing effort is as much called for as a religious duty for the salvation of the State as for the salvation of individuals. To enlist workers who would study social phenomena, and work as zealously to interrogate and to guide the democracy as they now do to save a soul or to run an institution, that is a great idea and one that is capable of realization. I have outlined this in the article I wrote for the *Contemporary Review*. It is the first distinct attempt to rouse the religious sentiment to establish the Kingdom on earth as it is in Heaven, working upon the whole community instead of solely upon individuals.

'THE CITIZEN CHRIST.' 'There flashed into my soul the great phrase, "The Citizen Christ". That is my special mission, to realise the Christian ideal. To be a Christ in politics. To be interested in all the ills and sores of the body politic, to approach the social organism as a healer with His sympathy, His love, His intelligence. To see the relations of things, to give eyes to the blind, to give hearing to the deaf, to make the lame walk. All this can be done by Christ, by the Citizen Christ. The vastness of the idea, the substitution of self-sacrifice in politics instead of selfish scrambling for place and power. The Kingdoms of the world will become the Kingdoms of God and of His Christ when men cease to be Christians and become Christs.

'I believe more than ever in the Spirit's leadings. I am not mystical. I am painfully prosaic, practical, matter of fact. Hence the leadings are to me usually drivings. There are signposts. But when God wills that I have to do a thing, He makes me. It is no choosing. By the back of the neck and the seat of the breeches out I am flung. "My place in life is seeking after Thee. Therefore be thou at rest from seeking after it.'' And my place in life has usually seized me in very peremptory fashion indeed. O God, make me willing to do Thy will! Idea just struck me. Why not write an anonymous article "The Citizen Christ". I let the Bible open itself and touched it with my finger. It came II Kings 7–20. "And so it fell out unto him: for the people trod upon him in the gate, and he died." The story is that of the sceptic who would not believe that God would work marvels and deliverance for beleaguered Samaria.'

One who was not in agreement with Stead's theology said to me on reading the foregoing, 'There was divinity in that man'.

THE PROPRIETOR OF THE *PALL MALL* ON WHAT IT 'IMPERATIVELY DEMANDS.' Stead, a month before making the diary entry, had received the following friendly letter from the proprietor of the *Pall Mall*, Yates Thompson, who had visited him in prison:

'Having exchanged views with you today and said all the worst I had to say in your clean cell I set myself to answer your letter of the 10th Nov. dated, "Dock, Old Bailey" in which you place your resignation in my hands.

'I am not in the least tempted or disposed to accept it and do not accept it. I think it is nobody's interest, yours, mine or the paper's that I should do so. What I ascertained from you today is that you entertain even a stronger sense than I do of the mistakes committed in connection with the Secret Commission. Whatever they may have been, however—and I demur completely to *your* expression of 'a discredited journalist' (as also, I may say, does Mr. Cook)[1] they occur to me to have been attached to one special subject presenting the greatest difficulties of approach and in which anybody was safe to make mistakes.

'I understand you to say that you will use your endeavours to recover and re-instate the paper even under the disadvantage of being, as you put it, to a certain extent 'shackled'. To me it seems that this phrase again is far too strong; but you will evidently be under certain limitations dictated by a consideration of what is fair and due to me and to the Paper; not 'double or quits' but a 'short turn' is what the necessities of the *P.M.G. imperatively* demand. The Revd. B. Waugh[2] says you neither can nor will get yourself or the Paper out of its present groove. I venture to believe the contrary. You told me you were ready to take this line last September. I believe you will take it, and take it successfully, in January or February next.

'Meanwhile as to Visiting Committee Regulations. As I understood Alderman Waterlow, you have (i) free communication with the outside world by letter, including of course the *P.M.G.*, but nothing from you must appear in it about anything connected with imprisonment, which seems to me to bar any such personal article as you meditate deprecating agitation for your release, etc. At all events no risks should be run. I have suggested

---

[1] E. T. Cook, assistant editor.

[2] Secretary of the National Society for the Protection of Children. An intimate of Stead's.

to Cook either to postpone it (supposing, that is, he receives it from you) with a view to submitting it to Colonel Milman or to make it impersonal. I can't understand however why what was said today is not enough:

MR. STEAD'S IMPRISONMENT

Mr. Stead was removed yesterday afternoon from Coldbath-fields to Holloway gaol, where he was accommodated in a room usually allotted to first-class misdemeanants. He was visited in the evening by the Rev. W. C. Talbot, Congregational Church, Wimbledon, who had a long conversation with him in the presence of Lieutenant-Col. Milman, governor of the prison. Under the altered circumstances Mrs. Stead will have the special privilege of visiting the gaol twice every week, and to Mr. Talbot the same privilege has been extended.

We have received this morning a very large number of letters protesting against both the sentence passed on Mr. Stead and the harshness with which, till the Home Secretary intervened, it was administered. While assuring our correspondents that Mr. Stead will feel deeply the kind sympathy which prompts their expressions of opinion, we cannot refrain from reminding them of Mr. Stead's strong and oft-repeated desire that popular feeling and popular energy should not be diverted from the main issues and the work which is waiting to be done by any personal considerations affecting himself.

There is such a thing as protesting too much. (ii) Stout or Cook may visit you three times each week. I fought hard for every day but could not get it. At all events three times a week is to be tried at first. No doubt an extension can be got later on if desirable. We may select the days. I may see you on application to the Governor but I understood this was to be used sparingly. (iii) The Governor offered to see himself about your having facilities for posting letters as late as could be allowed, 8 o'clock I think he said. We did not think it expedient to say anything at present about special messengers in the morning. That may be tried later.

Well, God bless you and keep you *from being melancholy*. Why should you not do some reading in gaol? Morley used to say *he* did not read enough and no other editor read at all. *Don't forget* if you want anything at once and in a hurry my wife or I can perhaps get it quicker than Mrs. Stead. My wife bids me tell you nothing would delight her more than to do some commissions for you. Telegraph to us without hesitation in any such case.

'NOT GOING MAIDEN TRIBUTING ANY MORE.' I have no letter from Stead to Thompson until January 13, the eve of his release, when he writes as follows to his proprietor:

'I am very sorry to hear what you say about the circulation and the advertisements. I had hoped that the former at least would not have suffered.

'I propose to come straight to the office on Monday, and as soon as I have written the leader and lunched, to go seriatim with you and the staff through all that requires settlement.

'I have borne in mind what you have repeatedly said to me as to the importance of publishing something which you could print as a proof that the sharp turn has come. I have therefore written an article (a proof of which I enclose) in order to comply with your wish. If anything is to be published, the day on which I emerge is almost the only time. The article entitled 'Mr. Stead's Release' sets forth what I hope will be in sufficiently emphatic form the doctrine of the sharp turn. The *Pall Mall* is to be what the *Pall Mall* was before July. We never boycotted any subject then and we shall not now. But we are not going Maiden Tributing any more. It is to be the old *Pall Mall*. I wrote the article to meet your views and I am perfectly willing to suppress it if you wish, merely preserving a proof as my conception of the fresh start.

'I am tolerably confident that by Midsummer we shall have more than pulled up lost ground. That will depend chiefly on three things, Distribution, Gossip, City.

'I am exceedingly sorry that the temporary reverse has been so severe. Mr. Leslie [the manager] informs me that the difference in advertisements in the last six months of 1885 and the same period of 1884 has been £2,500. This sum and any further sum that represents the balance of loss between what might reasonably have been expected as receipts if "The Maiden Tribute" had not been published, I regard as a debt which I owe you, and I shall not be a free man until the improved position of the paper recoups the whole of that sum and more. And, pending the recovery of that money, I am willing to pay you 4 per cent. interest on my debt. I do not regard this as a serious risk, for I believe that, after all allowances have been made, the advertisement of "The Maiden Tribute" represents an equivalent to a much larger capital expenditure.

PROFITS OF THE 'MAIDEN TRIBUTE'. 'And now I come to the question of "The Maiden Tribute" profit. [He means on the reprint.] After allowing £400 off for extra expenses, the general idea was that there would be £2,000 clear. Of this sum, believing it would be best spent from both points of view in rousing public attention and advertising the paper, I have spent about £800 in various channels. (1) In sending by post to all ministers of religion (40,000); (2) in founding the National Vigilance Association, including conference at St. James Hall, etc., (3) In the Hyde Park demonstration. I have also disbursed about £200 more in various expenditures growing out of the Secret Commission, but of this I will not speak. This money I drew from the Chief Director's Fund (of £10,000 raised by public subscription) to which it was to be recouped from the profits of "The Maiden Tribute". In addition there is an unpaid balance of £500 expenditure incurred in the Armstrong case, or arising out of it, which I will have to meet as it is not covered by the subscriptions. Mr. Leslie informs me that, after charging everything against "The Maiden Tribute" receipts, the actual profit will only be £1,200. The balance I shall have to make up as best I can. [I omit some details.] I acknowledge my liability to defray whatever further expenses may arise out of "The Maiden Tribute", Armstrong case or what not. You would then have absolutely nothing further to do with "The Maiden Tribute", and I can assure you that, so far as I am concerned, nothing would give me greater pleasure than never to allude to the subject in your hearing again.

'In order to avoid the nuisance of people coming to the office to see me,

I propose, if you do not object, to stay at Wimbledon for the rest of the month, writing my leaders as I do now and finishing my book.

'I need hardly say how bitter it is for me to have to write, for the first time in my life, to one who feels that he has suffered for trusting in me. It would overwhelm me, if I did not firmly believe that it is but for a time, and that by this time next year you will feel that you have not trusted me in vain.'

It is a curious fact that Stead was never formally appointed editor of the *Pall Mall*. 'When Morley left', he writes, 'Thompson became editor and I was assistant editor or acting editor. I never described myself as editor until I stood in the dock at the Old Bailey and then it would have been cowardly had I attempted to throw on Thompson the onus of his titular position.'

CHAPTER XV

FROM THE *PALL MALL* TO THE *REVIEW OF REVIEWS*

AN EDITOR'S GOOD RESOLUTIONS. There is nothing show-ing precisely what Yates Thompson's reply was. My next letter from Stead is written two years after having had the ad-vantage of a short holiday, a Swiss tour, 'the best holiday I ever had'. He was 'more worn than I imagined'. He is 'looking at the past and future in a very different mood from that in which I wrote last in this diary, but not I hope less devoted to the high purpose of being called of God with Christ Jesus. The first great lesson borne in upon my mind is the better disposition of my time. I ought to be up at 6 regularly on weekdays and have the children at least $\frac{1}{4}$ hour every morning before starting. That is of immense importance. I ought not to lunch out so much except on business and I ought to hurry home as much as possible. Always have biscuits and raisins, spirit lamp and tea in office in order to escape at two when possible. Seclude myself more so as to be more alone to my work during the morning. Read proofs carefully with pen in hand for $\frac{1}{4}$ hour before going to bed, for cutting down, etc. To take at least one week sub-editing. To avoid tobacco and all stimulants. To systematise visiting of friends and notables. Life goes too rapidly to be wasted by trying to do too much.

EFFECT OF IMPRISONMENT. 'I am now about seven months out of gaol. The curious effect it has had on me has been that I have lost to some slight extent the nerve and dash which used to belong to me. This showed itself oddly enough in a certain timidity in getting into a train in motion in the crowd that rushes for the first carriage of the morning train. Before gaol I never cared. More important than this is the slight loss of nerve that makes me less unhesitatingly impudent, if I may borrow my enemies' phrase, in tackling notabilities, etc. It supplies a palpable excuse for those who wish to evade me. Why should they see me or do what I ask them to do when, to a certain extent, I and my paper are under the cloud of imprisonment and social odium? I feel this the more because I see Mr. Thompson suffers from it. The devotion of per-sonal adherents ill counterbalances the general unthinking shadow of the world's displeasure, unless you can live solely among your

MRS. HENRY YATES THOMPSON

From the portrait by Helen Allingham, 1870. Exhibited as 'In a Hertfordshire Wood' and bought by George Smith, the publisher, Yates Thompson's father-in-law, who gave him the *Pall Mall*

These portraits are believed to be the only single portraits of Mr. and Mrs. Yates Thompson in existence

Both in the possession of Sir Christopher Chancellor

HENRY YATES THOMPSON

From the portrait by W. Dwight Morris, 1878. There is also an excellent portrait of him in the company of G. O. Trevelyan, in *The Life of Trevelyan*, by G. M. Trevelyan

devotees and avoid the constant struggle to be foremost in doing the world's work, not for the sake of being foremost, but because if you let others take your place they will use it for war not for peace, for tyranny not for freedom, for man not for woman. I shrink from demanding, as an obvious right, interviews etc., from persons whom I know will have heard the censure and may not know the praise. Of course they do not know me, those persons. With those who know me I stand in a different category. They see me as I am. Those who only know of me through common report are in a society that is preponderatingly hostile to those who meddle with its vices, and they are naturally disposed to believe that I am a somewhat bad fellow, whom they will do well to avoid. To live this down I must do something splendaciously, something that will give the silly world some other label to paste against my name than that of criminal convict.

'I am sorry for Thompson. I have injured his property and caused him untold pain. If God would only enable me to make him an immense return! But that must be as God wills. I will do all that mortal can. Before the end of this year I ought to see my way to placing the *P.M.G.* in a sound financial position. I wonder. I also wish, if God wills, that I may be able to do something to make my wife and family safe from monetary difficulties when I am called hence. If I could found them a little property? Nothing I have ever done for money has prospered. About public speaking, I feel as if I had said my say and had not to speak any more just now. I ought to write more religiously in the paper. Tolstoy attracts me enormously.'

RUSSIA: 'ANOTHER OF THE CRITICAL DAYS IN MY LIFE.' This is the heading to a diary entry of Sept. 25, 1888, noting that Yates Thompson had asked him to 'reserve half an hour for some serious conversation. 'Before I learn my destiny', Stead writes, 'let me briefly set down how it all happened. When I went to Russia in the early summer of this year I went to do certain things. I did them all except see Herbert Bismarck. Never since I was in gaol had I two months of such exalted enjoyment, such constant consciousness of being led. For years I had been abused and misunderstood and ridiculed for my firm faith in the Russians. It was the one point on which I stood most alone. The result was that I was afforded opportunities no one else had, first, of ascertaining the truth about Russian policy and, secondly, in obtaining a vantage ground in the confidence of the Tsar from which I could speak in favour of peace, liberty, justice and reform. I went with a consciousness that my visit had more to do with the internal affairs of Russia than her external. I saw the Emperor and most of

L

his Ministers. I stayed with Tolstoy. I lived among the cleverest people in P'burg, and got, I think, a firm grip. I wrote my articles as I had never written anything since "The Maiden Tribute." I achieved a greater personal success in higher spheres than ever before. It was to me a great signpost. When I left P'burg I felt more confirmed in my ideas that I had been led and helped and was to be used of God. My great ideal of journalism seemed to come nearer realisation. I was proud and happy and full of pleasant thoughts.

THE ROW AT THE OFFICE. 'I arrived at Queenborough not having heard from the office for a fortnight and expecting that the last of my articles would be appearing in that day's *Pall Mall*. I had had a rough passage. I opened the paper on the platform and discovered to my horror and confusion that the letters were being printed feuilleton-wise across the bottom of the page in small type and in small snippets. The series was not half through. I felt a sinking of soul indescribable. Instantly I said to myself 'Your work on the *Pall Mall* is done. You must now (1) go and edit the *War Cry*, (2) go to Russia to edit the Tsar's paper or (3) edit a morning paper. The calm ignoring of my express orders, the publication of my letters in a way which utterly spoilt them, and at the same time the structural alteration of the paper in such a way as to destroy the front page, which is to me the most important page, all showed that at the office they no longer cared for me or for my ideas, and that if they had their way they would leave them out altogether. I was awfully upset. I had been travelling continuously from P'burg, and was very weary and worn. Next day Hill[1] and Stout both came and both were full of indignation at the way in which things were going. I resolved that I would put my foot down. If I had to go, well and good. If I had to stop I would be master in my own ship. So I decided on reprinting the letters, re-setting them, and making a splash to recoup the damaging effect of their first publication. That night I could not sleep, and got up at one o'clock and wrote the leader which appeared in the *Pall Mall* on Monday.

'Then I got to the office. I found them quite unconscious of the mess they had made. When I told them what I was doing, it fell like a thunderbolt. Cook said nothing about the reprinting, but agreed in his usual curious, nonchalant way. When the proof of the leader came down he made no remarks. Mr. Thompson was then in Paris. He returned the next day. He was very indignant, said that I had insulted him, that I had destroyed his confidence in me, that he had more confidence in Cook than in me, and then harked back to the condition of the paper. Our stand regarding

[1] William Hill, news editor.

Trafalgar Square[1] hit us in advertisements and also in circulation. The *Star* starting soon after also hit us. The result is that we are now down to the figure that we were before, with fewer advertisements. This is failure, I admit. From my proprietor's point of view I have failed to make his paper a property. He has a right to send me away. He gave me notice from Oct. 1 and yesterday I got the letter saying that he wanted some serious conversation with me about it today.

'MY GREAT MORNING PAPER.' 'In June my head exalted almost unto the stars, now abased to the depths. "God keep me humble", my last words in leaving Russia, have been answered indeed. I have been humiliated. My whole future is overclouded. From the very pinnacle of success I have been hurled into the abyss of failure. And now I am utterly without resource. I am at Thompson's mercy. I had hoped that God was about to open a door to my great morning paper. So far he has given no sign of any such intention. All doors seem closed. All that I see is that by Oct. 1 I have to finish my book, *The Truth about Russia*,[2] and finish my term as editor. All my efforts to find new or even supplementary modes of support have failed. Outside the *Pall Mall* I do not seem able to earn a penny. Next year I shall be 40. If I am not a failure, if I am not useless as a journalist, O God, help me and keep me and give me might and courage and knowledge of Thy will.

'The house fixes the scale of living. If I cannot earn £1200 I cannot live there. But I have bought the house and so far as I can see I am meant to live there. Then, if so, God will find the cash and provide me with the work necessary. Again, O God, unto Thee do I cry. Hear my voice. Keep my feet. Show me Thy will and help me to fear not. "Only be strong and of a good courage".'

SALARY REDUCED. This is Stead's report of the interview with Yates Thompson on Sept. 19: 'He was somewhat brutal. I was enabled to be quite calm, self-possessed, and urged him to send me away, make Cook editor and make me only an outside contributor. He said that he was greatly puzzled about it. There were great advantages in my going. If I stayed I could only do so on condition I put the drag on, and whenever anything important

---

[1] The demonstration at which John Burns and Cunninghame Graham were arrested. 'The headquarters of the fight which raged round Trafalgar Square were at Northumberland Street', he writes. 'The *Pall Mall* held aloft the banner of popular rights before the *Star* had risen above the horizon. The question of whether I should take part in the meeting on "Bloody Sunday" was of importance to me because I had received an intimation from Thompson that, if I insisted on going into the Square, I must resign. Cunninghame Graham said, "You must not attempt it, because if we all get killed you are the only person we can trust to tell the truth about us".' At Bow Street Cunninghame Graham and John Burns got six weeks' imprisonment.

[2] Cassell, 1888.

likely to make mischief came up I was to consult him and Cook
and abide by their judgment. I had made the paper a property
before I began to play tricks. And to make an impression on me
I was to have my salary reduced to £1000. I had lost him thousands,
etc. I told him I was at his mercy, that if I had injured his property
I must stay if he thought I could mend it, but that I would practically not be myself, and if an opportunity arose for being myself
I should leave. I was only there on sufferance. The text that most
consoled me was Chron. 2.25.9, "The Lord is able to give thee
much more than this." '

Thompson's letter said:

I write in pursuance of our conversation to propose our new agreement:
(1) that your salary be £1,000 instead of £1,200, with three months'
notice on either side as before. (2) That, warned by the experience of the
last years, the present position is very critical and self-control on your
part is needed and willingness to consult others whenever emergencies
arise which specially enlist your sympathies.

It was followed by another letter when Stead suggested that
revenue might be increased by improvement in the distribution
of the paper and by the adoption of a syndicate arrangement with
provincial papers. Thompson wrote:

To my eye the vital point now is to *revert to the way of conducting the paper*
which succeeded so well in 1883–4–5. When you began with it in 1883
the average daily circulation was 8,360. In two years that rose to 12,250
for 1885 and it was still better in the first half of 1886. The means of distribution were no better then than now. My belief is that with similar conduct
of the paper there would be similar results. By all means let us try and
improve distribution but don't let us expect much money return from that.
Our plain interest lies in the vigorous but steady conduct of the paper.
From that we may expect and shall get a regular if gradual increase of
circulation. The vital point now is, can we regain the confidence of *our*
public—the penny as compared with the halfpenny public—which we
have to a great extent lost? I speak both of readers and advertisers. My
belief is that people's memories are very short, even advertisers', and that
the position is *recoverable with care*, but only with *care*.

I don't take to the idea of your working the syndicate business [with
provincial papers] on your own account as a quid pro quo.

But I will do this: To show that my move is the result of bona fide distress
and alarm at risks already run and losses realised, and more as an insurance
against such risks in future than anything else, I will undertake at the end
of 1889, if during that year the conditions of caution now agreed to by
you have been consistently carried out (of which of course I must be the
judge) to make up to you in one sum the amount (£200) by which your
salary will have been reduced for that year. And similarly at the end of
subsequent years.

RHODES AND HIS CHEQUE. The next thing of interest in the diary is an Irish M.P. speaking to Stead of the £10,000 Cecil Rhodes had given to the Irish Nationalists, and saying that he wanted power. 'Then', asked Stead, 'why does he not start a paper?' The M.P., Swift MacNeill, turned this over to Rhodes to whom he sent the *Contemporary* 'Government by Journalism'. The result was that Stead was asked by Sir Charles Mills to meet Rhodes. 'He did not impress me very favourably at first', writes Stead, 'but afterwards I liked him. He is the only man who has bigger ideas than myself. He has seized the idea of creating an immense Society of Jesus for the British Empire. He has left all his money to it, in trust to Rothschild, and he expects it will come to 4 or 5 millions. He had told no one but Rothschild, who merely sighed "Would that Beaconsfield had been alive!" Rhodes told me because he said he had read the *Pall Mall* and saw when I was in gaol that I was the man to run straight for a great cause. It is a great and fascinating conception. I told him I needed £250,000 for the voice of the secret society. He said that was too much for him to spare now as he had put money into Bechuanaland, but next year he could do more. At present he offered me £20,000 as a nest egg towards acquiring an interest in the *Pall Mall* or towards the newspaper. "Just think it over", he said. "I give it you as a free gift. I regard it as part of my plan of using my wealth to serve the Empire. I ask for no receipt and you must never say who gave it you. You can say an old man gave it you. I want to strengthen your hand and would rather you opposed this Charter [for the British Chartered Company] than that, if it ever came out, you should appear to have supported it from interested motives." I told him that as a Nonconformist I disliked endowments. He, as a clergyman's son, believed in solid cash down. He laughed and we parted.

'Next day the Irwin libel case against the *Pall Mall* mulcted us in £1,500 damages and about £500 costs. I at once sat down and wrote to Rhodes telling him that the verdict would render it necessary for me to resign. Would he let me have £2,000? I would not be disappointed if he refused. But it would not be candid in me not to tell him that the position in the *Pall Mall* was serious. He wrote back, "You can rely on me. When do you want it?" I replied, "Money must be paid tomorrow". I got back, "All right". I telegraphed Thompson, "I have found the money and costs. It will not cost you a farthing." Then I wrote him, saying, "It was my blunder. Under the circumstances I pay. Seeing the odium I have excited against the *Pall Mall* you may fear to publish with me as Editor. My resignation is in your hands. If not, until I work off mischief I have done your property, I remain." Rhodes sent me cheque. I paid it to Brett. Brett gave me a cheque of his own. I paid Brett's cheque into my bank and gave Lewis a cheque for £1,500. The £500 remains for costs. The importance of this is that it clinches me with Rhodes.

'I wrote an article for his special inspection called "Wanted, a *New Times*", which I have got in type. I feel convinced that June 30 sees me free from the *Pall Mall* and Jan. 1, 1890, sees the start of the new venture. It is a curiously precise prophecy as to dates.

'THE VERSE MY PIN PRICKED THROUGH.' 'Yates Thompson has further intensified my uneasiness at the *Pall Mall* by refusing to allow an article of Garrett's to appear, because it seemed to refer to "The Maiden Tribute".[1] There was one reassuring thing. The verse my pin pricked through to on July 5 was that joyous 103 Psalm that consoled Cromwell, "He suffered no man to do them wrong; yea, he reproved kings for their sakes." That was like my Jan. 1 text, about being called before birth to be a prophet to the nations.

'It may be. Only it will not come so soon. Whereas I formerly hoped that I should leave the *Pall Mall* by now and start the new paper on Jan. 1, I now feel as if I might have to go round the world before I start it. To create such a paper for the world, its conductor should see the world. In that case Brett and Willie[2] and a shorthand clerk should go with me. This is the new idea born from the disappointment of yesterday.

'The newspaper idea grows. I now see that I am called to found for the Nineteenth Century a city of God which will be to the age of the printing press and the steam engine what the Catholic Church was to the Europe of the 10th century. Round it endowment will gather and beneficent activities spring up. It will have its fellowships, scholarships, its missionaries. Men will endow correspondences as they used to endow fellowships. It will embody and render accessible for the meanest the ripest wisdom of the world. It will be father confessor, spiritual director, moral teacher, political conscience. It will be the great social nexus. It will be the mother of mankind. I am grieved to go away but it may be better for my wife that I should. Six months might take me round the world, or nine months not to hurry, and then I would still have another nine if the paper does not appear till Jan. 1, 1891. The twelve months' preliminary work would not be wasted. I begin to see daylight. Rhodes's offer of £18,000 may be used in this way. If only my wife were well. O God in mercy show me my path clearly before me now and ever.'

An entry in the diary of June 17, however, showed 'no signpost'. 'I have no hint, no light, no outward visible justification for the

---

[1] Edmund Garrett, see later footnote.
[2] Reginald Brett, afterwards Lord Esher, and Willie Stead.

SIR GEORGE NEWNES, PROPRIETOR FOR A TIME OF THE *REVIEW OF REVIEWS*. A CARTOON BY 'SPY' IN *VANITY FAIR*

faith that is in me. And yet I believe. For a month I have wandered in the Valley of Humiliation. In Isaiah's vision there comes a live coal from the altar and he went in the strength of the Divine burning. But I was not conscious of the coal. I only longed for it.' Two sheets more are given to his distress. On July 7 there is still no news. Beyond this, there is at home 'a shadow of great darkness that can be felt, entirely unconnected with the paper but neverthe- less intimately concerned with all that makes life and work possible.' His wife will not speak to him, and, for the first time since their engagement, has given him no present on his birthday, the anni- versary of 'The Maiden Tribute'.

MR. NEWNES OF *TIT-BITS*. About fourteen months after the letters from Yates Thompson to Stead on the new conditions of his employment the proprietor of the *Pall Mall* is writing to him 'in acknowledgment of *the accomplished fact* of your having arranged to edit a monthly magazine for Mr. Newnes of *Tit-Bits*. I very much wish you had consulted me first. I should certainly have said what I say now, that the editing of Mr. Newnes's magazine is quite incompatible with editing the *P.M.G.* Of course I am open to conviction on this or any other matter but I may as well say now that I don't, as at present advised, see the least prospect of my seeing my way to going shares in the Editor.'

Stead's reply by return is, 'I acquiesce in your decision absolutely and without a word'. And then Yates Thompson writes that if, as he gathers, Stead prefers separation on Jan. 1 1890 instead of April 1 he agrees. He adds:

Please remember that if the Newnes arrangement between now and then should fall through, or show signs of not coming up to expectation, and if for that, or for any other reason you are inclined even at the last moment to prefer April 1, I shall be perfectly ready to accept that date and Mr. Cook and I will both be pleased.

On thinking *calmly* over our conversation of yesterday I conclude that in the last twelve months we have been labouring under a serious mis- apprehension on both sides, and if you did elect to stay on I see no reason why the next three months should not be much more satisfactory to both parties.

If you leave the *P.M.G.* on Jan. 1, or indeed whenever you leave it, there is one point which I consider *essential*, that in the paper itself no notice whatever shall be taken of the event and that the precedent of silence set by Mr. Morley on the occasion of his leaving us shall be strictly carried out.

THE STARTING OF THE *REVIEW OF REVIEWS*. In Stead's memoranda from 1890–1901 there is this reference to his decision to leave the *Pall Mall Gazette* in order to start the *Review of Reviews*: 'The general feeling in the office was consternation. This seemed the maddest thing I had yet done.' He adds characteristically, 'Fortunately I had not the slightest doubt about its wisdom'. It seems that the magazine was at first to be called *The Sixpenny Monthly and Review of Reviews*. 'But at the last moment, on Sunday morning, Newnes came proposing to reverse the order, thus calling it *The Review of Reviews, the Sixpenny Monthly*.' From an artistic point of view the cover of the *Review* was deplorable. Stead, however, calls it 'a great triumph, the most effective cover in the magazine world'. Of the *Review* itself he writes: 'Boundless possibilities, the unexpected first step to a world-wide journalistic, civic church, with a faith and religious orders and endowments and all the rest of the paraphernalia of the Church Militant'.

THE WELCOME IT GOT. Nowadays when, as a matter of course, all sorts of articles in all sorts of periodicals are pithed in the Press and *Digests* of various sorts swarm, it is not easy to realise the novelty of the *Review of Reviews*. To Gladstone it was 'ingenious' as well as 'highly useful', Lord Salisbury expressed himself at length as sympathetical, and in the world outside politics there was hardly anyone who was not encouraging. 'Masha'Allah!' wrote Huxley, 'it is wonderful. May you have a full measure of success without the softening of the brain which, in my case, would certainly supervene from any long continuance of such work as the editorship.' The first number, for January 1890, produced in a rush within a month of the decision to publish, had a four-page appeal 'To all English-speaking Folk', a seven-page 'Character Sketch of the Month' (H. M. Stanley), nearly forty pages of magazines described, criticised and quoted by Stead himself, a careful record of the New Books and Blue-books of the Month and a painstaking seven-page index to the contents of the periodicals. The *Review* was at once successful and brought good wishes from the Prince of Wales, British Ambassadors and John Burns. He told how, unable to purchase a copy of a half-crown review, he 'looked through the first two pages on a bookstall at Charing Cross, the next few at Waterloo and finished the article some days later at Victoria, compelled of course to buy a paper to justify me staying the time at each'.

'Many publishers and periodicals', Stead had complained in his first issue, 'instead of co-operating in the production of what they will soon discover to be a valuable advertisement, took alarm and interposed obstacles, whereas, had they understood what was contemplated, they would have tendered assistance'. By the second number the publishers did understand. This issue was much improved typographically, and, with more time for the work, the reviewing of the reviews was done as well as it could be done, for Stead was a master at this kind of work. There was a page of

Russian and a page of German reviews, and only 'a typographical mischance at the moment of going to press', held over the French, Spanish, Italian, Dutch and Belgian. Stead enjoyed himself in his informed and vigorous nine-page 'Progress of the World', and in thirteen illustrated pages on his friend Mark Twain's *Yankee at the Court of King Arthur.*

'POURING OUT THEIR SOULS' GRIEF'. A feature of No. 2 was considerable extracts from a review which Gladstone had written forty years earlier, of a book called *Ellen Middleton* 'the tale of a tortured soul', by Lady Georgiana Fullerton. Stead said that what the woman in the tale needed was 'not a priest but a sympathetic, level-headed friend to whom she could have told her trouble'. And, practical as ever, he asked, 'Are there any among the readers of this *Review* who feel the craving for counsel and for the consolation of pouring out their souls' grief?' He asked sufferers to communicate with him—'I will respect confidences'. Apart from this, the editor desired to get into touch with 'a picked body of men, or women, if they are earnest enough, who will work with the *Review* and the ideals it upholds as zealously as hundreds of thousands are working for the ideals of the Churches and the shibboleths of Parties'.

By the third number, praise was forthcoming from the United States, from, among others, Oliver Wendell Holmes, Mark Twain, Whittier and Lowell; and the *Review* was taken in by the Royal Family and the Empress Frederick. 'Our Association of Helpers' had got started and was working on reading matter for workhouses. A London daily called the *Review* 'condensed culture, the swiftest, deftest and most complete achievement of sub-editing ever seen'. And so I would like to go on through the volumes of my set. The *Review of Reviews* eventually reached a sale of 130,000, a large one at that period. Readers were always sure of finding interesting, serviceable and stimulating things in it. Issue by issue of the *Review* there was some fresh idea—it might be only modest plans for child adoption or for village libraries or for collecting boxes outside railway stations for papers and magazines. Stead also wrote a large number of effective Christmas Numbers.

OVERSEAS EDITIONS. But within three months the partnership between Newnes and Stead had been dissolved. Newnes got almost as scared as Yates Thompson. He said Stead was turning his hair grey. It was a plain-spoken character sketch of *The Times*, after the Parnell Commission *débâcle*, that brought separation. Although Sir George Lewis scouted the notion, Newnes feared a libel action. The truth was that Stead and Newnes were incompatibles. They were good-humoured with one another but Stead was to Newnes an unbusinesslike flibbertigibbet, while Stead's imitation of the weighty basso profundo rendering of the business man in the following communication was worth hearing: 'There is one kind of journalism which makes and unmakes Cabinets, upsets Governments, builds up Navies and does many other great things. That is your journalism. There is another kind which has no such great ambitions. That is my journalism.' 'A journalism that pays,' the inventor of *Tit-Bits* added.[1]

I have a number of letters written by Newnes on the sale of his share in the *Review* to Stead. Sir George Lewis, concerned in the negotiations, reports that, though he found Newnes genial, he was 'a hard bargainer'. One letter from Newnes says: 'I would suggest that you should borrow £5,000 from a friend on the security of the *Review*. A property earning £4,200 a year ought to warrant such an advance, and you could pay the amount back in less than two years, perhaps in one year. This would leave you an ample margin of capital, £600, now that the business is in such splendid working order.' C. A. Pearson, who was formerly on Newnes's *Tit-Bits* staff, started an imitative *Pearson's Weekly* and worked himself into a position in which he became the proprietor of the morning *Standard* and achieved a baronetcy, was at one time with Stead and went to America for him.

A large and distressing correspondence between Stead and Dr. Albert Shaw, for whom he started the *American Review of Reviews*, leaves one with one's sympathies on Stead's side. In May 1901 Stead puts the circulation of the *American Review of Reviews* at 200,000, the *Australasian Review of Reviews* at 40,000 and the parent *Review* at not more than 70,000. The *American Review of Reviews* was finally amalgamated with an American publication.

'PENNY STEADFULS', THE *DAILY PAPER* AND MORNING BATHS. Not content with the *Review* and writing outside of it articles published at home and abroad, Stead produced books, booklets and pamphlets and papers like *Help*, *War Against War*, *Arbitrate before you Fight*, *Shall I Slay my Brother Boer?*—his manager

---

[1] Newnes was not a cultivated man but he was a remarkable man. He started *Tit-Bits* on limited means after two publishers had laughed at his scheme. Later, he was successively offered £16,000 and £20,000 for the paper. Within two years it had a sale not far short of a quarter of a million. He was fertile in plans to advertise it. The executors of everybody who had had a copy were entitled to £100 worth of insurance if the purchaser had been killed in a railway accident. Seaside donkeys were placarded, 'We don't read *Tit-Bits*'. There was the first of the 'treasure hunts', a seaside villa to be competed for with a story, and a procession of sandwichmen carried a series of boards, the first with *Tit-Bits* on it, the second with 'I like it'; the third with 'My Wife likes it', the fourth with 'My Daughter likes it' and the fifth with 'And so do I'. A prize of £1,000 for a story was won by Grant Allen. On the profits of the paper were built successively the *Strand Magazine* and *Country Life*, both of which broke new ground. The printers had an interest in the latter. Newnes was a Liberal M.P. for twenty years. He got his baronetcy after starting the *Westminster Gazette*, but this is anticipating.

said 'Mostly unremunerative, but he went gaily on'. He was
justifiably proud of *Penny Poets*, 64 pages crown octavo in a wrapper.
No fewer than five million copies were soon sold. He was glad
to think that he had circulated more first-class poetry within a
year than had ever been sold by any publisher in English. There
were also the *Penny Novels*, of 80 pages, condensations of Scott,
Dickens, Trollope and other out-of-copyright novelists, and the
penny *Books for the Bairns* which contained 64 pages, many of which
had pictures. Stead is remembered, as letters to me show, by
many grey-heads for the benefits he conferred on them in their
youth with his cheap books—*Penny Steadfuls*, *Punch* called them—
and the reading in the *Review of Reviews* articles of an informative
and cultural sort. An eminent man once said to me, 'To this day
I thank him for his *Books for the Bairns*, the only books that came into
an impoverished home'.[1] How Stead would have revelled in the
educational and publicity value of broadcasting! In his private
notes he is candid about the Penny Books. 'The *Books for the Bairns*
keep up to 150,000 a month, but the others—ahem!' He acknowledges that some of his views have 'injured my property'.

'TO RECOUP MY LOSSES.' He gives his reasons for starting
The Daily Paper: '(1) Chiefly to recoup my financial losses due to
opposition to the Boer War. (2) To provide for Willie and make
openings for the other boys and girls. (3) To create international
centres, Anglo-American to begin with. (4) To give me an opportunity of daily utterance in London on political affairs.' He estimates the cost of producing a modest 10,000 copies at no more
than £75! 'Like the foolish milkmaid, I count my chickens before
hatching them'; out of the profits his mother and his daughters are
to have £200 each, but the 'Bureau of Borderland'—spooks—is to
have £1,000 a year for 'international union'. 'I think', he says,
the venture 'promises well but, if it fails, I hope God will give me
grace to acquiesce patiently and even joyfully in His will'. *The
Daily Paper*, 'if it succeeds, may be duplicated in Paris and Berlin
and perhaps in Rome and Vienna, etc.' But there is also in his
mind, he states, a morning paper summary at 2d. a day, distributed
from door to door like the *Lokal Anzeiger* at 8 or 9 o'clock, 'substitute
for family prayers, etc.'

Among his papers I pick up in turn, the MS of 'Words of Comfort for Souls in Trouble, collected and edited by W. T. Stead',
128 pages, to be printed in 'two parts at a penny each', plans for
'The Bible Book of the English-Speaking Race' and for a quarterly

---

[1] And Sir Allen Lane, who has done such public service with his Penguins and
other beneficial books, writes to me, 'One of my first pointers to the particular
path in publishing which I have followed was my father's shelf of Stead's *Penny
Poets*.

review to supplement the *Review of Reviews,* and a note on the *Morning Paper:* 'the first halfpenny daily published in the capital of the British Empire, political but not partisan, Imperial but not Jingo, religious but not sectarian, in favour of municipal socialism but against collectivist tyranny, full of sympathy with all that minister to the welfare of the race'. Often one comes on the MS of an article. He writes, for instance, 'The Blue Water Cure for the Great White Plague, A Plea for Ocean Sanatoria'. A memo on Notable Things is: '(1) To remember to change underclothes every day, (2) Bath every morning, (3) Breathing exercises while drying, also repeat poetry'! And this: 'The more I see of men and women, the more I trust them. Individuals may be stupid and untrustworthy but the next one who comes along I find loyal and true.'

A £400,000 OFFER. Of all this some of the i's will be dotted and some of the t's crossed in chapters which are to follow on the *Pall Mall* editorship of Stead's second-in-command there, E. T. Cook. Meantime it may be recorded that I have a long unpublished typewritten account by Stead, which was new to his daughters, of how someone, after several conferences, offered him £400,000 for a new daily paper. With a sigh, Stead turned down the proposal, after consultation with Brett, on the ground of dissatisfaction with the fact that the proposed capitalist was living in adultery. The man's name is repeatedly mentioned in the memoranda but it does not appear in anything that has been printed about Stead and I may as well leave it unpublished.[1]

---

[1] THE BAD MAN. It is a melodramatic but truly Steadian story. The man was accused to Stead by letter of 'infamous conduct, blackmailing and cardsharping, of having had relations with a girl of thirteen and of being horsewhipped at Boulogne by her brother'. 'I went straight to him', writes Stead. 'He denied all but the intimacy with the girl but said she was not thirteen but fifteen and looked nineteen and that she had been previously seduced by —— [a Front Bench politician].

Sir Desmond MacCarthy called Prince Kropotkin 'that saintly revolutionary'

CHAPTER XVI

WITH THE GREAT ONES

TALKS WITH TWO TSARS. Stead's interview with Alexander III he was not allowed to refer to. All that is worth noting in it is Stead's apologia to the Emperor for the British attitude towards Russia during the Russo-Turkish war, the Tsar's declaration that the Dardanelles was neither for Russia nor Great Britain, and Stead's breach of etiquette in ending the interview 'when I had asked all my questions and knew that the Empress had been waiting for her lunch for half an hour'. The Tsar Nicholas was seen several times by Stead. (He also wrote to the Empress a number of letters from the Hague giving accounts of the Peace Conference.) The report of one interview fills eight closely typed foolscap sheets. It represents one of Stead's feats of memory, for it is all conversation in the first person. Stead has, of course, more space than the Tsar. One of the Tsar's observations was, 'I think the Dardanelles would be impossible for both Russia and England. We shall not take Afghanistan. I never understand why you cannot take it. It would be much simpler if the British and Russian boundaries were together.' The report of another interview fills twenty closely written quarto pages, but there is little in either interview that is of much interest today. The Tsar agreed to read the draft of a speech Stead proposed to make in Russia and to let him have it back on a particular day. The draft was brought back on the promised day, but the Tsar felt that 'in the disturbed state of public opinion' it would be imprudent for any view of his to be stated by a foreigner. Stead, in writing for England, said that 'the genial, kindly, sympathetic, kind-hearted man who received me at Livadia and Tsarskoe Selo wishes sincerely to do right' but that his 'incongruous position' is comparable with that of Mr. Forster when Secretary for Ireland. 'No one has a kinder heart than Mr. Forster but, when confronted with the Land League agitation, he became "Buckshot Forster" who crammed the prisons with untried men and brought the country to the verge of revolution.[1] The Tsar is an intelligent man, the sovereign of an empire steeped in ignorance, who has failed to impress anyone with the conviction that he has in him the capacity for heroic resolution. He said to me, "No one knows how difficult my position is. I would not inflict it on my worst enemy." Who is there, however, among the Grand Dukes

[1] But England owed to him the School Boards.

who would not be immeasurably worse? The Tsar would be delighted
if, by some act of Divine Providence, the burden of Empire could
be lifted from his shoulders and he could live the life of a country
gentleman with his wife and bairns. He is not a Hercules, physically
or intellectually. In all the world there is not a more pathetic or
tragic figure.' Stead's premonitions did not intimate to him the
end, the ghastly murder of the Tsar and Tsaritsa in Siberia.

CONTRADICTING AN EMPRESS. Stead saw the Dowager Empress at the conclusion of one talk with the Emperor. The conversation was of the frankest character, largely about the young man
whose charming character but weak will the Empress and Stead
acknowledged. 'He is so good-natured and so sympathetic that he
agrees with everybody', said the Empress. 'Now you have a very
different character from his, quite different. Look how you contradict me and I contradict you. We stand up and fight for our views.
He would never do that; it is not in his nature. Whereas you!
You must have a great influence.' Stead answered, 'I forget you are
Empress and only regard you as a woman'. Later in the talk
Stead asked, 'Who are your men, your Ministers? Who, by his
strength could supplement the excessive amiability of the Emperor?'
'I know of none', the Empress said; and then Stead made her laugh
by asking her, 'Why not give the women a chance?' for she had said,
'Our women are much superior to the men'. Stead said, 'Our
Queens have been better than our Kings—Elizabeth, Anne and
Victoria—and you have had your Catherine'. During the interview
the Empress mentioned that she 'continually received anonymous
letters of abuse from England, vile letters'.

ADMIRAL FISHER'S HELPFUL HORNPIPE. We hear of the
Tsar again in an account which Stead had from his friend Admiral
Fisher of the meeting of King Edward and the Russian and German
Emperors at Reval. Stead found Fisher in his shirt sleeves, and
learnt that he had been at work since four in the morning. Fisher
said that at Reval he made great friends with the Emperor's sister
Olga. 'The Empress suffered a great deal in one of her legs which
she was always rubbing, rheumatism, I think. At first we were all
a little bit stiff and standoffish, but I set myself to thaw them.
At the first State banquet I began telling stories. Olga is a very
hearty laugher. You know when you once get people laughing it
is not difficult to keep them laughing. The King shook his finger
at me and said, "Admiral, you forget you are no longer a middy
and that this is not a middy's mess", at which the Tsar and Tsaritsa
laughed heartily. Olga declared that it was the first time the
Tsaritsa had laughed for five years. Then after dinner the band
played *The Merry Widow*, and Olga and I danced. She is a splendid
dancer, and in that dance we put our hands behind our heads and

all the company formed a ring round us and watched us. Afterwards we went on deck and I danced the hornpipe, and everything went splendidly. Our King is not a clever man but he does the right thing on such occasions as this. At dinner the Tsar stretched his hand across the table and clinked glasses with the King and with me, and no one else. Then the King took out a card, wrote something on it in pencil and tossed it across the table. The Tsar picked it up and read it and his whole face shone. On the card the King had written "I appoint you an Admiral of the British Fleet". Immediately after the meal was over the Tsar ran up on deck, got an Admiral's flag, was rowed off to the *Minotaur*, hoisted his flag and made an official inspection of the ship, just like a boy with a new toy. Another thing the King did splendidly was his speech. The man who was told off to report the speeches broke his pencil

Signature of a letter from Admiral Sir John Fisher to Stead[1]

just as the King began to speak, so he had nothing. The King said he couldn't remember a word of what he had said. I said "Sir, do you mean to say that on an important occasion like this you don't prepare your speech?" "No," said the King, "I know what I want to say and I stand up and speak it right out. The only time I made a mess of it was when the French President was in London. I thought it was very important and spent twenty minutes in the garden making up my speech. When the time came, instead of saying what was in my mind, I was trying to think what I had thought of in the garden, and in trying to remember I quite put my foot in it." So there was nothing for it but for some of us to piece together what we could remember. In talking with me Prince Henry said, "What we are afraid of is another Copenhagen". Of course that is out of the question now, but we could do it if we had a Bismarck or a Pitt. Pitt laid down the law that when any nation built a sufficient number of men-of-war to be a danger to us we ought to step in and destroy them at once'. "Yes," said Stead,

---

[1] A letter before me from Fisher to Stead begins: "My Blessed Sheet Anchor!" Fisher became Lord Fisher of Kilverstone.

W. T. STEAD LATE IN LIFE, ABOUT 1907

'"and the Germans, judging us by themselves, cannot help wondering why we don't do it".'

TOLSTOY CROSS-EXAMINED. Stead spent a week with Tolstoy and said that he was the most interesting of all the many men he met in Russia. 'If you want to know the truth about Tolstoy', said Countess Tolstoy, 'you ought to come to me'. Stead asked her husband why he wasted his time making a bad pair of boots when he might have employed it in producing a masterpiece of fiction. He replied, 'When I am making a pair of boots I know I am doing good work, I am labouring with my hands; when I am writing a novel I do not know whether I am writing good or ill'. Tolstoy 'insisted on the absolute impossibility of convincing mankind of the truth of any new religion except by suffering for it. What converted Romans was the readiness of Christians to suffer the most cruel forms of death.' On the question of passive resistance, Stead asked if Tolstoy would carry his doctrine so far as to allow his wife and daughters to be carried off by Turks and submitted to outrage if by striking a blow he could save them. 'Certainly I would not strike that blow', he replied. 'To resist evil by force is contrary to the word of God. You can never convince a man by logic. He thinks that if a cleverer man came along he would answer you. So he remains unconvinced. But when he sees suffering for belief he thinks there must be something in that religion. Without persecution no success.' Stead's judgment is worth reporting, coming from him, 'Tolstoy was a charming host, a delightful conversationalist, a marvellous genius, but as a practical guide in the affairs of this life just a little too mad for anything.'

TALK WITH THE TSARITSA AND QUEEN ALEXANDRA. There are some eighteen pages of typescript giving an account of an interview with the Tsaritsa in company with Queen Alexandra and Princess Victoria at Buckingham Palace. There was an animated conversation. After a time the Queen and Princess Victoria—who said 'I very much wished to see you'—left Stead to the Tsaritsa. She now took an armchair in which she told him to sit and pushed it in front of a couch where she sat down. Of some canard in the newspapers she said, not too happily, 'It is like everything else you read in the newspapers'. 'Not everything', Stead rejoined. 'Well', she said, 'nearly everything'. She said she did not like a particular British Ambassador at St. Petersburg, 'smooth to your face but behind your back quite different'. Madame Novikoff had told her that Stead was helping her with her book. She spoke of a Russian Princess 'for whom I am very sorry because she has a most atrocious husband who dragged her about the room by the hair of her head; the police had to be called in'. Stead referred to the Tsaritsa's dead son of twenty-eight and asked if she had heard

M

from him since his death. 'No', she answered, 'never a word; I have never even dreamt of him'. 'Oh', said Stead, 'I have heard from my boy several times'.[1] The Empress had read Stead's *Julia*; 'my elder brother gave it to me. It is very wonderful, very wonderful'. On this subject the record of the conversation with the Empress gives half a dozen pages to Her Imperial Majesty to Stead's eighteen.[2]

WITH THE PRINCE OF WALES AND SIR FRANCIS KNOLLYS. In 1890 Sir Francis Knollys sent Stead a signed photograph of the Prince of Wales, afterwards Edward VII, and in 1898 an intimation that 'it will give H.R.H. much pleasure if you would have the goodness to call at Marlborough House at 3.15 p.m.' In the course of a long conversation, mainly about Russia, Stead reports that the Heir Apparent 'spoke as usual very rapidly and I spoke extremely fast, so we crowded a great deal into three-quarters of an hour. He said, "I have known the Tsar since he was a child; he is a charming fellow with a very simple, natural, and sweet disposition, but he ought never to have been a monarch." I noted that the Prince's mind does not work steadily, but flies back and forward. He does not show a habit of close attention.'[3] But Stead saw the Prince on another occasion, at Lady Warwick's, when he had his talk out. Before referring to an incident of this interview, however, something may be recorded of an hour's conversation with Sir Francis Knollys, before Stead wrote his character sketch of the Prince in the *Review of Reviews*. Stead told Knollys some of the stories which were current about H.R.H.'s relations with women. There was a report that, either at a Duke's shooting box or at Sandringham, he had seduced a chambermaid or a governess in distressing circumstances. The story came to Stead from Bradlaugh who believed that he had evidence to justify his sending in his resignation from Freemasonry when the Prince became Grand Master. Knollys gave Stead his word of honour that, as to Sandringham at any rate, there was no truth in the report. Stead said: 'I

---

[1] Willie Stead.

[2] INCIDENTS AT A SÉANCE. The subject was messages from the dead. Here, perhaps, I may drop in a new story. A colleague of mine on the *Pall Mall* was M. H. Spielmann, the art critic and author. His son, Dr. Percy E. Spielmann, tells me that his father, who had a knowledge of conjuring and its processes, 'became suspicious of some of the spiritualists whom Stead trusted, and attended several séances with him. On one occasion M.H.S. found a low panel of the door of the room loose. It was large enough for a small person to creep through; and outside the window was a fire-escape, screened by heavy curtains. At another séance Stead was allowed to lock the door of the room and to put the key in his pocket. Next day he was discussing the matter with M.H.S. with his hands in his pockets and took out the door key. Greatly disturbed, he said, "But I never unlocked the door before going out!"—a trick lock?' It was to Spielmann that Stead said that a medium had assured him that he would be kicked to death in Fleet Street.

[3] 'The German Emperor possessed almost every gift except the power of concentration'.—Dr. Eugen Schiffer in *Ein Leben für den Liberalismus*.

CARTOON OF THE PRINCE OF WALES (EDWARD VII) AFTER
THE BACCARAT SCANDAL, 1890

From the 'Review of Reviews' character sketch

fully recognise that a man in the Prince's position is run after by
women, and is quite as often seduced as he is the seducer, and I
had never said a word against ordinary immorality as a bar to
public life. It is only when it has a criminal aspect, and has been
judicially proved, that I have dealt with it. I have a horrible
presentiment that a day may come when I shall be confronted by
some scandal in which a ruined woman or an injured husband will
come to me, and I shall be driven, however much I dislike the
task, to go for the Prince as I have gone for Dilke; but hitherto no
such information has come before me, and it is a great relief to
me that the first occasion in which the Prince has got into a scandal,
it is about a matter on which I can honestly remain indifferent.[1]
The Republicanly-organised English-speakers far outnumber those
under the Monarchy. Has the Prince got the mind, has he got the
imagination capable of rising to the height of his opportunities?'

KNOLLYS' POSER. 'What would you have him do?' said Knollys.
'Whenever he does try to do anything the Government of the day
prevents him. He wanted to be on the Labour Commission, for
instance. He was not allowed. He attended every sitting on the
Commission for the Housing of the Poor, but whenever he makes a
move he is checked. He is never allowed to do anything that has
any interest in it. What can the Prince do?' Stead's rejoinder was:
'Why could he not make himself accessible to all Colonists, so that
they should feel in personal relations with the Heir Apparent?
And what I say of the Colonies, I say of the Americans also.'
Knollys replied, 'The Prince is going to see an American today,
and he will receive any American whom the American Minister
or the Secretary of the Legation presents to him'. Stead went on:
'Neither the Prince nor anyone else can afford to hide his light
under a bushel. *Réclame* is indispensable for all institutions. Even
le bon Dieu needs his parish steeples, said the Frenchman. It is a
great pity that, if the Prince is making himself this centre for
American and English re-union, he should not get the credit for it.
There is one thing which encourages me to hope, a remark I heard
he had made about the German Emperor. He said that his nephew
was able to order everything and do everything, while he himself
was not allowed to do the least thing. Now, the German Emperor
has nothing like the career and opportunities which the Prince
might have. He has the whole world before him, whereas the
German Emperor has but the parochial politics of Europe.'

THE PRINCE'S CHARACTER. 'True,' said Knollys, 'the Prince
has quite enough imagination to recognise that. But he does not
know what is going on. He is not allowed to know anything. For
my part, I think it is a great pity. It is much better that he should

[1] The Tranby Croft baccarat scandal.

take part in those things, but you must admit that it would be bad for the Heir Apparent to be in opposition to the Ministers of the Crown.' 'It would be very bad, but Prince Albert did these things.' 'Yes, but Prince Albert, being the Consort of Queen, was virtually a King, and a King is allowed to do a great many things which the Prince of Wales may not do.' 'Yes,' I said, 'that is true, but, on the other hand, if the Prince were really keen about things, and it was known that he was keen, he could do what he liked. Ministers jump upon him because they do not think he is in earnest about it. They say he has only a languid interest. It would be very different if the Prince himself were to be keenly interested in those questions, and were to make himself felt, especially if there was any strong expression of opinion on the part of the public that the Prince ought to take a more leading part. But it is no use making a chance for him if he has not got spunk enough to take advantage of it.' 'Well,' said Knollys, 'you may depend upon it that if public opinion should express itself in favour of allowing him to take more part, he will prove himself quite capable of responding.'[1]

Knollys went on: 'He is great friends with many women, and there are some women to whom it is impossible for the Prince to speak for five minutes without their imagining he means much more than he thought of. He was only lamenting to me the other day that it was quite impossible for him to speak to a pretty woman without being accused of evil intent. Now, I am a married man, but I greatly admire beautiful women, and I shall always continue to do so until I am a hundred years old.' 'My dear Sir, why should you not? I am always maintaining that doctrine, namely that a great deal of the joy and brightness of life arises from the freest possible intimacy between men and women, if only it does not degenerate into adultery.' The interview closed with Knollys promising to read the proof of the *Review of Reviews* article. Stead had several talks with Knollys and he was also on friendly terms with the Ponsonbys.

EDWARD VII AND GEORGE V. Stead had told Knollys that he had had some qualms about meeting the Prince because, he said, of 'a vulgarity which ought not to have appeared and led to the boycotting of the *Pall Mall* from the Service Clubs. [He had spoken of H.R.H. being known to thousands only as 'a little fat man in red'.] It was one of those grossly brutal things, which are true, and which, because they are true, ought not to be said. When I was writing, the idea presented itself to me, and I wrote it out

---

[1] Knollys could not say it, but it was the old Queen who objected most strongly to the Prince of Wales being brought into intimate relations with public affairs. The most important Ministers favoured the Prince's claim to facilities of apprenticeship to the Throne.

to see how it looked in print. When I saw it, I crossed it out, but I restored it when my staff protested that it was one of the best points of the leader, which it was, very striking and forcible.' Knollys said he was sure the Prince had forgotten it long ago. When Stead saw the Prince he said he had made some rather rough references to him, but the Prince said he was not to think of it, 'I am a liberal-minded man'. And Lady Warwick told Stead, after his talk with the Prince at her house, that H.R.H. thanked her for giving him the opportunity of meeting a remarkable man.

Stead saw the Duke of York, afterwards George V, and writes: 'He is not so nimble as the Tsar. If I had to describe him in a word I should say that he was George III come to life. The Duke did say that he was quite sure the Tsar did not want India; they had "often talked it over, and the Tsar said he could not conceive any more disastrous idea." He did not think the German Emperor ever received his letters unopened, but the Tsar always got his. "The Tsar showed me", he said, "a letter from a poor person in England asking for money. If his letters had been opened they would certainly have kept that one." The Tsar had never been to college and knew very little before he came to the throne, but he had worked hard. "Not that I have ever been at college myself. I went to sea when I was twelve. When you are at sea you do not learn much except about sea things. I suppose you learn without knowing it. It also broadens a man's mind and makes him understand the right proportion of things, but he does not get much book learning." The Lord Mayor was complaining to him that he was nearly knocked up after nine months of office because of the number of speeches he had to make. "Damn it", I said to him, "we have to be Lord Mayors all our lives". On Anglo-American relations I said he was the person of all others who had most to gain by the Anglo-American alliance; he and his family were at the top of the pyramid of the English-speaking races. He said, "I read your book about Queen Victoria and she had it read to her and liked it very much and was very pleased by the way you spoke of her!" He added he had seven cousins who would one day all be reigning. He went over them twice for me.' He little knew!

WHAT GENERAL GORDON WAS LIKE. This is the picture that Stead gives of Gordon: 'A little man and slight of build, with merry blue eyes and curly sandy hair, so simple and unassuming that I took him for a man-servant when he opened the door at his sister's house and helped me off with my overcoat. A man of profound piety, passing much of his time in prayer, he was also a fellow of infinite jest and of the merriest humour. No more delightful companion I ever had. His moods changed like the sky of an April day. Wrath as of the Berserker would flame up, to be succeeded

by the humble, self-accusing penitence of a man who feared greatly
lest he should have been unjust to his fellow man. No one was
more scornful or satirical when speaking of shams and windbags
in high places, but his whole face would glow with emotion as he
spoke of his "kings", the ragged urchins whom he had taught at
night school at Chatham.' Stead published three *Pall Mall* 'Extras'
about Gordon, the last being *Too Late*.[1]

A VISIT TO CARLYLE. When still editor of the *Northern Echo*,
Stead was taken by Madame Novikoff to see Carlyle. It was on an
October Sunday afternoon in 1877. He writes of Carlyle: 'His eyes
were bright, brilliantly bright, and blue as the azure lochs which
gem the hills between St. Mary's Loch and Hawick. I never saw
so rich a blue except in those lochs. Beneath the blue eyes were
ruddy cheeks, almost hectic in their colouring. On the left cheek
a vein showed out. His lips were rather fallen in owing to the lack
of teeth. His brow, although high and wrinkled, bore upon it none
of that weight of consuming care that oppresses you in his portraits.
The ploughshares of sorrow had passed over it but the furrows do
not show, and the expression is more that of benignant, placid
innocence. His head was covered with lovely grey hair as thick
as that of the young Carlyle of forty years ago. I appreciated for
the first time the exclamation of my companion when, in describing
Carlyle, she had emphasised her admiration for his "darling little
face". It *is* a little face. But in place of the infinite sadness which
I had believed ever brooded over the face of the author of *Sartor
Resartus* there was nothing but kindly mirth and ready sympathy.
Carlyle stood erect as if four score years did not rest upon his
shoulders and, although his long frail hands trembled slightly,
there was no other indication of failing strength. His hearing,
however, is not so good as it once was. You needed to speak
distinctly for him to follow you. He was wearing a long grey
dressing-gown.'

Stead saw Carlyle later on during a visit which he paid alone.
'Carlyle was dressed as before and sitting in his easychair, reading
a life of Edward III. He said: "The Turk has lain there for four
centuries and more without doing a single good thing for the world.
The only good thing he ever did was to destroy the Lower Empire.
They were a bad lot of men those Greeks, not much better than
the Turks, with the lawyer-like intellect wrangling and discussing
until the Turks swept them away."' The interview was interrupted

[1] THE FATE OF GORDON. It was not Stead's fault that Gordon came to grief. 'No
sooner had he gone', Stead writes, 'than the Government began interfering with
him in such a fashion that I was led to declare that they had much better stop him
before he got to the Sudan rather than send him with his hands tied behind his
back. When the time came for action to relieve him from the conditions which
their interference had created they refused to move until it was too late.'

by Lecky coming in order to take Carlyle to lunch. Lecky, Stead describes as 'tall, rather soppy-looking, large vacant eyes, light hair, awkward demeanour, and bashful appearance; more like a tallowchandler than an historian.' Well, Lecky did spoil Stead's interview!

GLADSTONE ON THE 'GREAT MYSTERY' OF MARRIAGE. Among Stead's notes of conversations with Gladstone is one undated extending to eleven closely typed foolscap sheets, from which I make a few extracts: 'Mr. Gladstone placed a chair for me near him before the fire. The only sign of age was that he was a little deaf. His head looked larger and his body smaller than the last time I saw him.[1] Several times his face lit up with that roguish smile which distinguishes him when he is pleased or much amused. He talked freely and affably. His courtly ways are as characteristic as ever. He spoke of his own "twenty years of Toryism, the first ten from 1832 to 1842 in which year I entered the formative period of my Liberalism. In financial matters I was quite a Liberal; I had always been in favour of peace and economy, had supported the admission of Jews to Parliament, and had voted in favour of Maynooth and the Dissenters' Chapel Bill. So I was looked upon with suspicion by the Conservatives, but I did not formally sever my connection with my former Party until 1859. The last thing a man does is to remove his name from his Club;[2] I suppose that took place that year. You must remember that I was educated to regard liberty as an evil. I have learnt to regard it as a good. I have never been much in favour of change, but the changes of the last fifty years have been almost wholly for the good. About divorce I hold to my old position. Marriage seems to be a great mystery, one of the most wonderful things in the whole world. I think that we must fall back on the old saying that marriages are made in Heaven."

WALKING BY FAITH IN POLITICS. The old man went on: "I do not consider myself as an optimist even in political affairs. The more I see of government the more I am convinced that the duties of government will always be more or less imperfectly performed and government will become rather more than less difficult. Still, political progress has been almost wholly good. Free trade, for instance, has been almost wholly good. The work of the last half century has been that of emancipation. We have been emancipating, emancipating, that is all. To emancipate is comparatively easy. It is simple to remove restrictions, to allow natural forces

[1] H. M. Hyndman in *The Record of an Adventurous Life* says that Woolner, the sculptor, told him that 'Gladstone's head between the dates of two busts he made of him had increased a full quarter of an inch in circumference'.
[2] The Carlton.

free play. We have to face the problem of constructive legislation."

'On another point Gladstone said: "I do not see a development of brain power. I do not think we are stronger but weaker than the men of the Middle Ages. The men of the sixteenth century were stronger in brain power than our men. Of course Napoleon's brain was the strongest and most marvellous that was ever in a human skull. His intellect was colossal. I know of none more powerful or immense."

'With regard to politics he said emphatically that "to men engaged in politics it is necessary to walk by faith, not by sight. Therein lies the power of the cause of progress. It is the party of faith." He added, "I have committed suicide more frequently than any man in politics." '

Stead hinted that Gladstone might have been more encouraging to Empire expanders. 'Well you know,' he said, 'if you have a son who is somewhat forward and is too self-complacent and you have frequently to chide him for that, you do not like to increase his complacency by sounding his praises too much. You may allow it as a treat, but it ought not to be his bread. When I entered politics the Duke of Wellington and others were anti-Jingo to an extent which you cannot now imagine. It was Lord Palmerston who changed that.'

CONCERNING SHORTCOMINGS OF THE CLERGY. Speaking of the Church he said: 'The Church has been entirely metamorphosed and its whole spirit transformed. It is a new Church from what it was fifty years ago. The clergy look at everything from an entirely different standpoint. I think, however, that the clergy are not severe enough on their congregations. They do not lay to the souls and consciences of their hearers the moral obligations, and bring their whole lives and action to the bar of conscience. The class of sermons which I think most needed are of the class one of which so offended a certain peer long ago. Coming from the church in a mighty fume he said, "I have always been a supporter of the Church and I have always upheld the clergy. But this is really too bad, to hear a sermon in which the clergyman actually insisted upon applying religion to a man's private life." ' Stead spoke of Spurgeon. 'Yes', said Gladstone, 'he was a good and brave man. There is not enough of that searching preaching.' Before he left the subject of religion Gladstone said, 'I not only believe in a personal God but in a personal Devil. On spiritualism I am in the same way as my friend Mr. Balfour who made an investigation, and I have come to pretty much his conclusion.'

The final words of the veteran were: 'I have come more and more to believe in the mass of the people. They take a clearer and juster judgment, it may be because they have been saved from the temptations which have beset the cultured and wealthy, or it may be because of their circumstances. There is no doubt that in the past the mass has taken a juster view than the educated and wealthier.'

LORD ROSEBERY ON HIS OWN IGNORANCE. Here are a few sentences from ten pages of typescript of an interview Stead had at and after lunch with Lord Rosebery alone when he was Prime Minister. Rosebery spoke of 'the waste of time and character' in the House of Commons. 'You take the best men you can in the nation and you keep them kicking their heels for eight months in the lobbies and smoking rooms, doing nothing but being ready to vote when the division bell rings.' Stead replied that he would write an article on 'The Wasted Wealth of King Demos'. He said how glad he was that Rosebery had municipal training on the London County Council before he became Prime Minister. Rosebery replied 'If you knew how I prefer municipal work. Do you know what troubles me most in my new office and is my chief difficulty? Ignorance, Sir, sheer blank ignorance. I am confronted with a sense of my own ignorance.' Stead speaks of Rosebery's habit of cutting the pages of books—books were uncut then—while he chatted. During the foregoing interview he cut the pages of six.

THE MEETING OF THE POPES. On Stead's talk with the Pope, which does not seem to have amounted to much, that versatile humanitarian, Henry Salt, wrote for Bernard Shaw a poem of which Dr. Lowenstein kindly favoured me with a copy. In the half I print Salt makes Stead advise his Holiness to transfer himself from Rome to the New World and supplies the Pope's reply:

> Pope Leo, that most holy man,
> Was sitting in the Vatican,
> One afternoon from callers free,
> Sipping his sacerdotal tea:
>
> When, lo! he hears with sudden dread
> The name announced of William Stead,
> That journalistic pope, who's rather
> More holy than the Holy Father.
>
> "Friend William, what you hint is true;
> The world's too small for me and you.
> There's this alternative at least,
> That you, good friend, should journey East;
> May I suggest that you should go,
> With your *Pall Mall*, to Jericho?"

CARDINAL MANNING AND PETERLOO. In conversation with Stead, Manning, who was a strong Liberal, said that he could remember that a chalk mark was placed on his father's house to guide the mob which was to fire it because of the paternal stand against the repeal of the Corn Laws. 'We washed out the mark and, as a child in my crib, I heard the mob go roaring by. I remember the burning of Bristol at the time of the Reform demonstration. I also remember Peterloo.'[1] Stead records that the Cardinal, who always spoke with the utmost freedom with him, 'praised Bradlaugh and Mrs. Besant and said he liked General Booth and they got on very well together'.

GEORGE MEREDITH: 'THE ENGLISH NEED MORE OF THE CELT.' When Stead paid his second visit to George Meredith one message he got was: 'I hold as strongly as ever I did to the general onward sweep and the advancement of the human race, but the English need more of the Celt in them.' Stead said Morley was

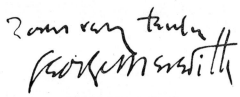

From a letter to Stead[2]

lacking in physical vitality and that if he could be crossed with John Burns it would be a good thing. Meredith said we ought to be 'the Eastern Star in the banner of the American Republic'.

RHODES'S WILLS AND STEAD'S PLACE IN AND OUT OF THEM. The facts about Stead's place in Rhodes's wills were kindly set out for me at length by Sir Francis Wylie, who was Oxford Secretary to the Rhodes Trustees from 1903 to 1931. Rhodes made seven wills. The six in Rhodes House Library, in Oxford, do not include the final one. Stead first appears in the fourth (March 5, 1891). In that will Rhodes says: 'I devise and bequeath my real and personal estate to the present Lord Rothschild and W. T. Stead of the *Review of Reviews* in equal shares as tenants in common, and, in the case of the death of either of them during my lifetime, then the whole to devolve on the survivor of them absolutely.' There is no 'trust'. The will itself says nothing as to how the money is to be used. This is characteristic of Rhodes in the drawing up of his wills. He meant those to whom he left the bulk of his property to have a free hand. During the year in which the will was drawn up,

[1] August 16, 1829. Several thousand people were peaceably gathered on ground now partly covered by the Free Trade Hall, Manchester, to petition for reform. Special constables with Hussars attacked the crowd. Eleven persons were killed and several hundreds injured.

[2] It has not seemed necessary on many succeeding pages to put a similar line below all the autographies reproduced from letters to Stead.

Rhodes sent Stead, as he had promised him, papers outlining his political ideas and hopes. This was meant to indicate what Stead should do when the fortune came under his control.

In 1892 Rhodes made his fifth will. It added Bourchier Hawksley (Rhodes's friend and solicitor) to the 'joint tenants absolutely'.

THE RHODES SCHOLARSHIPS. The next year Rhodes made his sixth will (Sept. 8, 1893). In it he instructs his trustees to found scholarships (36 in all) at Oxford for 'young Colonists'. (South Africa 9, Australia 18, Canada 6, New Zealand 3.) But, once provision is made for these scholarships, 'I give the residue of my real and personal estate unto the said Baron Rothschild, William Thomas Stead and Bourchier Hawksley'.

The final will (July 1, 1899) leaves Lord Rothschild out—he was put in to look after finance. The executors and trustees of this will, as first drawn up, were Lord Rosebery, Albert Lord Grey, Alfred Beit, Stead, Lewis Michell (afterwards Sir Lewis) of Cape Town, and Hawksley. They are to establish 100 scholarships for the U.S.A., 60 for the British Empire and, by a later codicil, 15 for Germany. There are other things they are to do, and legacies— but, after these are all provided for, the 'residue of my real and personal estate' is given to 'such of them as shall be living at my death absolutely as joint tenants'. Again no 'trust' as regards the residue.

'THE EXTRAORDINARY ECCENTRICITY OF MR. STEAD.' Stead remained in this will until Jan. 1901, when a codicil runs: 'On account of the extraordinary eccentricity of Mr. Stead, though always having a great respect for him, but feeling the objects of my will would be embarrassed by his views, I hereby revoke his appointment as one of my executors'. Milner was added by codicil in October 1901, and Jameson at the last minute of his life, in March 1902—he died on the 26th.

To sum up, Sir Francis writes: 'Of course both Stead and the other trustees, to whom the residue was left "absolutely", understood that that was done to give them a free hand in using it to further the purposes which they knew were Rhodes'. I remember Lord Rosebery saying to me in 1903 that, as far as he could make out, the trustees might vote each other their shares in the residue. And I happen to know that this is the view which the Inland Revenue took of the matter. So Stead was in that sense a "beneficiary" under four of Rhodes's wills—at any rate until the codicil of 1901. I wonder myself whether, had he chosen to—which of course he never would have done—Stead could, in law, have maintained that the codicil only removed him as an executor and trustee and not from the list of six or more persons to whom the "residue" was left.'

In *The Last Will and Testament of Cecil Rhodes*,[1] which Stead wrote, Hawksley is quoted as saying that 'the acquaintance of Stead, an acquaintance which ripened into a close intimacy and continued to the last, was sought by Mr. Rhodes. As Rhodes frequently said to me and others, including Mr. Stead himself, the friendship of the two men was too strong to be broken by passing differences on the South African War.' In a letter I have to Mr. Fairbairns Stead says, 'Although Mr. Rhodes removed me from being one of the executors, he didn't remove me from being joint heir to the residue of his estate. I may renounce it, but legally I am one of the heirs.'

WHERE DID RHODES GET HIS IDEAS? An American Rhodes Scholar, Mr. G. C. Huckaby, kindly sent me the following interesting extracts from a letter to him by Stead's son, the late Professor John Stead: 'My father developed Rhodes's ideas and grafted his own on them. This was one of my father's methods. When he found anyone who would work with him to forward his ideals and, as in the case of Rhodes, was in a better position to do so than he was himself, he managed to get them to work out his ideas by persuading them that they were really their own, and he let them have all the

credit because it was the end only that mattered to him. This was particularly the case with Rhodes's attitude to the U.S.A. Originally Rhodes's ideas were restricted entirely to the British Empire, but father inoculated him with the idea of extending it to the whole English-speaking world, and then gave him the whole credit.

'Rhodes would not have succeeded as well with his Chartered Company if it had not been for the support father gave him in England. Rhodes was bitterly disliked and distrusted by many of the leading people here, and, but for father's championship, he might never have got his charter, and never have acquired Rhodesia in the way he did. The obituary notice in *The Times*, which I am pretty certain was written by E. T. Cook, says, "The will of Rhodes impressed everybody with the marks of originality and imagination; it is not so generally known that the ideas were in a large measure

[1] *Review of Reviews*, 1902. This book, of 198 pages, has chapters devoted to the ideas, conversations, correspondence and speeches of Rhodes, with a large number of striking photographs of him from boyhood to the end of his career, and many photographs of the conspicuous South Africans with whom Rhodes was brought into contact. The photographs include portraits of the men associated with the Raid, and of Garrett, Milner and Hawksley.

Stead's." In H. W. Massingham's tribute are the words, "Without
Stead, Rhodes might have remained a local Colonial politician." '

After the death of Rhodes, Stead made close enquiry among those
who had been most closely associated with him from his college
days to the end of his life and found that to none of them had he
spoken 'as fully, as intimately and as frequently concerning his
aims and the purpose to which he wished his wealth to be devoted'.
Rhodes, 'brooding in intellectual solitude in the midst of the diamond
diggers of Kimberley', had been one of the most enthusiastic
readers of the *Pall Mall* from the day on which Stead became
editor in 1883 and began the advocacy of what he called 'the
Imperialism of responsibility' as opposed to Jingoism. Rhodes,
whose friendship with Gordon brought them closer, 'always
asserted', writes Stead in his full and interesting book, most of
which is devoted to Rhodes in other relations than his will-making,
'that his own ideas had been profoundly modified and modelled
by the *Pall Mall*'. On Stead's going to gaol over 'The Maiden
Tribute', the view of Rhodes was, 'Here is the man I want, one
who has not only the right principles but is more anxious to promote
them than to save his skin'. Rhodes went to Holloway Gaol and
drove away in a temper on being refused admission—an order
from the Home Office was required. He attended an Exeter Hall
meeting to protest against Stead's imprisonment and heard
Josephine Butler and Mrs. Fawcett. He was then thirty-five. An
illuminating account of Rhodes's ideas and personality, written by
Stead, appeared in the *Review of Reviews* as a Character Sketch in
October, 1899. Rhodes, in regard to his will, told Stead that he
was to decide as to the way in which his wealth should be used
and Rothschild and Hawksley were there to look after finance
and legal matters. 'I tell you everything, I tell you all my plans',
he said.

'WITH TENDERNESS'. TRAITS IN RHODES'S CHARACTER.
After the Raid, when the pair met, Rhodes, 'although more affectionate than he had ever been', did not disguise his disappointment
over Stead's having thrown himself so vehemently into the agitation
against the Boer War. He said: 'We three in South Africa, all of us
your boys, I myself, Milner and Garrett, all of whom learnt their
politics from you. We are on the spot and are unanimous in declaring
this War to be necessary. Instead of deferring to the judgment of
your own boys, you fling yourself into violent opposition. I should
not have acted in that way about an English or an American
question. I would have said, "No, I know Stead. I trust his judgment; he is on the spot?" ' Stead's rejoinder was that he had learnt
his South African politics from Rhodes who had always contended
that South Africa could not be ruled without the Dutch; 'I am

true to the original Cecil Rhodes'. 'Taking my hand in both of his with tenderness, he said: "Now I want you to understand that if in future you should unfortunately feel yourself compelled to attack me personally as vehemently as you have attacked my policy in this War, it will make no difference to our friendship. I am too grateful to you for all I have learned from you." ' Stead said that when Rhodes removed his name from the list of executors his phrase was 'I was too masterful' to work with the others.

Stead prints in full in his book Rhodes's correspondence with Parnell and the Liberal party in connection with his gifts in support of Home Rule, and typical extracts from his speeches. Old General Booth and his son and successor, Bramwell Booth, Stead says, were greatly impressed by Rhodes, and Bramwell spoke of him as having 'a great human heart, hungry for love'. Just as Gordon had always with him a little pocket edition of Thomas à Kempis, so Rhodes carried a dog-eared and pencil-scored Marcus Aurelius. Light on the man's character is to be found in a story told by Lord Grey which Stead records. Grey had ridden out into the country with Rhodes in order to tell him bad news. 'I must give you a rather ugly knock', he said. 'Out with it', said Rhodes. 'Groote Schuur (Rhodes's house in which he delighted) is burnt down'. 'Thank God, thank God!' exclaimed Rhodes. 'I thought you were going to tell me Dr. Jim was dead. The house is burnt down—what does that matter? We can rebuild it but if Dr. Jim had died I should never have got over it.' He had known Jameson for many years and his affection for him was not abated by his 'upsetting the apple cart' with his Raid. A favourite saying of Rhodes's was, 'Do the comparative thing; always do the comparative'. Stead reports him: 'When inclined to take too tragic a view of disaster, I reflect on what the Roman Emperors must have felt when (as often happened) their legions were scattered and they fled from a stricken field. It must have seemed that their world was going to pieces around them. But the sun rose the next day, the rivers flowed between their banks, and the world went on very much the same. And thinking of this I used to go to bed and sleep like a child.' Rhodes 'as a millionaire, a bachelor and a man of charming personality', Stead chronicles, 'was absolutely hunted by many ladies', but was singularly free from any sex scandal.

His death was a distressing one, with agonising pain from his heart. One of his last exclamations was, 'So much to do, so little done!' His last word was 'Jameson'. He lies in a wilderness of granite in the far Matopo Hills, at a commanding spot which he had named 'The View of the World'. The Matabele, whose first monarch, Umzilikazi, is buried there, call it 'The House of the Guardian Spirit'.

ANGLO-AMERICAN UNDERSTANDING. RHODES OR STEAD?
'I have always felt most strongly', wrote Professor John Stead in a
letter to the Rhodes Scholar in Louisiana, Mr. Huckaby, to whom
I have referred, 'that full justice has never been done to the part
played by my father in moulding and influencing Rhodes's ideas.
There is a simple explanation of this. Rhodes died just after the
end of the Boer War and was at the time one of the most popular
persons in England. Father had been the leading pro-Boer in the
country, with the result that he was anathema to most people.
Therefore there was the natural endeavour to minimise or ignore
the relationship between one who was looked upon in the light of
a hero and one of the most disliked men of the time. This attitude
lasted for a long time after Rhodes's death. A result was that in
the various biographies of Rhodes my father is ignored or only
given a slight mention. Only in the life by Mrs. Millin is father
given any considerable space, but even she does not do him full
justice. This belittling of my father seems to have continued, because
when I had a talk with Lord Lothian when he was secretary to the
trustees, he seemed to have little knowledge of the relationship of
my father to Rhodes. I did persuade him to let me present a
photograph of my father to Rhodes House.[1] It is absolutely certain
that it was my father who persuaded Rhodes to include Americans
in the scholarships, and was responsible for arousing Rhodes's
interest in the United States.' Ultimately, Stead writes in his book,
that Rhodes became 'colour-blind between the British Empire and
the American Republic, the first statesman to grasp the sublime
conception of the essential unity of the race'.[2]

Sir Francis Wylie tells me that, when Stead spoke to the Rhodes
Scholars, 'his emotion was obvious'. What was the effect on the
execution of Rhodes's purposes of the elimination of Stead from
the list of executors of Rhodes's will? On this Professor Stead writes
in the long letter to Mr. Huckaby to which I have referred; 'My
father always said that he was very glad Rhodes had removed him,
as he was certain that he would always have been up against his
co-trustees because he was imbued with Rhodes's ideas and was

---

[1] Sir Francis Wylie writes to me: 'It hangs in the left wing occupied by the
Warden (who is also secretary to the Rhodes trustees).'

[2] *Rhodes Scholars' unusual qualifications as drafted by Rhodes:* There are several pages
in Stead's book giving an account of conversations between Rhodes, Hawksley
and himself and, later, Lord Rosebery, as to the qualifications for a scholarship.
Rhodes is thus reported: 'My three things, you know how I put them. First, I
am all against letting the scholarships merely to people who swot over books,
who have spent all their time over Latin and Greek. But you must allow the
element which I call "smug", which means scholarship. That is to stand for four-
tenths. Then there is "brutality", which stands for two-tenths. Then there is tact
and leadership, again two-tenths, and then there is "unctuous rectitude", two-
tenths. That makes up the whole.'

the only person with whom Rhodes had discussed them fully, and the others had only a superficial knowledge of them. On one occasion my father was asked to address the scholars on Rhodes and his ideals. He came back absolutely disgusted. Firstly, because most of the men got drunk, but chiefly from conversations he had with some of them; they seemed to know nothing of Rhodes, his ideals or the reason why he founded the scholarships. He protested to the trustees. They were apparently only interested in carrying out the material side of the scheme and handing out the money and were not interested in the ideal side. My father vowed he would never go to another Founder's Day and, as far as I know, he never did.'

WHAT THE RHODES FUNDS ARE DOING TODAY. On this Sir Francis Wylie writes to me:

It is within my own knowledge that the trustees have created a number of new scholarships over and above those left by Rhodes—seven annual scholarships (tenable nowadays for two years, with the chance of a third year if recommended) in Canada; four in South Africa; one in New Zealand; as well as triennial (if that means filled up every third year) scholarships for Malta, East Africa, India, Pakistan. Scholarships are now worth £500 p.a. instead of the £300 of Rhodes's Will. (Four of the new scholarships in the British Empire came out of money saved by the cancellation of German scholarships during the 1914–1918 War. On the other hand, in 1929, the trustees created two annual scholarships for Germans. I suppose it is possible that they may do that again when sufficient time has elapsed since the war with Germany.) The trustees have also made some large donations to the University of Oxford (as well as one or two minor ones). They founded a chair of Roman Dutch Law (to attract legally-minded Dutch students from South Africa); they gave £100,000 to the University Appeal Fund; and they built Rhodes House, of which the main part is for the benefit of Oxford, including the Library which houses a section of the Bodleian and is staffed, warmed, lighted, etc., by the trustees. They also make a yearly contribution for the purchase of books. They have evidently regarded any improvement of Oxford as in the interests of Rhodes Scholars.

I have also this letter from the present Secretary of the Rhodes Trust, Lord Elton:

If Stead expressed misgivings as to the use by the Rhodes Trustees of funds outside the Scholarships themselves, they have not been justified. There have never been very extensive funds available for use apart from the Scholarships, save, in comparatively recent years, in South Africa. Here there is a fund which, under South African law, can only be used for charitable and educational purposes in South Africa, and out of it grants have been given to a number of schools and universities and good causes of various kinds, including the furtherance of native education and welfare. The extra-scholarship funds in England have been comparatively limited but have been available for a considerably longer period and, apart from giving occasional assistance to deserving cases among Rhodes Scholars themselves, they have been used, broadly speaking, to promote the welfare of the British Commonwealth and its good relations with the U.S.A. This has covered grants for research, the Imperial Institute's lectures scheme, the welfare of overseas troops during the war, and numerous kindred objects. These grants cover many individual organisations but have not been publicised. Also from time to time the trustees have made themselves responsible for more conspicuous charitable or educational undertakings, such as the Rhodes lectures delivered in Oxford on a number of occasions before the War by lecturers of world renown such as General Smuts, or the Rhodes Travelling Fellowships which enabled Oxford dons to visit and study various parts of the Commonwealth, or the foundation of two Chairs in Imperial subjects.

Lord Freyberg, Governor-General, New Zealand, made a plea on July 25 this year for adherence 'closely to the terms of the will of Rhodes. It is not the concern of the scholarship trust board to extend the boundaries of knowledge and science. Rather the trust should seek out, encourage and send forward good all-round men —men of the stuff of which leaders and teachers are made.'

LADY DILKE AND HER HUSBAND. On this subject there are half a dozen foolscap pages in the handwriting of Stead's secretary, Underhill. Most of the pages are occupied by an account of a long and painful talk with Lady Dilke, who had asked Stead to see her. He told Lady Dilke that, if her husband remained a private citizen, discharging his everyday duties, he would not say another word in the *Pall Mall*, but that, if he took his position as a public man in the House of Commons, he was compelled to protest. 'All I ask', said Lady Dilke, 'is silence and hope'. Stead was very gentle with her. At one point she said plainly that 'a heavy burden lay on her heart because she had brought all this trouble on her husband by trying to wean him from his worldly life; that, if she had only let him go on with his intrigues and life of pleasure, none of the trouble would have come upon him; and it made her doubt whether it was not better to let men go on in their vice rather than try to raise them to a higher life.' 'It was pitiable, ghastly', Stead writes, 'to see her sobbing.' He adds that, when he dined with his friend Lewis, who was his own solicitor as well as Dilke's and a friend, Lewis said, 'I would wish you to believe that Dilke is innocent, but, as an honest man, I cannot tell you that I think he is'. Stead records that Reginald Brett said to him that 'he was very certain nothing could be done for Dilke. He was quite sure that he had always been a very sensual man and that his forwardness, to use no stronger word, to Lady Randolph Churchill led to a vehement attack by Lord Randolph on Dilke in the House for which no one was prepared. Dilke was excluded from the Churchills' house.' Moreton Frewen, a brother-in-law of Lady Randolph's, said to Stead that 'he knew two or three other ladies who had been treated in the same way'. Sir Charles Mills believed that 'Dilke had had six intrigues going on at once'. By the way, in another note, Stead mentions that John Morley told him 'as a great secret' that Sir Charles Dilke, who was well-off, had it in mind at one time to start a London evening newspaper, with a preliminary six months' experience in the *Pall Mall*, the *St. James's* or *Globe* office. Stead adds that Brett told him that 'one of the Queen's ladies mentioned that Her Majesty, who read the *Pall Mall* every night, sympathised very keenly with "The Maiden Tribute".'

Sir Henry Irving

CHAPTER XVII

LETTERS FROM THE FAMOUS[1]

1. POLITICIANS

GLADSTONE'S OBJECTIONS TO A WOMAN ON A ROYAL COMMISSION. Gladstone's correspondence with Stead is remarkable. It began in 1876 when Stead was the young editor of the *Northern Echo* and it continued for fifteen years. Stead writes at length but Gladstone writes at length also. There are several dozen letters from him. Many extend to more than four pages of ordinary letter paper and one or two to several sheets of foolscap. The courtesy of the old man and the characteristic way in which he never spares words in order to convey the impression he wishes to make are noteworthy. I have room for little more than isolated phrases: 'I will, with your permission, be silent.' 'I have been too much in personal conflict with Lord Beaconsfield to be altogether a fair judge of incidents connected with his utterance!' 'I drop these remarks, from which it may be better not to quote now as my name is rather often before the public, but the acute discernment with which you write needs no help from me'. 'Were I in the place of editor of your paper I should take the following for my general clew' (*sic*). 'There is great force in reserve'. 'To me it seems to pour water on sand'. 'My hopes as to Russia are that she will make a clean job of Slav redemption, that she will not be unkind to the Hellenes, that she will secure ample recompense for good, gallant, glorious Montenegro, that she will not mar a glorious work by taking back the little Danubian bit of Bessarabia'. 'We have behaved extremely ill to Russia'. 'You will, I presume, come up to town to prosecute this matter and I shall be most ready to see you'. 'My Eastern papers will be left in such a state that you can see them even when I am out of town.' 'Lord Grey is one of those whose displeasure I can always bear without anger because any emotion of that kind is at once suppressed by my admiration for his unflinching courage and unvarying rectitude of purpose'. 'I do not know whether you will have the desire or the courage to face a further supply of Eastern letters which I found since seeing you'. 'Old heads are not the best for taking in new ideas, nor is an overfilled warehouse well adapted for receiving at once additional

---

[1] This is the pith of a few of the hundreds of letters received by Stead which I have had the satisfaction of reading—often, it is true, with some trouble with a magnifying glass. They were written to Stead at various stages of his career.

and large supplies of goods'. 'I am conscious of having fallen behind the age in point of Colonial information'. A very long letter is on the Baccarat affair, 'a serious event', Gladstone calls it. He has had proofs of Stead's *Review of Reviews* article on the Prince of Wales. 'Though I am an obsolete Prime Minister this subject has weighed incessantly on my mind. I should send proofs to Lord Salisbury and should put it to him that the public is entitled to know what advice he, as Prime Minister, tenders in the Tranby-Croft case.'

ON A 'LYING WENCH'. A letter of Easter Sunday, 1887, says: 'Rumour is, to speak plainly, a lying wench and well worthy to be the wife of the Father of it. She has moreover a special spite against me and has given me from many sides a heap of this material for our Easter Sunday treat. She fibs.' A sentence from one of several well-filled postcards has the sentence, 'I am afraid you err in estimating my capacity of work by your own.'

Miss Mary Gladstone says her father would like to know if a pension would be acceptable to Octavia Hill, the housing reformer. There is also a private and confidential letter from Sir Francis Knollys saying that the Prince of Wales, 'of his own accord and in furtherance of what he considered would be for the advantage of the Royal Commission for the Housing of the Poor', wrote to Gladstone urging him to put Octavia Hill and Goschen upon it, and that Gladstone replied stating that 'for various reasons, the principal one being that the Government thought that it would form an inconvenient precedent were a lady to be placed on a Royal Commission, he hoped the Prince would not press the matter. Mr. Goschen has, however, been invited.' In a letter from Lord Rosebery is this passage: 'I am glad you gave it to the wily old man. Alas! superior in guile to the editor of the *P.M.G.*'

LIVELY SCRAPS FROM LORD ROSEBERY. The stack of letters from Lord Rosebery from which I take scraps numbers eighty-three. Four-fifths are in his own hand, and in every other letter there is an invitation to Stead to come to see him—'my convenience must meet yours'. Among letters begging a visit is this: 'I think our meeting will never come off unless I take a stand-and-deliver line'. Another time it is, 'I shall sit in the porter's chair till you arrive for I have a footman of phenomenal perversity'. Again, 'as soon as I return to London I shall send you a summons'. 'Nothing under a corporal's guard with fixed bayonets would make me face a camera'. He has 'a particular reason, which I will tell you, why I would rather not have my picture of Charles I photographed'. In a heavily black-bordered letter he says, 'I cannot follow you into Borderland'. 'I am very doubtful as to your seeing Dawson [his trainer] for he is ill, unnerved and 75'. 'I cannot agree with

you in wishing Ladas [Derby winner] had never been foaled. He
has afforded me the few gleams of sunshine in my life during the
last eighteen months'. 'I enjoyed our talk very much, more than
any that I have had for a long time, for it was very human. Brett
and Lady Warwick are here, so you have a good percentage of
friends on the spot'. 'At times one is haunted by a word or a saying
and then it dies away and gives place to another or a blank. Since
I have been Prime Minister the word most present to me is Pitt's
saying that the quality most required is patience'! 'I see that in
your irrepressible passion for paradox you have been standing up
for H.M.'s First Minister. This is going too far and may lead you
into trouble'. In reference to a Keir Hardie proposal he says, 'I wish
I were unemployed'. 'I hear you are not well: a steam engine like
yourself has no business to be out of gear.' 'I cannot promise a
regular contribution for three years to the Women's Liberal
Federation, but I send a donation of £100.' One appointment is
for 'my dressing room, Berkeley Square'. 'A drawback of indisposition is a chronic chaos of papers. They lie like a miser's treasure,
in old stockings, beds, chimneys and so forth. Berkeley Square is
no longer an address of mine—it is merely a whited sepulchre.'
'I am strong enough if I could only get regularly half a night's
sleep. I have tried every opiate but the House of Lords. Exciting
talk is one of my banes! The world is tumbling about in great
billows, one ugly crest after another. We may be on the brink of
immense events [the date is April 1895]. All this does not aid
sleep, but then vigilance is required, and vigilant means wakeful.'
'John Burns was here at The Durdans yesterday—very pleasant and
indeed fascinating'. 'I did at length face the huge shapeless bale of
printed matter (proofs) that you sent me. I found that by taking
it out shooting I could read it at the covert side'. 'I have enquired
twice as to your arrival in London. It appears to me you come to
London when everybody else leaves it.' 'I enjoyed our last talk;
it was so downright, and I should like another'. 'You need not be
afraid of my shutting myself up in London Society unless under
judicial sentence to that effect'. 'I saw Rhodes in Paris.' 'I have
reason to believe that you are a traitor and have been planning a
character sketch of me. Such a sketch, heinous were I in public
life, is criminal now that I am out of it!' 'I trembled when I saw
your envelope for I feared you were asking me to declare my faith
in the United States of Europe.' (The date is 1898.) 'I wrote to
you some time ago to suggest a talk, a proposal which you ignored.
Nevertheless I now propose a meeting some time in the week
beginning May 1.' 'I can well understand a lover of liberty following
Cromwell up to the time when he cut the King's head off, and then
becoming his opponent.' 'You take a somewhat one-sided view of

the horrors of war.' 'Many thanks for your benevolent letter!' He is obliged by a copy of *Review of Reviews* 'disagreeing with me; I wish you could have sent me a number in which you agreed with me, a rarer number!' Afterwards he writes: 'I have been a regular sub- scriber from the beginning, disinterested homage which I think you should appreciate'. Of a speech at Sheffield: 'If I had denounced Chamberlain I should have elicited great enthusiasm, but I am not much in the philippic line and I am less and less so every day I live.'

LORD SALISBURY'S CONFIDENCES ABOUT CHURCHILL AND RUSSIA. In reading the letters of Lord Salisbury one feels that he had respect for Stead, believed in his sincerity and, perhaps remembering the freedom he himself took in his early days of *Saturday Review*-ing, understood his onslaughts. In a letter of 1892 he says: 'I should be very unreasonable indeed if I had any fault to find with your estimate of my work. I have been very fortunate in one respect, the singular calmness and discernment of the states- man who had charge of Russian foreign policy. In one respect I was very unfortunate. During the first six months of the six years foreign affairs were in the hands of Lord Iddesleigh, whose powers were already seriously weakened (though I did not know it) by the disease which killed him. The consequence of this was that the first division between us and Germany [in Africa] was not well managed and we lost Kilimanjaro. Of course I was constitutionally responsible.' In one letter he thinks Stead underrates, in reference to a certain Bill, 'the conversational powers of the House of Com- mons'; in another he says he has 'never had experience of a more imaginative body of men than telegraphic correspondents'.

To a seven-page letter about Lord Randolph Churchill's resigna- tion, is appended 'Not confidential, but do not say or let it be known that I have been in communication with you'. The letter runs:

Rather more than a week ago he informed me that unless the total of the Army and Navy Estimates was very considerably below the total of last year, he would not continue to be Chancellor of the Exchequer. After considerable discussion with the Departments he resigned his office in a letter I received on Tuesday. [The letter is dated 'Friday.'] I answered his arguments and said that I could not take the responsibility of refusing the heads of the War department and the Admiralty the sums which, after prolonged consideration, they thought necessary for the defence of the country. Least of all could I refuse the funds necessary for defending our ports and coaling stations—which was the point to which Lord R.C. had taken the most objection. He replied by a letter, which I received here after one o'clock on Wednesday night or Thursday morning, in which he confirmed his intention of resigning and mentioned, much in the language used in the communiqué to *The Times*, his dissatisfaction with our legislative intentions. He had not before alluded to this subject to me in connection with his resignation. A few hours later I saw the announcement in *The Times*.

It is not the case that the Estimates proposed by the War Office and Admiralty were very large. My only fear on hearing of them was that they were insufficient.'

BALFOUR, MORLEY AND STEAD. I had not realised until I came upon a large envelope full of letters from A. J., afterwards Lord Balfour that he and Stead were on such cordial terms. Here, for example, is a letter from Stead (1887) on Balfour's appointment to the Irish Chief Secretaryship:

Quintus Curtius Balfour henceforth to be known in History! My dear friend, permit me to congratulate you with sorrow not unmingled with pride. I am proud to think of your heroism. I am sorry for your fate. Oh why did an unkind Providence make you so sensitive, so delicate and then thrust you into the navvy's work of Irish Administration! I took the news to Morley and we both were very sorry.

I am in the opposite camp—perhaps one of the most truculent of your opponents. But I want to help you more as a man than I want to mar you as a Minister. To do the first I will now really try in earnest, which will enable you to leave the Irish Office with honour before it kills you. And in the meantime if I can help you in any way, or can be useful in any humble conduit-pipe capacity, so as to lessen the friction and the wear and tear of an impossible position, pray remember that I am yours to command.

Three years later there is this, 'I lunched with Morley and it was very curious to listen to his emphatic eulogy of yourself'.

One letter from Balfour begins, 'A great many more people will read your electoral programme than will read my speeches', a second, 'I am surprised to hear that you desire to see so humble an individual after having associated with all the crowned heads of Europe'.

THE TRUTH ABOUT CHAMBERLAIN AND THE JAMESON RAID. It was a feature of the friendship between Balfour and Stead that they spoke their minds to one another. In one letter, for instance, Balfour charges Stead with 'what theologians describe as "invincible ignorance" in regard to Chamberlain and South Africa'. 'I believe I know all the facts about his conversations, telegrams, etc., before, during, and after the Raid, and I can assure you that the idea that he was in any way connected with it is wholly illusory'. Stead writes to Balfour, 'Since Dilke took the Sacrament to prove he did not commit adultery there has not been anything quite so bad as Chamberlain's evidence yesterday [at the South Africa Committee].' Stead writes further, and the letter is worth reproducing in full because it states clearly what many people do not know, the gravamen of the charge made against Chamberlain:

So far from alleging that Mr. Chamberlain was privy to the Raid, I have contradicted that in the strongest possible terms. What is not covered by your letter is the fact that Mr. Chamberlain and the Colonial Office—meaning by that Sir Robert Meade and Mr. Edward Fairfield—were continuously informed as to the preparations to support the insurrection in Johannesburg from the outside by aid of the Chartered Company and the mounted police, which were made over to Mr. Rhodes in order that they might be used for that purpose.

Mr. Chamberlain, not content with assenting to Mr. Rhodes's plan for supporting the insurrection from the outside by stationing troops on the frontier, spoiled the plan by insisting that the movement should take place under the British flag. Thereby he did his best to convert a movement for obtaining a reformed Republic, with political rights for the Outlanders, into an attempt to seize the Transvaal for Great Britain. This it was that wrecked the whole plan. But for that fatal insistence on the British flag—which, apart from any private knowledge which I may possess and which therefore cannot be used, seems to me the only possible inference to draw from the few cablegrams which were produced when they are read in connection with subsequent events—the plan might have succeeded.

I make one more appeal to you to see for yourself Mr. Fairfield's memorandum upon the cablegrams, of which Mr. Chamberlain produced only one, and the Hawkesley correspondence, which you have refused to produce in the House of Commons, but which afford written evidence as to what Mr. Rhodes believed to be the truth of the matter.

It is a thousand pities the conspiracy did not succeed. At least one-half of the Boers would have been delighted to have seen General Joubert become President in the place of Kruger, and in that case all our subsequent difficulties would have disappeared. But that bright hope was blighted by the insistence upon the British flag. The matter is very serious, and every day the War lasts it will become more serious, for this affair is not going to stop where it is.

One would like to know what Stead proposed to say to Chamberlain in the interview he sought in 1898.

A REMARKABLE LETTER TO CHAMBERLAIN. This was written by hand on Dec. 15:

SIR,

I am in receipt of your letter stating that you do not think any useful purpose would be served by a personal interview.

This I can understand, because you do not know why I wish to see you or what I have to tell you.

Believe me when I assure you that personally I shrink from meeting you on many grounds, but as an Englishman I am ready to submit to any indignity or humiliation you may choose to inflict upon me, if only you will allow me to see you and to explain certain matters which I can only tell in confidence. I think it due to the country which we love that a Minister of the Crown so influential and forceful as yourself should know at first hand how things actually stand.

I have had one hour and 25 minutes with Lord Salisbury, two hours and a half with Mr. Balfour, an hour and a half with Lord Curzon, an hour with Lord George Hamilton and three quarters of an hour with the Prince of Wales whom I have to see again next week.

I shall be in Birmingham tomorrow and if you will re-consider your decision and telegraph me to the Post Office, Birmingham, I will wait upon you when and where you please.

Only I implore you for the sake of all the causes to which you are devoted, do not refuse me the opportunity of seeing you and delivering to your own ears what I have to say.

I do not ask you to say one single word by way of greeting, or of farewell, nor do I wish to ask you any questions. The audience can be conducted on your side in absolute silence.

I am,
Yours truly,
W. T. STEAD.[1]

In an early letter to Stead (1885) before the Crawford case, Sir Charles Dilke speaks of the *Pall Mall* 'attacking with extraordinary bitterness and unfairness a man to whom I am bound by the closest ties of personal affection' i.e. Chamberlain. But he adds that 'as that friend told me of his having forgiven you, there is no reason why I should not correspond with you if you please to honour me with your confidence'.

SHADES OF THE EMPRESS CATHERINE AND BEACONSFIELD. A letter from Stead to Balfour after some jar says: 'I am so sorry. I thought I wrote in love. But do not let the old year end without receiving my sincere expression of regret if I have said one unkind word of one who has been a good friend'. In January 1909 Stead writes: 'You remember I spoke to you about the Empress Catherine. She wrote the enclosed article automatically by hand, in the second part of which she allowed my personality to obtrude more than in the first part and the third. I put the statistics in the third part, otherwise it was all written automatically.' Towards the end of the year Stead writes about 'a series of communications which have been received from 'the august shade of Lord Beaconsfield'.

CANDID 'C.B.' There are two dozen cordial, candid, and often witty letters from Sir Henry Campbell-Bannerman in a pleasant

---

[1] VAN DER POEL'S EXPOSURE. After this book had gone to the printers Jean van der Poel published a scholarly, temperate survey of the now available papers of two men who have their place in South African history, Sir Graham Bower and Sir James Rose Innes, *The Jameson Raid* (Oxford University Press, 1951). These papers are a devastating exposure of the exaggerated grievances of the uitlanders and the humbug about the danger to 'the girls of the gold-reef city', of the knowledge possessed by official and unofficial London of the plans being made against the Transvaal from the Chartered Company's territory, of the extent to which, in his public statements, Chamberlain economised the truth, and of the way in which the South Africa Committee in Westminster Hall hushed up the facts in the mistaken belief that revelations would make international difficulties.

handwriting. They go back to 1900. What Stead proposes to print on one matter is, C.B. says, 'sufficiently near the truth'. Something else C.B. has sent to Stead is 'written merely to confirm you in the faith'. He stands sturdily by his phrase about 'methods of barbarism' in the Boer War, and adds, 'I am still, after all said and done, more concerned about the state of things the war will leave behind than about the war itself.' An article Stead has written about him 'makes me almost proud of myself'. He is going to do what he can about the indexing of *Hansard*, he is grateful for a packet of some specific, and, as to an article sent him, 'I hasten to acknowledge it before I have time to read it lest I should have to say I differ from it'. He understands Stead's 'general rule against dinner engagements' but three Ministers are coming to his party 'and if you saw your way to make an exception, you would meet good men and give me much pleasure'.

MRS. ASQUITH ON HER HUSBAND, MILNER AND STEAD. 'Someone pulled your leg', she writes from Downing Street in pencil, 'when he said my husband was merry. You cannot exactly say this, can you? You could say he has not high vitality but is a very real hero and saint. Next time you write about my husband put as his motto the Scottish phrase, "They have said, what say they? let them say"'. And this note goes on: 'I don't want to be loved at memorial services. Give it all to me here now and say what you like when I am gone. The reason the dead are praised is often funk. Men like those we were speaking of don't see people or things whole but scarlet if they hate them, mauve or grey if they are indifferent, and silver or gold when they agree with them or like them. Now you have always known that Gordon was a

confirmed opium eater, and consequently often muddled, although always a great or a rare man. I have never known the West End right on any subject. I like lots of people who never agree with me, and I am even fond of Milner with whom I have never agreed on anything. I like you but do I agree with you? People's opinions should not become obsessions and go to their heads and poison their blood and turn good people into malignants.'

In a note in January 1909, marked 'Strictly Confidential' Mr. Asquith says that if Stead is contemplating an article on 'mutual disarmament between Germany and England I would venture earnestly to urge you to abandon it or postpone it. I speak with full knowledge and an equally full sense of responsibility when I say that the cause which you and I have at heart is at this moment more likely to be prejudiced than advanced by public advocacy.'

'THE CHRISTIAN MEMBER FOR NORTHAMPTON' AND THE PIGOTT CHILDREN. Henry Labouchere, 'Labby', proprietor of *Truth*, the Puck of F.C.G's cartoons, 'the Christian member for Northampton' he was dubbed when Bradlaugh was his colleague in its representation, was always sending House of Commons gossip. In regard to one piece of information, sent in 'the strictest confidence' he says: 'I rely on your denying that you got it from me even if on the rack. Might it not be brought into a leading article?' He says with his accustomed candour, 'Very few Englishmen care for Home Rule, but will vote for the Bill in order to get rid of the subject and the Irish'. Stead was trying to get some money together for the children of Pigott, the man over whose forged letters *The Times* got itself into such trouble. Sir Henry James (one of the counsel in *The Times* case) was very sorry for the children and said he would give something but did not wish it to be known. 'I told him', writes Labouchere, 'that I thought that *The Times* ought to give something, and he rather agreed with me but said that it might imply collusion. I think I will try and arrange something. Parnell thinks that Archbishop Walsh would be a good man ultimately to send the money to. I enclose my cheque. These Catholics have a lot of institutions abroad and they might send the children there, for they will remain marked in Ireland, poor creatures!'

PARTY-LESS CHURCHILL. Lord Randolph Churchill writes in purple ink from Egypt: ' "To play the great game" in Ireland to which you invite me two things are essential, a party and a majority. I have not even the first. Lord Salisbury has both. Why don't he begin?' He adds, 'If ever you want to spend a pleasant six weeks of winter, life on a Nile dahabeah is an ideal existence.'

THE CONFIDENCES OF JAMES BRYCE. James Bryce wrote many letters when in office and when Ambassador in Washington. I have looked through at least sixty, all marked by regard and respect. He recalls the fact, interesting to note along with the story told on another page, that as early as 1883 he urged the Oxford authorities to make arrangements for attracting American and Colonial students, 'but to no purpose. Rhodes's ideas are his and yours.' He says (1894) that Chicago is 'an extraordinary phenomenon, not less wonderful than Babylon must have seemed to an envoy from the court of Hezekiah'. He is interested in Stead's publication *Help*, and likes not the least the parts which will be called 'unpractical'. He thinks courage 'the finest gift a public man can have'. Speaking of Stead's editing of Madame Novikoff's reminiscences, he says 'the period of resistance to Disraeli's pro-

Turkish policy was practically the last time the Liberal Party acted as a whole. There were a good many Tories, like old Spencer Walpole, who entirely disapproved of Disraeli's policy. Mr. Gladstone never did anything better or more finely in manner than in stopping the pro-Turkish movement. The Boer War has made me feel what a pernicious power the Press has in conveying wrong impressions of facts; it is not the arguments of the papers that work the mischief. Your collection of South African facts will one day bring shame to many a cheek'. He listened to Stead at some public meeting and writes, 'Your speech was as impressive as any I ever heard'. Bryce had heard, of course, the best speakers of his time on both sides of the Atlantic.

HALDANE ON 'JOHN BULL'S UGLY UNDER-JAW'. From a batch of letters from Haldane, who says that for ten years he has been 'living more or less in the executive engine room': 'For you the cause is want of morals, for me want of knowledge'. 'John Bull has an ugly underjaw, concealed by the pot out of which he is generally drinking peacefully, while his leaders are preaching to him. He needs a great deal of teaching, guiding, leading. He counts by deeds, and deeds are difficult in the doing. Well, we have got to do them—that's all.' On shields for soldiers, 'The shields stop bullets, but their weight and expense are disadvantages which, in the opinion of the Master of the Ordnance, preponderate over any advantage they would afford'.

REDMOND, GEORGE WYNDHAM AND THE IRISH. John Redmond, M.P., leader of the Irish Nationalist Party, often wrote to Stead, who had written in the *Review of Reviews* of George Wyndham's scheme to 'prepare for the advent of the new day when Ireland will be the landing stage and central clearing house of the commerce of the Old World and the New, the prosperous and flourishing middleman between Uncle Sam and John Bull'. There are a dozen pages of quarto in the handwriting of Wyndham when he was Chief Secretary for Ireland, written in anticipation of a walk. He hopes Stead's *Daily Paper*[1] will be 'an instrument of grace to the graceful, ingenious, contentious, fascinating and exasperating grown-up children of Ireland who

> Fight like devils for conciliation
> And hate each other for the love of God.'

2. AN ARISTOCRAT WITH A HEART AND ASPIRATIONS

WARWICK CASTLE AND EASTON LODGE. It is like my old days in Essex to come upon a large packet of letters from the late Countess of Warwick—whom my wife and I consider to have been

[1] See page 246.

the most beautiful woman we have known—a woman with a large heart, an endowment of brains and no notion of economics, ever eager to be doing a good turn for somebody or something and not always quite knowing what it ought to be.[1] One early note to Stead, when she was still Lady Brooke—she is his 'in true friend-ship'—says, 'I can never be thankful enough for a friendship that helps me more than you can imagine to lead the life I wish in the future'. Another note testifies to 'some words you said when we last met which have sunk into my heart'. Some verses sent to Stead from China 'I handed to the Prince who will give them to his son. My "Parishioner" [her usual name to Stead for the Prince of Wales, afterwards Edward VII] was very glad to spend those few quiet days at Easton, but I think he is rather jealous of your influence on my life and thoughts!' As Lady Warwick she says that 'the average Englishman is behind in enthusiasm for our American cousins', and that Lady Randolph Churchill is keen about something Stead has written. 'She comes here [Warwick Castle] on Wednesday, also the Duchess of Marlborough, Lady Essex, Mrs. George N. Curzon, and Mrs. M. Herbert, all lovely American ladies to meet the Parishioner! So we ought to do something. Can't you write me a letter to show? The Russian Ambassador, the Duke of Devonshire, George Curzon and Henry Chaplin are also coming'.

I find a memorandum of hers pencilled before the days of Women's Institutes entitled 'A Rough Idea of a Victorian Associa-tion of Women, with a Central Board in every County and Branches in every Parish, members in every home, to be what the Queen has been to the realm at large, a centre working for Peace, Progress and Social Well-being'. The Countess has been reading *Borderland* which Stead has sent her, and says she feels she is too practical a person for spirits to feel much sympathy with her. She asks for a few notes of what she might say in the local paper 'about standing as a Guardian here'.

In May 1900 she has not been in London for ages 'except to see Mr. Rhodes', whom she thought depressed, and has just come back from a co-operative conference at Leeds—'how delightfully enthu-siastic the North Country worker is!' She has 'the Australian Federa-tion delegates coming to Warwick Castle and I want to welcome them under this old roof that has sheltered so many great deeds and dark deeds, but is now gathering all that tends to goodwill and

[1] Her engaging book, *Life's Ebb and Flow* (Hutchinson, 1919) begins: 'I am descended on one side from Nell Gwyn; on the other from Oliver Cromwell. The Nell in me is all discretion. The Noll would fain be heard.' When as Lady Brooke she was eighteen, Queen Victoria favoured a marriage with Prince Leopold but Lady Brooke preferred the manly, handsome Earl of Warwick, and she was married, with Prince Leopold as best man and in the presence of half a dozen other members of the Royal Family, in Westminster Abbey.

peace'. Will Stead not think out a pretty sentence or two of welcome? He has a standing invitation to Warwick and Easton.

'SPLENDID PAUPER' AND ELINOR GLYN. In 1896 she says:
'I so thoroughly respond to your further advice and admonition
to the "splendid pauper", and what a difference it would make if
it was acted on! I will re-double my efforts this winter. You always
"enthuse" me by your writings and personality.' A letter from Stead
to Dunrobin arrived 'just as my sister[1] and I were poring over our
copies of the most interesting number of the *Review of Reviews* you
have sent out'. From Sicily she tells 'My Very Dear Friend' that
she has 'torn up two letters' to him. She continues to be unbelieving
in spooks. 'I *won't* write you "automatically" nor must you to me.
It is not a bit all right. Besides I want my letters to you to be me
and yours to me, the same, and I won't write with your hand. It's
all too stilted and forced'.

Her 'Labour Salon' in London, she goes on, 'is to be very cautious
at first, as I must learn so much. But I have their confidence because
I have no axe to grind, no sect to run, nothing but disinterested
friendship and genuine interest in all that affects the working classes.
So I pray I may help them.' With regard to a Salvation Army
address of Stead's she feels 'one has no right to call anyone a
"wastrel" '.

In a long letter she mentions her neighbour in Essex, Elinor
Glyn. 'She is pretty clever, but I disapprove of her writing; too
stupid, silly and vicious for words. She portrays a Society not really
so stupid and silly and vicious as that which I meet daily in London
and country and, thank goodness, see less and less of. And the
bulk of it is around our King and that is "a fact, dear friend".'
She says she will return from Italy 'more Socialist than ever'.
'What have centuries of greatness in rulers, aristocracy, genius, art,
done for the country one sees today? Bad government, bad art,
bad ideals, an effete and miserable aristocracy, an ignorant,
depraved, servile democracy living in conditions no better than
animals and crushed by ignorance and taxation. One valuable
asset is the sun.'

'JULIA'[2] AND JOSEPH ARCH. In a letter of twelve pages
from Dunrobin she tells how ill she has been when the newspapers
were giving the impression that she was taking part in all sorts of
frivolities. 'I have never read so much, French and English, and
have been working at Italian.' She speaks of so many peers' inability
to do more than make ends meet; 'the landed gentry and aristocracy
with incomes of about £20,000 in good times now find themselves

[1] The Dowager Duchess of Sutherland from whom I have a kind letter now
and then from Paris.
[2] Stead collected his colloguings with his spectral friend under the title of
Letters from Julia.

with about £10,000 [the year is 1893] and their expenses and obligations just as heavy.'

Turning to *Julia* she says, 'There is something wrong somewhere with spooks. They tell us nothing new, they reveal nothing of the future, which alone could interest. For ordinary life I prefer a genial human companion to a spook. The only mysticism I should like to cultivate would be the power to communicate in spirit with someone one cares most for in the world when one is at a distance. I want to be receptive of his thoughts and aspirations.' Meantime her chief requirement is the right kind of woman as secretary, for she wants 'leisure to read and think'. She ends, 'Don't commune too much with Julia but write occasionally to a flesh and blood friend, and above all, don't give up your splendid work of pointing out to English men and women how to live and work, how to bring to light wrongs, and help to higher and better things. Don't forget us all toiling to find our ideals, and to whom your encouragement means much, or forsake us for spirits who have had their day on earth and need your help and sympathy less than we do!' She sends a photograph of the interior of the cottage of the farm workers' leader, Joseph Arch, a Warwickshire Primitive Methodist, for whose memoirs she wrote a preface.

'THE PARISHIONER' AND THE QUEEN. The 'Parishioner' is not out of the picture: 'I can see him any time. Shall I ask him to write the letters you require? Would you be able to see him on his return to London?' She implores Stead to take care of himself; 'no one could stand the immense amount of labour you give yourself.' Her own work has been added to by her husband becoming Mayor of Warwick, she tells him in a letter from Chatsworth. The Mayoress is 'helping to re-organise my school needlework scheme'. Of a vigorous letter of hers to *The Times* she says, 'Society will sneer because its creed is that woman ought to be content with clothes, admiration and diamonds'. In Paris, 'after long daily sittings to the painter in a stuffy studio', she has 'daily got on my bicycle and sped away for air and exercise and all kinds of adventures. Alas, I cannot write to you through the medium of a prim young lady stenographer in an office!'

She is very pleased with the series of articles Stead wrote in the *Review of Reviews* on the Queen. 'You have written so beautifully, so simply and so humanly, if I may say so, and there is not a word I wish altered. "The Parishioner" wants you to "make a book" of the series and let him have them all. No one has treated the Queen in the way you have done.' She thinks Stead 'will have to come and live in the house in Warwick Castle park'. Lord Rosebery, the Asquiths and Arthur Balfour are coming to stay with her, but she wants to know Tom Mann; 'will you bring us together?'

And she is anxious to 'stir women up as Poor Law Guardians at the elections in the spring as there are many Boards with no women on them'. 'The Parishioner' 'wants me to invite all the big "Colonials" to Warwick, but I suppose I must see Chamberlain (Colonial Secretary) about this.' And she does not like him. Stead's letters 'have been such a pleasure' to her. Will he give her 'a couple of quiet hours soon?' One letter lets us learn that Mrs. Stead has been with him at Warwick. An 1896 letter says, 'Don't forget luncheon on Tuesday as the Prince is coming and looks forward to meeting you.'

I had no idea I should copy out so much. But what a representation of part of the later Victorian period one gets, and how the letters bring home to us the way in which Stead, despite all the ways in which he laid himself open to criticism, endeared himself to people with hearts in their bodies!

SCANDAL. Because at Great Canfield my wife and I knew Lady Warwick well—I come on several letters in which she addresses me as 'My dear John'—stayed with her at Easton and Warwick and in Mull, had visits from her and, with the aid of the acetylene lamps of her car for our stage, turned an Easton barn into a theatre and produced Barrie and Synge and an Essex play by my friend Bensusan, there is something that I think I ought to add. One day in Mull she said to my wife, who had helped her with her book, *Life's Ebb and Flow*, that she wanted to open her mind to her. It was about her relations with men about which the world had gossiped so freely. She wished to say solemnly that, though many men had made love to her and some had tried hard to have relations with her, and though one or two guests, mistaking her feelings in inviting them either to Easton or Warwick, had even endeavoured to enter her bedroom—they returned to town the next morning[1] and she never received them in any of her homes again. She spoke to me once of the way in which her guests would leave her with Albert Edward, Prince of Wales, who used to be boresome as he sat on a sofa 'holding my hand and goggling at me'.[2] But who today cares tuppence for Victorian era scandals?

3. THE REPUBLICAN IN HIS CASTLE

CANNY CARNEGIE. No letters are more interesting than the large collection from Stead's faithful friend and counsellor and constant informant on what is happening behind the scenes,

---

[1] I heard of one.

[2] 'A benign and hardworking old woman, who had gained respect by sterling public spirit and an element of genuine conviction and sincere reforming zeal.'—*Beatrice Webb's Diaries* (Longmans, 1952).

'Reggie' Brett, afterwards Lord Esher. Half the letters are addressed to 'My dear Friend'.

In December 1899 Brett wrote concerning Andrew Carnegie, the Scots-American millionaire who lived most of the year at Skibo Castle in the Highlands; 'Mr. Carnegie must be a firstrate business man to have made all those millions. He has wealth like Monte Cristo. He wants power. Why don't you suggest to him quite straight (1) that he should put down £500,000 (a trifle to him) for a big Liberal paper, (2) Vest a fifth share in you and another fifth in me, keeping three-fifths for himself, (3) Massingham (or anyone else) for editor, (4) the management to be distinct from editorship, (5) Carnegie to redeem the two-fifths at any time upon terms to be settled beforehand, (6) the paper to be run on Anglo-American Liberal lines. This is the psychological moment. No delay is possible. For the thing is sure to be done. I think we could in about three years or less make this the biggest thing in newspapers ever seen and knock Harmsworth clean out. If Carnegie really wants "power" and possesses imagination I think he would probably say "Yes" quite simply'.

SUPPORTED NEWSPAPERS AND 'A SQUELCHED EDITORIAL GENIUS'. But when Stead wrote to Carnegie he replied, 'Cannot agree with you about supported newspapers to support an idea; they never amount to anything'. Some years later, in a long letter, in which Carnegie calls Stead 'one of the original geniuses to whom I am attracted', there is a reference to some Stead plan for an evening paper to stimulate a taste for reading especially among the young. 'You credit me with good Scotch sense. Very well, here it is at first glance. There is something incongruous in a daily issue stimulating young people to read. Then it appears, say, at midday, just the busy time. I feel that your daily issue prodding me to read would have the contrary effect; I should get so tired of the missionary periodical. Truly, though not an editor I have always felt that my true field was to be one. It is as a squelched editorial genius that I say that no paper is worth much which is devoted to one cause. The converted read it but the sinners don't. Besides everyone knows that what it says is the word of an advocate, not a judge. The same money paid in advertising our views in ordinary periodicals would have much greater effect. My opinion is dead against your scheme. I should be sorry to see you put your earnings in it.'

'EGOISM FIRST, ALTRUISM AFTERWARDS.' He adds personal counsel: 'I think the example a man sets is a great good, and it is a good example to provide for those depending on you. No higher, better, more noble duty is ever performed than to take care of those of your own household. There must be egoism first, altruism afterwards. Assure me that your family is assured of means to live, modestly and comfortably, and in independence, and then I rest easily and "let genius do its worst".'

Referring in 1902 to the free library buildings he gives away, he says the work 'places within the reach of the poorest the only true riches, knowledge of the best from the Masters of the Race'. The next year, writing from New York, he says that his secretary tells him that he has spent or committed himself to spending on Empire libraries, not including Canada, over a million sterling. 'Don't you think upon consideration that instead of prodding a willing horse you should have mercy?' In the last letter about money I come on he says: 'There is nothing that robs a righteous cause of its strength more than a millionaire's money. It makes a serious, holy cause simply a fad. Its life is tainted.'

Stead, he declares, resembles Chamberlain in that 'both lack business instinct'. 'The *Daily Paper* idea[1] is madness. I do not wish

to do another stroke of business in my life—neither buy, nor sell nor lend. You can borrow on your property in *R of R* or otherwise; you have no need of my aid as a friend. If W. T. Stead ever needs means to live or his wife, then *as a friend* I shall not need any application from either if I know the situation. I ventured to say this to your genuine friend, Lord Esher. You are one of the elect, that rare thing, a man true to his convictions, with the true martyr spirit and "shall not want" while I have ability to succour, but no business with Your true and "good sense"-friend always.' He invites Stead for a week's yachting. He begins one letter 'My dear Erratic Genius, 'What can you expect of a man who talks with ghosts, or, what is worse, allows ghosts to talk with him?'

'MISSIONARY MILITANT FOR BRITISH AMERICAN UNION.' Letters from Carnegie range from January 1898 to January 1912. One from Cannes reports Gladstone 'to be a sick eagle, sick of 88 years'. Carnegie invites Stead to Skibo Castle for a week, and speaks of being 'so impressed by the talk of two young men in a small fishing village that I sent them to London to see you and others. It is to the young men we have to look.' Mrs. Carnegie thinks from something she has read of Stead's, that 'you are a greater man than she expected from your modest demeanour'. Some of Carnegie's letters are in pencil. One of them is about

---

[1] This and the *Review of Reviews* belong to the later stages of Stead's career, but it is convenient to have all the Carnegie letters together.

being plagued by an alleged blackmailer who came to him on an introduction from—Herbert Spencer! Two years later Carnegie says he knows 'two geniuses, one Kipling, who has a strain of coarseness in him, the other a tendency to sensationalism and going to extremes, slops over, but the true fire is in him'. He expostulates with Stead for not giving Herbert Spencer the credit to which he is entitled. 'He published before Darwin and is the philosopher, Darwin the collector and prover only'. In a 1903 letter Carnegie hails Stead as the 'Missionary Militant for British-American Union' and points out that Stead was 'the Prophet in Excelsis before Mr. Rhodes rose to the ideal of Race re-union; it was your words that developed him; you were his leader. I am, as you are, a Race Imperialist.' In 1906 he writes: 'It is really true that nothing will keep the West from improved spelling. I hope, however, for a joint Commission, comprising the two Branches, and a moderate beginning.' Carnegie hopes to see Stead in Pittsburgh, and provides him with 'transportation from your home on any ship and return'; his baggage is to pass without examination. A note to Stead when he gets to America says, 'I think you can be safely left to your own devices; even if you cannot be, genius is not to be controlled.'

In 1908 Carnegie is delighted with penny postage to the United States, 'in every way a great advance, very great'.

'TO FORTIFY THE MOON FOR PROTECTION AGAINST MARS.' The following year there is this postscript: 'No flying madness for me. I want to keep my feet on the earth and let you and other flyers go up in the air.'

In 1910 he says: 'There is no such thing as lawful war. Every war is lawless. The invader of course should be repelled. That which makes it a duty to defend our homes makes it also a duty not to attack the homes of others. Civilised nations have banned war between individuals and all we have to do is to extend that to nations. The fact that men have always killed one another is no reason why we should not denounce war as what Wesley calls "the sum of all villainies". Men used to eat their fellow-man, yet we denounce cannibalism. Men used to sell each other, yet we denounce slavery. They used to put garrisons to the sword, fire on unfortified places, poison wells, kill the commander of the opposing forces by treachery.'

In 1911 he is writing: 'We find our Motherland, like dear old mothers in general, very slow in adopting the improvements of the age'. He thinks that there should be displayed in every civil chief's room a quotation from Lord Salisbury, "I should not be surprised if my military advisers proposed to fortify the Moon for protection against Mars".'

'THE CAPITAL OF THE UNITED ENGLISH-SPEAKING WORLD.'
He asks for the authority for the statement that Rhodes said that, if
Anglo-American Union could not be obtained otherwise than by
applying for admission as a State federated with the American Union,
he would apply. In a later letter he says: 'Lord Rosebery, the Orator
of the Empire, is the man. He would be willing to have the capital
of the United English-speaking race midway which is Washington,
3,000 miles from Britain and an equal distance from the Pacific
Coast. And some day all under one Government, for I hold to my
prophecy in the last chapter of *Triumphant Democracy*.' But he
mentions that Morley once said to him, 'Look at Cain and Abel,
brothers fighting'. 'The reunion of the English-speaking races is
the greatest cause in the world', and he confidently believes in
'the brotherhood of man, the federation of the world.'

'LET WORKING MEN NOTE.' He goes on to quote from his
Problems of Today: 'Seldom, if ever, to the palace or stately home of
wealth comes the messenger of the gods to call men to such honours
as follow supreme service to the race. Rank has no place. Wealth
robs life of the heroic element. Let working men note how many of
the exceptionals who have carried the race forward were workmen.
There is not one rich or titled leader in the whole lot. All were
compelled to earn their bread.' He tells Stead that his firm has
made it a rule to give the men half of the advantage of improved
machinery. He says that as a child in Scotland he was brought up
among Chartists and Republicans, and had an uncle in gaol for
holding a prohibited meeting; 'my childhood's desire was to get
to be a man and kill a king'.

4. THIRTEEN AUTHORS AND A PAINTER

CARLYLE AND 'MY OWN LITTLE DEARIE.' Froude vouches
to 'My dear Stead' for the authenticity of a letter from Carlyle
to his wife in Scotland: 'Oh dear, oh dear! not a little sleep
yet in spite of the kindnesses. Nevertheless, hold on to your
milk, to your dietings, to your bathings, poor little heavy-laden
woman! Yes, but it is for ever true, the Eternal rules above us
and in us and round us, and this is not Hell or Hades but the
place of hope. The place where what is right will be fulfilled. And
you know that too, in your way, my own little Dearie, and you will
not and must not forget it; forgetting it one might go mad.' He
speaks of a particular doctor 'passing his life in silent company
with facts—what a different man from a thousand ones who are
always on the stage. I beg him very much to survey and investigate
your case and throw what light on it for us he can. I suppose there
is but little light except what our common reason might lead us to,

"time and the hours" which wear out the roughest day, and what I have looked to mainly from the first.' He goes on: 'I intend to work with double energy; no other resource for me to keep the Demons chained in their caves. Taking no damage, were my poor sick Dear well back to me. Don't mind writing me beyond a word when you feel weary, one word (as you say) to keep me away from gloom. Adieu, my love'. There is an addition: 'The Poulterer was discovered to be right and I have paid accordingly. Every Monday I am to count and reckon, and will.'

'A FAR CRY TO LOCH AWE.' Writing while Minister in England, James Russell Lowell says: 'Yours is a beautiful dream [of Anglo-American union], and most good things begin with that—a dream for which all good men should pray and which I more than half believe will be realised one day, though "it is a far cry to Loch Awe".'

LETTERS FROM E. A. FREEMAN AND FROUDE. The many hearty letters from J. A. Froude and E. A. Freeman begin in *Northern Echo* days. Freeman mentions that he once told a Continental statesman that the *Northern Echo* was 'the best paper in

From Letters from the Historians to Stead

Europe'. He says that when Greenwood edited the *Pall Mall* he 'sent him an Occasional Note most days. Because of his attitude to Russia, however, I dropped him silently. But I am bound to say that as an editor he was perfect. When Morley came into power I began again, but presently he dropped me. He has many merits but no sense of fun, nor any general interests.'

J. A. Froude caught something of Carlyle's style in a letter in which he says of politicians that 'the Devil will take them away at last'. He 'learns from an absolutely trustworthy source that the Queen is warmly seconding the Beaconsfield attitude' on Russo-Turkish matters.

GEORGE MEREDITH. 'The advantage of the eminence of sixty-two', Meredith writes, 'is that we are in no one's way and have a better animation than the desires. Do not send the *Review*; I get it. The cover is cold to the eye. The foreign department should be done in pointed, terse, elucidative sentences, not examining but exposing. I congratulate you on the fruit now showing of your long and strong advocacy of concord with Russia. English journalism will have to acknowledge your dues in this respect when time is riper.' If Stead can come for a week-end 'I will get a bed for you at our neighbour inn'.

EARLY LETTERS FROM BERNARD SHAW. There are letters of 1894 from 'G. Bernard Shaw', as he signs himself. In *Arms and the Man* Stead will 'see soldiering treated with some reference to reality'. G.B.S. says—and one thinks of Dubedat's farewell confession in a future play, *The Doctor's Dilemma*: 'Wagner once wrote a sketch called "The End of a Musician in Paris", in which the hero, at the point of death, says his creed, "I believe in God, Mozart and Beethoven". You were brought up to believe in God but not in Mozart and Beethoven, whereas I was brought up to believe in Mozart and Beethoven but not in God. I think you ought occasionally to try the influence of art, just to see what it is like.'

In a post-card he points out that in a *Review of Reviews* article someone has 'perpetrated a most frightful libel on my mother, who is still living and is quite respectable, little though you might suspect it from your knowledge of her son; her relations with the gentleman you accuse her of cohabiting with were as innocent as yours with Julia.'

The same month he says: 'What a man you are to talk of making a round of the theatres as if they were brothels! Why, how many years do you suppose it takes to hear and see in a theatre? You had better begin with the most serious attempt yet made to treat the theatre as a temple—I mean, of course, Bayreuth.' He offers him four £1 tickets and proceeds: 'Remember in *Parsifal* the Holy Ghost descends. Ober-Ammergau [which Stead had vivified] was a miserable, genteelified, Sir Noel Patonesque, Sunday school piece, Illustrated Bibleism. Bayreuth is very different.' Stead accepted the offer. 'Most noble of you', wrote Shaw, 'and I believe you will not repent it'. He did not.[1]

OLIVE SCHREINER ON MARRIAGE AND NON-MARRIAGE. What am I to do with two large envelopes bursting with letters from Olive Schreiner to Stead, a third of which are undated and all in a vile but sturdy penmanship? Bearing in mind, that is, one's

[1] SHAW IN THE 'PALL MALL.' The student of Shaw will be interested in what his 'historiographer and remembrancer', Dr. F. E. Lowenstein, kindly told me of the following contributions to the *Pall Mall*: 'The Surrey Hills', signed 'S,' appeared April 28, 1888. [It is a sharp criticism of life in the country.] From May 16, 1885, to December 26, 1888, there were pretty regular but anonymous reviews of books. Shaw signed himself 'A Firm Believer' and 'An Inveterate Gambler' in reviews, and Archie Mackintosh, Horatia Ribborson and Jesse Sodd in letters. An article entitled 'Failure of Inept Vegetarians' (26.1.86) appeared as 'By an Expert', and there is an article by 'Our Special Wagnerite'. 'The Amateur Boxers at the "Imperial" ' is also by Shaw. In an anonymous note (17.9.88) he complains about a rubbishy book sent to him for review. Shaw was one of the contributors to the *New East* I founded and edited in Japan.

obligations to *The Story of an African Farm* (1883), two other books and public service in South Africa? Also did I not once meet the determined little German-Jewish genius paddling about in the rain in the Strand, and do I not every day of my life see her portrait at the door of my study? I have loyally got all the correspondence into heaps from 1889 to 1914, and noted bits down. She is Stead's 'always with respect and affection' or 'ever and ever'.

In an early letter (1890) 'to my dear friend' she says: 'No woman dares in my presence to discuss other people's private concerns. *I will not stand it.* Four times have I ordered women out of my room. The only kind of personality I like is when people tell me of *themselves*, their own thoughts, their own feelings.'

In 1891 she writes: 'I am glad you have made an alliance with Rhodes, your genius is eminently fitted to harmonise. He seems to enlarge the horizon. He has the strongest antipathy to me, but it does not in the slightest degree affect my sympathy with him. I am able to sympathise with and love so many people who will never be able to sympathise with and love me'.

Before marriage she writes: 'Having a child seems to me the one compensation the gods give women for being a woman. The

only thing that makes me sad, in thinking I shall have to live all my life alone, is the thought that I shall never have a child. Marriage seems more and more an impossibility. If by any possibility one did at last find a human being for whom one could feel so absolute an affection as would make marriage right, one would be sure to find that some other woman loved him. Close knowledge and friendship ought to precede all thought of marriage, and that is very difficult for men and women to attain to in exacting circumstances. I believe in marriage. Some years ago I could not see a little tiny baby without an inclination to burst out crying hysterically, and to see a happy husband and wife with their children seemed to make in me the same unaccountable feeling. Now I have entirely conquered it. I know my work and have accepted my little part in life.'

A HUSBAND WHO CHANGED HIS NAME. In 1894 she tells Stead of her wedding to Cronwright, who changed his name to Cronwright-Schreiner. The next year she writes: 'I don't see how the relations of married life can be well, nobly, in any way ideally arranged where there is not perfect and profound union of aim. Where that is not, in the case of intellectual and mentally active people, I should say the marriage was a failure. Where there is complete unity there never arises the least difficulty regarding friendships with persons of the opposite sex. My marriage has not touched any of my friendships, and there is something almost comical in the idea that it might. Where a man and a woman marry, feeling that life with its highest personal and impersonal duties can best be carried out in each other's company, complexities and difficulties cannot arise. Where men and women marry without this the sooner they part the better. Perfect marriage of mind and body is such a lovely and holy thing that, rather than a travesty of it, none was better. Mental union "for the begetting of great works" constitutes marriage. Physical union, even with absolute fidelity, is a repulsive and degrading thing in men and women capable of the higher form of union. Of course there are thousands of millions, even in the most civilised communities, for whom physical attraction and fidelity must constitute marriage. Continuance of the physical relation where the highest mental relation is not possible and where affection is given elsewhere seems to me a more terrible because a more permanent prostitution than that of the streets.'

Three extracts from letters run: 'It has been a great pleasure to my husband and myself to see your boy, manly, straight, sincere'. 'What a beautiful soul Josephine Butler was!' 'Physical strength to do one's work is the first of the good things of life, after the power of loving nature and folk, which is perhaps even the greater good.'

THE RAID FROM THE JOHANNESBURG SIDE. In 1897 Stead receives a letter beginning, 'I, Olive Schreiner's mother, send you an illuminated scroll from the *Cape Times* in honour of our "King of men, the Amalgamator and Pacificator of South Africa", as Olive in her better days used to call him'. Olive Schreiner's brother, writing from Johannesburg, speaks of the ignominious collapse of the Raid: 'A sense of consequent humiliation is general. Johannesburg was practically sold. The capitalists for two years or more had been assiduously smuggling arms into the mines, and maturing their plans. They were going to achieve gigantic success in one brief hour. They would provoke the Boers into making an attack. Then they would fire in self-defence, and in no time, Jameson and his column being already with them, thousands of armed men would pour in from Rhodesia and Bechuanaland and, before you had time to say Jack Robinson, the Boer Government would be no more. Then the Transvaal would be annexed to the Chartered territories and every one of us would be glad to bow the

knee to the Colossus. Only five or six in Johannesburg were in the
secret, but, as soon as the scheme failed, the famous "Manifesto",
which was only a blind, was made the rallying-point and all the
prominent men in the town were invited to join a Reform Committee which was also a blind. The Transvaal Government are
behaving most magnanimously and exercising marvellous leniency.'

In one of her last letters Olive Schreiner says, 'Rhodes's career
is ended and the terrible thing to us who have admired him is to
have to say "It is well so".' Her friend, Havelock Ellis, tells her of
Stead's 'splendid, fearless stand against the War'.

AN AUTHOR'S RECEIPTS. In the batch of letters is one from
Fisher Unwin who published *The Story of an African Farm* stating
that *Peter Halkett* (1897) was not a great business success for the
publisher. 'However, I paid the author four figures and am quite
prepared to pay four figures again if she will give me a good long
novel'. This is in 1904. 'I find it difficult to believe', writes Mr. A. D.
Marks, of the Quality Press, to me, 'that Fisher Unwin ever put
down £1,000 for anything. It is possible that he really means
that over a course of years the royalties on the sales amounted to
£1,000. Fisher Unwin often stipulated that a substantial number
of copies had to be sold before any royalty was paid at all. As for
The Story of an African Farm, the original publication was through
Hutchinson and of course it is possible they got it outright for a
small figure. Fisher Unwin took it over long after first publication.
The book was pirated in U.S.A. However, ethics were above law
and the author was paid a royalty on every copy sold and this
must have amounted to a tidy sum.'

H. G. WELLS ON HIS BOOKS. In letters from H. G. Wells
there are these passages: 'I have a great belief in the Endowment
of Motherhood, and left the Fabian Society because they would
not incorporate it in their Basis. *The New Machiavelli* is not a
sexual book but it is not sexless. A firm which publishes genteel
pornography has turned it down. It's just about as clean and
just about as dirty as Michelangelo's Adam on the Sistine Chapel
roof, i.e. it shows what has to be seen. *Anticipations* is designed,
with another book, as a sketch of a possible New Liberalism
that might usefully supersede the chaotic good intentions that
constitute contemporary Liberalism.' 'Coming up to London
disturbs the course of my work for many days—my sense of proportion won't stand travelling'. But he looks forward to seeing Stead
when he does come.

GEORGE MOORE ON 'ONE-NESS OF CHARACTER'. Moore is
attracted by Stead's 'courage and one-ness of character'. Here
are isolated sentences from several letters of his earlier years: 'I
write a great deal that I do not believe to be true, paradox and

ideas that I sympathise with; you may sympathise with much that you cannot under penalty of lunacy believe in.' 'I have always held the increase of the population to be the vital question, the rest is ephemeral and circumstantial. That a young man should

Most sincerely yours

George Moore

take a young girl on his knee seems to me of no moment; that he should marry her and have a dozen children seems to me of very great moment. Regarding *La Terre* I used my best endeavour to prevent Vizetelly from publishing it. It is a horrible book!'

GRANT ALLEN, 'UTOPIAN BY BIRTH'. Grant Allen sends advance proofs of *The Woman Who Did* and says the book is written 'straight from my heart; we two alone have realised the horror of prostitution'. Writing at another time he says: 'I have lived more than half my life in two Colonies, Canada and Jamaica, and only a quarter of it in England, but Colonists are the thinnest-skinned people on earth and I never wrote anything about either Colony without hurting some tender susceptibilities. It is all a question as to what you consider civilised and what you consider wild. I am a Utopian by birth.'

CONAN DOYLE ON 'PILL AND SALVE SELLERS'. Conan Doyle, on the basis of his medical knowledge and experience, declares that 'secret remedies are usually impositions and deceit. It would be better for the public to miss one real cure, to break down the farce, and keep off the pill and salve sellers who trade on the hopes of sufferers and the love of relatives.' He has been 'studying eyework in Vienna' and is 'off to Wimpole Street as I found literature incompatible with general practice'. He is dictating *The White Company*. Stead's 'mission is grand, to find some sort of voice and expression for all the dumb strength which lies in noble England'. He gives him a reminder:

'I dedicate what I thought was the best book I had ever written to "The hope of the future, the reunion of the English-speaking race", because it seems to me the greatest cause in the world and I wanted to identify myself with so glorious an aspiration. By reunion I did not of course mean a reunion of Governments but a restoration of racial patriotism, a reunion of sympathies, an earnest endeavour to clear away prejudices and to see things from a common point of view. What was then only a glimmer in the distance, is now a bright beacon in sight of either nation. The danger is lest we go too fast. That which is built to last must be built solidly and gradually. To go too far is to come back again.

But let-it-be Anglo-Celtic and not Anglo-Saxon reunion, please. Why should a race which is shot through and through with the Celt continue to call itself by the name of two German tribes.

A Conan Doyle.

WILLIAM ARCHER, REVIEW BOOKS AND PUBLISHERS. William Archer, in his clear bold hand, tells of his system with books he gets for review. 'Poetry and novels I almost always sell; history and general literature I keep. Publishers have no right to complain of the sale of a book which has been reviewed. Selling a book which has not been reviewed is unfair if it fetches anything more than its price as waste paper. When it comes to doing, say, three-volume novels in a column I look upon the right to sell as a set-off against the time it takes to read them. I do not pretend to read every word on every page of a three-volume novel but I always look over the whole of it. The sale of books brings me in on the average £6 or £7 a year.'

Archer is convinced that the censorship is 'perfectly futile as a safeguard against indecency, while in other respects a source of the gravest inconvenience and injustice. The existence of the censorship deadens the public's sense of responsibility. The New York public is a better censor than our Great Irresponsible.'

FREDERIC HARRISON AND THE RIGHT KIND OF PILGRIMAGES. Frederic Harrison writes in warm approval of pilgrimages to spots 'consecrated by great memories'. He has himself 'had scores of such parties. But pilgrimages may easily fall into the hands of agents of hotels, railways, and so forth, or pass into holidaymaking trips in the absence of any real control and inspiring spirit. Our pilgrimages have always been guided by an historical social and religious system behind them, and were real pilgrimages. They were regarded as genuine parts of religious education and even of religious worship.'

'ONLY A PAINTER'—G. F. WATTS. G. F. Watts often wrote. He says: 'I don't know why Sir Edward Grey is so desirous of coming so far to talk with me. I am only a painter.' Again, 'No doubt our opinions on many subjects may differ, but I quarrel with nothing but violence, rancour and malevolence. Conflict is the principle of sociality! Again, gambling I feel very strongly about. The habit is utterly destructive to national character.'

5. PRO-CONSULS AND GENERALS

VISCOUNT MILNER'S APPRENTICESHIP AND COLLEAGUESHIP AT THE *PALL MALL*. Letters from Viscount Milner go back to the days of his appearance as a journalistic novice at the *Pall Mall*. One of April 1882, to Stead as assistant editor, says: 'I don't want to give myself up to journalism, but it would be helpful to me to give some time to it and I would rather do it regularly than spasmodically. I will regard attendance at 9 a.m. as imperative and get up my newspapers beforehand. Besides *The Times* I thought the *Standard, Morning Post* and the *Daily News*. The foreign papers I see at my club'. Later, he is a little critical of Morley, then editor, as a judge of lighter topics. A week or two afterwards he writes: 'I am proud of my connection with the *P.M.G.*' On mourning paper he refers to the death of his father, 'all that was most precious to me on earth'; his mother was 'my most constant ideal of all noble virtue, uniting the spirit and courage of a man with the tenderness and patience of the best women'. In reference to some articles he is sending from Germany he hopes 'you will amend and amputate freely; I am not touchy about my writing'.

Five years afterwards he is speaking of a leader he has done in Stead's absence, 'much what you would have said but not with your vigour and incisiveness'. Another day he says, 'We made a blunder yesterday in guessing Sir Charles Dilke and not Northbrook for India, and of course that is the one thing Thompson remarks on in the whole paper. There is a long account against Thompson for the Day of Judgment. But he is most good-tempered, helpful, too, in his little way, absolutely submissive. We had a fight between Hill and Charles Morley almost ending fatally, and delayed the paper till about 1.40.' The readers of the *Pall Mall* accepted it whenever it was ready to come out. Charles was John's nephew.

During Stead's holiday Milner wishes 'I was there to bathe and play with the children and drive about in your pony cart'. He has been doing City Notes and mentions that '45 minutes is too little by half for me to write the leader in'. Another day there is 'a good paper on the whole, though the leader, an ambitious one, is as usual, rather *manquée* for want of time, and some of the Notes are bad'. 'Hurrah' begins another letter, 'I am so glad you are staying away. The paper can better afford to be dull for a day or two than to part with you to the majority. Besides there is lots of matter of all sorts.' The last letter of this period, written from Balliol in July 1885, is one in which Milner proposes to resign after Cook and Stead have had a month's holiday, one after the other. On 'The Maiden Tribute', he writes, 'You have realised your principle of "frank brutality" to the full. . . . I hope you will achieve all the good you hope for and will not be too knocked up in the effort.'

On one of Milner's visits to Stead at Wimbledon he took Arnold Toynbee with him. Milner, when he gets to Somerset House, sends long letters of information but 'you must conceal the source'. He will be delighted to come down to Wimbledon 'for a long talk about anything and everything except spooks'. Regarding Stead's praise of his *England in Egypt* he mentions that 'an admirable critic who knew me at college says I have "a good grey style".'

LORD DUFFERIN AND AVA. Speaking of his rectorial address at St. Andrews, this genial diplomat says 'it is no joke to address a parcel of hard-headed students many of whom are probably better educated than I am'. In a letter, when he was Ambassador in Russia, he says: 'I do not know what could have induced Sir Edwin Arnold to put in that absurd story about the Russian officer and Lionel Tennyson's death—a pure invention'. He mentions that at the ceremony he had 'not put on a cloak because I thought it would encourage the troops, who had to remain in such discomfort all day long, if I took the punishment they were getting!'.

In a letter written in 1897 he expresses the opinion that 'it has begun to dawn on a considerable body of educated Americans that a Constitutional Monarchy such as ours is a cheaper and more convenient instrument of popular government than their own unwieldy mechanism. Moreover before long they will begin to revolt against the platform of luxury and ostentatious extravagance on which the rich folk are trying to establish themselves above their fellows.'

Lord Dufferin says that 'They also serve who only stand and wait' has consoled him for many an unaccomplished task and useless endeavour. Stead was evidently writing to well-known people for their inspiriting quotations. Mr. Goschen is inclined to attach importance to 'All comes to him who knows how to wait', but a principle he has often held is, 'Resist the interviewer and he will fly from you'. An Admiral says that what most influenced him in 'his striving time' was Johnson's, 'He that aims at excellence is sure to attain mediocrity, but he that aims at mediocrity will probably sink far beneath it'. 'The resource and stay of all life which is active' within the Bishop of Durham is St. John 1, 14, Colossians I, 19, 20. Sir Theodore Martin, the Prince Consort's biographer, says that no maxim has been kept before him more persistently during his life than 'to let no day pass without having something to show for it'. Max O'Rell (Paul Blouët) would like to see 'engraven on the cranium of every living creature, "Nations are not better or worse than others; they are only different" '.

SIR HARRY JOHNSTON ON TWINS AND 'THE MISMANAGE-MENT OF THE UNIVERSE'. A note on *Review of Reviews* paper by that great authority on Africa and valiant but diminutive fighter against Arab slavers—I remember that when I saw him in his chair his feet did not reach the carpet—is, 'I just called to see you, that's all'. A letter says, 'I wish very much to talk to you about Africa generally. The prematurely bald young men at the Foreign and Colonial Offices think it a horrid bore doncha know. An East, West, and South African empire is to be shaped or smothered. Whereas we are for ever doubting our worthiness and right to rule, less scrupulous nations step in and supplant us. It is sickening. I shall always be pleased to come and see you at Wimbledon, in Central Africa or in Northumberland Street.' He has an aversion to lunching and never eats in the middle of the day. He is troubled by the birth of twins which lived only a few hours. Another note says:

Name	H. H. Johnston
To see	Mr. Stead
Subject	The Mismanagement of the Universe.

Following this we have: 'I really thank you, my dear Stead, for the pleasant intercourse we have had. I must come to you for further education. I am a working man and his ideals are very much mine and mine are his. The Liberal and the Labour Parties *must* work together. Your kind letter has put heart into me.' He says he has been 'for some years a fanatical teetotaller'. Stead is to come and dine with him and 'an intelligent black man'.

'BOBS' ON HEALTH. Lord Roberts confides: 'You are quite right in thinking I must have had a very tough constitution. Before I left India, when 15 months old, I had a very severe attack of brain fever which resulted practically in the loss of my right eye. I doubt whether I was really strong until I went to India at 19. Even then I had constant attacks of fever, to which I was more or less subject throughout my career there, but by taking care and by being moderate in all things I found myself able to do what most men could do, even when I was much older in age than they were.'

PLAIN SPEAKING BY LORD WOLSELEY. Cordial letters from Lord Wolseley[1] arrived from 1887 to 1903. In an early one he retains 'the deepest and pleasantest recollection of our thoughtful conversation'. He 'would much like another'. In a letter of 1887

---

[1] 'I always thought he was by far the cleverest man in the Army and the most farseeing.'—Sir Frederick Ponsonby in *Recollections of Three Reigns* (Eyre and Spottiswoode, 1951).

on grogshops and brothels in Egypt he bespeaks attention first to conditions in London, 'a pesthouse of infamy, of terrible immorality. I cannot go a hundred yards without seeing a public house, and outside I see a dozen or so of the persons who have voices in the management of public affairs more or less tipsy. Take a turn in the Strand or Piccadilly at 9 or 10 p.m., what do you find? Prostitutes of all ages. Ask the police and you will find out the brothels of sodomites. Look at your thieves' quarters.'[1] He wishes Stead were in Parliament, offers to touch up proofs, wants him to see 'one of the very ablest of our officers, Colonel Maurice', and says 'the Tsar stands in no need of his enormous army, for no one wants anything he possesses'.

6. CARDINAL, CANON AND SALVATIONIST GENERAL

CARDINAL MANNING AND GENERAL BOOTH. Cardinal Manning was for Stead a kind friend, counsellor and admonisher during the whole *Pall Mall* and *Review of Reviews* period. His regard for him and confidence in him were great. The straightforwardness of their correspondence and their consideration for one another commend both men to us. I have had the privilege of reading not only a score or two of the Cardinal's letters but a number from Stead to Manning, evidently returned at Manning's death. Letters showing the way in which the Cardinal stood by Stead in 'The Maiden Tribute' experience have appeared on previous pages. In one of the remaining letters he says, 'I shall be happy to meet General Booth. Choose some neutral place which will be acceptable to him. To me it is indifferent, if not public.' About a woman whom Stead is befriending, the Cardinal says, 'If it will quiet her to lay her case before me let her do so and relieve you'. In reference to a leading article of Stead's he writes: 'Take care or you may die a Papist. None are so near as those who think themselves safest.' There is a letter explaining that 'the whole Episcopate in all countries is in close correspondence with Rome in Latin, Italian and French. Every week my secretary and I write in these languages on all manner of business. Every Bishop uses one or all of these languages not as a *lingua franca* but as a living language. Every nation has its College in Rome. If the Pope is not polyglot Rome is.'

When Stead retires from the *Pall Mall* the Cardinal says: 'I think you have outgrown it. What your next work will be is not so clear to me but I hope it will be a new *kind*.' He has some acute typographical criticisms of the *Speaker* (the forebear of the *Nation*

---

[1] 'The ravages of venereal disease in the Army and Navy had become in the sixties a cause of great anxiety. It was said that a ship which came into Portsmouth Harbour with its full complement would hardly be capable of putting to sea two or three weeks later.'—*James Stansfeld*, J. L. and Barbara Hammond.

and *New Statesman*) and underlines 'that it will not live unless it becomes lighter'. He has read Stead's sketch of John Morley 'with interest and sympathy. You will not let an old man say that neither of you has as yet reached your last analysis, but I see with great joy that both of you for the Truth's sake would make war upon the world.' He proposes to enlarge upon this in talk; meantime he says, 'To be a Christ [Stead's phrase] demands not only faith in Christ but the faith of Christ pervading the intellect first and reigning over the will.' In the Parnell crisis he says that Parnell will not last. 'He has nothing to rest on in morals or politics. Ireland has been drugged by politicians.' There is this personal message: 'I am afraid for you. No man can do the work of two. He may for a time keep it up, but it cannot last, and it breaks with a great recoil. Do not let your will outrun your reason. Work less and you will work longer, and in the end lay up more work in quantity and in quality.' In one letter he says that he will be glad to see Mr. Rhodes and in another sends this list of books for him:

> Bishop Stubbs' *Constitutional History of England*
> Freeman on *The Growth of the English Constitution*
> Thorold Rogers' *The Economic Interpretation of History*
> Bryce on *The American Commonwealth*
> Bagehot on *The English Constitution*
> Marshall's Political Economy *Principles of Economics*
> Lilly *On Right and Wrong*.

On the Reunion of Churches he says: ' "One" cannot be reunited, for it can never be plural; but I rejoice to see the desire of unity. I will send you an old book of mine on Unity written before the Flood, the last part in haste and in error. I came to understand the Temporal Mission of the Holy Ghost. That changed everything.' He finds Stead's sketch of Leo XIII 'very true and just, confirming your estimate of the goodness and greatness of the man'. Manning says that if Stead will send one hundred copies of his May and June numbers of the *Review of Reviews*, done up ready for post, 'we would with pleasure direct, stamp and post them to our Bishops of the United Kingdom and our chief Colleges, etc.' He feels that Stead has done his sketch of the Prince of Wales with great sincerity, 'and it was both wiser and safer to be severe. Your defence is very good. His position is intolerable. As you say, there is a non-political world of intelligence and action in which he would be a centre of public business'.

On the subject of Ireland: 'The Irish are to be judged in Ireland. Not even the Tyrolese compare with them in chastity, generosity and faith. Their faults of rebellion, sedition, deceit, falsehood, etc., are the demoralisation of an oppressed and persecuted people.

P

They are what the English have made them. The Irish driven over to Liverpool by poverty and starvation fall into all the vice and crime. It is injustice to compare the proportion of Irish criminals in England with ours. Look at Ireland with nine judges having no crimes to try. Look at the rising Irish in our Colonies.' He concludes about a particular critic: 'He is a sample of an intellectual convert. Life without love has no place in God or Heaven.'

When Stead goes to Rome the Cardinal writes of him: '*Homme d'insigne intelligence and de rectitude morale. Il est sincèrement croyant et de religion Dissident, néanmoins pour l'Eglise Catholique juste et respectueux.*' Manning's usual signature is as in the reproduction, but sometimes he is 'Yours ever' with initials, a common signature of Stead's to the Cardinal. The Cardinal always uses the spelling 'inclosed'.

SPURGEON IN A LETTER OF THE TIME. In one of his letters from the Metropolitan Tabernacle Charles Haddon Spurgeon invites Stead, as he has evidently done before, to his Pastors' College supper. 'I give my daily thoughts to this work of aiding my Master's young servants to know the way of God more perfectly and to preach it with greater clearness. We have sent more than seven hundred men into the field. The Lord has very signally blessed this service, although it is not without its trials and disappointments.' In another letter of the time, he says, ' "There is a fountain filled with blood" has spoken to my heart as no other hymn has done'. The day after the death of Spurgeon I happened to pass the Tabernacle in Newington Butts, and saw an intimation that 'our beloved pastor entered Heaven' at a particular hour in the afternoon.

CANON LIDDON'S JUDGMENTS. Stead's friendship with Canon Liddon began in the *Northern Echo* days and there are letters from 1876 to 1899. There would have been more Liddon letters had not the two friends taken frequent walks along the Embankment. A letter of 1877 says: 'Lord Beaconsfield delights in the sensational in all its forms. Still I cannot but hope and think that while Lords Salisbury and Carnarvon are in the Cabinet the criminal project of a war against Russia will not be carried out. After all this is a free country, and in free countries it is impossible to go to war when a large minority of the people (if it be a minority) thinks the proposed war not merely uncalled for but criminal.' He encloses £3 'to assist you in distributing Lord Derby's speech on the subject of the threatened war', and thanks Stead for his 'consistent courage and great ability in the *Northern Echo*.'

Cromwell, of whom they had been speaking, was 'probably a very mixed character, unduly praised and blackened. If I thought force was as admirable as pure goodness I should admire him enthusiastically.' 'The objection that the roughs have to the

Salvation Army is certainly not an ecclesiastical objection'. 'There are worse things than Disestablishment and Disendowment, and one of them is a cynical contempt for truth in the real or supposed interests of property'. 'Politically speaking, most clergymen are Conservatives'. 'Dante lived through the reigns of fourteen Popes, praises two, blames five and says nothing about seven'.

GENERAL BOOTH DISCIPLINES HIS DAUGHTER. One letter from General Booth, the founder of the Salvation Army, dates back to the days when his letters were headed not 'International Headquarters, Queen Victoria Street' but 'The Salvation Army, called The Christian Mission, 272, Whitechapel Road'. Stead has a letter later on in which the General deplores his daughter, La Maréchale, having left the Army. 'Your sorrowful father feels that no advantage could result from any intercourse at any rate at this time.[1]

7. ALL SORTS AND CONDITIONS OF MEN

CHURCHILL AND SOUTH AFRICA. Winston Churchill, writing in 1906 concerning a letter which ex-President Steyn had written to Stead, on a subject which has relevance today, says: 'I should certainly not be forward in pressing upon the South African Colony views in regard to native franchise which they are at present not ready to accept. But our responsibility for the native races remains a real one.' In his life of his father he says, 'He would, I believe, have opposed the Boer War.'

EDITOR'S COWHERDING. Sir Robert Donald, editor of the *Daily Chronicle*, and formerly of the *Pall Mall*, gives this account of his early difficulties: 'I left school when I was ten and, commencing as a cowherd in a dreary part of Banffshire, worked four or five years as a farm servant. I was then sent off to learn a trade and bolted to Aberdeen and, after struggling through various grades of clerking, formed a slight connection with the Press.'

A LORD CHIEF JUSTICE'S DISTINCTION. A letter of 1887 from the excellent Lord Chief Justice Coleridge, great nephew of the poet, making an anonymous gift of £5 to two ladies whose sad case had been reported in the *Pall Mall*, says 'Lord Coleridge is very glad to know Mr. Stead but the Lord Chief Justice respectfully declines all communication with the editor of the *Pall Mall*'.

IN PRAISE OF MORMONS. Moreton Frewen thanks Stead (1911) for something he has said about the Mormons and says: 'They have converted a desert into a fruitful field, and the distribution

[1] *In Darkest England and the Way Out*, not to be confused with the volumes of Charles Booth, *Life and Labour of the People*, bore the name of General William Booth, founder of the Salvation Army, but was largely written by Stead, without remuneration.

of wealth through the Church has absolutely extinguished poverty. I have known the community very intimately for thirty years and no attack can be fairly made upon them either on the religious or social side. The real objection to Mormonism is that the Church, with its immense endowment and cohesiveness, is a political machine which dragoons the community.'

THE KAISER'S ANECDOTE. Otto Beit told Stead about his chat with the Kaiser, who said that when Rhodes saw him he put his hand on his shoulder several times. One of the Kaiser's stories to Beit was about two waggoners who met in a lane too narrow for them to pass one another. Each called to the other to go back and each refused. Then one said, 'If you don't go back I will do as I did yesterday when I met a cart in the same way'. 'Very well,' said the other waggoner, 'I will go back', and he backed out of the lane. When he had done so he asked what the waggoner had done yesterday. The reply was 'I backed out myself'.

MRS. BESANT AND HER WISE FRIEND. One of the most interesting women Stead worked with and befriended was Annie Besant. She first came into notice as the unfortunate wife of a clergyman, unjustly deprived of her children. Then for thirteen years she shared with Bradlaugh public opprobrium in respect of atheism and a pamphlet on family limitation, *The Fruits of Philosophy*—it is difficult for the present generation to realise the horror

Producing Mr.
Annie Besant

of the crinolined for a book which would today pass unnoticed— edited the halfpenny *Link* ('a journal for the Servants of Man'), unselfishly succoured and comforted girls in trouble, was an energetic member of the old London School Board—at the *Pall Mall* I used to sub-edit the notes she brought in of its proceedings—was the ardent, concerned advocate of India, and at the end of her life high priestess of theosophy. Her letters fill two envelopes. Stead is 'Dear Sir Galahad', and she is 'your dear friend' to him in English, French and Italian. It is plain that in 1887–8 she was in love with Stead, and that he was her wise friend. Her relations with Bradlaugh, whom I remember as towering over six feet and with a 48-inch chest, gave his wife anxiety, but no fault could be found with his behaviour. This fact did not prevent gross imputations being made.

BOTHA AND SMUTS. General Botha writes about the things done in concentration camps 'which should not be done by any civilised people believing in God and Jesus Christ. I am sure that

God cannot otherwise than punish such cruel behaviour.' Smuts,

remembering the Afrikaans proverb, *Alles zal regt kom*, says 'Right in the long run always becomes Might'.

'HOLY, HEAVENLY WHISKY, BLESS US.' When Stead advocated a 'model pub run on Christian principles' Sir Wilfrid Lawson wrote to him in rhyme:

> Here am I, send me, dear mother,
> Send me to that Christian brother,
> Thither to and fro I'll toddle,
> Bringing whisky from the 'Model',
> Stead, with every charm has graced it,
> On 'a moral basis' placed it,
> Every joy shall now possess us,
> Holy, heavenly whisky, bless us.

A BROTHER'S TESTIMONY. In a Christmas letter Herbert Stead, whom I knew when he was doing valuable work as warden of the Browning Settlement in South London, writes to his brother of 'the wars which you have had a part in staving off, and improvements you have made in international relations. Particularly, you have done more than any other man to create a feeling of unity with the United States. But that is not the thing I recall with greatest pride and thankfulness. Cleverness and valour won't unite men. Only love will overcome hatreds and bitternesses. The work you have done has been done by your warm brotherly heart. It is the old affection which made that home of ours at Howden, with all its ructions and excitements, one of God's hotbeds of love, whence he has planted out seedlings and saplings which have been for the healing of the nations. There are many men who would gladly have died to have been used, honoured, and loved as you have been. I would like to have told you how much you have been to me and done for me, but I am but one small unit. God bless you, and gather about your heart the love of all that is lovely and the joy of all whom you have made glad, and the happiness of unnumbered homes which know not that you have saved them from the misery, outrage and murder of war.'

———————

When Boswell said to Johnson that he was afraid he had put in too many little incidents Johnson encouraged him. Here then are snippets from letters:

Janet Achurch is 'immersed in gardening which I love even better than acting' . . . The South African millionaire, Sir Abe Bailey, says: 'You are splendid if you will only continue to give me good advice'. . . In 1890 Hilaire Belloc has been to shops in order to choose Stead the best possible bicycle. 'The price at which you get most for your money,' he advises, 'is £12, with ball-bearings everywhere'. . . A note from the outstanding Paris correspondent, Blowitz—he does not use his criticised 'de'—congratulates Stead on a 'brilliant article' . . . A day of my life I remember was enjoyed

[handwritten signature: Truly yours. Blowitz]

at Crabbet Park with Wilfrid Scawen Blunt. He wrote to Stead, 'Even the Turks have never been able to make soldiers out of Bedouins. They fight well in their own way but you cannot get them to accept discipline. What is wanted for Egypt is not a clever administrator but an honest man.' . . . Letters from Bright are written between 1876 and 1879 while Stead was editor of the *Northern Echo*. Speaking of work with Cobden, he says, 'In our great fight we gave tracts to every elector in some counties.' . . . A close friend, Colonel Brocklehurst, Queen Alexandra's aide, asks if there is any other country in which its Sovereign is head of the Church. . . . Philip Burne-Jones is 'most grateful for your kindness to the poor girl: she has been literally starving'. In another letter the same month he introduces another 'poor girl who has been deserted by her husband' . . . General Botha, in congratulating Stead on the twenty-first birthday of the *Review of Reviews*, says: 'Whenever you have defended any cause you were always moved by a noble sense of justice, and you have consistently striven to promote the welfare and happiness of mankind'. . . . That remarkable Northumberland miner M.P., Thomas Burt, who once stayed at our house when I was a boy, speaks of the gratifying way you 'beamed on me' and is 'Yours ever, with affectionate regards' . . . Hall Caine, writing early in 1908, on the paper of '*Household Words*, founded by Charles Dickens', will 'gladly go' to a peace meeting, but J. K. Jerome, the humorist, is all 'for armaments as affording honourable employment to a large number of men', and puts on paper the view that 'war is itself a good thing'. . . Marie Corelli, with a gay silvered mono-

gram on her paper, asks: 'Can I see you in private on a matter of importance? The affair admits of *no delay*'. She speaks of herself as 'a woman who is womanly and happy in having home influences and home love' . . . The one-armed Irish patriot, Michael Davitt, will 'always gratefully remember your manly defence of the weak and oppressed everywhere', and speaks of the efforts John Dillon and he are making 'in the Talking Shop to expose the barbarous qualities of the Mark IV bullet, which some experts tell me is worse than the Dum Dum' . . . John Dillon praises 'a wonderful letter for a man of his age with the hand of death already laid on him', written by Gladstone . . . Mrs. Drew, who sends occasional book reviews to the *Pall Mall*, says, writing in 1888: 'My father scarcely ever goes to bed before twelve, nor does he eat anything before church next morning' . . . Lord Derby points to the difficulty in Imperial Federation that 'the Colonies would be outvoted by the thirty-two millions at home' . . . In one of several amiable letters, Sir Morell Mackenzie, who had such a rough time of it with the German doctors about the Emperor Frederick's cancer in the throat, writes, 'I can give you a lot of information about the Emperor's character and you have an extraordinary memory.' . . . Sir Gilbert Parker gratefully remembers the help given him twenty years before by 'England's greatest journalist'. . . W. R. Hearst, who died last year, wants signed editorial articles from Stead and says: 'Newspaper prejudice against the *Journal* is caused by its irritating success, and as your contributions would add to the success they will add to the prejudice against the "yellow" rival'. He writes of the first article, '*A tour de force*' . . . Oliver Wendell Holmes looks forward to the *Review of Reviews* as an 'indispensable guide and

companion' . . . G. J. Holyoake in a letter about Stead's action on
behalf of Mrs. Langworthy is 'Yours anyhow'. 'No act of like

generous peril has occurred in my time in journalism', and he
quotes Morley on Voltaire and Calas . . . Professor T. H. Huxley
expresses his views on the place of 'the exactions of industrialism
and international commercial competition' in the production of
militarism . . . Sir Henry Irving says, in reference to a 'most admirably done' interview, 'What a memory you have—you'd have
made a first-rate actor'[1] . . . Rudyard Kipling writes, 'You are
entirely at liberty to use *Recessional* as there is no copyright' . . .
Lloyd George, 'ever sincerely', says that during a twenty-five years
period of the *Review of Reviews*, 'brilliantly and forcibly written, it
has combined the widest possible scope with the most consistent
unity and control' . . . Elizabeth Robins, 'Yours always' to 'My dear
Friend', sometimes signs 'Hedda' in remembrance of the first
production in England of *Hedda Gabler* . . . Ruskin sends a letter he
intended for the *Nineteenth Century* but 'Master Knowles, objecting
to the introduction of the name of the *Pall Mall*, I damned his
eyes and send it to you' . . . G. W. E. Russell says 'I know that I
am a bore but there is no other way of being a Reformer' . . .
Mark Twain frequently wrote to Stead. In one note from Paris
he mentions that someone is 'coming here to photograph my

From a letter from Mark Twain

hands, back and front'. He asks for back numbers of the *Review of
Reviews* . . . John Wanamaker, of the Stores, has desired for a long
time to meet Stead and is his 'with great respect' . . . Canon Wilber-
force says 'You I can never forget.' . . . Israel Zangwill has a

---

[1] Stead says, 'Was not particularly taken with him; liked Bram Stoker, his
manager, much better; there is a certain artificiality in Irving; his mind is not
very nimble; was more impressed by the mobility of his lips than by anything else.'

play 'dealing with sexual equality, called "The Marriage of Tomorrow" . . . One of several letters from Arnold White is an
invitation to lunch, 'subject to your knowledge of the fact that I
would have hanged you if I had had the power to do so for some
of your actions'.

George Brandes

CHAPTER XVIII

MEMORIES AND IMPRESSIONS OF STEAD

I. BY ESTELLE STEAD, EDITOR OF THE *REVIEW OF REVIEWS* AFTER STEAD'S DEATH

LIFE AT WIMBLEDON. The name Stead is of Swedish origin. I believe one branch of the family came over in the fifteenth century and settled in Yorkshire. Father had the blue eyes and rugged features of the North, quite a Viking type. His mother belonged to Northumberland. As a boy he was fond of birds and painted them. The story that in *Northern Echo* days he used to ride into Darlington on a donkey is not quite correct; it was a pony!

He read the *Spectator* to us on Sunday afternoons, ending up with the Bank Rate! My mother followed with stories. To ensure that we had been listening, each of us in turn had to fix on some name or episode mentioned; also after chapel at our meal we had to do the same, taking the sermon as our subject. It was a game very much in the manner of 'Twenty Questions'. Every morning each child had to bring to the breakfast table an interesting fact chosen out of the morning newspapers.

Father had fluent but ungrammatical German. He saw to it that all his children had a really good knowledge of French and German. He adored children and had a wonderful way with them, as he had with grown-ups. His *Books for the Bairns* were the genuine result of his affection for children.

He was continually bringing people to Cambridge House, our home at Wimbledon, not only to dinner but to stay. There always seemed to be visitors and my mother's life was not easy, for he would telegraph at the last moment—there was no telephone then—that he could not get away from the office, and she would have to entertain strangers, about whom she knew little, to dinner.

Though in many things my father and mother were not sympathetic, there was a strong bond between them, and I remember him saying that he would not have married anyone else. He gave mother a valentine every year.

'PESTERED AND PLAGUED BY WOMEN.' He was always being pestered and plagued by men and women who appealed to him, for he was most sympathetic and soft-hearted. He gave his money away with goodwill to everybody who asked and seemed deserving.

[I have a number of letters to Stead from women—some not
unknown—thanking him for money help.] One of the worst cases
was that of a Russian Princess who told him that she had been sent
to him by the Tsaritsa. In all she must have got £15,000 from him,
on, it appeared, the security of estates that she owned in Russia.
The way he parted with his money was so notorious that the time
came when mother had to see that he went out with very little in
his pockets. My mother undoubtedly had a better flair for character
than my father. She died at eighty-two in 1932.[1]

My father was a demon for work. In the early morning, before
going to the office, and after dinner at night, he would be writing.
He seldom had much time to spare for holidays, but once he went
with my mother on a tandem tricycle to the Lake District. Whenever
possible, he would retire to our cottage at Hayling Island and
plough through masses of arrears.

RECREATIONS. He was fond of sailing and the coastguards said
they always kept a sharp look-out because he was so venturesome.
But he never had an accident, whereas my brothers had several,
and at times my father had to go to their rescue. He was a strong
breast-stroke swimmer, a keen walker and, to the scandal of
Wimbledon in the early days when we were small, would make us
all run down the hill on the way to chapel. At one time he was
very keen on photography and the walls of our cottage at Hayling
were adorned with the results. He also liked gardening. He would
have left a fine library had he not lent his books to all and sundry.
He had the ability, when in good health, to go to sleep at any time.

He was very sensitive and it hurt him that so few of his *Pall Mall*
staff fully sympathized with him.[2] It is well that it should be explained that he was subject to terrible fits of despondency, when he
felt that he had not the power to go on. Then he would suddenly
recover.[3] Harmsworth and a brother came to him for ideas before
starting the *Daily Mail*. Many people got ideas for their schemes from
him for he never minded having his brains picked. His motto, 'The
union of all who love in the service of all who suffer', was chosen

[1] 'About my father's relations with women', writes Miss Stead to me, 'I have no
doubts whatever. I expect you remember that he had a way of making whoever
he might be talking with feel he or she had wholly his regard and attention. So he
or she had for the moment. My father was intensely interested in women and most
sympathetic—rather too sympathetic—so that some women thought he was in
love with them and were hurt when disillusioned. My mother understood and
trusted him but was not sympathetic, and therefore he was, as you say, more than
ever thrown on his female friendships and a few he treasured and confided in.'
[2] EDMUND GARRETT. It was a great pity that constant illness so greatly shortened
the colleagueship of this fine spirit. His life was written by E. T. Cook (Arnold,
1909). Except on South Africa and 'spooks', Garrett completely sympathised.
I knew him intimately and hope to include recollections of him in an autobiographical volume to be published next year.
[3] 'Subject like most men and all editors to fits of despondency.'—*Herbert Paul.*

when he was discussing with Mrs. Besant the idea of a Civic Church.

MY FATHER'S HABITS. I never remember him giving much time to preparing his speeches. He would think about what he was going to say but seldom make notes. He had such a wonderful memory.

He took to smoking cigars in the *P.M.G.* days because when interviewing he found that if he smoked with people he could get them to talk more freely. When in South Africa he began smoking a pipe, using Boer tobacco, but as he could never keep it alight he gave it up.

With regard to *The Daily Paper*, his idea was, as he wrote in the *Review of Reviews*, 'to band together all the readers in a great co-operative partnership for the achievement of common ends; to make the newspaper itself not merely a nerve centre for the collection and distribution of news but for the inspiration, direction and organization of the moral, social, political and intellectual forces of the whole community.' He particularly wanted to interest the housewife and so he arranged for delivery in mid-morning after the men had gone to work. *The Daily Paper* experiment was a complete failure. After seeing the first number to press he broke down completely. By the loyal support of those around him the paper was kept going for some weeks but it was soon clear that it was impossible to continue. The doctor advised a voyage to South Africa. Nothing seemed to rouse him until we got to Teneriffe when he suddenly decided that there was a good reason for the failure. After that he worked hard, reading and dictating in the morning and romping with the children on board in the afternoon.

When in South Africa, Lord Milner would not receive us because of a speech that father made in Cape Town. [So Campbell-Bannerman's private jest to Stead that he was glad that he had escaped a dungeon under a *lettre de cachet* from his old assistant was not so far out.] Rhodes had long been dead and we stayed at Groote Schuur with Dr. Jim. We also stayed with Smuts, Botha, ex-President Steyn and Hertzog, and there is no question that the work that my father did helped to make a good settlement. Hadley tells me that, when Stead returned from South Africa, he went straight to Campbell-Bannerman and so much impressed C-B that he sent him to the King. In the great settlement for which C-B got the credit, Stead had therefore his part.

'THE SENIOR PARTNER.' When I wanted to go on the stage my father took it very badly and sent me to South Africa again, this time to tell stories in connection with the *Books for the Bairns*. When I came back and still persisted he gave way. Up to this time, of course, he had never seen a stage play. Benson said, 'Send her

o me and I will put her through it good and strong', so I joined
Benson's company.

My father always felt that he got his directions straight from
he 'Senior Partner'. He talked about the 'Senior Partner' long
before he took up spiritualism. How did he get his directions?
No doubt it was something like the way in which the Quakers feel
hey get a lead. His visit to the Tsar was one of the instances in
which he felt that he had a clear lead.

It was well perhaps that my father died when he did. Had he
lived he would have been a disappointed and thwarted man. His
physique would not have stood the conditions in which he found
himself. His head worried him. He felt he could not do as much as
he used to do and that he had lost his influence.

His intention, if he had come back from America, was to have
written his memoirs, which he was always looking forward to doing.
He could have kept in touch with people he could help and might
have recognised that he had done his share and could well be quiet.
But would he have been willing?

A portrait of my father was offered to the National Portrait
Gallery and refused. There is a copy of the Thames Embankment
plaque in New York.

THE FAMILY. When my brother William died in 1907 my father
was just going to make over the *Review of Reviews* to him. Henry
edited the *Australian Review of Reviews* for some years and died in
1922; he is buried in Tahiti. Alfred, who had a brain more like
father's, was not sympathetic to him. He travelled a great deal
and wrote several books.[1] Jack, who hated the idea of journalism,

---

[1] STEAD'S FAMILY. Stout wrote to me: 'Alfred Stead deserted his wife and family
in Capri, bounced about Roumania in khaki with decorations for doing nothing,
and died in 1934 in Germany. One day a German woman turned up at the Steads
in London to say that she had been living with Alfred who had left her all his
money, and she had come to realise the estate. She was surprised to learn that the
estate was comprised of liabilities and went back disillusioned. Later on a parcel
was delivered from the docks with a bill from the Customs for expenses. The
parcel proved to be a casket of Alfred's ashes. It was returned to the Customs.
It was next delivered to Jack, who had no love for the "remains", which we must
suppose were finally buried at sea by the Customs.' I have no confirmation.
Of Stead's children only two survive, Estelle and Pearl, who married the late
J. M. Gilliland of the *Daily Telegraph*. (Miss Christine Stead, author of a number
of novels, Sir Charles Stead, Archdeacon Stead and Professor Gilbert Stead were
not relations of Stead.) Mention has already been made of the late Herbert
Stead, head of the Browning Settlement, Stead's brother. Another brother was
John Edward Stead, F.R.S., who, his nephew, Professor John Stead, told me, was
like Stead in looks and character. 'From 1900, or even earlier, until his death in
1922, he was the most distinguished metallurgist in England and had an international reputation. Apart from his research work, he carried on a crusade to
persuade manufacturers to make full use of scientific knowledge in their businesses.
It was due to his efforts almost entirely that a large number of firms installed
research laboratories. At the same time he carried on a most successful business
as an analyst and was a wealthy man. He was given the honorary degree of D.Sc.
by Leeds and Manchester Universities and that of Doctor of Metallurgy by

became a professor at the Royal Naval College at Greenwich and
died in 1949.

II. By Theodora Stead

THE CHILD BOOK TASTERS. I remember being with my uncle
at Hayling Island and that among his boats were a catamaran
and other craft. He was fond of wading in the mud collecting
cockles. Collectors who did well were rewarded from a 4-lb. jar
of sweets on the dining room mantelpiece. When the children
were assembled in an ex-Navy houseboat a prospective *Book for
the Bairns* was tried out on them. As we were bored uncle decided
not to accept it. When one of us asked if the author would mind
and we gathered that he would not get any money we wept. Uncle's
pro-Boer sympathies led to a crowd getting hold of his garden
roller and dumping it some distance away.[1]

Sheffield University, was awarded the Bessemer Medal by the Iron and Steel
Institute, of which he was President, and was also chairman of the Chemical
Section of the British Association in 1910.'

EDITORS OF THE 'REVIEW OF REVIEWS' AFTER STEAD. Willie Stead was to have been
his father's successor as editor of the *Review of Reviews* but this young man of promise
died in 1907. After the *Titanic* disaster Alfred became editor but he soon grew
tired of the post, and John, afterwards Professor Stead, became editor. He was
glad, however, to give it up and take his part in the 1914 War. For three months
Charles Peers was editor, and then Mrs. Stead asked her elder daughter Estelle
to succeed him. Miss Stead occupied the editorial chair for 3½ years, raised the
sale and sold the *Review* for £25,000 for her mother. For a short time Sir
Philip Gibbs was editor and Daniel O'Connor proprietor. In 1923 Mr. Wickham
Steed became owner-editor. Mr. Lovat Dickson succeeded him in 1930. Mr.
W. W. Hindle, formerly of *The Times*, was editor from 1933 to 1936. The *Review*
then for about three years came under the direction of Mr. Vernon Bartlett as
the *World Review of the Press* and was published by Chatto & Windus. Mr. Bartlett
had been running a magazine called the *World*, consisting entirely of translations
and cartoons from the foreign Press. Sir Roger Chance and Mr. J. W. Wheeler
Bennett were among those associated with it. In 1940, under the proprietorship
of Mr. Hulton, the periodical was named the *World Review*.

[1] THE ADVANTAGE OF BEING MOBBED. Stead describes in the *Wimbledon Annual*
how during 'The Maiden Tribute' someone hung an effigy of him to one of his
trees. During the Boer War his garden was invaded by a yelling and groaning
crowd which trampled over the flower beds, pulled up the plants and flung
stones into the greenhouse. A hole made in the window of his drawing room he
refused to have mended. It is typical of Stead that he writes that he was 'grateful
to the revellers, for in that waking moment I was able to seize the exact sensation
which the seigneurs of the Middle Ages must have had when the Jacquerie surged
in tumult round their chateaux'. Among these reminiscences is a recollection of
John Morley 'coming up the carriage drive with a ghastly expression of pain and
horror on his face'; he was bringing news of the murder of Lord Frederick Cavendish
and Burke in Phoenix Park, Dublin. Stead also speaks of driving about in his
pony phaeton with Lord Milner, 'a delightful companion who sat bareheaded
with his hat on his knees'. Incidentally, in reference to his own health, Stead
recalls the fact that in his *Northern Echo* days, when he was full of local work his
doctor said to him, 'You can give up your editing and stick to your local duties,
you can stick to your editing and give up your local duties, or you can stick to
both of them and give up your life.'

II. By W. W. Hadley, Former Editor of the *Sunday Times*

STEAD AND THE NEW ORDER IN JOURNALISM. By his genius and creative energy, Stead was the greatest journalist of our time. If he had known how to make terms with capital he and not Northcliffe might have led the newspaper revolution at the turn of the century. In his prime he could have been in the first flight of almost any calling he chose to follow: in the Church a great preacher; in politics one of the most compelling orators. In politics, as in journalism we cannot think of him without a challenging 'if'. Newspapers in his time were demanding more and more capital, and he would not submit to the mildest restraints. Yet I have known no man with whom it was a greater pleasure to collaborate. His magnetic personality, compounded of idealism, abounding faith and dauntless courage, drew to him those who shared his aspirations. With them he was never 'difficult', never arrogant, and those who came near him soon discovered a vein of true humility that others never suspected. He was essentially a crusader. It was the cause for which he lived and worked; and for those who were prepared to work with him he was a good comrade as well as an inspiring leader.

He stood at the beginning of a period in which newspaper circulations were to be counted not in thousands but in millions. He could have no place in this new order, for the Cause always meant more to him than sales or profit. Though Northcliffe and others exploited his early seminal achievements in journalism, it is impossible to think of him as one of their executives or as editor of any popular daily paper in our generation.

AS PREACHER AND SPEAKER. As we walked away from a meeting one winter night in 1905 he told me he was going to Russia. An invitation from the Tsar had reached him through a friend at Buckingham Palace. Replying to my question, he said he could not say how long he would stay. I knew that his business affairs were in a bad state. The *Review of Reviews* had suffered severely as the result of his uncompromising opposition to the Boer War. The collapse of the *Daily Paper* had involved him in further heavy loss. I ventured to ask whether, in view of this, he was justified in leaving the country for an indefinite period. 'That,' he replied, 'I leave to the Senior Partner'. Knowing nothing of a partnership I repeated his words—'Senior Partner'? He stopped and gravely raised his arm and pointed to the stars. 'Yes', he said, 'The Senior Partner'.

On the platform, as at his desk, he had a rare power of quickly mobilising all the resources of his mind. On an autumn Sunday in Rochdale, I was told that he would preach in the evening at a

mission hall maintained by one of his friends. I arrived as the firs
hymn was being announced. He took the whole service. Lessons
prayer and sermon, all in harmonious sequence concentrated ou
minds on the ingathering of the harvest. The sermon reached ɑ
high level of glowing eloquence. I told him afterwards how it had
moved me. 'Thank you', he replied, 'but I wish they had told me
it was a harvest thanksgiving. I didn't know till I came in and saw
the pumpkins'. It was a marvellous improvisation. He could call up
all his powers at a moment's notice. If he had disciplined himsel
as a speaker he could have been a great orator. As it was he wa:
one of the most impressive speakers of his time.

What one marked in him was his extraordinary benevolence, to
which there was no limit. If a poor girl came his way he would
put aside everything to help her. There was one case in which he
got a young woman to Hayling Island, brought her work, saved
her life and gave her a career. [I have several letters from grateful
women.]

One morning I took him to a secondary school where he addressed
the senior girls. His theme was woman's place in the world, past
present, and to come. He didn't talk down to the young people
but gave them of his best. They listened intently with shining eye:
and I am sure that, though they might forget his words, the
memory of the man and his inspiring message would alway:
remain.

Of another meeting, recollection is specially vivid because of ɑ
distressing duty it imposed on me. The town hall was crowded
and many notables were on the platform. The audience was spellbound—and so was Stead. Unconscious of the flight of time, he
went on till the chairman became restless, for important local
people had been asked to speak, and they must not be crowded
out. Something had to be done, and sitting just behind Stead]
tugged at his coat-tails. He turned on me with blazing eyes and
then, with only a few seconds' pause, in which I suffered an agony
of remorse, he uttered a few more sentences and sat down. To me
he made no complaint, but at his host's table an hour later he told
how 'the devil put it into Hadley's heart' to ruin the climax oɪ
the speech.

'JOE' AND 'WILLIAM'. Those who knew him well cannot forget
his jovial moods. We were sitting by the fireside one night after a
meeting in Northampton. Finding that I had no fixed habit oɪ
physical exercises he told me what his morning exercises were.
'First', he said, 'I use my legs—six kicks forward with each foot, and,
to put vigour into them, I say with each kick, "That's for Joe!"'
"Joe" of course was Chamberlain. 'Having finished with "Joe" ', he
went on, 'I think of myself and give two half-dozen kicks to the rear;

kick my own behind and repeat each time, "William, be humble!" '[1]

WITH THE KAISER. He watched with grave foreboding the great expansion of German naval power in the early years of the century and joined whole-heartedly in efforts to prevent Anglo-German relations getting out of hand. In 1906 he was chiefly instrumental in bringing German editors to London; and in the following year he was the outstanding member of a large party of British journalists who toured Germany. They included J. A. Spender, A. G. Gardiner, Sidney Low, Clement Shorter, J. S. R. Phillips, Herbert Sidebotham and other newspaper notables. Everywhere it was Stead whom the Germans most wanted to see and hear. One beautiful summer morning we watched an imposing military display at Potsdam, with the Kaiser very much in the picture. After luncheon we were drinking coffee outside the Orangery when, with two equerries, he rode along the garden path and joined us. Spender and Phillips were presented. To Phillips, a Cumberland man, he talked with animation about the Lonsdale country which he knew well. 'Aren't you going to talk to Majesty?' I asked of Stead. 'No', he replied, 'when I did wish to talk with him he wouldn't see me, and now in this place I don't desire it.' Two other memories of that German visit: One of a great feast given in Berlin by the important Chamber of Commerce. Stead made a stirring speech in German. His grammar, a friend told me, was terrible, but he was never at a loss for a word, and the Germans were greatly impressed. A few days later we were in a village south of Munich. It was a gala day and all the afternoon Stead was the life and soul of the party, talking with everybody and romping with the children.

IV. BY JOHN MORLEY

'THAT COCKATRICE'. 'You mean when I hatched that cockatrice', Lord Morley is reported to have said of Stead to a friend after the appearance of 'The Maiden Tribute'. Morley's tribute in *Recollections*[2] is: 'Stead was invaluable; abounding in journalistic resource, eager in convictions, infinitely bold, candid, laborious in sure-footed mastery of all the facts, and bright with a cheerfulness and geniality that no difference of opinion between us and none of the passing embarrassments of the day could ever for a moment damp. His extraordinary vigour and spirit made other people

---

[1] Mr. E. S. Hole tells me that, during his term on the *Review of Reviews* 'often when the tram came to a stop at Aldwych, Stead would say that he would beat me up the steps, and frequently did so, though he must have been double my age. Once on the way to Waterloo with him we came level, on the bridge, with an old woman who was carrying a heavy bundle of washing, and Stead took it from her and carried it as far as the station. He would not let me take it.'

[2] Macmillan.

Q

seem wet blankets, sluggish, creatures of moral *défaillance*.'

An early impression is that in Morley's letter to his sister on Stead's arrival at the *Pall Mall*, 'A queer child of nature but a nice and good fellow'. Morley also wrote: 'He was surpassed by no journalist in any country in his sense of the commanding duties and responsibility of the mission of the Press. His temperament was eager, but he had a passion for being right, and to be right in facts and information was with him the foundation of serviceable opinion and popular instruction'.[1] In a letter to a sister in 1881 Stead says: 'Mr. Morley said that if I had not come up the *P.M.G.* would have collapsed, that I had saved the paper, and that, in short, I had exceeded his utmost expectations. If I were to leave he would leave instanter'.

V. WICKHAM STEED, FORMERLY EDITOR OF *THE TIMES*

ADVICE TO A WOULD-BE JOURNALIST. Mr. Wickham Steed, as a young man, had this advice from Stead: 'How can I know whether you are fit to be a journalist? To be a journalist, not a mere cumberer of the ground, you must have something to say. You can only find out whether you have anything worth saying by trying to say it and by seeing whether anybody will print it. But this I can tell you. When you have found something to say and have written it down, imagine it has to be telegraphed to Australia at your own expense. Telegrams cost, I think, five shillings a word. Then, when you have cut out every superfluous word and spoiled all your favourite phrases, copy it out legibly and send it to an editor. If he rejects it try somebody else. If nobody will accept it you are probably not fit to be a journalist'.[2]

Writing to Stead in 1899 from *The Times*, of which he was to be editor from Feb. 1919 to Nov. 1922, Steed says: 'You at least *payez de personne* in your work for peace; twice across Europe and up and down England in six months is not a bad record for a man who is not a Queen's Messenger but a hardworking and overworked apostle'.[3] He refers to the bi-lingual paper Stead is running at The Hague during the Peace Conference and regrets the cessation of his *War against War*.[4]

[1] *Early Life and Letters of John Morley*, F. W. Hirst (Macmillan, 1927).

[2] *Through Thirty Years* (Heinemann, 1924).

[3] For example to find a series of nine Stead articles, 'On the Eve of the Parliament of Man', dated respectively London, Paris, Rome, Vienna, Berlin, the northern capitals and so on, one of them being 'The Sacrosanctitude of Holland'.

[4] In a letter sympathizing with my difficulties in bringing out my review in Tokyo, *The New East*, with compositors who knew no English, Stead's son Henry, who was editing the Australian edition of the *Review of Reviews* in Melbourne, wrote of 'the trouble I had in producing the *Courier de la Conférence* at The Hague, a daily written in English, translated into French, and set up by compositors who knew only Dutch.

In a letter to me in 1944 Steed speaks of seeing Stead when he
was in Rome organizing support for the Conference:

He had just seen the Tsar and he told me the whole of his conversation.
He was entirely devoid of reserve or reticence and he trusted my discretion.

He spent some days with me, and left me a little bewildered by what I
felt to be a curious amalgam of sensational journalist and political seer.
He had the gift, which I think essential to good journalism, of seeing things
as they might be and ought to be, though he was too unacquainted with
foreign countries and languages to detect the presence of dangerous lions
in the path. In his way he was a great man.

The last time I saw him was in 1911. He turned up suddenly in Vienna,
with a notion that struck me as impracticable, but was characteristic of
his disinterested enthusiasm for what he thought good causes. The Young
Turks were massacring the Albanians and were threatening to do likewise
to the Greeks, Bulgarians and Serbs. Stead thought that the Emperor
Francis Joseph could put a stop to all this by proposing a 'new deal'—
those were his actual words, long before President Roosevelt used them—
by which Austria-Hungary and Russia would prevail upon the Balkan
peoples to sink their differences, would check the misdeeds of the Young
Turks, and generally inaugurate an era of peace and prosperity in South
Eastern Europe.

I have always kept a warm corner for Stead in my memory. British
journalism has many reasons to remember him—despite his vagaries—
with admiration and gratitude.

VI. By the late J. A. Spender, Editor of the *Westminster Gazette*

'ALL ENGLISHMEN HAVE CAUSE TO CHERISH HIS MEMORY.'
'Stead and I were, I suppose, about as unlike each other as two
men could well be', Spender once wrote; 'but he was a continual
inspiration to me and helped to supply a great deal that was
lacking in my own temperament.' Spender unveiled the memorial
to him on the Thames Embankment and said:

He was a master of his craft, with daring and original ideas, and he loved
journalism and left a permanent mark on it. Coming on the scene at a
time when it was in danger of being entangled in its own traditions, he
broke its bonds and enlarged its sphere to embrace a great new range of
human interests and emotions. He brought to his work an overflowing
vitality, a limitless curiosity, a vehement crusading temperament, a positive
preference for shocking and even scandalising the inert multitude, provided
only he could make it think. For pointed and animated writing, for the
discovery of the human interest which lurked in the heart of the most
forbidding subjects, for arresting phrases and unflagging vivacity in what
other people thought to be dull times, Stead was unequalled among his
contemporaries, and has not been approached by any of his successors.
But journalism with Stead was no mere craftsmanship. His great

journalistic qualities were the qualities of a mind full to overflowing of honest emotion and conviction, a mind to which journalism was always a means and not an end. Again and again he staked his whole fortune and career on forlorn and unpopular causes. And when his impetuous disposition and warm chivalry for man and woman brought him into conflict with worldly opinion and authority, he never resented any criticism but one, which was that he had done what he had done in order to sell his paper. He was one of the masters of our calling and an example to us of high faith, courage, and integrity in pursuing it. Not journalists alone, however, but all Englishmen have cause to cherish his memory.

'A PERMANENT MARK ON ENGLISH JOURNALISM.' Spender had already written in one of his own books:[1]

He was in his prime the greatest journalist in this country. In fertility of resource, in originality of ideas, in controversial dexterity, in the power of vivid presentation, in the instinct for study, he had no equal among his contemporaries. He was also one of the few men whose innovations have left a permanent mark on English journalism. But though he took a keen pleasure in procuring interesting and exclusive features and in tricking them out with journalistic arts and graces, he regarded all this as only leather and prunella. The ship, he used to say, had to be kept afloat, but the thing that mattered was the guns that it carried. He valued his newspaper and his review as a platform from which to fire hot shot, as a pulpit from which to preach hot gospel. Journalism happened to be his trade; his mission was that of a crusader. Sometimes he was on the popular side; more often on the unpopular side; and he always felt a little uncomfortably uncertain, as he was fond of saying, when the case was the former. The lines of his favourite poet which perhaps most often came to the point of his pen were:

> Then to side with truth is noble when we share her wretched crust
> E'er her cause brings fame and profit and 'tis prosperous to be just.
> Then it is the brave man chooses while the coward turns aside,
> Doubting in his abject spirit till his Lord is crucified.

The secret of Stead's success, alike as a journalist and as a preacher, lay in his strong and intense personality. His preaching was passionate and emotional. It may be doubted whether any of his contemporaries other than Disraeli or Gladstone excited in equal measure among so many people feelings of admiration and of personal antipathy. But few of those who had conceived a dislike for Stead on his public form were not disarmed if they chanced to come into personal intercourse with him, and those who enjoyed such intercourse liked him best. It would be impossible for the history of Stead's time to be written without frequent mention of him. There was no opinion to which he would not give a charitable hearing. Hardly ever have I known him wrong about a fact, and his power of reducing masses of detail to brief and lucid statements was unequalled.[2]

---

[1] *Life, Journalism and Politics.* (Cassell, 1932.)
[2] Several people have testified to the speed at which Stead could 'gut' a blue-book. He once spoke of driving his mind through a blue-book 'with the rush of a buzz-saw'.

VII. By the late C. P. Scott, H. W. Massingham, T. P. O'Connor, R. D. Blumenfeld and Kennedy Jones

'TO BE HIMSELF.' C. P. Scott of the *Manchester Guardian* paid a tribute in August 1899 to Stead's services respecting the Hague Conference. 'Three men's work for four or five months! That the Conference was ever held at all is due as much to you as to anybody. As to the account between us it can only be imperfectly liquidated by our hearty thanks. As to payment, would £300 be satisfying at the rate of £30 a week or £5 a column?' T. P. O'Connor said to Stead, 'You are too good a fanatic to be a real journalist, too real a journalist to be a true fanatic'.

H. W. Massingham is quoted in *Everyman Remembers* by Ernest Rhys[1] as saying: 'He will live in history as the man who made of modern journalism a powerful personal force, the instrument of one intensely individual mind. His main conception of an editor's duty was to be himself. His temperament was that of the great pamphleteers. In his boldness and versatility, in his faith in the constructive power of his pen, in many of his opinions, even in his championship of women, he resembled Defoe.'

R. D. Blumenfeld, editor of the *Daily Express*, who was no sentimentalist, called Stead 'virile and courageous'.

No one would have taken Kennedy Jones for an idealist after Stead's pattern, but in *Fleet Street and Downing Street* he wrote: 'It is easy to find fault with Stead, but his work in the bulk has stood the test of time, and his influence is still apparent.'

VIII. By J. P. Collins, Formerly Literary Editor of the *Pall Mall Gazette*

IN DEFENCE OF A BOOKSELLER. I can say that nobody will read your *P.M.G.* study in better heart than I, for I admired the old man from the first, certainly long before I came to London. The first time I ever saw him was at Bow Street, when he came forward to speak for Dobell, the poet-bookseller, for championing the cause of his craft, after it had been shifted to Charing Cross Road, and the police objected to the display shelves protruding more than so many inches across the footpath.

Charles Morley used to talk about the days when he went to Holloway Gaol at an early hour to discuss the day's paper with the convict-editor, and take him all the morning's correspondence. C.M. assured me that he never came away without a lighter heart

---

[1] Dent, 1931.

as a result of the man's marvellous courage and determination of character.[1]

We had in our house a helper, an estimable old widow, who had been in service in Stead's home. She said: 'There was never a better master or a better husband or a better father. I never knew him lose his temper with any of us, however impatient he may have been. And on the one Sunday in the year when he used to keep open house, it was a regular sight to see all sorts of people come crowding in to talk with him; and there he was in his prison dress, because, you know, he was sent to gaol for something—I could never understand why, because I am very sure there never was a kinder or better man'. She finished with a full downpour of tears, and there was sincerity in every word. How many great editors, I wonder, would leave such an impression on a domestic help? [W.A.Y. sends me a story of a village shopkeeper and postmistress who had had Stead staying with her and said, 'Do you know I always thought he was a wicked man but he wasn't!']

IX. BY S. R. LITTLEWOOD, FORMERLY EDITOR OF THE STAGE

AN INTERVIEW WITH THE SPIRIT OF GLADSTONE. Stead struck me as a great journalist and at the same time a great innocent. I remember being told off by the late Sir Robert Donald, then editor of the *Daily Chronicle*, to get Stead to interview the spirit of Gladstone. I found Stead hard at work, coat off, and in a grey flannel shirt with the sleeves rolled up. I told him my mission. He said, "It's a tough job, but give me a couple of hours and I'll try". I came back in a couple of hours and found him still at his table. It was littered with papers, all of them covered with his own handwriting. He said, "I've had a wonderful interview, but I've got to sort these out. Give me another couple of hours". I came back in another couple of hours and he had the whole thing in order and sub-edited. It was certainly a remarkable Gladstonian survey of the political situation. The great phrase was, I remember, 'Do not precipitate a crisis'. I am certain that Stead sincerely believed he had, in effect, interviewed Gladstone. Morley was very different—far more learned, far more sophisticated, but without the simple-hearted genius and journalistic ardour of his successor. In place of Stead's brotherly blue eye and instant understanding and sympathy, Morley was questioning and quizzical. I might have been talking to a solicitor.

[1] Morley, sent on a trip to New York at the instance of the *Pall Mall* to inspect newspaper offices, says in a letter to Stead: 'You have nothing to learn from the New York Press as far as conceptions and ideals go.' The long letter ends in capital letters NEVER FEAR.'

X. By the late Edwin H. Stout of the *Pall Mall Gazette*
and *Review of Reviews*

MEMORIES OF THE MORLEY-STEAD PERIOD. When Morley
arrived at the *Pall Mall* in the morning he would thresh out the
policy of the day for an hour with Stead, then write the leader,
and after that consider the proof with him, sometimes taking so
much time over this as to cause the paper to miss the trains. Then
he would go off to lunch at the Athenaeum and Stead would start
going through the provincial papers. I was with Stead as a reporter
during 'The Maiden Tribute', 'The Truth about the Navy', and
the General Gordon campaigns. I had £100 a year and at no time
more than £250. I had come to the paper as a junior reporter
under Morley. Newspaper staffs were small then, and I was
additional to William Mackay, who had a weekly paper of his
own at Chatham. The sub-editor was Bayne. I stayed at Stead's
home for six weeks, was drawn into the family life and later became
editor's private secretary. I recall a Quaker lady overhearing
Stead use the word 'damnable' and saying to him, 'William, thee
shouldst not swear'. Stead rejoined, 'Even Jesus Christ swore'.
The Quakeress's reply was, 'Thee should leave it to Him'. Stead
tried many mornings to take his small folk for a donkey drive before
he went off to the train for the office.

In my day the printer was Lambert—his photograph is in the
Review of Reviews—and he was succeeded by Thomas Hunt of
your time.

With regard to Stead's later period, after he had left the *Pall Mall*,
I disbelieved in spiritualism for two reasons: First, the sealed packet
left by Sir Oliver Lodge containing what he would say if he spoke
after death had never been appealed to. Secondly, in view of
Stead's ardour and his long experience of my unbelief, he would
certainly have got through to me and he didn't.

THE SCENTED GARDEN AND SILK HATS. The following
experience had nothing to do with spiritualism. After Sir Richard
Burton's death Lady Burton got into touch with my friend, W. A.
Coote, secretary of the National Vigilance Society, founded during
Stead's purity crusade, and handed Burton's MS. of *The Scented
Garden* to Coote with permission to destroy it. One Saturday after-
noon Coote, a Camberwell man, and I went down to that borough's
incinerator and consigned the book to the flames.

It was the custom for reporters to wear silk hats, and I remember
that, when my hat got the worse for wear, a Press friend and I
bought new ones and took the old hats out to Clapham Common
and played football with them. Reporters were more simple-
hearted in those days. My memory goes back to the election of

1867, before the Ballot Act, and the hustings in the High Street of my Hampshire home, and seeing a distribution of pheasants and hares after the election to men who had voted for the successful candidate.

I recall reporting in the House of Commons a Budget speech by Gladstone, and that at one point the old man raised his hand, showing the black cloth patch over the stump of the left hand forefinger that had been blown off in a shooting accident, and begging honourable members to consider for one moment the appalling fact that the national expenditure was rapidly approaching one hundred millions a year!

XI. BY THE LATE JOHN BOON OF THE EXCHANGE TELEGRAPH COMPANY

'HE OUTSHONE THEM ALL.' 'Stead was himself alone. Frowned upon by many of the journalistic pandits of the time, he outshone them all. I have heard his style described as crude. For my part I admired his nervous English; it had much of the quality of the old puritan divines, with considerably more than their sense of humour. He excelled in attack; but that was the nature of the man. He was a reformer and he achieved much that was to the nation's benefit in his time. He, like other men, had been described as a champion of lost causes. Yes, but he was a champion who led them to victory. I regarded Stead with both admiration and affection. There was much of the seer in his composition. In the same year with him died that very remarkable man, General Booth. Stead was one of his champions from the start.'[1]

XII. BY ADMIRAL LORD FISHER

THE H.M.S *INDOMITABLE* EXPLOIT. 'Stead was absolute integrity and he feared no man; I have known him tackle a Prime Minister like a terrier a rat. I have known him go to a packed meeting and scathe the whole mob of them. He never thought of money; he only thought of truth. He might have been a rich man if he hadn't told the truth; I know it. When he was over sixty he performed a journalistic feat that was wondrous. By King Edward's positive orders a cordon was arranged round the battle-cruiser *Indomitable*, arriving late at night at Cowes with the Prince of Wales [afterwards George V] on board, to prevent the Press being a nuisance. In the dark Stead, in a small boat,[2] dropped down with

[1] *Victorians, Edwardians and Georgians.* (Hutchinson, 1927.)
[2] John Stead, who as professor at the Royal Naval College, Greenwich, would have access to the best information, told me that the boat, which was hired from Southsea, 'went about a mile in the dark in weather not too good, and that his father reached the boom by a rope ladder which was very wobbly, and he was then distinctly stout'.

the tide from ahead and swarmed up a greasy pole, known to sailors as the lower boom, talked to one of the officers, who naturally supposed he couldn't be there without permission, and the *Daily Mail* the next morning had the most perfect digest I have ever read of perhaps one of the most wonderful passages ever made.[1] (This big battle cruiser encumbered with the heaviest guns known, and with hundreds and hundreds of tons of armour on her sides, beat the *Mauretania*, the greyhound of the seas, built of gingerbread, carrying no cargo and shaped for no other purpose than for speed and luxury.) No other paper had a word.

'CROMWELL AND LUTHER IN ONE.' 'Stead always told me he would die in his boots. Strife was his portion, he said. Stead was a pro-Boer and so was I. Of course every genius has a strain of queerness. Esher loved Stead as much as I did. We felt a common affliction when he died. That's why I wrote to Esher: "This loss of dear old Stead numbs me! Cromwell and Martin Luther rolled into one. And such a big heart. Such great emotions. All I've read quite inadequate. The telegrams [in accounts of the *Titanic* disaster] say that he was in the forefront with the women and children, putting them in the boats! I can see him! And probably singing Hallelujah and encouraging the ship's band to play cheerfully. A fine death." As a boy he had threepence a week pocket money. One penny bought Shakespeare in weekly parts, the other two pennies went to his God for Missions. He was a missionary himself all his life. Fearless even when alone, believing in his God—the God of truth—and his enemies always rued it when they fought him. He was an exploder of gasbags and the terror of liars. He was called a "wild man" because he said "Two keels to one". At Berlin the All Highest said to him, "Don't be frightened". Stead replied, "Oh, no, we won't, for every Dreadnought you build we will build two!" That was the genesis of the cry, "Two keels for One". I have a note of it made at the time for my *Reflections*.'[2]

XIII. By Viscount Esher

'OWING TO A BAD CONSCIENCE'. When I was a boy, Stead used to come down to stay for the weekend with my father, and I was immensely struck by that jovial, exuberant bearded man, with his loud laugh and inexhaustible enthusiasm. At that time he was absorbed in spiritualism, and he used to gather us all round the instrument that spelled out words from the spirit world. He was

---

[1] The Admiralty kindly informs me that on the voyage there had been an unofficial endurance and speed trial. *The Times* gave the land-to-land average speed as 24·8 knots.

[2] From *Memories*. (Hodder and Stoughton, 1919.)

in such deadly earnest and so anxious to get results that I remember cheating in order to satisfy him. In consequence he considered our house unusually favourable for séances, and wrote about our experiences and successes in the *Review of Reviews*. Perhaps this has stuck in my memory owing to a bad conscience. But after more than fifty years the whole atmosphere of the man, his total lack of self-importance, his charming inclination to treat all human beings, however young, as his equals, and his Gargantuan appetite for ideas, comes back to me redolent of his powerful vitality. As one looks back it is strange how un-Victorian the Victorians were.[1]

XIV. By the late Lord Snell, Chairman of the London County Council

THE BRAVEST, MOST TOLERANT MAN I HAVE KNOWN. I knew Stead more particularly as a visitor to his home. I had a great regard for him. He was a wonderful talker and a generous, impulsive and understanding and most loyal friend, one of the bravest, most tolerant, and most provokingly self-willed men I have ever known. He frequently distressed his friends by declarations that appeared to compromise both him and them. He ran for years a "two keels to one" Navy campaign while supporting most of the peace societies. He was at one and the same time a democrat and an imperialist. He defended Russia under the Tsars while fighting the slightest deviation from democratic standards in his own country. All this pleased his critics and tried the patience of his friends. He was not really, however, so inconsequential as his political activities suggested, and he certainly was not merely perverse. There was in him a unity of purpose which only those who knew him well could see. He was a deeply religious man, and the clue to his character and purpose was on the moral and spiritual rather than on the practical side. He was a moral rather than a

[1] 'ONE OF THE FEW REALLY GOOD MEN.' This is what Lord Esher's father, Stead's faithful friend, Reggie Brett, called Stead. He added 'and truly A MAN'. To Mrs. Stead on her husband's death, he wrote, 'No one loved and admired him more than I, who have been his friend through every hour, dull or bright, for thirty years. He was one of the few very honest, very single-minded and really good men I have ever known. There was nothing he ever undertook which he failed to talk over with me. Often and often we differed in opinion, as you know, but it made no difference to our friendship or intimacy. It was not only a privilege but an honour to be admitted to his confidence. No one was ever more faithful than he to his ideals. How often we talked about you, and I know how profound was his admiration as well as his love for your character, and how grateful he was to you for your lifelong devotion and charity.'

In a letter years before Stead's death, Esher had written to Lady Esher: 'Stead is off to Russia to see the Tsar again. He is wild and odd as ever and thinks he has inherited the spirit of Charles II, who—through him—is making amends for his previous life on earth. If he wasn't so sane in other matters he would have to be shut up.'

political thinker. I never knew him to deviate from his allegiance to his conception of religion and duty.[1]

XV. By the late Sir Peter Chalmers Mitchell

STEAD'S PLACARD. Sir Peter Chalmers Mitchell in *My Fill of Days*[2] has several stories of Stead in the United States in 1907. 'In Philadelphia, Stead and his wife came across the hotel lounge to where we were sitting at the far end, Stead almost at a run, stooping forwards, his beard untidy, his strange blue eyes making a rather commonplace face more than striking; Mrs. Stead ambling behind with a motherly, humorous smile as of one affectionately and protectively tolerant of anything her husband might do. After shaking hands, she gave Stead a piece of cardboard about a foot square, with a ribbon arranged as if it were to be hung on a wall, like a text in a cottage bedroom, and then went off to the lift. Stead settled himself in an armchair, and hung the placard round his neck. There was printed on it: "W. T. STEAD, London, England". "What on earth?", I began to say. "The Press will be seeking me," he answered; "the reporters don't know me by sight, and I like to save them trouble". The Press was there and did wish to see him. As soon as the placard had been noticed, young men seemed to spring up from every part of the hall and came running across to Stead. Never can there have been a kinder-hearted, more unselfish man than the great English journalist, nor one who at all times was more alert to do some good turn in a great matter or a small matter to those about him.'

XVI. Other Memories

WHO INVENTED THE 'NEW JOURNALISM'? Most people think of Harmsworth. The truth is stated by the great authority on the British Press, Mr. Stanley Morison, in *The English Newspaper*:[3] 'Stead created the "New Journalism". By the introduction of one innovation after another—the gossip column, the interview and the cross-head among them. The vogue spread not only to the new evenings but to the crop of new dailies that began during the next two or three decades'. Writing to me about the present book, which he was good enough to term a 'thoroughly admirable

---

[1] Lord Snell adds in his *Men, Movements and Myself* 'His beliefs helped to sustain him in great emergencies, and I recall that on our way back from Brookwood cemetery, after the funeral of his eldest son, he said to me: "I shall have him daily at my side as usual". When I said: "It is in any case a great thing to be able to believe that you will," he replied: "I did not say 'I believe': I said 'I know.'"'

[2] Faber, 1937.
[3] Published by *The Times*.

project', he said, 'I have studied the *Pall Mall* in some detail. Journalism owes far more to Stead than has ever been acknowledged. He seems to me to have been a man after Tom Barnes' heart, though certainly writing for a different public. Neither was the type of man to twaddle about chrysanthemums or spin rigmaroles about the fashions at Goodwood. He anticipated all of Harmsworth's and Pearson's journalism.'

A veteran author of several volumes on Fleet Street, the late Hamilton Fyfe, wrote in his authoritative 'How the Press Revolution Came'[1]: 'Stead invented what Matthew Arnold called the "New Journalism", full of ability, novelty, variety, sensation, sympathy, and generous sentiments'. Northcliffe said Stead 'effected a revolu-

Before and after the peerage

tion in journalism. For instance, Stead took up interviewing, till then unknown in England. He made his paper livelier, more outspoken than his rivals. They never startled or surprised anybody; what he would say or do next no one knew.' Sir Edward Cook writes somewhere: 'If an intimate, well-informed history of British journalism during the eighties and nineties is ever written, Stead and his school will be recognised as the innovators'.

With reference to Matthew Arnold's word 'sensation', R. C. K. Ensor in *England 1870–1914* in the *Oxford History of England*[2] distinguishes. 'Stead's "sensations" ' were like the sensations of Delane and Barnes of *The Times*. They 'always made a direct appeal to men dealing with public affairs. The key feature of the "New Journalism" (Ensor is now thinking of Harmsworth) was not sensation but commercialism. It ran its sensations, as it ran everything else, to make money. The indisputable pioneer of *this* school was Harmsworth'.[3]

[1] In Chapter III in his *Press Parade*. (Watts, 1936.)
[2] Oxford University Press, 1936.
[3] 'Northcliffe, who was gifted with an uncanny sense of the ordinary citizen's state of mind, gave orders in 1917 that no articles in his *Daily Mail* should exceed three hundred words in length, and set the example by writing a large number of condensed and pithy articles himself.'—Wickham Steed in *The Press*. (Penguin.)

A writer in the *World's Press News*, with some knowledge of London Press history, Mr. F. G. Mansfield, corrected Mr. R. J. Cruikshank's statement that the "New Journalism" was born on January 17, 1888, when the first number of the *Star* was published, and quoted Bernard Shaw who speaks of the *Star* 'growing out of the "New Journalism".' 'The distinction of originating the "New Journalism",' Mr. Mansfield said, 'belongs without doubt to Stead'.

FIRST THEATRE-GOING AT FIFTY-FIVE. Stead was fifty-five when, at the urging of Sir Henry Irving, William Archer and Elizabeth Robins, he took the decision, in his thorough way, not to visit one theatre but several. He would make an 'investigation' and write a series of articles in the *Review of Reviews*. His first play was Beerbohm Tree's *Tempest*, seen from the front row of the pit with Miss Robins, whom so many of us gratefully remember in Ibsen. 'If all plays are like this play', Stead reported, 'the prejudice against the theatre is absurd'; Tree was doing 'a national service'. A Pinero play he was ashamed to find himself laughing at. It is worth turning up an old number of the *Review* to read honest theatrical criticism of a new type. It was characteristic of him that, once having realised the potentialities of the playhouse, he should launch a scheme for 'English Plays and Players on the Continent'. J. T. Grein, who is remembered for the good work he did in offering worth-while theatrical fare in London, was chairman of 'The English Players'; Stead was hon. secretary. A bundle of letters contains cordial messages, in their marvellously varied handwriting, from the chief actors and actresses and theatrical managers and playwrights of the time. There was an 'honorary committee', joined by John Walter of *The Times*, ambassadors on the Continent and literary people at home including Wells, Galsworthy, Frederic Harrison, J. M. Barrie, Sarah Grand of *The Heavenly Twins*, Conan Doyle and Jerome K. Jerome.

Before this adventure Stead had attended at fifty 'My First Ball', the title of a paper of fifteen pages quarto he wrote for Mrs. Tickell, one of his most knowledgeable secretaries, and she has kindly let me see it. The ball took place in Holland during the Peace Conference at The Hague and most of the delegates were there.

BALFOUR'S FOOTMAN AND STEAD'S BOOTS. Mrs. Tickell, who is a grand-daughter of T. H. Huxley and a cousin of Grant Allen and Grant Richards (who was at the *Review of Reviews* for six years), writes to me: 'I retain a great affection for Stead. He was a most lovable man. I am one of the women who did not fall in love with him, but he was very much my friend. I had a great job managing him. One day he was going to see Balfour and I insisted on his getting a new hat. The next day I noticed when he stretched out his legs and crossed them that the soles of his shoes were badly broken. "Yes", he said, "when I went to Balfour yesterday the footman told me to go to the side door." I can confirm the statements as to his belief that he would die a violent death. He often told me that he thought he would be kicked to death while supporting some unpopular cause. As for the clothes Stead wore, he once told an interviewer that he could dress from top to toe in five minutes. On which someone said he was 'the only man in London who dares to dress as he does'.

HAD STEAD A SENSE OF HUMOUR? Could he have had? A man who knew him very well for twenty years was positive that he was without a sense of humour. That 'he thoroughly enjoyed fun with children' there is plenty of evidence. But that is not humour. Professor John Stead, of whom I saw a good deal, put in writing for me the following: 'I have never met a human being who had a keener sense of humour. When he came home from his travels the account he gave us always contained humorous details. He appreciated humour when it was against himself. Often the humorous side appealed to him much more than the serious. He told Mark Twain that, as a schoolboy doing a general information paper, I had written that Twain was the author of *Paradise Lost*.' Then J. S. R. Phillips, in the fourteenth volume of the *Cambridge History of Literature*, asserts that Stead was 'possessed of much humour'. Surely the truth is told in one of the kind letters Miss Stead has written to me: 'I don't think my father had a strong sense of humour. Had he had it would have saved him a good deal of worry and unhappiness. Someone said of him that he was too much of a realist to be witty. He was very fond of children and loved playing with them—he had the heartiest laugh I have ever heard—and in that way obtained relaxation. But, once convinced that a cause or a case was right and that it was the "Senior Partner's" wish that he should fight for it, he was deadly serious. You don't find touches of humour in his writings. Had he had a greater sense of humour it would have helped him over many things that hurt him sorely, for he was extremely sensitive, though he seldom showed it. I know people who say he had a strong sense of humour, but I think they were mistaken.'

RELATIONS WITH WOMEN. Few men can have had more women friends and acquaintances in all classes of society. To few men have more women been indebted for intimate counsel or for cash. At few men have more women, in the common phrase, flung themselves. I have hundreds of women's letters to Stead. Both in my house and in Stout's, towards the end of Stout's life, we spoke at times of Stead's moral conduct. Neither of us had heard a scrap of evidence to impugn it. I as a Rationalist and Stout as a life-long

practising Methodist—he told me that in his young days he was
once so much shocked by seeing Stead kiss Marie Belloc that he
remonstrated with him—may be fairly considered to offer between
us a responsible opinion. Havelock Ellis, the most scientific student
of sex in this country in the time of Stead, knew him well. Twice
in conversation with Ellis when Stead was discussed between us,
Ellis said to me that he was in no doubt as to the self-control he
exercised. It was the control of sexuality, Ellis contended, that
supplied no small part of the driving force with which he accomplished so much. I believe that Stead's experience with Madame
Novikoff was a lesson to him. The 'confession' I have reproduced
I only read lately, and Stout had not seen it.

STEAD AND MONEY. What is the truth about Stead when there
is applied to him another touchstone of character, that of money?
It is beyond doubt that no man thought less of money, spent less
on himself, or, in proportion to his means, gave more away with
an honest heart. From his boyhood until his death his spending
was all for what he conceived to be the public welfare, and he was
not content with spending. His mind, his sympathy, his physical
strength went with it, to the utmost of his powers and with no
regrets.

I was jarred when, at the end of a letter to me from a conspicuous
figure in public affairs, the late Marquis of Crewe, there was a
phrase to the effect that Stead had 'all the qualifications for a
great career except commonsense'. No doubt judgment was in the
writer's mind, and we have already had E. T. Cook's view. The
debt of the world to the lack of what so many of its inhabitants have
regarded as commonsense is immeasurable. Stead had genius,
and a price had to be paid for it, by himself and other people.
It is the mark of men of genius that many of them have little regard
for money and small qualifications for handling it. Stead conformed
to type. To incapacity for looking after his money there was added
impulsiveness—which often seemed like waywardness—reluctance
to act on the advice he so frequently sought, a firm belief that all
he did and—may it be said?—wanted to do, was directed by a
'Senior Partner' who would see him through every difficulty.
To these characteristics there must be added an acknowledged
satisfaction in the privilege of sharing in the direction of the
destinies of the world.

Something of the man may be seen in his handwriting. There is
not a flourish anywhere. It is the writing of an earnest, honest,
indomitable, working, striving man, sure of his goal, often under
illusions but in control. It is noteworthy that throughout his life
the handwriting never varies. In its grip and its absence of flourishes
the writing has a curious resemblance to Gladstone's. Stead and

Gladstone were equally determined, centred characters. When they
let themselves go they were under a conviction that what they were
doing mattered greatly. They could also be both cogent and prolix.

When the outcry was loudest against Stead, Benjamin Jowett
merely observed, 'I believe Stead to be an honest man'.

Cardinal Manning said, 'When I read the *Pall Mall* it seems to
me as if Cromwell had come to life'.

Lord Northcliffe, after the death of Stead, wrote that he was 'an
affectionate and true friend'.

W. M. Crook, of the Eighty Club, who was well known for his
useful letters to the newspapers, wrote of Stead's 'lovableness'.
'He was of the stuff of which the early Christian martyrs were made.
He was natural, simple, and had no trace of self-consciousness.'

Sir Horace Plunkett, who did not fling his praise about—I knew
him well—spoke of Stead being 'marvellously informed'. Dr.
Jameson said, 'I sit in his big armchair and he paces up and down
and in an hour I have learnt more from him than from any man
in London'.

'The most interesting man I ever met' is the description of Stead
given me by John Morley's nephew, Mr. Guy Morley.

Mr. Hesketh Pearson in his *Bernard Shaw* says 'Stead's exposure of
the white slave traffic aroused Shaw's enthusiasm to such an extent
that he offered to sell copies of the *Pall Mall* in the streets because
the bookstalls had boycotted the paper'.

In an account of Stead done by a skilled woman journalist,
Mrs. M. C. Braby, who, after she had interviewed him when she
was twenty-five, he called the best interviewer he had ever met,
one reads of 'a joyous gentleman whose white beard alone hinted
at advancing years, whose cheerful, healthy countenance glowed
with the joy of living, in whose bright blue eye there shone fire,
whose whole mien was one of overflowing, irresponsible gaiety
and innocent gladness'.

*The Countess of Aberdeen's facetious signature to Stead when
she was Vice-reine of Ireland*

CHAPTER XIX

A CHAPTER IN STEAD'S PRIVATE LIFE

'THE MOST MOMENTOUS OF ALL HUMAN ACTS.' There is an entry in Stead's diary in which he gets clear away from journalism. He makes a revelation, at first sight surprising, of the intimacies of his married life and parenthood. It is in keeping with his character and temperament. He says, 'I do not like to write of these matters'. But here before me is what he has written. I do not think that, if he should now be sensible of what is going on in the world, as he believed he would be, he would disapprove of my including it in this book. In the time in which he lived it would not have been possible to print any of it. The facts of 'The Maiden Tribute' were one thing; this personal intimacy is another. Since his day, however, the world has grown up many years; a library of books on marriage and parenthood has been published and widely read. My task is to furnish, as far as I can, a complete picture of the man who has so great a part in the story of the paper the history of which I am trying faithfully to present. As Froude said, 'It is worse than useless to attempt the biography of a man unless you learn or think you know what his inner nature was'. Attentive readers have no doubt wondered more than once about an aspect of Stead's life on which nothing has been said so far, thoughts on which follow naturally on what he has let us know in earlier pages about his wife and himself. Here is what he records on January 20, 1889, reduced somewhat in detail:[1]

'I stand at the point of one of the most momentous, perhaps the most momentous of all human acts, the begetting of a new soul. Poor little creature yet unconceived. Why do I have to face the frightful responsibility of saying that thou shalt be? Because it would seem God hath need of thee. I did not intend thee to be born. I have brought five into the battlefield and I thought five is enough. But it would seem that I was mistaken. All my five have grown up well. The youngest is five. Happier children I never knew. Life to them has been a gift of joy. So far they have had no reason

---

[1] Some time after the completion of the typescript from which this chapter was printed I had a letter from a kind helper who typed it. She wrote: 'The more I think about it the more certain I am that you do well to include all that matters about Stead's private life. He emerges as a really human being. He was so many-sided that it is necessary to show him as such.'

R

to curse me for begetting them. Now God seems to want another soldier.

A MARITAL HISTORY. 'I will set forth simply what has taken place. I have from the birth of Willie practised simple syringing with water. Of late always withdrawal. We never used anything but this. Intercourse limited to twice a week, and withdrawal, taking place just before the supreme moment, never did me any harm. The pleasure I think is rather greater than when the emission takes place in the natural way. If thrice or four times in the week I got deaf with apparent wax formation in the right ear. Desire increased with years rather than diminished, and the last twelve months I worshipped my wife with my body, as the Prayer Book has it, more than ever before. She also was responsive and affectionate. The pleasure was far greater for her than when she was first married. (For me it was immeasurably so.) Nor could we say positively that the interruption did her harm. It did not interfere with her satisfaction, rather enhanced it.

THE DESIRE FOR CHILDREN. 'In July happened the carriage accident, following which came her acute despondency and absolute loathing of me. Melancholia culminated in her going to Heywood Smith's hospital. There she had some cautery performed. She was better when she came out. But when in the hospital and all intercourse ceased for six months ovarian pain began to develop. Dr. Smith said pregnancy would give the ovaries rest and Dr. Gale strongly recommended a child.

A WANTED CHILD. 'We had never decided definitely to stop breeding. My wife's passionate love for babies always made me feel that there was a lurking desire in the heart to have another little one. When she began to see that her health seemed to stand in urgent need of recovering by conception, she said she would like another baby. I was for a time somewhat dismayed. The sorrow and the struggle and the agony of the world, the sense of its sin and its despair made me reluctant. But I thought we could bring up six as easily as five. Willie is now getting up to 14. The little one would be a great blessing to Emma. It may be that God may not make my seed quicken. That is for Him to decide. We both prayerfully hope that he will not unless He will take the child for His very own and use it for His Service from the womb up. We prayed about it and it seemed to come quite clear. So this night we shall have uninterrupted intercourse for the first time for five years, in the hope of getting a daughter who may, I hope, be the Lord's from her conception, and may do valiantly for the Lord and for her sex. Perhaps by the time she comes to womanhood the lot of woman may not be so hard as heretofore.'

On Sunday night, April 15, 1889, there is an entry from which

I make this complementary extract: 'My wife is away. She seems to have conceived, and next October there will probably be another soul born into the world. So far her health is somewhat improved but all the year she has been a more or less constant invalid. Since she conceived I have read to her Ibsen's plays, Tolstoy, *Faiths of the World* and part of Gogol. I shall read Goethe, Shakespeare, etc. She is still various in her moods. Now and then a week or a fortnight of her old self but on the whole year not one month herself. Intercourse almost suspended. Three weeks' interval intermitted from fear of pain in ovary, resumed at her wish with great passion of desire [on my part]. Only once this year has she had fierce, strong longing. I had been preparing myself for apparently endless abstinence when suddenly it came on her in my absence. I noticed the change when I returned. She told me and was very loving. How rare are such moments. How longingly I remember them. Ah if she were but always so!'

CHAPTER XX

CATASTROPHE

THE *DAILY PAPER* FIASCO. The canny Sir William
Robertson Nicoll, of the *British Weekly* and *Bookman*, is
quoted[1] as saying: 'I never could understand that awful
mess of Stead's *Daily Paper*. Stead seemed to me always to be
dreaming of some millionaire who would give him *carte blanche*,
and this prevented him from doing what he might very easily
have done. He might have established a weekly with a world-wide
circulation, telling immensely upon opinion.' In a letter to me,
W. W. Hadley says: 'When Stead started the *Daily Paper* he
had arranged with me to edit a national weekly which was to be
launched if the daily caught on. It was plain that he had no sure
confidence that success would be achieved. The enterprise, he
said, would leave him very soon a millionaire or a pauper. He
ought to have put the weekly first; it would have been a more
manageable enterprise and would, I think, have succeeded. It
might, indeed, in time have provided capital for the other and
far more hazardous project. He was to send me a telegram and
I would leave Rochdale for London as soon as possible. The
telegram never came.'

Before Stead started the journal (E. H. Stout once said to me)
'he sent me a pitiful estimate of probable receipts and expenses
and asked my candid opinion. I replied, "If you do this, in under
six weeks you will be a bankrupt." "Very well", he said, "I think
you are wrong, but you take no responsibility; you look after the
Review of Reviews and I will look after the *Daily Paper*." One of
Stead's prodigalities was to take leases of shops all over London,
and some of these leases are still running. The paper was to be
delivered by girls from these shops. When premises could not be
got for seven years, they were taken for fourteen, and when they
could not be got for fourteen they were taken for twenty-one. Therefore Bourchier Hawksley, the solicitor of the Chartered Company
of South Africa (his faithful friend who kept him out of no end of
trouble), and Alfred Beit were for years afterwards settling claims.'

I have before me in Stead's handwriting his preliminary memorandum on the *Daily Paper*. The results of efforts of Lewis & Lewis with
it he describes accurately as 'a document the like of which does

[1] *William Robertson Nicoll: Life and Letters*, T. H. Darlow (Hodder & Stoughton,
1925).

not exist in Somerset House'. There are a dozen or more 'Objects' the type of which is indicated by the first two:

(1) To reduce or alleviate wrongs and hardships of all kinds, whether public or private.

(2) To expose, denounce, remove or put down abuses and objectionable habits or customs, and to caution and warn the public against dangers, perils and risks and to prevent and avert the same.

On getting down to business one reads: 'Mr. Stead's shares shall always confer on him the right to ten more votes than the aggregate number of all the votes conferred by all the other shares, and a new office is created which Mr. Stead is to hold for life'. The declaration of this Governing Director 'as to the amounts of the net profits shall be conclusive'.

The New Daily Paper

Mr Stead's Company Limited

The Powers of the Governor Director

In Stead's handwriting

WHAT THE NEWSPAPER WAS LIKE. There were really two *Daily Papers*. The first was the specimen of October 1, 1893, which was never published. It was about 10 inches high and about $7\frac{1}{2}$ inches wide, and contained 40 pages. They included, besides the normal features of a newspaper, a page on the Church Congress, a page on 'Is Dissent Doomed in Rural England?' a page of Notes, a 2-page 'automatic interview' with Lady Warwick on 'The Failure of the Aristocracy', a page of 'In Place of Morning Service', a page of 'The Saint for the Day, St. Francis of Assisi', a 2-page interview with Elizabeth Robins on 'A National Theatre of the Press', a special correspondent's two-page account of

GREAT NAVAL BATTLE OFF SALAMIS
TRIUMPH OF THE GREEKS
THE PERSIAN FLEET DESTROYED
TERRIBLE CARNAGE
XERXES IN FULL FLIGHT
THE STRATEGY OF THEMISTOCLES
INTERVIEW WITH THE GREEK ADMIRAL

by Edmund Garrett, a 2-page interview with W. H. Smith & Sons, 3 pages of 'The Romance of the World from Day to Day', 2 pages of 'How to Make and Lose your Money', 2½ pages on 'Wanted, an English Bible' ('for English literature and history what the editors of the Sacred Canon did for the Hebrew Scriptures'), and a page of 'A Crusade against Bad Cookery'. There were also a page on 'Advertising as a Fine Art', a page on 'The Latest Invention in Sewing Machines', a page on 'Pegamoid, the Industrial Earthquake', a page on 'The Milk of 30,000 Cows and What is Done with It', a page on 'Cancer, its Increase and Cure', a page on 'How to Cure Drunkards: A Crucial Test' and 'A Bicycling Tour on the Continent'—all ingenious interviews with advertisers, evidently by Stead—and finally four pages of ordinary advertisements. Illustrations were frequent throughout the 'dummy'.

The actual paper, *The Daily Paper*, which ran for five weeks, closing down on February 9, 1904, was a little more than 20 inches high by about 15 inches wide, that is, approximately the size of the *Evening News*, and had twelve pages. There were in the last issue two cartoons, five portraits and eleven illustrations, all of some size. An illustrated page was headed 'London Fog, which means Waste of Carbon and Sulphur, Half Stoppage of Business and the Pressing of Sewer Gas to Breathing Levels. 260 Tons Belched from London Chimneys Daily. Death Rate more than Doubled by long Peasoup Fogs.' Advertisements filled a page and a half and there was £100 insurance for readers killed on the railway. It was a pitiful production.

STEAD'S BREAKDOWN AND FAREWELL. The most important thing in this last number is a column and a half 'Farewell or Au Revoir' signed 'William T. Stead', three-quarters of it 'To My Readers' and about a quarter of a column 'To My Dear Bairns'. He said in the course of the leader for the grown-ups: 'The attempt to improvise everything out of my head proved too much for my head. After seeing the first issue through the Press I was prostrated by a severe nervous collapse. My doctor ordered me away instantly and predicted that, if I did not obey, I might wake up one morning with my memory completely gone. I continued to edit the paper after a fashion from Wimbledon, and then, when the perpetual clang of the telephone drove me farther afield, from my seaside cottage. The task of bringing out the paper was undertaken by my staff, to whose loyalty, zeal and affection I cannot pay too high a tribute. My share in the work was limited to writing the leader, some of the Notes and compiling the daily Matins. Despite the unwearying devotion of my wife and family my health did not improve. A long sea voyage and complete abstention from journalistic work are prescribed. I am off to South Africa on Thursday [two days later]. This breakdown has been a great disappointment. To have a daily paper that would be all my own, in which I might hope to realise some at least of the ideals which have haunted my imagination from my youth up, has been the dream of my life. But I have lived long enough to know that the things which we most desire are often not the best things for us. I am content to wait.' He concluded with the two mottoes on his office door: 'Thy place is seeking after Thee. Therefore be at rest in seeking after it' and 'Call not your burden sad or heavy; if your Father laid it upon you He intended neither', and these lines:

> Yet the high soul is left
> And Faith, which is but Hope grown wise, and Love
> And Patience, which at last shall overcome.

Stead's plight on the breakdown of his health is reflected in a few sentences from one of his letters to Brett before closing down: 'The result is rather serious for me, for whereas I had hoped I should have been able to launch the paper successfully upon £25,000, it will require double that amount and I am in no condition of mind or body to go seeking it. Hence the prospect before me is rather blue. I do not see how I am to avoid going under. I leave the destinies of the *Daily Paper* and my own future in other hands than mine, where indeed they have been, of course, from the first.' The *Daily Paper* was unquestionably an act of folly. Where Stead got the money it cost I do not know. The beneficiaries may be supposed to have been rich men who were in no way incommoded. But Stead's lack of intelligent foresight was none the less deplorable.

FINANCIAL RELATIONS WITH HIS WIFE. Some confidential letters which Stout placed in my care just before his death are distressing reading. They cannot be suppressed in the honest presentation of Stead's character and temperament at which I aim. With genius there must go not only exaltation but unhappiness. It was in 1892, eight years after the death of Gordon and the publication of 'The Truth about the Navy', seven after 'The Maiden Tribute' and the imprisonment, four after the visits to the Tsar and the Pope, and a short time after the starting of the *Review of Reviews* that Stead wrote to Stout this curious letter about his financial position and his wife. It was written preparatory to coming to Stout's house for a talk which he hopes 'may be able to get things in a more satisfactory condition':

My salary, £1,200 before you came, was divided as follows. I paid my wife to keep the house and everything going £1,000 per ann. while I retained £200 to pay interest on mortgage loan, railway fare, dinner, etc. I at that time drew £120 per ann. from a Russian review and about £50 per ann. from miscellaneous contributions.

No sooner was the change made here than my wife informed me that it was absolutely impossible for her to continue to make both ends meet on £1,000, and that she must have another £200 per ann. I begged her to try and wait until we got through our difficulties. She refused and insisted upon receiving the increase at once. I thereupon handed over to her the whole of my income and trusted to meet my own engagements by borrowing for a time from my friends to whom I could explain the circumstances. About this time, owing to the press of work on the Lantern Mission, I was compelled to drop my Russian work. My miscellaneous earnings remain about the same, and for the last eighteen months they have constituted my only source of revenue. As things stand at present I have to pay interest on mortgage and other debts £160 per ann., railway fares to Wimbledon £10, lunch etc., £50, travelling expenses, say 20 meetings at £4 per meeting £80, to say nothing of all other expenses whatever, such as cabs, presents, etc.

Nor is this all. My wife insists that I must pay the French teacher because that is an added expense since her allowance was fixed. I had to pay the children's holiday railway fare and last night she wanted to know what I intended to contribute to the expense of levelling the lawn, a project of hers which she has at last carried out at a cost of £90.

Under those circumstances you can understand that I am in a pretty tight fix. Add to that I shall have to contribute to keeping my sister, and it seems to me that unless the *R. of R.* can be made to contribute to the maintenance of its editor and proprietor, that unfortunate individual will have to go into the Bankruptcy Court! At present not only every penny of his salary is attached by his wife, but at least £100 per ann. is thrown upon his shoulders in addition by her method of construction of the contract.

Stead had confidence in Stout as a business man—he alone had a cheque book—but they did not 'click'. To the end of their relationship it is 'Dear Mr. Stout' and 'I am, yours truly'. Stead felt that Stout was not in sympathy with many of the things he thought he ought to do. He also knew that Stout did not at all believe in spooks. Stout's appreciation of Stead has been quoted, but he lost patience with him over the way in which, as he held, Stead was fooled by the Russian Princess of whom we shall hear again shortly —there is a large package of letters from the lady—and by some other people. In Stout's last letter to me he says: 'I have made at least one great mistake in my life. I ought to have left the *Review* and gone to work somewhere in peace. Nobody but my wife and I know what I had to put up with. As for Mrs. Stead, there is this to be said about her. She probably thought that if she did not get more money it would go to other women. I don't blame her.'

A LETTER FROM STEAD'S SON. The financial trouble at the *Review* office was indeed continuous. Twelve years after the date of the Stead letter just reproduced, young William Stead, whom Stout liked, writes two pathetic letters within a month to Stout, beginning 'Dear Stout' and ending 'Yours very sincerely'. They are about the critical position brought about by the failure of the *Daily Paper*. One letter runs:

Something must be done about money and that at once, I fear. We cannot carry on and the sooner father recognises the fact the better. Personally I cannot stand the strain very much longer. What do you think can be done? Anything is better than the present state of things. I am down in the depths of despondency. What do you think can be done to meet present liabilities supposing we stop now? I suppose something like seven thousand pounds would be required. Can this be obtained on the security of the *Review*? If not I do not see what is to prevent a smash.

In the second letter, on *Daily News* Book Department paper—William had evidently left his employment on the *Review*—he says:

I have been turning over my father's letters—not a very grateful task. I fear we cannot get much assistance from them. The fact of the matter is that my father placed X [of the *Daily Paper*[1]] in sole control, and it was only with difficulty that I got him excluded from the editorial department. But any passage setting forth that point I fear would only emphasise his power as business manager. The only saving clause in father's letter to X is that the business had to be reorganised in consultation with him, and against that I suppose X would say that first he did so consult and second that my father was too ill to be consulted with. As I told my father at the time it was a fatal appointment and destroyed any small chance there was of the paper pulling through. I don't see how we can get away from the two facts (1) my father's letter to X appointing him his representative and alter ego and (2) my father's announcement in the last number of the paper that he would be responsible for all engagements entered into on his behalf. If Y and Z can depend on X to back them up it looks as if we could do very little. There is only one thing worse than having to clean up this desperate mess and that was to have to live through it. It was a perfect nightmare.

Five years later William's father discusses his will with Stout. This is an extract from a letter:

There would be no anxiety on your part as to the dead hand in the *Review*. Even if I did say anything as to policy it would only be as a wish not as a condition. I agree that it would be unwise to make the R. of R. a Labour organ. Neither need you be under any apprehension as to the business passing into the hands of outsiders. My idea is that I should leave the business to be carried on by my executor, subject to certain charges. I don't think I could improve upon your suggestion that you should represent Mrs. Stead and the others, while Harry [Stead's son] would represent himself

He adds provision for the members of his family and for certain

---

[1] There seems to be no object in giving the names of the persons mentioned by William Stead.

copyrights going to Stout, and proposes his son Henry and Stout as joint executors and managers. He adds 'I don't smile on the idea of a partnership'.

THE RUSSIAN PRINCESS TRAGI-COMEDY. Eight letters from Stead to Stout are of the year 1910, long after the *Daily Paper* disaster, when the *Review* was twenty years old. I think I can best reflect the hectic conditions in which Stead was living by running together extracts from all the letters. The Russian Princess who is the centre of the picture was introduced to Stead by the Tsaritsa as being in difficulties until there was a settlement of her Russian estates. The sums advanced by Stead were, as has been stated, considerable. The Princess's son married the daughter of a prosperous business man in London.

The Princess's trustee has died and she is tied up at present. She is in town today trying to realise sufficient money on a £35,000 diamond pendant. If she does she will pay, if she does not I fear we must wait a bit. I am awfully sorry for her. . . . The Jew would not part with the guarantee, would only accept the £500 as payment on account and stayed proceedings. The Princess seems very confident that she will be able to raise money next week to pay us all off, so I live in hope. . . . I have not parted with the other £500 yet. The solicitors of Mr. A. want to know from you when that insurance policy in the New York office was released from notice. If you could let me have the information I shall be obliged. . . . The bill for £1,100 with the three days' grace falls due today. I wrote asking him to make it payable at his bank but he did not answer. A's money is due on Monday and this would meet that nicely. The Princess says she expects to settle up on Tuesday. The Princess or I have to pay £900 tomorrow or the next day to that moneylender. [Somebody whose name I cannot make out] showed me that circular from the New York offices showing that £1,000 or £1,100 is due as bonuses in April. Will you be so good as to arrange with the Bank by means of a month of two's bill for the sum due on bonus so as to let me have that money tomorrow or the day after? I suppose you could draw a bill on H. or S. making over to them the bonus. If the Princess pays the £900 then you take the £630 which you advanced her out of the bonus and give me the balance. If she does not let me have the £900, take balance. . . . The wife has come home. Do you think you could let me draw £100 on my private account to bring the wife's monthly money up to the sum I have always paid her? As you know I appropriated one month of it to the Bureau and have more or less had to dodge things ever since. . . . I am awfully sorry if, as the result of reading this letter to you, you feel that it is your duty to resign the post which you have held so long and which I hope you will hold till death us do part. I shall lament your decision but I shall not blame you for deserting me. This preamble is to introduce the fact that by some means or other I must have £1,000 first thing on Tuesday. Unless I pay £1,515 to the moneylender on Tuesday he will take out a writ and in eight days he can compel me to pay it. It is of course the affair of the Princess. If I get the £1,000—I can raise the other £515 myself—I receive in exchange a bill for £1,515 at twelve months from Mrs. M. [a well known public man's sister] with as collateral a first mortgage for £2,000 on an estate valued at £16,000 for which £14,000 is now offered. If I do not produce the £1,000 on Tuesday I shall have to produce it a week later, by process of writ, and in that case I should have no bill on Mrs. M. and no collateral security. Under these circumstances I hope that you will in some way or other raise me the £1,000 either on my insurance policies or in any other way your judgment deems best, but get it first thing Tuesday. If we manage this through, I think we shall be able to recoup ourselves in a very short time for all the money we have advanced. If we cannot get that money by Tuesday another £1,515 vanishes with no prospect of recovering anything.

I am awfully sorry to bring your holiday to so disgusting an end and, as I have said, if you decide to chuck me up as an entirely impossible person I shall not complain or be surprised, although I should be put in an abominable hole. If you don't chuck me up I promise this shall be the very last of these adventures. . . .

The moneylender is obdurate. He refuses to take the ring, insists upon his money. I must send him cheque for £520 tonight. I have drawn a cheque for £500. The remaining £500 can remain over till the end of the month. Please send me cheque for £520. My head is too bad to remain here [at the office]. I will go to Smith Square and finish 'Progress of the World'. . . .

[Same day] Have to see the moneylender at 11. If I cannot get the ring out by then I may have to pay £1,520 today. Please let me have three or four blank cheques. I shall do my best to induce him to take the ring if I can get it. If not make some other arrangement. I understand that with the £1,000 you loaned and my £550, I have that amount to draw upon. . . .

I have never thanked you as I ought to have done for contriving how to extricate me from the hole I found myself in last Monday. I am very grateful to you and feel very sad when I reflect upon the trouble I have occasioned you all in this and other matters. How did you manage it? And what has it cost in discount, etc.,? . . .

[Next day] Could you let me have the £500 I have to pay to the new moneylender in two cheques to self today of £300 and £200? It is rather urgent that I should have the £300 by 10 o'clock, the other £200 can wait. I am sorry to trouble you but I hope this will be the end of this. . . .

The sum Stead is supposed to have lost by the Princess was £15,000! £53,000, WHAT HAVE WE DONE WITH IT? A year afterwards, on July 15, 1911, Stead thanks Stout for his kind letter 'with figures, which fill me with dismay'.

In ten years we received £53,000. What have we done with it? I have lent the Princess £5,000 and have wasted another £1,000 on speculation, etc. But apart from this, even if we add another £4,000 to my drawings, there is £40,000 to be accounted for. It looks, I am afraid, that we have so run our business in England as to lose £40,000 net in ten years, which is a showing which makes me sick to dream of, especially when I have never had more than £1,200 per ann. and £200 as salary.

Don't bother about it or write me about it. But I am afraid when the wife read's J's letter she will think there is something wrong somewhere if with all that money coming in there cannot be enough saved to get her the motor car she has been so anxious about so long.

This is the letter Stout wrote in reply:

I have received your letter in which you are dismayed that in ten years over £50,000 from America in respect of the *American Review of Reviews* has been dissipated. I can assure you that it distresses me very much and it gives me very anxious hours. I am not so surprised as you appear to be, because it will be easy for me to show you when and where. I shall not bother you with the statement until you come back, but another letter received from America makes it imperative that I should let you know of the latest development, even though nothing need be done until you are back in London.

There have been times in the history of this concern when one event after another has seemed to point to the necessity of taking some fresh action and making a fresh start. The present appears to be such a time. I have £2,500 of liabilities, with £1,000 in the bank to meet them. I want £1,500 to feel comfortable. In the last thirteen months I have paid a thousand pounds for life insurance, to bring up your policies to £15,000; I have paid £200 on your acceptances for Miss B and Mr. C; and I have received £920 less than we expected from America.

Stout goes on to discuss relations with the *American Review of Reviews* and the necessity for having Stead's position legally recognised and defined. But, he says, partnerships are tricky things and he suggests, as a possibility, selling out for £50,000 to America, and with a portion of this money as capital 'starting your business again, remodelled to suit existing conditions'.

'WOE IS ME!' There is no surviving letter of Stead's but one of December 11 of the same year, in which gratitude is expressed to Stout:

Woe is me for I am an unprofitable servant!

I shall not be surprised if you should have lost confidence in me when I feel so utterly incompetent myself. If only I had been born different or had made myself different how much easier it would have been for everybody! But, alas, I am what I am and as I am, and I should not blame you in the least if you were to say that you were sick and tired of trying to save your old chief from the consequences of his own faults.

I have had a wretched night, horribly reminiscent of the *Daily Paper* breakdown, but I hope I shall be well enough to come to the office today.

If there was any phrase in my letter which implied that I was ungrateful to you for your long and devoted service I regret that I used it. But I do not think there is. For my starting point was that you had had such a long spell of work and worry for me, I was most grateful. Only I felt that you might have begun to lose heart and confidence in the *Review* and in me—small blame to you if you had—and as I felt we should have no chance of success unless we believed in the possibility, I wrote as I did. The one dread I have is that I may lose faith in myself, in my own health, in my own work, for if that goes all goes so far as I am concerned. I hope however that the New Year may bring new hope.

By the bye did [his son] tell you that Bottomley was promised £200 towards his accounts by the end of this year? I told him we could not pay it until the American cheque arrived. But I said he should have it by the end of the year.

The remarkable thing is that in this final letter Stead's handwriting goes firmly, in perfectly level lines, right across the page, as it has always done. There is nothing drooping or downcast in it. Bottomley I hear of for the first time, and I can learn no more.

And there, because of non-existent letters—a mass of Stead's correspondence was destroyed in the bombing of London—we must leave matters.

'COMPANIONS OF THE MERRY HEART'! Stead's experience in no way quenched his spirit, however. In a letter to Brett he says:

Slept badly, had a vivid but broken dream, the gist of which was that the great work I had to do was to found a new order of Knight-errantry. The Helpers were to be amalgamated in it but not to be conspicuous. It began somewhat as this:—Let us create a new Order of Poor Knights: then it varied into: A Simple Company of poor Knights: then a Secret Order of Poor Knights: variations being run on adjective and substantive but Poor Knights remaining. The object of this Order was to be of simple service day by day. The old motto "Union of all who love etc" sufficing. Then it varied into the Companions of the Merry Heart. The Company of the Joyous Life. And its obligations were two:

   1. To laugh heartily at least once per day. And
   2. To try to make another sentient thing smile. Sentient thing needs to be correlated to 'make happy,' 'make another smile'.

The Knight-Companions of the Joyous Life, or the Poor Knights of the Merry Heart.

Motto: Rejoice evermore.
Doctrine: Joyousness is the Test of a religious Life.
Eligible: Everyone. No subscription.
Badge: A small red cross with white enamel ground.
Duty: To laugh heartily once a day and to try to make another smile.
Ritual: To ask every night, have I laughed? Have I made another smile? *To compile text-book from Bible and Master.*
Love and Service bind this being to the world's sad heart.
Rule: No money to be asked, or received, or accepted as discharge of duty.

The heart of every reader, who by this time knows Stead thoroughly, realises his high spirit, his goodness, his integrity and his skills, his strength as well as his follies, must go out to him when, after attempting so much, achieving so much and failing so much, there comes home to him some of the bitterness of defeat and of advancing years. His beliefs, his faith in Another as his sure Counsellor and Guide, the Partner in all the efforts he made—on the inside of the door of his private room at Mowbray House were the words, 'In all thy ways acknowledge Him and He shall direct thy paths'—do not allow Him to feel forsaken; but the way, which had often been hard, becomes harder. There is a Scots phrase, *sair forfauchen*, which means sore jaded, fatigued, exhausted, worn out. Towards the end of his life Stead must have been feeling the strain of the tremendous labours he had imposed upon himself. His last portraits show traces of the wearing life he had led of work, emotion and ever new projects. He had had many rewards but many disappointments, many blows. There is a sapping of his physical and mental vitality. The aspirations and hope of the reformer rise high, trust in his God sustains him from time to time, but he has only a human frame. He has bright as well as dark hours but 'the clouds return after the rain'. Stead as he embarks for America still looks in his photographs a remarkable man. But he also looks a tired man.

DEATH IN THE *TITANIC* DISASTER. In 1886 Stead had printed in the *Pall Mall* a vivid imaginary account of the foundering of a mail steamer in mid-Atlantic, with an appalling death roll, and had added to the narrative the sentence, 'This is exactly what will take place if liners are sent to sea short of boats'. About a quarter of a century later, on April 15, 1912, he was himself drowned in the sinking of the *Titanic*, after it had struck an iceberg. Nearly fifteen hundred lives were lost. There were not enough boats.[1]

Stead was one of the few passengers on deck at the time of the disaster. One of the rescued, a New York lawyer, Mr. Frederick Seward, said, 'I was thoroughly scared but he preserved the most beautiful composure'. Mrs. William Shelley, another survivor, also marked his 'superhuman composure'. 'My last glimpse of the *Titanic*', she stated, 'showed him standing in what seemed to me a prayerful attitude of profound meditation'. W. W. Hadley, writing as an experienced journalist, told me that he thought that

---

[1] Many variants in the figures have been published. The Cunard Steamship Company has been good enough to give me the exact totals as recorded in the report of the Inquiry:

	Passengers	Crew	Total
Leaving Southampton ..	1,308	893	2,201
Saved	499	212	711
Lost	809	681	1,490

the most credible story of the end, among all the reports that came to hand, was that Stead, a strong swimmer, finally plunged overboard and, when he found the boat or raft to which he swam could not take anyone else, perished in the icy water. 'It is unlikely', E. T. Cook wrote in the *Contemporary Review*, 'that we shall ever be told how he died; but those who knew him will be in no doubt. He must have faced his doom unflinchingly, for he knew no fear, and he did not believe that death meant separation. And, if occasion arose, he must have comforted any weaker brother within his reach. It was what he was doing all his life.'

Stead's premonition during many years that he would not die in his bed was realised. 'His grave, midway between Britain and America', wrote J. L. Garvin, 'is where he might have chosen it, in the full stream of their intercourse, in accordance with his view of things.'

The late W. H. Fairbairn wrote to me to say that, on a visit to America the year after the disaster, he met Mr. Frederick Seward, who had sat at the same table as Stead on the *Titanic* the night before the vessel went down. Seward spoke of 'the extraordinary impression made by Stead's conversation on all the other men'.

Hadley reminds me that it was by chance that Stead was a passenger on the *Titanic*. He had booked his passage on a North German Lloyd boat when an official of that line, who was a warm friend and admirer of his, suggested to him that the first voyage of the *Titanic* would be much more interesting. Stead accordingly transferred to the new British liner, and went to his death.

Stead, who, before his departure from England, had had communion in his Congregational Chapel, set out on his third voyage to the United States in response to an invitation to speak in New York at a meeting of the Men and Religion Forward Movement. But he had evidently in mind further work in America. He said to his daughter Estelle that he had a feeling that he should be like Saul, the son of Kish, who set out to seek his father's asses and found a kingdom.[1] 'What the work is, journalistic, spiritual, social or political, I know not. I await my marching orders, assured that He who has called me will make clear His good will and pleasure in due season.' He had once a thought of starting a *Daily Paper* in Chicago.

THE MEMORIALS. I was at a garden party in Tokyo when I was stunned by the news of Stead's death, and, as I was to remain in Japan for more than four years, I heard only by post from England of the impression it made. 'Do let the family know how much I grieve for them', said Queen Alexandra. The number of newspaper and magazine articles in the home Press alone reached

[1] *My Father*. Estelle Stead (Heinemann, 1903).

five hundred. They are collected in a volume kindly lent to me on my return by Mr. S. G. Jones of Hayling Island. On Stead's house at Hayling Island I found two inscriptions:

This house was the seaside residence of Mr. W. T. Stead, Journalist and Social Reformer, who lived here from 1895 to 1912.	This Balcony was erected in 1922 by Mrs. W. T. Stead in loving memory of her husband, W. T. Stead and her two sons, Willie and Harry.

The memorial on the Thames Embankment bears these words:

W. T. STEAD

1849   1912

This Memorial to a Journalist of wide renown was erected near the spot where he worked for more than thirty years by journalists of many lands, in recognition of his brilliant gifts, fervent spirit, and untiring devotion to the service of his fellow-men

There is also an inscription on the Manse at Embleton where Stead's father was minister. Largely attended memorial services were held in London and New York. The service in London closed, as Stead would have rejoiced to know, not with the 'Dead March' but with the 'Hallelujah Chorus'.

'UNBALANCED'? I have now told all there is to tell of Stead, hiding nothing—I think of Carlyle's exclamation, 'Biography, bless its mealy mouth!' No true admirer of Stead can wish, I think, on consideration, that I had omitted any detail set down. Burns, paraphrasing Ecclesiastes and taking counsel of his own nature, gives us the needed reminder:

> The cleanest corn that e'er was dight
> May have some pyles o' caff in.

'Unbalanced'? How many of us are not, in some degree or other? As Burns goes on to say in the well-known lines:

> One point must still be greatly dark,
> The moving *why* they do it:
> And just as lamely can ye mark
> How far perhaps they rue it.

> Then at the balance let's be mute,
> We never can adjust it;
> What's *done* we partly may compute
> But know not what's *resisted*.[1]

'We have treasure in earthen vessels.' Most of us in our time have done imprudent or imperfectly considered things, things which

---

[1] The italics are the poet's.

fuller information or greater experience would have led us to do differently. The trouble with Stead was that when he did such things he did them within the public view and was accordingly discredited. When account is taken of all his faults, the fair and pertinent question to be asked is surely, Just where should we have been without him? One of the last friends to see him said to me with deep conviction shortly before he himself passed away, 'His works follow him'. Did Stead, within the full measure of his education,

Never shrke deel to a fear
Emerson
William T. Stead
March 18 1893

his endowment and strength, and within his limitations, further goodness, help to his utmost the development of civilisation? That he did do so is the evidence of all his contemporaries who knew him best and of what he has himself written in his private papers. It must also be, I hope and believe, the finding of everyone who carefully considers the facts I have brought together. 'In righteousness that he hath done he shall live'.[1] Keats spoke of 'the glory of dying for a great human purpose'. Stead once said he would jump down Etna for a great public good, and meant it. As a practical man, seeking the utmost results from his actions, it would never occur to him not to arrange to have the deed properly reported.

[1] The last words in a letter from Stead to me late in his life are: 'I am very sad, but though I may stand alone today, there will rally round me all that is best'.

SIR EDWARD COOK

CHAPTER XXI

STEAD'S SUCCESSOR

APPEARANCE AND CHARACTER. Stead was in Holloway Gaol when I first came in contact with the fourth editor of the *Pall Mall*, Edward Tyas Cook, afterwards Sir Edward. It was in an odd way. The paper had lost touch with Henry Norman (later Sir Henry and a junior Minister) who had been despatched, with rather loose instructions, on a trip round the world—quite a piece of journalistic enterprise in those days—and, in Burma I think it was, he had evidently gone off prospecting on his own account. A friend of mine in San Francisco had seen in one of its journals something about his adventures, and in a few lines covering an article I had sent to Northumberland Street I had happened to mention what he told me. I received from Cook a note of thanks beginning 'Sir'. That was rather of the times, but I thought also told me something—something but not much—of the shy, reserved Cook, for by this time I had had half a dozen 'followers' in the *Pall Mall*.

No one can look at his fine face in the portrait I reproduce (taken later in his career) without realising that here was, as I soon had the gratification of discovering, an outstanding man. The portrait accurately portrays the large head, strong chin and nose, and the level eyes of the arduous, serene, kindly, wise worker who in the familiar lines,

> Took measure of his soul and knew its strength,
> And by that silent knowledge, day by day,
> Was calm'd, ennobled, comforted, sustain'd.

He edited in turn the *Pall Mall*, the *Westminster Gazette* and the *Daily News*, and, beyond a persuasive, responsible journalism of distinction, gave years of his leisure not only to the editing of the vast quarto 39-volume *Works of Ruskin*, a subject on which he was an astounding authority, but to books of quality I enumerate.

But he did not 'wear his mind any more than his heart on his sleeve'. His silences were not more disconcerting than his lifeless handshake. We have his wife's authority for it that 'Teddy made few friends'. He looked like being the despair of his biographers. There seemed to be a chance that the world might be left without a convincing picture of an unusual man. The moral and mental lineaments of Cook were accurately preserved, however, in a large, carefully filed correspondence and in diaries of individuality, interest, and humour. The devotion of the 'few friends' who felt his charm, valued his powers and marked his achievement has done the rest. The biography by the late Saxon Mills, who was with Cook on the *Daily News*, served very well for a time and I am indebted to it.[1] But it was published more than thirty years ago. Today Edward Tyas Cook is confounded as often as not with the E. T. Cook who wrote the gardening books, or Sir Theodore Cook, author of *Spirals in Nature and Art* and *Leonardo da Vinci, Sculptor*, who served, for a short time, I remember, as an editor of the *Field*, or Edward Dutton Cook, who was dramatic critic of the *Pall Mall Gazette*, or E. T. Cook, the musician, or the E. T. Cook who is E. Thornton Cook, author of a number of stories. There is also a Sir Edward Cook, C.S.I. Saxon Mills did his best, but relatives and friends felt that the book might have been more intimate. It is time to try again.

I have more than three hundred letters of Cook's to various people, I have had access to many volumes of diaries, I have copied from letters to him from people of importance in their day which lie in the manuscript department of the British Museum, I have my own and other people's memories of him, and all his books. It would be strange indeed if, after all my years with Cook, I did not wish to do what I can to give him his honourable place in the minds of a generation which knows little of him. Nothing made a greater impression on me as a youth in Northumberland Street than his tranquillity, courtesy and application, and the wondrously neat slips of 'copy', done overnight, which with a book or two in a neat cotton strap, he brought down to the office every morning. All his life through, Cook was helped to success and public esteem by rectitude, sound judgment, a power of clear exposition and a restful, abounding urbanity, but most of all by untiring industry. 'Thou, O God, sellest all good things at the price of labour.'

WINCHESTER AND OXFORD. The industry began at Winchester where, owing to some weakness in his back, he had a special chair. He was never, however, crippled and he did not show, in after life, signs of his youthful ailment. His devotion to Ruskin began at school. But as editor of the *Wykehamist* he read bluebooks, and was journalistically enterprising enough to get into correspondence

---

[1] *Sir Edward Cook*, J. Saxon Mills (Constable, 1921).

with the Tichborne Claimant.[1] He had a medal for his 'particularly promising' English, he was head of the school and an able debater, and an obituary notice in the paper he had edited speaks of his 'fiery eloquence and independence of thought in rather Conservative surroundings'. Later, he became a Fellow of Winchester and was active in its interests until the end of his life. I have to thank the Right Hon. H. T. Baker for this transcript of the tablet in Cloisters:

IN MEMORY OF TWO BROTHERS
SCHOLARS OF THE TWO COLLEGES
OF SAINT MARY OF WINCHESTER
PREFECTS OF HALL

ARTHUR KEMBALL COOK   EDWARD TYAS COOK
ASST. MASTER 1875–1911   FELLOW 1903–1919

LOVERS OF ART ACCOMPLISHED IN LETTERS
IN THE SERVICE OF THIS COLLEGE
WISE AND DEVOTED

As Edward and Arthur were much alike and attached to one another it was a happy thought to commemorate them together. E.T.C., who was born in Brighton in 1857, had a second brother who was a schoolmaster, A. M. Cook, St. Paul's surmaster. Another brother was Sir Charles Cook, Charity Commissioner. One sister married Mr. J. E. Vincent of *The Times*, another Mr. A. G. Leach of the Record Office. Cook's father was secretary to the Seamen's Hospital at Greenwich. His mother had a preparatory school, attended by, among others, two boys who were to become a Provost of Oriel and an Oxford Professor.

At Oxford, as President of the Union, Cook was an unemotional, logical and at times cutting expositor of political principles and, with Curzon and Milner, was marked for distinction in public life. To cope with his narrow means he took a pupil. While he had neither a physical aptitude nor a taste for games he did credit to New College with a first in Greats. But it is told in the Records of the Meetings of the Warden and Tutors that on June 11, 1879, Cook and another Scholar, having failed to satisfy the examiners in 'the Rudiments of Faith and Religion', it was agreed that they should each forfeit £10 from the emoluments of their Scholarship for the ensuing year. At a later meeting a communication was received from Cook. It was agreed, however, to reply that 'The Warden and Tutors have considered Mr. Cook's statement, but

---

[1] Arthur Orton, a Wapping butcher who had emigrated to Australia, came back to England with a claim to be Sir Roger Tichborne, the missing heir to the Tichborne estates, maintained his chicanery with such audacity as to delude thousands of people, and eventually, after a prolonged trial, enjoyable alike to the public and the lawyers, was sent to fourteen years' penal servitude. On his gravestone he is still dubbed Sir Roger

see no sufficient reason for remitting the penalty'.[1] In the following
year, I note, Cook was awarded a prize of £4 worth of books
on the result of the Lent Term Examinations in Literae Humaniores.
He was unsuccessful in efforts to secure a Fellowship at All Souls
and other Colleges.

MILNER AND COOK AT THE *PALL MALL GAZETTE*. In
London at the end of 1881 he ate his dinners in the Inner Temple
but was not called to the Bar, and was offered a place in the Civil
Service, which he had the foresight to avoid. He sent in paragraphs
to Labouchere's *Truth* and, after an interview with John Morley
at the *Pall Mall*, began to contribute careful 'Occ. Notes'. He
became and remained for some years secretary for the London
University Extension lectures and was identified with Toynbee
Hall. His first leading article, a judicious and forceful piece of
writing from the Liberal standpoint, with no little resemblance to
his adult journalism, I have looked at in the *Oxford Chronicle* of
Jan 7, 1882. He had German enough for a study of German editions
of Aristotle's *Poetics*, and meditated but did not write a book. He
tried for a Professorship of English at Nottingham, and in 1883,
on Morley's assurance that he was 'a young man of great ability—
a good past and a promising future, a prize', offered himself as
private secretary to Andrew Carnegie, the Pittsburgh millionaire
resident in Scotland. There would have been an amusing conjunction.

In August 1888 Milner, writing at the request of Stead, offered
a part-time post on the *Pall Mall* editorial side, and when Milner
retired from the assistant editorship Cook succeeded to it. The
Congregationalist Stead had had a Rationalist to work with in
colleagueship with Morley; now, for nearly seven years, he was in
harness with a Liberal Churchman.

Cook, with his noteworthy gifts as a speaker and a debater, had
been, as far back as 1880, among the Parliamentary candidates
chosen for consideration for Oxford, but he was without funds. Six
years afterwards Milner put before him the prospects of 'a safe
Liverpool seat'. Later still, a third electoral opportunity presented
itself. But Cook definitely turned his back on the House of Commons
and made his decision for journalism.

At the age of twenty-four there had been an engagement to
marry which was broken off. In 1884, when he was twenty-seven,

---

[1] 'My recollection', writes the Warden of New College, who kindly sends me
the above extract, 'is that when I came to the College as a Scholar in 1902 there
was still this rule about fining Scholars who did not pass the examination which
we called "Divvers". I remember that I was fortunate enough to pass it with the
aid of a special cram book by a man of the name of Hawkins, to which we all
resorted. Since that time the examination itself has been abolished, and with it
the danger to Scholars of a fine.'

he entered upon a happy married life with a Northumberland
girl of talent and charm, Emily Constance Baird, the second of
the seven daughters of John Forster Baird. The eldest became the
wife of A. L. Smith, the future Master of Balliol. Another was
Dorothea Baird (wife of Sir Henry Irving's son, H. B. Irving), the
nakedness of whose feet in *Trilby* the Princess of Wales and other
well-intentioned people found objectionable but the Heir Apparent said to Millais pleased him. Lilian married B. R. Wise, New
South Wales Agent General, and Evelyn Sir Richard Threlfall,
scientist.

In his first days at the *Pall Mall*, when the interview was still
something of a novelty, Cook received 'with consternation' Stead's
instructions to interview the Archbishop of Canterbury. He was
to show in that early piece of work that, like his chief, he had an
unusually tenacious memory, a sharp eye for essentials, and a sense
of timeliness. A thing which stands out in my memory of his assistant
editorship and editorship is the assiduity with which he kept on
derisively pasting on the door of what we called 'the big room'
newspaper cuttings about pushing people we knew. Afterwards,
at the *Daily News* he had three boxes filled with cuttings and
correspondence labelled 'The Age of Puff'.

RELATIONS WITH RUSKIN. A testing time was 'The Maiden
Tribute', during which Cook's friend, Milner, left the *Pall Mall*.
There must have been occasions when a man of Cook's temperament felt the strain, but he was a man of honour and clarity of
mind and supported his chief. His loyal energy and the grip and
sober tone of his leading articles when Stead was in gaol were
invaluable to the paper. The prisoner wrote to Cook wishing him
'the happy fate of a term in gaol'. Stead had previously thanked
him for his House of Commons Guide, which went through many
editions as a *Pall Mall* 'Extra'. The pithy 'Mems about Members',
written on the basis of wide enquiries and of scraps of information all of us collected, were something livelier in reference books.
Stead spoke of his high sense of Cook's 'journalistic judgment,
industry and tact'. He added, 'I know of no instance of so young
a man so suddenly entrusted with the conduct of a London paper
at a critical time, and I know of no one, old or young, who could
have come better through the ordeal'. As for the 'Mems' about
M.P's, I remember that one legislator pointed out that it was
unfortunate that his former Sunday school teaching should have
been mentioned as he now sat for a sporting constituency; another
M.P. suggested that mention of the fact that he also had been a
Sunday school teacher would help him as he sat for a Nonconformist constituency.

Two later Extras, the *Fall of Mr. Parnell* and a most successful one, *The Best Hundred Books*, which is still quoted, were also Cook's work. The number of prominent people who were 'drawn'—prominent people were not so pestered then—surprised us. The Prince of Wales's note was on Dryden. Some of the originals of the letters are to be found in the Cook collection at the British Museum.

Cook owed to Stead his valued introduction to the prophet of his boyhood, Ruskin, for as an undergraduate he had been asked to report the Oxford lectures for the *Pall Mall*. His summaries, afterwards the basis of *Studies in Ruskin* (1890), were so well done that when the Master was in London he asked Cook to call. Ruskin, who was afterwards to say that Cook knew more about his works than he did himself, told him, in reference to some letters that had come into the hands of the *Pall Mall*, that it was very welcome to print them: 'all the world may read any letters I ever wrote'. He also undertook to write a preface for Cook's *Popular Handbook to the National Gallery* (*1888*)[1] and volunteered permission to him to cut it as he had a mind. This book went into edition after edition. A volume on the Tate Gallery and a *Pall Mall* Extra, *Half Holidays at the National Gallery*, followed. In the Preface to the *Popular Handbook* Ruskin commended the author's care, industry and good sense.

He also told him that the *Pall Mall* was 'the only paper with a conscience'. Although he did not like 'The Maiden Tribute' and some other things it printed, he was warmly appreciative of Stead and deplored the number of prostitutes in the streets of the West End. Among the Cook memorabilia in the possession of Lady Hartley is a letter in which Ruskin is solicitous about Stead's health. 'It is best', he writes, 'not to be teased by letters of inquiry when one is resting. I hope he *will* rest whenever he ought and that you may both reign over Northumberland Street, a new Downing Street of great efficiency'. In a letter for publication Ruskin supported Cook's editorial stand on the right of public meeting in Trafalgar Square.

Writing three years later to Cook from Sandgate, Ruskin says about a visit to London: 'I've only National Gallery work and to have my teeth knocked out, and then down here again as fast as I can. But next time it will be, I hope, for British Museum MSS. and then it must be the greatest good and help to me to be with you both (Cook and his wife), only my man Edwin is rather a rough diamond, horsey and boaty—I would make him keep out of the way till after my breakfast—and I am sorrowfully obliged still to have it in my room. In hope of a chat in my little room at

[1] Cook also wrote a *Popular Handbook to the Greek and Roman Antiquities of the British Museum* (Macmillan, 1903).

Morley's' [the demolished hotel in Trafalgar Square and the Strand]. He signs 'Affectionately yours'.

LETTERS FROM SWINBURNE. One of the letters addressed to Cook which he gave to the British Museum is from Swinburne exhibiting the poet's respect for Ruskin: 'My letter to Ruskin I do honestly think utterly unworthy of the very great honour you design for it. [Evidently Cook proposed to place it among the notes in the *Works*.] However if Mr. Ruskin thought it worth keeping it it not for me to object. I had a most valued and treasured letter from him about the attack on me and my poems. I made myself quite ill yesterday hunting for it. But I have been cursed from birth with the unutterable curse or tendency to lose or mislay things I prize most dearly. Even this is not the very worst instance. But what am I to say of Ruskin's magnificent and incredible generosity in praise of me? I could not have believed it possible, even of him'. He adds: 'I think I know English and French pretty decently, and I learnt to write verse in Greek and Latin at Eton like a not exceptionally stupid schoolboy. But as to being a scholar!' Later he asks, 'if not very egotistic or exacting', for a few copies of what Ruskin had written 'with such superb extravagance of praise'.

In another letter Swinburne is equally characteristic. He protests against an extract from a book of memoirs 'containing an obvious invention regarding my humble self. "Mr. Nemo Nameless" gives an account of my imaginary behaviour as a drawing room spouter of unsolicited verse (!!!) on the authority of Mr. James Anthony Froude. This authority, I see with surprise, is not backed up by the support of another eminent autobiographer who was present on the occasion—the "high and well-born" Baron Munchausen. Surely without such affirmation Freiherr von Froude can hardly be regarded as worth a rotten fig's end.'

GLADSTONE AND RANDOLPH CHURCHILL. Ruskin was not the only celebrity the *Pall Mall* helped Cook to see. His admirably written diaries record, often word for word, what was told him in confidence by Gladstone, Salisbury, Balfour, Lord Randolph Churchill and 'Old Morality' (W. H. Smith), who began, 'Mr. Stead tells me I may speak to you in perfect confidence'. Which reminds me of when I was doing the daily 'Round the World' for the *Westminster*, and the French Ambassador, M. Cambon, said to me after a long chat, 'Of course, Mr. Robertson Scott, if you write any of this in the paper I will say you were never here'. Lord Randolph Churchill, the Chancellor of the Exchequer who did not last long enough to produce a Budget, Cook saw often and liked. 'I've tried every form of excitement in my time from tip-cat to tiger-shooting', 'Randy' wrote, 'but there's nothing like an exciting division in the House.'

I hope you have been heading a good time, and will come back an Atlas, refreshed ready once more to take the world for our produce. You will be delighted to hear that I have had two or three inquiries, expressing a hope that "Round the world" is not dropped

Yours very truly

E.T.Cook

AUTOGRAPH OF E. T. COOK

The reference is to a daily feature I did on Foreign and Colonial Affairs in the 'Westminster Gazette' from the first number

Gladstone was attentive in correcting—without publicity—errors in the Press. A letter in the Cook collection is in reference to a statement that at Bradlaugh's funeral 'the floral offerings included one from Mrs. Gladstone: this was not so, but Mrs. Gladstone called with me at the Bradlaughs' residence on the day preceding the funeral to express our sympathy.' On a sheet of stiff quarto are a few lines of notes by Gladstone for his speech on introducing the Home Rule Bill of 1893, the small letters of which are a quarter of an inch high. Two years later, in June 1896, the old man's writing quavers to such a degree as to be barely legible. He seems to say: 'Please be so good as to publish enclosed without any indication other than what it contains. Of course I shall support it should there unhappily be any need.'

One of Cook's letters is from George Meredith who says 'Browning's death takes me with a choking'.

Cook was to write much about Florence Nightingale. In a closely-penned four-page letter stressing her belief in women's suffrage she says: 'It is so important for a woman to be a "person", as you say, and I see this most strongly in married life. If the woman is not a person it does such harm to her husband. And the harm is greatest when the man is a very clever man and the woman is a very clever woman.'

CHAPTER XXII

EDITORSHIP OF THE *PALL MALL GAZETTE*

EDITORIAL QUALITIES. On June 25, 1889, the entry in Cook's diary is 'Crisis at *P.M.G.* begins'. It was over the way in which Stead's Russian letters had been printed, an account of which has been given. Cook resented the admonition of his superior officer and wrote to Stead gently (signing himself, as was his fashion, 'Yours truly'). Yates Thompson, in his dealings with Stead, no doubt felt that he had Cook in reserve. Cook manfully did what he could to heal the breach, pleading with Stead not to step down in journalistic rank and influence; but he also told his proprietor that, if it became necessary, he would be willing to succeed. On New Year's Day, 1890, he sat in Stead's chair.

Stead evidently felt that he had been hasty and, after Mrs. Thompson had received a letter from him,[1] the proprietor suggested to Cook the engagement of his old editor as a salaried contributor. The prudent Cook objected to this as 'putting me into a false position, since my long subordinate position and Stead's intrinsic weight would virtually make him editor'. Yates Thompson agreed that there was a good deal to be said for this view, but Cook, on consideration, characteristically seeking 'an end to the bother', fell in with the plan. 'I remain nominal editor with Stead as political director', he says in his diary, 'a bad plan, I think, and an unpleasant, but I must do my best to give it a fair trial'. Stead used to come to the office daily and naturally the situation was sometimes delicate. Within a few weeks Yates Thompson objected to an interview he had given to the *Star*, Stead never returned to the office, and Cook reigned alone.

The impression given of Cook as editor by J. A. Spender in his *Life, Journalism and Politics*[2] was very much ours at the *Pall Mall*: 'Cook was the most efficient and methodical editor of his time. He was at work all the morning and most of the afternoon, and, except when he was dining out, during the evening at home. He had a mind in which everything seemed to be indexed and was at once available whenever it was wanted. For the office he invented a system of what he called "clag-books"[3] in which clippings from

---

[1] See Stead's references to Mrs. Yates Thompson, pages 115 and 143.

[2] Cassell, 1932.

[3] The clag-books were invented by Stead, and were kept, with reference books, by the devoted Miss Hetherington. The editor of the *Northern Echo* kindly confirms my impression that 'clag' is north country for stick. 'I believe that in the pits it is used in relation to a roof of a mine to which the coal clings'.

all sorts of newspapers and periodicals about things and persons were daily pasted. In addition, he had his own private "clag"—clippings made with his own hand and stored in envelopes which he kept at home. Finally he kept a diary, one of the most intimate records of his time. On all this side of him he was the perfect machine. He was never flustered, never late, and wholly free from the uncertainties, irregularities and lapses from the normal which commonly afflict the writing tribe. Also he had an extraordinary gift of silence. Members of the staff would go in to interview him and come out reporting than in a quarter of an hour he had done nothing but nod his head and say "Yes" or "No". At first this was rather frightening, and against his silence even the most moderate talker felt garrulous. But gradually one discovered that these were only the mannerisms of a shy man. After a few weeks the reserve broke and he was no longer the editor giving orders but a kind and warm-hearted friend whose talk was free and witty, and whose interests ranged over a wide field in spite of his methodical way of bringing them under discipline.'

Massingham's jest on the succession of Cook to the editorship was that the *Pall Mall* was a 'trifle steadier than in the days of Stead'.

'THE BEST EDITOR I HAVE EVER HAD.' It was not long before the new editor had to deal with the O'Shea–Parnell divorce suit and the trying political complications it brought about. One of the aliases the Irish leader had used during his intrigue was 'Mr. Fox', and the unblushing fashion in which one day he tried to draw his followers' attention from his offences by an unscrupulous attack on Mr. Gladstone, who had made such great sacrifices for Ireland, shocked public opinion. I usually did the day's contents bills—the papers had such things then—but one morning Cook had it ready. I think Charles Morley had suggested it. It was of two lines only. (To fill in the space across the page I have ventured to place alongside the bill one of mine—in pigeon English. It announced the escape of Sun Yat Sen from the Chinese Legation.)

MR. FOX *PALL MALL GAZETTE*	CHINEE LEGATION NO HAB GOT PLISONER WALKEE *PALL MALL GAZETTE*

On the problem of Ireland the *Pall Mall* undoubtedly maintained the standard set by John Morley of sound information and sober, sympathetic comment. When Gladstone met Cook he took his hand warmly and said, 'Let me pay you a well deserved compliment; your paper under your management has been very good'; and Stead reported that Yates Thompson had said to him, 'Cook is the best editor I have ever had'. Stead's successor could not have been more ably served by an assistant editor than by the man he chose to take his old place, Edmund Garrett. When tuberculosis took Garrett from time to time to Nordrach and Egypt, Spender was Cook's aide, and of him also and his editorship of the *Westminster*, and of Charles Morley I shall write in another book.

The *Pall Mall* was original in what was written, inside and outside the office, for its editorial columns, and in the cartoons of the man who stood out in his field, the kindly Frank Carruthers Gould from the Stock Exchange. F.C.G. was as keen and good-tempered a politician as David Low and the people he pilloried eagerly bought his sketches. Then there was the sapience with which, in what the *Pall Mall* called 'political meteorology', Cook, by a cool consideration of previous pollings in a constituency and some acquired knowledge of local conditions and personalities, made fortunate shots at the probable results of bye-elections.

T. Fisher Unwin, 1908

MR. A. J. BALFOUR IN SIR F. CARRUTHERS GOULD'S *FROISSART'S MODERN CHRONICLES*, 1903–6

'Sir Arthur de Balfour bethinketh himself that he will resign.'

SOLD! Things were not going at all badly with us in our tenth year under Cook. Sailors speak of a happy ship and, as Cook has noted, the small company in our shabby, inconvenient office in Northumberland Street was singularly devoted to 'the old *Pall Mall*'. The editor was not the only member of the staff who had declined the chance of a Parliamentary seat. We felt that we were on a paper with a mission, quality and self-respect, and our zeal was not abated by the fact that higher salaries were to be got elsewhere. On the business side our journal was below what would nowadays be reckoned efficiency; I never knew the name of the man who looked after what advertising we had—I now learn it was Taylor.

What a development in advertising and what an increase in advertising agencies there has been since then!

Something happened, however, that none of us had ever thought possible. We knew the paper did not pay, but Yates Thompson was a well-to-do man and had no children; we did not dream of his following his father-in-law's example and parting with it. But the paper *was* sold, and to whom nobody knew or seemed able to find out. The reputed purchaser, a T. Dove Keighley of the National Liberal Club, was clearly an intermediary. Even a person who appeared to be behind him, one Löwenfeld, the owner of a non-intoxicating beverage called Kop's Ale, whom Cook described as 'Polish by birth, Jewish by race, and Roman Catholic by religion', was not believed to be the real investor. There was talk of one Steinkopf, a man who had bought a house in the West End and, when he did not like it, pulled it down and built another in its place. He had worked with George Smith in floating Apollinaris. All that Cook could get out of 'Thompy', as we had all, in a kindly way, called Yates Thompson, was that he had had the opportunity of selling for £50,000 what had cost him, in financing his father-in-law's gift of twelve years before, £20,000, and that the purchaser was probably a well-to-do man who wanted a paper 'as a man might want a pony.'[1]

What aggravated editor and staff was not only that the paper had been sold over our heads, but that it had been done with no care that its politics and social outlook should be as they had been. Yates Thompson, who will be more fully discussed in the next Chapter, did not lessen our feelings of discomfort appreciably when, in a parting speech, with 'big tears on his cheek', Cook chronicled—I happened to be on holiday—he promised to give us, as he did, greater financial compensation than we were legally entitled to.

PROPOSALS. In interviews with Cook we learnt that Dove Keighley and his lawyer, Adams (afterwards Sir John Coode-Adams) got the worst of it. They wanted him to remain but without definite assurances. He wished to have—and as newspapers are so frequently bought and sold it is worth while setting the terms down—'absolute control over the whole paper, and appointment of editorial staff, assurance of harmonious relations with manager, and a year's engagement'. As to salary, he said he was not likely to quarrel over what he was receiving, £1,200, but Adams's suggestion of three months' notice was, of course, out of the question: did not Adams know that, by the custom of the profession,

---

[1] One is reminded of what Northcliffe, before acquiring *The Times*, wrote to Buckle: '*The Times* is, in fact, in my life what a yacht or a racing stable is to others—it is merely my hobby'. *The History of 'The Times'*, Vol. 3, page 640.

an editor's notice was twelve months? A friend of Cook's, the admirable Maxse, whose politics were Unionist, tried persuasion. 'Why should I not write on neutral subjects: would I do so for a few months at £200 a month or any other sum I liked?' It seemed clear that Cook would very likely be a stopgap and that a suitable successor had not really been secured. Cook was not to be trapped. As he said at the dinner that was given to him, with Morley in the chair, he 'did not object to being a humble penny-a-liner if the line was straight, but he would not consent to be a mercenary curvilineator'. He walked out of Northumberland Street with most of his staff, as Greenwood had done before him. Lord Rosebery, taking up the issue of October 21, 'said with a groan "Cook's last number" '.

Shortly after the sale, Yates Thompson suggested to Cook that he should start a paper on his own account. This was also the notion of Charles Morley and of Henry Leslie, the manager. It was proposed that Cook should found a weekly to be called the *Weekly Review*. Cook himself thought of selling his house and buying the *Speaker*[1] and another paper, and combining them, he to put in £2,500, and Morley, Leslie and himself to be content at the start with salaries of £250 each. Reginald Brett suggested buying what had been Frederick Greenwood's *St. James's Gazette*. There was a project with which the name of the Marquis of Ripon was associated, to start a publication for Cook, but it came to nothing. It may be that it was after he left the *Daily News*—but this is taking us years ahead—that there was a scheme for a Liberal *Daily Graphic*, capital £80,000, which Cook wisely said would not be enough. Cook has a reference to 'an Imperialist weekly'. There is nothing in any of Cook's diaries about Rosebery being identified with any journalistic plan for him.

[1] The predecessor of the *Nation* and the *New Statesman*.

CHAPTER XXIII

THE SCHOLAR WHO FOUND HIMSELF A NEWSPAPER PROPRIETOR[1]

AN HEREDITARY BOOK COLLECTOR. The truth about Yates Thompson is a new and an interesting story. In justice to him and to our indignant selves in Northumberland Street it is well that it should be known.

He missed the reign of William IV by two years. His father was a Liverpool banker and his mother a woman of ability. She was a daughter of Joseph Brookes Yates, who is remembered not only as a merchant and philanthropist but—and this is a point in heredity—as a book collector. Yates Thompson did not bear the name of Yates until after the death of his maternal grandfather in 1856. J. B. Yates made bequests to two of his grandsons with the proviso that they should adopt his name. One of them accordingly became Yates Thompson and the other Thompson Yates (a parson who was a collector of bindings). Yates Thompson was head boy at Harrow and won a prize for Greek. At Trinity, Cambridge, he gained the Porson Prize for Greek verse, defeating Jebb, and took his degree as 16th classic. He became a student at Lincoln's Inn, but was not called till 1867, for he decided to see the world. He was in Palestine, India, the United States and the West Indies. On his return home, in the year in which the *Pall Mall* was founded, he stood for Parliament as a Liberal in South Lancashire, but unsuccessfully. Later attempts, also in his home county, were no more fortunate. In 1868, however, he became private secretary to Earl Spencer, Viceroy of Ireland, and the experience in Dublin made him a confirmed Home Ruler. After the fall of the Liberal Government in 1874 he spent a year in India. For many years he was a director of the Lancashire and Yorkshire Railway.

During his visit to America in 1863, at the time of the Civil War, he developed a great interest in the United States. I have seen no reference in any English newspaper account of him to his attempt, long before the Cecil Rhodes scholarships were thought of, to endow at Cambridge a lectureship for 'the history, literature and institutions of the United States'. The facts, which present a rather amusing picture of the sixties, will be related later on.

[1] If it be preferred not to interrupt the narrative, this Chapter may be read after Chapter XXXII.

THE SALES BY SON-IN-LAW AND FATHER-IN-LAW. But to our grievance against 'Thompy' at the *Pall Mall*. In transferring the paper to its political opponents he had done, as I have said, what his father-in-law had done twelve years before. But we felt that Yates Thompson was not precisely in his father-in-law's position. George Smith, a Liberal, if an old-fashioned one, had for years put up with Greenwood's swinging of the paper farther and farther into the Conservative camp. He had no doubt felt that, though the *Pall Mall* had become a supporter of Disraeli, it had many merits as a newspaper and some standing. The time had now come, however, he argued, that his son-in-law and their common party might well gain the advantage of having the paper within the Liberal fold. So the Conservative *Pall Mall* became the Liberal *Pall Mall* it had been more or less planned to be originally. Its Liberalism under John Morley's direction was to be, no doubt, of a somewhat newer brand; but it was Liberalism, not Conservatism.

For Yates Thompson's action, however, we could find, in our wrath, no apology. He had been given the paper with a view to its ceasing to support the Conservative Party. By turning it over to that Party he had dealt a blow at the political cause of which he was a professed adherent. Further, Cook speaks of the profits he had recently drawn out of the paper, so it was beginning to pay. Even if it were losing a little it was not a matter of great consequence to him. Nor could he plead that the ownership of the paper was giving him anxiety on other than financial grounds. Cook was a man with whom he got along easily. His work was distinguished and his character and temperament were much in accord with his own. Cook had also the advantage of possessing the full confidence of the chiefs of the Liberal Party.

One excuse made for the sale was that it became possible to avoid the capital expenditure required for the renewal of the obsolete printing plant. And Yates Thompson appears to have said more than once, with engaging candour, that the Party had never done anything for him.[1] Still the proprietorship of the *Pall Mall* had its social value and there is reason to believe that he soon regretted selling it. He said to Cook, 'Please tell Mrs. Cook I hardly dare face her; I can hardly face my wife'. An excuse he offered was that he felt he ought not to miss £50,000 for what he might never be offered £18,000. He said indeed that the paper was bought from him without the purchaser seeing figures. As to who that purchaser was, the negotiator, he declared, 'lied to him to the last'. After the sale Yates Thompson gave a farewell dinner to Cook and the staff

[1] Mrs. Yates Thompson told a friend of mine that he was offered a peerage and declined it. This was not during his proprietorship of the *Pall Mall* but later, in recognition of public services of which I am about to give some account.

T

at which a silver inkstand and candlesticks were presented. Looking back on Thompson's action with the knowledge I now have of him, I feel that, though he may have acted precipitately, even ill-advisedly, he was not so much to blame perhaps as was believed by our little journalistic company, all keen Liberals and Radicals.

SIR CHRISTOPHER CHANCELLOR ON YATES THOMPSON. But Yates Thompson was not really known to us. His turn of mind and disposition are stressed in a felicitous letter written to me by Sir Christopher Chancellor, his great-nephew.[1] Chancellor spent much of his childhood in the home of the Yates Thompsons, who were his guardians during the 1914–18 war when his parents were abroad. His closest association with his great-uncle was between 1914 and 1924, that is when Yates Thompson passed from seventy-five to eighty-five. Sir Christopher says:

'I very seldom heard my great-uncle, who died in 1928, talk about the *Pall Mall*: it seems to have been almost a passing episode in his life.[2] His real interest (and his consistent activity) lay in the creation of his famous collection of books. He had no real taste for being a newspaper proprietor. I remember him saying that he took Stead on the *P.M.G.* after half-an-hour's conversation. This was characteristic: he was prone to act on impulse and I do not think he often reflected about the consequences of action or speech. He often gave offence to people by things said and done—unintentionally: he had no malice. But, being singularly free of prejudices in an age of prejudice, he had a way of brushing aside the prejudices of others.

'The public odium and social ostracism resulting from 'The Maiden Tribute' he felt deeply, but he paid regular visits to Stead in prison and supported him loyally. When Stead was drowned in the *Titanic* he wrote these lines about him:

He devoted his life to the good of Humanity
A wondrous amalgam of genius and vanity—
A man of so deep and such matchless emotion—
To drown him—it needed the weight of the ocean.

A dexterous journalist, steeped in 'sensation'
He firmly believed in his own inspiration
And whether he wrote from a Palace or Prison,
We felt that his equal had never arisen.

[1] In 1944 Sir Christopher Chancellor became the head of Reuters, that famous international news agency, founded in 1851, which is now the property of the entire British Press and of the Press of three members of the Commonwealth. He received a knighthood last year, when a thousand of us gathered at a dinner to celebrate the Reuter Centenary.
[2] The Morley-Stead-Cook editorship lasted twelve years, 1880–1892.

> As he lived without fear, so he died without panic
> And he has for his coffin the mighty *Titanic*,
> The dark depths of ocean around and above him,
> And friends without end to remember and love him.

'A RICH MAN'S LACK OF IMAGINATION'. 'Yates Thompson was no journalist. He was a scholar and an antiquarian. T. P. O'Connor wrote of him: "Though the face was handsome and the manner thoroughly courteous he gave the impression of dryness. This was the reason why, in spite of his great wealth, his fine intellect, and his transparent integrity of character, he was always an impossible Parliamentary candidate. But he was conspicuous in his epoch among collectors of rare books".

'I regard him as a typical Victorian of his class. He was a rich man with a rich man's lack of imagination, but there was no trace of the hypocrite in him. He disliked the ordinary conventions and enjoyed flouting them. He hated humbugs and took pleasure in shocking people. He was original in outlook and, above all, tolerant and a humanist. He valued men for what they did. His interest in human nature was deep and wide. He had wonderful health and in this, as in other ways, he was spoilt all his long life. A Liberal of the *laissez-faire* school, he thought there was equal opportunity for all. Yet his generosity was unbounded and much of it anonymous. His conversation was original, witty and spiced with classical allusions. He knew Horace, his favourite poet, by heart. But his interests were wider than Greek and Latin. He was hurt because the Liberal leaders, after his failure to win a seat in the Commons, took little notice of him. He never seems to have been in the inner councils of the Liberal Party. He lacked the fire of a true politician: his convictions did not move him sufficiently to action. But his friends, Morley, Bryce and G. O. Trevelyan, active in Liberal politics, were always close to him. Among those who came to 19 Portman Square in the 1914–1924 period I remember John Burns well. My great-uncle and great-aunt had a gift for friendship: they loved conversation and their house was always full. I recall Henry James, Anstey Guthrie of *Punch* (author of *Vice Versâ*), H. A. L. Fisher, Hugh Walpole, John Sargent, Andrew Carnegie, and Tom Jones. But I saw only the tail-end of the procession.

THE ILLUMINATED MSS. 'His book-collecting took Yates Thompson all over the world. His friends were the keepers of every great library in Europe and America; he belonged to an international circle of scholars and booklovers, and this was the company (except for intimates of Harrow and Cambridge days) that he enjoyed most. His collection of manuscripts was a daily delight to him, and in the pursuit of books he gratified his taste for scholarship and his acquisitive instinct. He limited his Illuminated Manuscripts to one hundred. "My plan", he said, "has been never to buy any additional volume unless it was decidedly superior in value and interest to one at least of my original hundred, and upon its acquisition pitilessly to discard the least fascinating of the said hundred". This was the main activity of his life and in the result he assembled a collection which for uniform perfection of quality has probably never been excelled.

IN AMERICA WITH LINCOLN AND GRANT. 'I must add a word about one aspect of his life which has always interested me. When he left Cambridge, his father sent him to visit America. The young man was strongly in sympathy with the North and he felt keenly about slavery. He travelled all over the Northern States, conversed with the intellectuals of Boston, met and admired Abraham Lincoln, and saw the war at close quarters. He witnessed the three-day battle at Chattanooga and listened to General Grant giving directions to his staff. I have his eye-witness description of the battle and his daily diaries of 1863—enthusiastic, whole-hearted Unionist and emancipator, thrilled by America and convinced of her great destiny.

'This enthusiasm for America never left him during his long life. He made regular visits to the United States, and American friends were always at 19 Portman Square. He was intimate with successive American Ambassadors in London—he would ride in Hyde Park with Joseph Choate, and Walter Page was a close friend of his later years.

A COMEDY OF CAMBRIDGE. 'In the first flush of his American enthusiasm my great-uncle was ahead of his time: in 1864 he went about England lecturing on Chattanooga, praising the Northern cause and striving for Anglo-American understanding and friendship. In seeking at once to give some practical advancement to the cause in which he so fervently believed, he received a rebuff from his beloved University. The *American Historical Review* (April 3, 1918) recalls this episode under the title: "The Thompson Readership; A Forgotten Episode of Academic History".

Young Thompson (it writes) convinced of the widespread and deplorable ignorance of the United States which characterised especially the upper classes of his countrymen, addressed, on Dec. 24, 1864, a letter to Edward Everett. 'My wish', he wrote, 'is to endow a Readership, at Harvard University, its object being the delivery of a biennial course of twelve lectures during a residence of one term at Cambridge in England on the "History and Political Institutions of the United States of America", such Reader to be appointed biennially by the President and Fellows of Harvard (subject to the veto in each case of the Vice-Chancellor of Cambridge), and his sole qualifications to be American citizenship and the opinion of his appointers that he is a fit person to deliver such a course'. The Readership, based on an endowment of $6,000 of United States Government Stock, was to carry the donor's name.

There were difficulties both at Harvard and at the English Cambridge. The plan was without precedent. If its direct benefit to Harvard was not easily discernible, neither was it clear in what way a such course of lectures could find a place in the rather inflexible curriculum of Cambridge, although Mr. Thompson argued that it might 'form a very suitable addition to the lectures of the Professor of Modern History'. However, with a distinguished American as first lecturer—the donor had in mind such men as Agassiz, Lowell, Longfellow and Holmes—he was sure that the plan would prove in the end to be of international usefulness. On April 29, the corporation (of Harvard) sanctioned the plan. On May 8 President Hill sent to the Vice-Chancellor of Cambridge a discreet letter of approval, with a suggestion that Charles Francis Adams—then our Minister to England—might be a desirable choice as first lecturer.

In October Mr. Thompson printed in a pamphlet portions of the correspondence and his own reflections in order to provide every voting member of the Senate with definite information. The Council of the Senate took its first formal action on Dec. 4 by calling attention to sundry difficulties and communicating these to Mr. Thompson. He in turn suggested that a preliminary trial be made of the plan for one year. Altering the title of the Readership to one on the History, Literature and Institutions of the United States, he printed a leaflet in addition to the pamphlet. On Feb. 9 there appeared a broadside, written by Charles Kingsley, Regius Professor of Modern History, which commended the project.

'The circumstances of the test vote on Feb. 22 were recorded briefly in *The Times*: "At a Congregation this day the grace for allowing the use of a lecture-room for the trial of the proposed lectureship on American history, institutions and literature was rejected by the Senate by 107 votes against 81. A great many flysheets on the subject have been circulated in the University during the last day or two, and a great many non-residents came up to vote. The strength of the opposition seemed to be mainly due to a fear lest the lectures should be made a means of diffusing Unitarian opinions." As is explained in Maitland's Life of *Leslie Stephen*:[1] "The drum ecclesiastic was resoundingly beaten. 'Are members of the Senate aware', wrote one of the drummers, 'that Harvard University, as far as it professes any form of religion, is distinctly Socinian, or if Americans prefer the term Unitarian?'" Another gentleman thought well to say in print that by receiving a lecturer from Harvard we should "pander to that which is perhaps the worst vice inherent in the North-American character, namely SELF-CONCEIT".'[2] To Lowell

---

[1] Duckworth, 1902.
[2] There is also a reference in the *Life and Letters of Sir R. C. Jebb* to 'the narrow and bigoted party in the University.'

the result was evidently not surprising. 'I doubt', he said, 'if the lectureship could have done much good; England *can't* like America and I doubt if I could, were I an Englishman.'

'LES HÉRITIERS DE MES GOUTS.' 'Towards the end of the 1914–1918 war', Sir Christopher continues, 'Yates Thompson's sight began to fail. This was a great grief to him; he could no longer handle and enjoy his books. He decided to sell the collection now that he could not see it. Certain directors of museums and librarians remonstrated with him: he was unmoved—his books, he said, should go to *les héritiers de mes gouts*. After three sales, he was successfully operated upon for cataract and once again could see his books. He at once cancelled the remaining sale and started buying books again—he was then eighty-two. It was in the end a splendid, glittering, collection of manuscripts and printed books that he left to his widow. In 1941 Mrs. Yates Thompson died and in her will she bequeathed the complete collection of Illuminated Manuscripts to the British Museum, thinking that this would be a fitting and worthy memorial to her husband.

'Returning to your theme, the *Pall Mall*, I feel it would be wrong to gloss over the feelings of the staff when the paper was sold over their heads. But it would be equally wrong to judge the character of Yates Thompson by this action alone. It was typical of him. He would act so often on quick impulse without pausing to consider or reflect on the effect of his action upon others. The best example I know of this habit of his is the fact that he purchased his country house (and also in fact his house in Portman Square) without consulting his wife beforehand—to her consternation! He liked to play the rôle of *enfant terrible*, but not with intentional unkindness. He was a warm, erudite, original, easy-going, cultivated, generous, yet insensitive man.'

I showed this faithful testimony to Sir Sydney Cockerell who knew the Yates Thompsons well—he once had a bedroom in their house which he could occupy whenever he pleased. 'They were immensely hospitable,' he kindly wrote to me in a character-istically interesting letter, 'and had a particularly nice circle of friends. On the point of "honours" H.Y.T. had not the smallest touch of snobbery. The reference to his flouting "the ordinary conventions" must not be misunderstood; he answered letters, kept a butler-valet, and pursued a regular and honourable existence. His generosity should not be overpraised, for his wife, he told me, was as rich as himself. He gave liberally, no doubt, but it was from his superfluity, not always, perhaps, quite without a touch of vanity. His interests were those of a well-bred scholar, but what did he do in scholarship? He did not start collecting until he had sold the *Pall Mall*, presumably with the proceeds. His earliest appearance in the sale room that I can recall was in March 1895 when he bought a very fine Parisian Bible of the 13th Century (No. 1 in his catalogue, Vol. I) which he ceded to me at cost price in 1914, having then acquired a Bible that he liked better. In 1897 he purchased *en bloc* from the Earl of Ashburnham a large portion of his collection of MSS. known as the Appendix. He sold at Sotheby's the items that he did not wish to retain and then started collecting the finest illuminated manuscripts with great zest. He had inherited a very few MSS. from J. B. Yates in 1856, and eventually sold all but one of them—and as I have stated he did not begin to collect MSS. until forty years later. There were four volumes of the Yates Thompson Catalogue with seven larger volumes of illustrations. There were also a number of separate monographs on MSS. of outstanding importance.'[1]

It may be added that among Yates Thompson's gifts was a statue of Tennyson, a Trinity man, to his old college, and the Art School to Harrow. He was munificent to Liverpool and a benefactor to the London Library, and he gave a psalter of the fourteenth century to the British Museum and an ancient volume to the Louvre which was acknowledged with the Legion of Honour.

THE ANNEXE TO WESTMINSTER ABBEY. On one of the occasions on which the cry went up of lack of burial space at the Abbey—it was before the days in which cremation is taken as a matter of course—he offered £35,000 to build what was described as 'a kind of additional Valhalla', with, some thought, a not too tactfully expressed condition, that his name should appear on the building. The proposal was declined on its merits, but it was noted as characteristic of Yates Thompson's width of mind that, when the buildings round the Chapter House were demolished, he said that the refusal had been justified.

Sir Charles Hagberg Wright concluded his obituary notice in *The Times* with this: 'In his private charities Thompson sometimes anticipated a request by an astonishing offer. Any appeal for a deserving object, especially one unlikely to meet with enthusiastic support, was fairly sure of his contribution. He had great indulgence for the ebullitions of youth; he had indeed a curiously playful side to his nature; sometimes one suspected that his bluntness was sheer premeditated mischief. In his later years he loved his game of billiards or bowls. But life itself was always the greatest game of all.'

I have read somewhere—I think in a letter from Cook—that

---

[1] Further particulars of the Yates Thompson MSS. may be found in *The Times Literary Supplement* of May 20 and 27 1949. Any visitor to the British Museum, however unskilled, may realise something of their beauty by looking into the glass cases to the right of the reading room.

John Morley said to him, 'I like Yates Thompson; he is a gentleman'.

It is stated by someone in the third volume of the inimitable *History of 'The Times'* that Yates Thompson was one of the men whom Moberly Bell saw with reference to capital for a *Times* purchase scheme to counteract Arthur Pearson's. Bell eventually succeeded with Lord Northcliffe, the chief investor, along with Harold Harmsworth, Kennedy Jones and Sir John Ellerman.

Yates Thomspon once told me at his house of a remarkable gathering-up he had made of first numbers of newspapers. What happened to it? Nothing is known of it at Colindale or the British Museum. Is it in America? The Press Club has a 1708–1929 collection.

I must not omit to mention among reminiscences that on one occasion, as a substitute for his father-in-law, George Smith, Yates Thompson took Matthew Arnold to Epsom, where the poet, while being blarneyed by a gipsy woman, had his watch stolen. 'G.S.', he remarked to Yates Thompson, 'would have taken better care of me'.

RUTH DRAPER, ELIZABETH ROBINS AND MRS. YATES THOMPSON. Mrs. Yates Thompson, Sir Sydney Cockerell once said to me, was 'the finer character of the two'. 'A radiant personality' was the description I had from the late Mrs. Reginald Smith, George Smith's daughter, who gave me so much information for *The Story of the 'Pall Mall Gazette'*. A vivid impression of her is to be found in *A Portrait of a Lady* by Elizabeth Robins, whom so many of us remember with admiration in the first presentation in London of Ibsen's plays.[1] I have permission to quote from it. 'Accustomed to the society of elderly men in George Smith's circle, she married a man sixteen years her senior when, at twenty-three, she wedded Yates Thompson. But Mrs. Yates Thompson shared her husband's interests as a collector, and Elizabeth Robins, when a guest in their house, once came upon them early in the morning in the billiard room with a folio and other books "doing their morning bit of Dante".' Mrs. Yates Thompson was a good horsewoman, gave Eton and Harrow cricket luncheons, had pleasure in her Jersey cows, and built several cottages in the village of Oving. She spoke of a forebear who was one of the first Virginians to free his slaves. She had much to do with the discovery of Ruth Draper and helped her greatly at the beginning of her career. From this gifted artist who as the granddaughter of C. A. Dana, has some association with the Press, I have the following letter:

My mother, Mrs. William H. Draper, was a beloved friend of Mrs. Yates Thompson, and I first knew her when I was, I think, six. I 'recited'

[1] Published for private circulation, 1941.

informally at parties in her house as early as 1912 and 1914. At one of these the gathering included Henry James and John Sargent. She was deeply interested in my 'career' which began in 1920, and from that time on came constantly to my shows, bringing her many friends. I very often performed at her house in the early days, and their many interesting friends made up the company. Emery Walker, Sydney Cockerell, Lady Ritchie, the Darwins and Sir Hagberg Wright I can recall, and I feel ashamed to think I have forgotten so many names. Men from the London Museum, the British Museum and the *Pall Mall*, and all the names that you have at your finger tips, would probably ring a bell in my proud memory.

I used to look at the lovely illuminated MSS., with Mr. Thompson telling me the story of their acquisition, their romance and history, and I can feel the thrill to this day of taking the treasures from his hands and holding them.

I was very fond of Mr. Thompson as well as Mrs. Thompson, and was always interested in him as a character, though it was she who was my close and devoted friend. Their house was very much a centre for me, and the good talk that I always found there remains a standard in my life.

LADY CHANCELLOR'S PICTURE OF MRS. YATES THOMPSON AND A VANISHED LONDON. An old friend of Henry Sidgwick, Yates Thompson was for many years a Governor of Newnham, and the present Newnham Library was the gift of himself and Mrs. Yates Thompson. Miss Sylvia Paget, daughter of Sir Richard and Lady Muriel Paget, a student at Newnham, knew Yates Thompson by repute as a benefactor of her college, and had a close association with Mrs. Yates Thompson for eighteen years. She has been good enough to write to me as follows about her great-aunt by marriage, for her husband is Sir Christopher Chancellor. The account is interesting not only for what it tells us about a remarkable woman and her literary associations, but for its picture of social conditions no longer surviving.

Self-effacement was deeply rooted in the character of Mrs. Yates Thompson and, if she thought about herself at all, it was only in relation to her husband, her family and friends. Defiance of fatigue, and stoic indifference to pain, led her, while suffering acutely from arthritis, to ignore all warnings until it was too late. She became completely crippled and the last years of her life were spent entirely in her chair.

Mrs. Yates Thompson was the eldest of George Smith's three brilliant and beautiful daughters. The sisters were united by bonds of deep affection and close understanding. They saw each other almost every day. Notes were constantly exchanged between Park Street, Green Street and Portman Square.

In such fragments of time as she could spare from her husband Mrs. Yates Thompson entered with eager interest into the lives of his countless nephews and nieces. She loved to help us, however little we might study to deserve it. She thought of everything. Jersey butter if we were thin; a weekend at Oving if we were tired; a dress for our first ball; a pram for our first baby. All this was planned and executed at the cost of endless trouble to herself. She tied and addressed each parcel with meticulous care. She wrote innumerable letters, which she often delivered in person, in her brougham or victoria, as the season might dictate. The weekly clatter of the horses' hooves down our small street behind the Edgware Road persists among the happy memories of my early married life.

But her generous solicitude extended far beyond her family, to a circle that widened quickly and steadily as the years went by. Every morning found her writing ceaselessly at her desk in the window of the library at Portman Square or in the window of the Oving billiard room. By lunch-time the envelopes had risen to a steady pile. Each was a work of art in itself, for it was addressed in her exquisite handwriting—the finest I have ever seen. Letters of admission to schools or hospitals, subscriptions to libraries, seats for Ruth Draper's performances, tickets for the Zoo—all were promptly and unfailingly supplied. She was incredibly reticent, almost furtive, in the execution of these tasks. It was only rarely, and by accident, that one heard of the boys whom she had quietly sent to schools and colleges and finally despatched (again in secrecy) to hopeful posts in every corner of the world.

She loved to entertain her friends but, though a technically accomplished hostess, was fundamentally diffident and did not do herself justice in company. She was shy and sometimes appeared to talk too much. But her dinners were perfection. The food was delicious, the service perfect in its unobtrusive solemnity. However apparently undistinguished the guests or dimly distant the relatives who might at times unaccountably assemble, the high standard of excellence invariable prevailed. Punctuality was rigidly enforced. The butler's awful words 'Dinner is on the table', uttered at the striking of the clock, never failed to awe our youthful hearts.

After her husband's death, she still gave large and frequent dinner parties for, in her devouring modesty, she could not believe that anyone would want to visit her if she were alone. To find her alone was a rare, and rewarding, experience; but a long visit was needed before she would consent to shew herself, momentarily, as the brilliantly gifted daughter of a distinguished man. Her relationship to her father was of abiding significance in her life. She had been his favourite child and he had intended her to run his business if she had not married at the age of twenty-three. From her childhood she had heard and read the best that had been spoken and written in her time. Thackeray had sat her on his knee. Later she had ridden regularly with Trollope 'in the Row'.

To her Victorian parents she owed also those moral standards by which her life was governed—inexorable standards from which she allowed herself no respite, relaxation or appeal. Her devotion to duty was absolute. She never lectured, but she never failed to practise what she did not preach. She was deeply versed in humility and devoted her formidable intellect to the most trivial tasks. But her diffidence was not to be confounded with timidity. She was forceful—sometimes vehement—in argument, and she would make short work of the visitor who unwittingly questioned some fact or theory that she had long believed to be beyond dispute. Her prejudices were vigorous—and refreshing. Certain persons were 'foolish', certain books 'unpleasant'—and both were likely to remain so. Her life was so busy that early judgments and habits persisted unrevised. But the habits that dictated the rhythm of life at Portman Square were in need of no revision. The machine functioned almost perfectly. Sometimes a faint creak was audible. The housemaid was cross: a footman gave notice; a guest was late for lunch. But such occurrences were rare.

Mrs. Yates Thompson could never have survived the life we lead now. So we must be thankful that she was not asked to endure it, and that she has left so much for us to remember, now that we are aunts and uncles in our turn.

Mrs. Yates Thompson died in 1941, at the age of eighty-six. Her husband, who survived until 1928, had passed away at the advanced age of eighty-nine.

CHAPTER XXIV

THE EDITOR OF THE *WESTMINSTER GAZETTE* AND HIS FRIENDS

E-ENTER 'MR. NEWNES OF *TIT-BITS*'. How Fleet Street
was to absorb the *Pall Mall* staff no one could see. But it was
not put to the test. 'Mr. Newnes of *Tit-Bits*', who had by this
time added the *Strand Magazine* to his properties,[1] reappeared. 'I have
heard', he wrote to Cook, 'that the *P.M.G.* is to become a Unionist
organ. Would you be disposed to enter into an arrangement to
start another penny evening on the old lines?'[2] The baronetcy to
come may or may not have been in his mind when he added,
'I think the scheme would find favour with leading men of the
Party'. But that is harsh, for Newnes was a Liberal. So, however,
was Yates Thompson.

Cook at his very first interview with Newnes had no difficulty in
getting better terms than he had required from what, it soon came
out, were the representatives of William Waldorf Astor, of Berkeley
Square, father of the present Lord Astor. He was conceded 'full
discretion as to the political policy of the paper and general control
over the contents, on the understanding that it shall be conducted
on the same general lines as those of the *P.M.G* under my editorship
thereof'. But, taught by experience, he stipulated—and again this
is of interest to hardly-pressed editors—'that before any offer for
the purchase of the paper be accepted the purchase be open to me
for fourteen days on the same terms, and the engagement to be
for three years, but with option on my part, after the first year, to
terminate the agreement at three months' notice'. Newnes made
no difficulty about all this except that he said, 'You could turn it
into a Tory organ.' 'No', said Cook, 'that is governed by "on the
understanding"'. He did not desire, he added, to be a 'mere
Daily News—independent support is the best support'.

Liberals who realised what the financially unrewarding but most
politically persuasive *Pall Mall* had meant to their party, had been
as perturbed by its sale as the Tories were when it went Liberal
under Morley. They were now, like Cook, in buoyant humour.
But he had had his time of anxiety before Newnes came on the
scene. I am struck, however, as I read his private memorabilia,

[1] Ceased publication last year.
[2] The idea seems to have been put into his head by a friend and a neighbour
of his with whom I was acquainted, L. R. S. Tomalin, the prophet of Jaeger.

by the indications of continued interest in what he saw of wild
life in the Parks and by his appreciation of outstanding architecture
in London, 'How pretty the blue mist is in London on fine days'
is a typical note.

Apart from its politics, the new journal got wide notice by being
on green paper, the colour, it said, of the sea, the fields and the
billiard table, and of help to the eyes. The office interior was a
light green. While the office was being built we occupied the
evening *Sun* premises opposite the site. They were the *Daily Telegraph's* second string in case of fire. In the first number there were
some measured words on the sale of newspaper properties. A
departure, in a journal of its class, was a serial story, a political
one by Justin McCarthy, author of a convenient *History of Our Own
Times*, and the troubled leader of the anti-Parnellite M.P.'s. There
was so little space available for the tale, and we had to print in
such short instalments, that it ran on interminably, and finally on
publication as a book, was brought rather abruptly to an end.
Some time afterwards, on Saturdays, we had Anthony Hope's
Dolly Dialogues, which had some imitators. Twenty witty, scathing
verses, 'Athanasius up to Auction', by Edmund Garrett, on the
sale of the *Pall Mall*, were much to our minds. Cust, Cook's successor, was sporting enough to print them. Two were as follows:

> Come gentlemen! what offers? I am authorised to sell
>   Without reserve, each stick and stone that can be sold or bought,
> That valuable property which is known as the *Pall Mall*
>   Names, fame, and all the fittings of a 'Medium of Thought'.

> 'The staff, sir'? No, the Staff, ahem, together with a few
>   Small matters (you remind me of a detail I forgot)—
> A few small matters of ideas that appertain thereto
>   Are not included in this unexceptionable lot.

Cook must have been glad of a Newnes request to remember
that on matters which required an immediate decision in his
absence he had 'absolute discretion to do what you think best, and
I shall approve'.

COUNSEL OF G.B.S. In the way of advice Bernard Shaw was
at his most pungent. 'Get rid of the infernally friendly terms you
are now on with everybody. Everybody says you are a very nice
fellow. They always said Stead was the damnedest scoundrel and
hypocrite. Until at least a thousand men turn white with rage
and hatred whenever your name is mentioned I shall not believe
in you a bit as an editor. You have a tremendous chance. And you
are throwing it away because you wish to behave as a gentleman.'
A friendly journalistic view of the newspaper is expressed in Saxon
Mills's satisfaction with its 'equableness, its statesmanlike tone, the

variety of its interests, its impartial devotion to politics, literature and art, its high moral and literary stand'. It was 'essentially E. T. Cook's; London had never been provided with a better, wiser, more brilliant and attractive journal.' When the Jameson Raid happened the *Westminster* said at once that it was the action 'not merely of an unscrupulous freebooter but of an utter madman'.

FURTHER TALKS WITH GLADSTONE. Nothing was set down in the Chapter on Cook's editorship of the *Pall Mall* about his social life. There was no mention of the interesting personages he was meeting, of the many 'good things' he heard, of the extent to which the intricacies and personalities of the political situation were exposed to him. It is now convenient to bring together, from the volumes of the diaries which Mr. D. G. Duff generously sent to me, some notes on the friends his uncle made during both the *Pall Mall* and the *Westminster* periods.

On two occasions Cook found Gladstone talking about Pearson's *National Life and Character*, with the author of which I remember having a friendly correspondence. But who reads the book now? 'Pearson', Gladstone said, revealing once more something of his own mind,[1] 'would disappoint the very sanguine believers in progress, but I have never been one of them'. A question of Gladstone's, in his stately English, was 'What oculist do you employ?' It was illustrative of the old man's attentive interest in everything he came across that he had for years made a study of bus horses. He was satisfied that they did not have a bad time, compared, at any rate, with tram horses. When he lived in Lord Aberdeen's house at Dollis Hill he and his wife would count the buses; there used to be sixty, now there were eighty. Cook noticed that at dinner the octogenarian had two glasses of both claret and port. He said: 'We're not sherry drinkers. Take fire and water and that is sherry'. Political talk was forbidden at Hawarden at dinner. The octogenarian (who, at other gatherings, 'punctiliously waited for the noble lords to go in first') remembered that Wordsworth when he dined with him at Albany disparaged Tennyson, and deplored such newspaper vulgarisms as 'lengthened'.

When Cook was at Hawarden, Gladstone's daughter, Mrs. Drew, said that she made it her business to open her father's letters and that she flung half of them in the wastepaper basket. On Lord Salisbury a remark of Gladstone's was, 'He is a man of very great power, very remarkable parts, but what a training the *Saturday Review*-ing was for a politician! His writing in the *Saturday* was however entirely honourable to him—it was to support his family, for his father had behaved very badly to him.' Cook did not mention at Hawarden that one day in 1888 he had followed

See page 170.

behind the old man from St. Martin's Lane to Parliament Street. Dressed as Gladstone was in old-fashioned clothes, he attracted the attention of small boys, one of whom cried 'So they've let him out!'

George Russell told Cook that the G.O.M. had a full journal written right up to the day of his resignation, and that he had once said, 'You know, there are many transactions in my public life which have been the subject of much animadversion and I have thought it right to have on record my view'. Lord Rosebery, who was present when this reminiscence was offered, said 'That sounds like some garbling of history'.

The veteran was much in favour of the green paper of the *Westminster*. The pink of the *Globe* and of telegraph forms ought, he said, to be abolished. The secret of clear writing, he went on, was 'space between your letters and words'. Gladstone asked Cook if he walked to his office. 'Yes, sir', said Cook, 'reading *The Times*'.

In an hour and a half's talk before dinner, at Hawarden, Gladstone said that he wished 'the English language had a larger and a stronger vocabulary' with which to characterise the atrocities of the Sultan; 'no such Sovereign ever committed such murders as he had'. Gladstone praised Alexander III; 'never was there a monarch with whom it was possible to act better'. As to the broken promise not to go to Khiva, 'Why, it was an utterly impossible promise'. With regard to Austria-Hungary and Germany, 'if it was a question only of moving a grain of sand in the cause of philanthropy and humanity, they could not be relied on for aid'.

In order to save his eye-sight, Gladstone was translating Horace from memory. On one of his journeys he took a pocket Herodotus with him but found he could not read it. It was very difficult for his family to help him for he could not bear to be read to; but music was a solace. When someone said to him that there was no reason why he should not live another ten years, he said, 'God spare me from such an event'. He was 'thankful' when the doctor told him that recovery was impossible. In spite of all the inconvenience and distress he suffered, the weakening old man's state of mind, Mrs. Drew said, was 'one of serene joy'.

Gladstone's mention of Salisbury is a reminder that the Conservative leader once said that there were only two offices in the Cabinet that mattered, the Prime Ministership and the Foreign Secretaryship, and so he combined them. Cook, who was at more than one Hatfield garden party, heard of Lord Salisbury putting off a meeting of the Committee of National Defence because the Duke of Devonshire was going to Newmarket 'to see which of two quadrupeds could run faster'.

LORD ROSEBERY'S GOSSIP. Rosebery said to William Watson when he gave him the Civil List Pension that the office of Laureate should follow 'the Court Fool into oblivion'. One of Rosebery's chance sayings was that Sydney Smith was 'the wisest politician of the nineteenth century'. Cook noticed at Mentmore that Rosebery's books had his index at the end, not like his, at the beginning.

Towards the close of his life, Rosebery, in search of sleep, was taking, Cook was told, 'every sort of drug and narcotic, enough chloroform to send ordinary people to sleep for a week'. Sir William Broadbent said 'a man in such a condition must get sleep, die or go mad'. A statement of Rosebery's was 'I lie awake all night thinking of my mistakes'. Joseph Chamberlain told Cook that he himself, by changing his thoughts, could sleep at will. As to the duration of his night's sleep he could manage with six hours, but he preferred seven and liked eight.

Cook's friendship with Rosebery grew—Sir Harold Hartley remarked to me that 'they were kindred spirits in many ways'. When the busy editor had forgotten an appointment the Foreign Minister wired, 'You didn't come; it was like missing the morning sun'; on the death of Cook, Rosebery described his friend as 'singularly gifted and delightful'. Rosebery once asked him to go with him to the Derby, but warned him that in that milieu he would 'have to play second fiddle'. Cook met at The Durdans, as a fellow guest, Tod Sloan, the jockey, of whose brains Rosebery spoke highly—'he can put us right on most things'. With regard to his own interest in racing, Rosebery said that the only drawback was that his son might become addicted to it, which he should regret. I thought it would be interesting if the present Lord Rosebery would care to tell us exactly what his father said to him on the subject. But Lord Rosebery cannot remember his father saying anything; 'he constantly took me racing as a boy'.

Rosebery did not at all believe, as Reginald Brett suggested, that there was something derogatory in a Minister writing for the Press. What was the difference, he asked, between writing an article for a paper and speaking from a platform? As we know, Rosebery found his Prime Ministership a trial. He called it 'a perpetual nervous strain, a crucifixion'. Sympathy, he declared, was 'deserved by a Prime Minister shut up in the House of Lords with 400 Tories'. He was all for a Single Chamber, and Cabinets of a dozen were wrong—they are now nineteen. 'Nothing human or divine' would make him sit again in the same Cabinet as Sir William Harcourt. Yet he also mentioned that once, when Harcourt had written to him asking for his aid in getting him appointed a Trustee of the British Museum, he had replied that he was delighted to have the opportunity of doing something for him. On the remark by some

SIR GEORGE NEWNES

Proprietor for a time of the *Review of Reviews* and, later, of the
Westminster Gazette

Liberal to Rosebery that Harcourt was a good fellow at bottom, he rejoined that 'they might as well expect you to live with Jack the Ripper by telling you that each murder cut him to the heart'. But Rosebery told Cook he did not believe that abuse ever hurt anybody, quite the contrary. He declared that he had no support 'except from the *Westminster*, and that one of Cook's articles—Cook is not given to noting commendations of himself—was 'the most brilliant thing in journalism for many years'.

Once, in London, Cook found Rosebery 'at the top of a high house writing at a washing table'. Rosebery was well pleased with the work he had to do as chairman of the London County Council. 'It might not be high work but it was something done. When you went to bed at night you could at least say to yourself, "I've put up that pump anyway, and men, women and cattle are getting water from it". But at the end of my term in Downing Street, where will be my pump?' He took to the County Council as a result of his experiences in the United States in 1873. 'Bad roads, full of holes—why? Answer, nobody can trust anybody else with eighteenpence to put them right.'

There have been various anecdotes about Sir William Harcourt's devoted son, Lulu. Cook's story is that when someone said to Lulu, 'Let's take a cab', he replied, 'I never go into a cab; one doesn't know who may have been there before'.

LORD RANDOLPH AND WINSTON CHURCHILL. In Stead's time, as has been noted, Cook had seen a good deal of Lord Randolph Churchill. His son, speaking to him in the year in which the first Great War broke out, said that Rosebery and Lord Randolph were 'two tragedies of modern politics'. As for Lord Randolph, Winston quoted Dryden's well-known lines:

> Happy the man, and happy he alone,
> He who can call today his own;
> He who secure within can say
> Tomorrow do thy worst, for I have lived today.
> Be fair, or foul, or rain, or shine,
> The joys I have possessed, in spite of fate were mine.
> Not Heav'n itself upon the past has pow'r
> But what has been, has been, and I have had my hour.

Winston said Lord Rosebery had 'great faults, great defects; he kills conversation at his own table, not by his talk but by his silence'. (Of himself his view was that the public being accustomed to one mattered a great deal; 'I am just as ill-educated as before but people are used to me'.) Balfour extolled Lord Randolph Churchill as a conversationalist. Of a Conservative member of whom he disapproved Lord Randolph said, 'A regular snarling old

U

Tory of the worst type'. Goschen, who was promptly to succeed him when he threw up the Chancellorship of the Exchequer, was 'the croaking, hissing, scolding, old raven with no future I can see'.

Mrs. Asquith told Cook that Balfour 'played the game to the last point'. Cook met Margot in her younger days. He and his wife heard her lightly debate whether she should marry Rosebery, Balfour or Asquith. Which reminds me of what the late Countess of Warwick told me that, at a house party in the Highlands of which young Winston Churchill was a member, there was a discussion as to whether he should throw in his lot with the Liberals or the Conservatives.

MINISTERS AND MONARCHS. Cook was once told of Mrs. Asquith weeping over her husband's troubles as Prime Minister. Meeting Cook at dinner, the Prime Minister told him of Jowett saying that he would have known that George Eliot's books were written by a woman because, with all the knowledge and love of the country exhibited in them, there was nothing about sport. One is curious about what really happens at Cabinet meetings: Asquith said on the same occasion that twenty minutes was occupied at one Cabinet meeting in considering whether *Hoc volo sic jubeo* or *Sic volo sic jubeo* was right, and there was a division of opinion. On the selection of the members of a new Ministry Cook had Admiral Fisher's view that, as far as the Admiralty was concerned, 'It doesn't matter a damn; send us your great duffer, deaf, dumb and blind if you like'. A pleasing story was of Haldane after being made Lord Chancellor. Having answered seven hundred letters of congratulation, he went off to Scotland for the Sunday to show himself to his old mother in his robes.

During a walk with Bonar Law, who had a sovereign on the result of the 1906 Election, Cook said to him that Lloyd George's wild man style on the platform increased the effect of his reasonableness when people met him, for they said, 'He's quite a moderate man after all'.

One of the noteworthy things of the first World War was the way in which King George tried to set a useful example by banishing intoxicants from his table. Cook was told that he had been rushed into his temperance pledge by Lloyd George without consulting Asquith. Only lemonade and barley water were provided.

Lord Lonsdale, who had been conspicuous in his association with Kaiser Wilhelm, was asked when war was declared what he thought of him now. He replied, 'It only shows how careful one must be in picking up acquaintances on the Continent'.

Reaching back to the Victorian era, Cook was told how Disraeli, on the failure of his *Endymion*, took back to Longman £10,000 of the £15,000 that had been given him. Longman refused to accept it but enjoined secrecy on Dizzy. During the afternoon, however, Longman found the matter in the *Pall Mall*.

'DE MORTUIS NIL NISI BUNKUM'. Cook does not say where he heard this adaptation. Kitchener, he reports, was 'rather repellent to look at, a sort of squint, red face and slightly blotchy nose, but a fine figure of a man'. Rhodes's expression was 'not quite like his pictures; in some phases more sinister, but when smiling more simple; a curious squeaky voice'. Swinburne was 'short and rather fat, nearly bald, talking in a curious falsetto, his hand shaking violently at meals'.

The famous advocate, Sir Charles Russell, told Cook that throughout his career he had never had a case in which he disagreed with the jury's finding. He would rather have a jury than twelve judges. How about the Maybrick case?

In view of Cook's youthful application to Carnegie for a post, it is of interest to read what he thought of Carnegie in later life: 'A tiresome little man with a tendency to spout on the smallest provocation', is his report; 'it was pathetic his attempt to reconcile his millions with the higher life'. There was an assembly at which Sir Edwin Arnold, of *The Light of Asia* and the *Daily Telegraph*, said that his own motto was never to say anything against anybody, and was smitten by Carnegie with 'That's why you say nothing worth saying'.

Cook listened to no end of after-dinner and after-luncheon speeches, and was struck on one occasion when he was an auditor of Yves Guyot by what he calls the superiority of French speaking. 'English, when the matter is good, is stiff and like a performance; French is genial and the speaker enjoys it, throws his whole self into it'.

At an Authors' Club dinner he heard a story of W. D. Howells, to whom the author of a number of books had said, 'I don't know how it is but my later books do not strike me as being as good as my earlier ones'. Howells's reply was 'My dear sir, they are quite as good; it's your taste that has improved.'

To Milner, first Sir Alfred and then Viscount Milner, Cook's colleague on the *Pall Mall*, there are many references. When a peerage was first proposed he said he preferred the G.C.B. 'I can manage very well in chambers but do not quite feel security as holder of a peerage. I certainly will never guinea pig'. He told Cook he would not sign a letter on a memorial to Stead, 'even if John Morley wrote it'. 'This is a pity', writes Cook; 'his bitterness is his weak place'.

On meeting Mrs. Sidney Webb after the visit she and her husband paid to Australia, Cook said to her that it was a pity they didn't write a book about that country. When she replied that they were there a few weeks only, he said, 'But you could have written what struck you, not what other people told you'.

A TALE OF KINGLAKE AND NAPOLEON III. The famous solicitor, Sir George Lewis, said to Cook something for biographers, 'Did you ever know anything that did not come out?' Apropos, Mr. Tedder, so well known as librarian of the Athenaeum Club, told Cook that 'the hostility of Kinglake to Napoleon III was due to the French Emperor having taken his mistress from him'. On this Yates Thompson showed Cook a note he had from his father-in-law, George Smith, based on what he had heard from old Mr. Procter. The story was that Omar FitzGerald had begun to tire of a pretty girl, his mistress, and that Thackeray, perceiving this, invited her, FitzGerald and Kinglake to dinner, and that Kinglake was so much taken by the girl that he got her to come and live with him and sent her to school. But FitzGerald appeared at the school and she had to be removed. Whereupon Kinglake apprenticed her at a milliner's, and there she fell into the hands of Napoleon. A story, Mrs. Yates Thompson interjected, which explained FitzGerald's views on the woman question. But Kinglake was 'a kindly man, very good to children', and when he was to be operated on for cancer, Madame Novikoff told Cook, 'went to his death with a joke'.

Of the difference between Cook's time and our own there is a reminder in the fact that he dined in a house in Amen Court—in 1894 I think it must have been—which 'had not even gas'. But there is this resemblance between 1894 and 1952 that Korea, which has large headlines in the papers on the day I am writing this paragraph, was to the fore one day at the *Westminster* when I had my usual morning few minutes with Cook. I was rather full of the subject—I referred to my daily 'Round the World'—and Cook startled me by asking me to do the leader. So I set to, and had my first experience of leader-writing for a London daily and of sending up my 'copy' to the printers one or two sheets at a time.

LAST THOUGHTS ON RUSKIN. The diaries are, of course, full of odds and ends about Ruskin. One gets the impression that Cook feels that, with all Ruskin's devotion to his parents and the many ways in which he used to fall in with their views, he had a quiet smile over some of their suggestions, requirements and demands. From his books Ruskin is stated to have had for an unspecified period £3,750 a year. Cook was occupied with his thirty-nine volumes from December 1902 to May 1912. The later two-volume *Life* took five months and had to be repeatedly cut down. Of the hero of all this print Cook says that he was 'never at a loss for the fitting word', that 'no literary man of his time reached anything like the same output and all the while he was no less indefatigable as an artist than as an author'. His immense production was due in no small measure to early rising. He would be 'up with the sun'.

CHAPTER XXV

EDITOR OF THE *DAILY NEWS*

THE *WESTMINSTER* 'VERY UNINTERESTING'. Newnes had been 'hugely pleased' when Rosebery mentioned that Cook was 'the only person connected with the Press who had my confidence', and the day came when Newnes told Cook that the ensuing twelve months would see the end of his losses with the *Westminster* and the *Weekly Dispatch*.[1] In 1894, however, there was a conversation between Newnes and Cook which was 'not pleasant'. Newnes told him that the paper was losing £250 a week, and said that 'while he wanted to retain its seriousness, he wondered whether it could not be more interesting'. A month or two later Newnes again said that the *Westminster* was 'very uninteresting, that he could find nothing of interest in it. He had put in £45,000 and £35,000 was gone.' Cook, who says he was 'very angry'—none of us, I think, had seen him so[2]—agreed to keep down expenditure by about £25 a week, and no doubt Newnes was gratified by his baronetcy. He told Cook that he had been rather afraid the papers would have a jeering reference to *Tit-Bits*.

I can understand that, as a business man, Newnes did not like to see his money going—the *Westminster* cost him in all £100,000—when he felt, on the basis of his experience with his other publications,[3] that there was a large and increasing public to which, in his view, the paper did not sufficiently appeal. Looking back, I think that if we had all been called into council, had taken complete stock of things, had put our wits to work and had sought new fields of interest, and had been encouraged to speak or write our minds freely, the *Westminster* might have had many more readers.

RESIGNATION. When in 1896 Cook's first three years' term provided for in his agreement with Newnes expired we had a

[1] Published in the same building.

[2] On one occasion Cook writes in his diary that someone 'exploded' at the *Pall Mall* office; 'I declined battle and left him to cool down'. See page 302.

[3] Miss Friederichs' *Life of Sir George Newnes* does not tell the history of *Country Life*. Hudson's, a firm of printers, acquired with Newnes a paper called *Racing Illustrated* and turned it into *Country Life*, a publication which has been highly successful because its conductors, having produced a good thing, have had the commonsense to leave well alone. After a few years as a joint concern with Hudson's, Newnes sold his interest to George Newnes Ltd., whose buildings tower at the corner of Southampton Street. A public-spirited scheme of Newnes' was the starting of the hillside railway connecting Lynton and Lynmouth, which was the making of those health resorts. Date of baronetcy 1895.

28 Dec 1894

Dear Tomalin.

You asked me to write you when Lord Rosebery's letter came. It has now arrived. "The baronetcy is "to commemorate not only political services but the good work done in the cause of healthy popular literature".

This is particularly gratifying as it is not a mere party honor.

I am faithfully yours.
Geo Newnes.

It is still necessary to keep it quiet till the official announcement.

A LETTER FROM GEORGE NEWNES ON HIS BARONETCY

shock. He was appointed editor of the *Daily News*. He had only to walk across the street from Tudor Street to Bouverie Street, up which his *Westminster* window looked. He sent a handsome letter to Newnes in acknowledgement of what he had done in starting the *Westminster*, and said that on his part he had striven to the best of his ability to give it 'a position of credit and respect'. Newnes wrote in his turn of relations of 'a very agreeable character'. But there was something unsaid on both sides.

MORNING *VERSUS* EVENING PAPER JOURNALISM. Perhaps Cook ought not to have left the *Westminster* for the *Daily News*; I never fully penetrated his mind. In the eyes of many journalists, no doubt, it is preferable to edit a morning than an evening paper. But the *Pall Mall*, *St. James's* and *Westminster Gazettes* were journals of a rank and influence of their own. Some of us might scoff at the *Daily News* as of the past, but it still had a standing, a following and an influence. Some attractions of its editorial chair to Cook are not difficult to understand. I doubt whether financial considerations were foremost. But the fact that the *Westminster* was still only a three-year old which had not yet reached the paying stage may have been. Maxse, in a note to Cook, was glad that his friend was 'relieved from his early morning drudgery and was to take it at the other end of the night when a man has best command of his faculties'. Well, like the Quaker of the tale, 'I've tried both'. As Sir Harry Lauder sang, 'It's fine to get up in the morning'. It is a good and rewarding habit, but in the winter in London early rising may have had its drawbacks for Cook, who was frequently late up at night. At the *Westminster*, however, Cook had not to begin the day as early as some members of his staff. When, after leaving Tudor Street, I was at the *Daily Chronicle* and lived near Epping Forest, I had to walk to Liverpool Street from Fleet Street, after tiring nights, at three in the morning. On the whole the conditions of afternoon paper work seem to be preferable. One works in the daylight and has one's evenings free. Evening paper journalists have also the advantage of being able to see what London and provincial papers have said on some of the happenings of the day. For a man of Cook's judicious temperament, an evening paper which people have leisure to read, was possibly the better platform. Lord Layton records the view that 'while a morning paper is the greater tie, an evening paper is the more taxing'.

If it were profitable to dwell on might-have-beens, the thought might be indulged that a combination of Cook, the rarely endowed and very human Edmund Garrett, physically fit and given his head, with F.C.G. as cartoonist, sub-editors and reporters of quality, and a management which believed in them all and knew its business, could have produced a paper of distinction with a sound

commercial basis. Garrett in normal health could have supplied
and got others to provide a touch right through the paper that
neither Cook nor his assistant and successor, Spender, was quite
able to give. The constituency of the *Westminster* had its limits, but
I doubt whether the circulation and advertising were ever what
they might have been made. Sir George Newnes declared that he
did not dare to go into the office! Cook was like Morley in resenting
intrusion—as Spender says, he was 'firm on the point that a proprietor should not walk into his editor's room unannounced'—but
Newnes, with the resources, intelligence and information available
to him might possibly have done more or got others to do more on
the business side of the paper.

CHOOSING EDITORS. Some correspondence between Lord
Rosebery and Sir George Newnes which Sir Frank Newnes has
kindly let me see shows not only the position of influence the
Westminster had made for itself under Cook but the attitude of
its proprietor to his leaving, to the editorship in the future and to
the possibility of improving the paper. Lord Rosebery, writing on
Jan. 7, 1896, in a letter marked 'Most Confidential', says: 'Do not
think me impertinently intrusive if I express to you my ardent
hope that under its new editor, whoever he may be, the *Westminster*
may continue on its present lines of pre-eminent usefulness to the
Liberal party. It would be difficult to exaggerate the opinion of our
best men as to its helpfulness. I have had letter after letter spon-
taneously expressing this feeling. It would be almost impossible to
over-state my own sentiment on this subject. The *Westminster*
appears to me to guide stimulate and instruct the Liberal Party
throughout the country to an extraordinary degree. It is moderate
and therefore strong, it gives the tone that is wanted, and inspires
the provinces. I cannot but feel anxiety as to what course you may
be contemplating in regard to this indispensable journal.'

Sir George thanked Lord Rosebery warmly and expressed his
mind to him: 'This is an important moment in the *Westminster*
history, as the compact which I entered into with the staff of the
Pall Mall Gazette has now been broken by the decoying of Mr.
Cook to the *Daily News*. I do not complain as I suppose the necessities of great journalistic properties sometimes bring about the
effacement of sentiment, but I must say that I did not expect that
the compact which I made under peculiar stress of circumstances,
from a Party point of view, would be shattered by the Maxim
guns—not moral Maxims—of Mr. Arnold Morley and the *Daily
News*. As to the future my first thought will be to preserve the
influence of the *W.G.* and also if possible to make it more newsy
and popular. This will add to its influence, and the two can be
continued. Great pressure has been brought to bear upon me to

appoint Mr. Herbert Paul, and several members of your Administration have written urging the claims of the Apostle Paul. He has
written many of the leading articles for the *D. News* for years past.
It has rejected its own apostle and has taken my ewe lamb. I do
not propose to retaliate.'

In the course of a second letter, Lord Rosebery speaks of 'Cook's
right hand men at the *Westminster*, F. C. Gould and Charles Geake:
I rejoice that Mr. Gould is to take a more active part. I consider
him a unique member of our Party, and so was delighted to show
him what attention I could. Geake is a capital fellow. I am grateful
for your confidence and should like to have a talk with you next
week.'

The reference to Gould is explained in a note by him to Newnes
stating that he had been spending a night at Mentmore. He states
that Rosebery 'holds a very strong opinion that "next to *The Times*,
the *W.G.* is the most important and valuable power in the London
Press". This tribute was entirely voluntary and expressed with a
great deal of earnestness'.

CROSS CURRENTS IN BOUVERIE STREET. At the *Daily News*
Cook had four persons instead of one to get along with or, counting
the veteran manager, Sir John Robinson, five. The four were an
ex-Postmaster General, Arnold Morley (no relation to John),
Henry Oppenheim (Frederick Greenwood's friend), Lord Ashton
(a rich industrialist), and Lord Brassey (seaman). It was Arnold
Morley who had first sounded Cook as to whether it would be
worth while making an offer to him of a paper, 'not an evening
one and not a new one'. The fly in the ointment at the *Daily News*,
beyond a difficult member of the staff, was Ashton—'slouching
clothes, bitten nails, not quite sure about his h's'—wrote Cook, a
person who was to pronounce some of Cook's leaders 'worse than
Toryism'. Cook this time agreed for two years instead of three,
and for a notice, on either side, of six months. It was conceded by
letter that at times of crisis the proprietors should have a voice,
but they were all of them hearty Liberals.

Rosebery said to Cook that he had his Sir William Harcourt in
Herbert Paul, who perhaps looked to having his place. He did not
take the Cook line on South Africa and other subjects, and represented what Thackeray, during his editorship of *Cornhill*, called
'thorns in a cushion'.[1]

---

[1] HERBERT PAUL. Lord Crewe in the *D.N.B.* notes that at Oxford Paul obtained
a first class in *literae humaniores*, that he was for three years M.P. for South Edinburgh, that he wrote lives of Gladstone, Matthew Arnold and Froude, a *History
of Modern England* and a study of the age of Queen Anne, and that he had in 1907
a nervous collapse, and in his writing was 'often sub-acid'. John Morley in a
letter to Campbell-Bannerman (March 6, 1907), which I read in the British
Museum, says: 'I hope you won't let Herbert Paul slip out of your thoughts for

Cook's major problem was the direction of a Liberal Party, some of whose members were for Harcourt and some for Rosebery. It was also a Party whose possible leaders took to resigning,[1] a party which was divided in its sentiments about foreign policy and a Party some of which was Nonconformist and some Church. Cook had rather a time of it with the various sections, but he gained general applause in a direction for which no one suspected he had willingness as well as talent; he settled disputes in the engineering and building trades.

SOLD AGAIN! He ran into heavy weather, however, over South Africa. Milner and Garrett, now editor of the *Cape Times*, were his friends and he accepted their views and drove the paper according to their way of thinking.[2] He even drafted in the *Daily News* a despatch which, if adopted by Chamberlain, the Colonial Secretary, would, he thought, bring Boer and Uitlander together. When he went to see his friend Lord Selborne, Under Secretary for the Colonies, to find out what had been done, Selborne said, 'Mr. Chamberlain told me to give you a hint that your despatch had been adopted. I drafted one and you drafted one, and in some respects the Cabinet preferred yours.' Cook's comment in his diary is that 'this is probably the only occasion on which an editor of the *Daily News* drafted a despatch for a Conservative Government'.

Things moved to a crisis not only in South Africa but on the *Daily News*. By this time I was on the *Daily Chronicle*. What eventually happened was that Cook lost his post on the *Daily News* through being a Milner-Garrettite and trying to make its readers Milner-Garrettites, and I resigned from the *Daily Chronicle* because the paper, from being 'pro-Boer', so-called, under Massingham, went into the opposite camp under W. J. Fisher.

The money for the purchase of the *Daily News* from Cook's proprietors had been largely contributed by George Cadbury, and Lloyd George is alleged to have been the agent. Cadbury and his associates were dead against the South African War. At a *Daily News* dinner in 1912, the printer of the paper told the story of its sale, and that accomplished journalistic hand, S. K. Ratcliffe, has kindly repeated it to me. Murch said that on coming on duty

the Civil Service Commission. When I first came to London to make my fortune this post was regarded as *a sort of perquisite for men of letters*. In my moments of giddy ambition I used to aspire to it myself. Now Paul has a really high sort of literary position. 'Tis true, as you said, that he has some biting peculiarities of temper, but in private he has fundamental amiability, and I believe that hard times have humbled him down to office pitch. Excuse me but I am keen about my trade, and P. is the most eminent man in the trade who is available.'

[1] Balfour on Rosebery, 'He had the worst of all things, a resigning mind'.

[2] Cook's *Rights and Wrongs of the Transvaal War* (Arnold, 1910), was described by a political opponent, H. W. Nevinson, as 'an admirable exposition of the case from the Imperialist point of view, as was natural in a writer of such integrity and industry, a friend of Milner, and possessing very similar qualities'. See p. 354.

one evening he was told by the commissionaire that the paper was sold and the editor was leaving. He went into Cook's room and said, 'Mr. Cook, is this right, the paper sold and you're leaving?' 'First I've heard of it, Murch,' said Cook, who in his turn went off at once to Sir John Robinson's room. On coming back he said 'Murch, you're right'. Arnold Morley, who had been the chief proprietor, had lost interest in and hope for the paper. It was 'costing money', the circulation was almost the same as when Cook came to it, and some of the owners deplored the editor's attitude towards the Boers.

The new owners, like Dove Keighley before them at the *Pall Mall*, tried to get Cook to stay on with 'a little give and take'. But he was no more inclined to what he termed 'a little trimming' than he had been when it was proposed to him in Northumberland Street. He once put in writing the view that 'an independent journal which leaned to (a very different thing from adhering rigidly to) neither side and to no organised group or party would not be a very influential organ'. In his farewell leader he said that in the cause of 'sane Imperialism and social reform the New Liberalism may hope to regain the commanding position of the Old'. It was a pious hope that was not to be realised in his generation or the next.

POTBOILING. A scheme for 'a new Liberal weekly' with a capital letter for 'new' no doubt, came to nothing, and Cook had to accept a position offered to him as leader writer most evenings in one of the cubby holes of the now Milner-and-Garrettite *Daily Chronicle*. It seemed to the discredit of rich Liberal politicians that Cook, at the height of his journalistic career and after all his experience and sacrifice, was suffered to drudge for ten years for a paper which, in his words, 'knew no better than to mangle my work unmercifully and very crudely—I felt very angry and humiliated'. Rosebery once wrote to him of his *Chronicle* leading articles, 'I see you shed a tear sometimes'. A *Chronicle* editor is reported as saying to Cook, 'We must bow to the winning side; we must say nothing until the Cabinet decides'. Cook appends the word 'Sickening!'

One day when he had walked away from a Hall Caine luncheon with Harmsworth that Press magnate said to him: 'If you get tired of Lloyd's [the *Chronicle* proprietary], for Heaven's sake come and help us. Commercially, I am sure we could do better for you than any paper you have had yet.'

The breaking of Cook's connection with the *Chronicle* is thus recorded in his diary of July 25, 1911, 'Last night on coming home to supper and leisurely opening letters found one giving me three months' notice'. It shows how much Cook was liked personally in Whitefriars Street that he felt that he had to write thirty-eight letters of thanks in acknowledgment of a parting gift. A short time after his work at the *Chronicle* ended he met Yates Thompson who said, 'You must be very glad to get rid of the *Chronicle*'. To which Cook adds, 'A rich man's view'.

He records a profit on the *Chronicle* and *Lloyd's News* of £100,000 in 1911. When in 1919 the paper was hit by the competition of a rival which was getting circulation by pandering to low tastes, Frank Lloyd said, Cook notes: 'I can't help it. *Lloyd's* shall remain a clean paper'.

Cook also contributed leaders to the *Sunday Sun*. It appears from his diary that before he came away from the *Daily News* an effort was made to buy the *Chronicle* and make Cook its editor. The story ran that Frank Lloyd wanted £400,000, with *Lloyd's* thrown in. The *Daily News* had been bought by the Cadbury syndicate for a fourth of that sum, or twice what Yates Thompson got for the *Pall Mall*.[1]

Cook once wrote, repeating, unconsciously perhaps, very much what John Morley has been recorded as saying, that 'the best preservation against the worry and responsibility of journalism is not to take the work too seriously'. But he did take it seriously. 'Whether one agreed with its politics or not', the Conservative *Pall Mall* had said generously on Cook's retirement from the last editorial chair he was to occupy: 'The *Daily News* in his hands became one of the most varied, coherent and altogether delightful papers ever published. There has been no happier union in recent journalism of political instinct, fine literary judgment and interest, and an excellent news service combining to produce a paper that was always individual and amusing, and often brilliant, and that made itself a power by the pungency not the partisanship of its leading articles.' In the same high fashion Cook, when his political opponent, Massingham, left the *Chronicle*, wrote to him: 'Your courage in asserting and maintaining the most honourable traditions of our profession commands the admiration of every journalist. It certainly commands mine.'

TALK OF PAPERS. But, on getting his freedom, after so many years, from what he called in a note to Miss Violet Markham 'the daily grind', and Harmsworth termed 'a terrible grind', one can understand the note in his diary, 'Loose-endish'.

An interesting thing is how much Cook saw of Yates Thompson

---

[1] Among Cook's newspaper gossip is a note that Harmsworth's offer for the *Standard* was £450,000. Arthur Pearson who secured it paid, he stated, 'not far short of £700,000,' but this price included several valuable freeholds. The circulation was 80,000 and a year's profits were reported to have been £10,000. 'They were once £100,000.' For figures in relation to *The Times*, see the third volume of *The History of 'The Times'* on which Stanley Morison has been engaged since 1933.

after his disappointment with him as proprietor of the *Pall Mall*. He frequently lunched and dined with him. Yates Thompson said to Cook that 'Gladstone might have kept the *Daily Telegraph* and *Chronicle* if he had baroneted Lawson and Lloyd'. He also confided that, in Lord Astor's absence, he had got someone to show him his remarkable estate offices on the Thames Embankment. There was, he said, no plot of ground in London on which so much money had been spent. A metal screen cost £600, a weathercock £120, which were then considerable amounts. Yates Thompson consulted Cook as to whether he should finance a useful municipal weekly run by Robert Donald (afterwards Sir Robert) called *London*. He got it for £500, with an editorial salary of £350 to Donald.[1] When the *Westminster* was announced he asked Cook to let him see over the new office, and before long was telling him that if Newnes got tired of the paper he might purchase it. In later years he put it to Cook whether he would like to edit the *Star*. Between the sale of the *Pall Mall* to Astor and the retirement of Cook from the *Daily News* a number of offers of editorship and other journalistic and literary employment came Cook's way. He appeared to have been sounded about both the Johannesburg *Critic* and the Johannesburg *Star*. Milner, who was privy to the second offer, said to him that, in command of the *Star*—the paper that was offered to me, and Monypenny ultimately accepted—'you have South Africa beneath you'. Then there was talk of Cook's taking the *Cape Times* which Garrett had edited, but he had already backed Saxon Mills's application. In one of Cook's diary entries there is a reference to a possible London correspondentship for the *Star*. But none of these things fructified. In January 1908 he had a midnight call regarding the editorship of Thomasson's unfortunate *Tribune*, for some Liberals had made it a condition of helping with funds that Cook should be its head. 'The gossip was', he writes, that 'five of the capitalists all demanded baronetcies beforehand', which may be one of Ben Trovato's efforts.

The most remarkable overture of all, to use Cook's word, was that made to him by Astor to edit the *Pall Mall* again, on independent lines. An intermediary said that he thought Astor meant to go into politics as a Roseberyite. Cook writes, 'See correspondence', but it has not been preserved.

As far back as 1902 the editorship of *Black and White*, a weekly established in rivalry with the *Illustrated London News* and the *Graphic*, was proposed, first at £1,200 and then at £2,000. Cook also seems to have been approached regarding the editorship of

[1] I remember hearing Robertson Nicoll, of the *British Weekly* and *Bookman*, who brightened the former publication with his 'Man of Kent' [*Scottice*, man o' kent, man of understanding], tell Donald that an editor should always have in his paper a personal column of his own.

another long-since-departed periodical, the *English Illustrated Magazine*. For a time he acted in a consultative capacity for *Cornhill*. One day his suggestions were 'The classics on the model of Prothero's book on the Psalms', and three articles 'A Day in the Life of the Prime Minister', 'Torpedoes', and 'Japanese Flowers in English Gardens'. He notes that the number of unsolicited MSS. received by *Cornhill* in a twelvemonth had been 2,050, of which 51 were used.[1]

In the way of writing, Cook seems to have been approached by Bell's with a view to writing a 'popular life' of the Duke of Devonshire. Milner said that 'though Holland's life was a ghastly failure' he would be ill-advised to take on the job. 'Personalia would be difficult to get, and politics of Lord Hartington's days had no relation to present day politics.'

[1] Mrs. W. L. Courtney, in her book about her husband, *The Making of an Editor* (Macmillan, 1930), says that during his editorship of the *Fortnightly* 'something like a hundred articles a month were sent in on chance. Not more than fifteen or so were printed, and these included a good many definitely arranged for and consequently seldom counted'.

CHAPTER XXVI

RUSKIN IN THIRTY-NINE VOLUMES

THE TEN YEARS' TOIL WITH WEDDERBURN. The thirty-nine volumes of Cook's monumental effort, *The Works of Ruskin*, which have been so frequently referred to, are about $9\frac{3}{4}''$ by $6\frac{1}{2}''$, run up to six hundred pages each, and occupy nearly eight feet on my shelves. Some possessors of the tomes know little of Cook's colleague in the enterprise, Wedderburn. He was of the well-known Scottish family, but like many Scots, spent his life in England. He went to Haileybury and, later, to Balliol under Jowett. Ruskin was then Slade Professor of Art, and Wedderburn became one of his most ardent and active disciples, and took part in the Hinksey road-making. He frequently visited Ruskin at Denmark Hill and was often at Brantwood. He helped with *Arrows of the Chace*, and Wedderburn's son, Mr. A. H. M. Wedderburn, who has the manuscript of the Preface, was taken there as a child. He remembers two things, he tells me: the house was on the hillside and red squirrels came in at the dining-room window and were fed.

Cook describes his colleague, who from his youth had been a Ruskin collector and brought some useful Ruskin material to the partnership, as 'kindly, courteous and cultivated'. Saxon Mills says that during the execution of the big work Cook and Wedderburn met twice weekly. They would work from ten to one o'clock, and then from two to seven, after which Cook would do his night's work for the *Daily Chronicle*. Wedderburn has been described to me as endowed with a zest for life, a fine sense of humour, restless energy and unbounded industry. He met with considerable success at the Parliamentary Bar, and had spared time to produce in *The Wedderburn Book* a genealogical work of merit. His delight in and service to Ruskin continued throughout his life, and at Ruskin's death he became, with Mrs. Severn—to whom he owed his introduction to his wife—and Charles Eliot Norton, one of the three Ruskin literary executors. In this capacity he proposed colleagueship with Cook in the monumental edition. Cook was nationally known for his devotion to Ruskin and wide knowledge of his books, and for his practised literary skill. Wedderburn's work in the partnership seems to have been the collation of no end of papers, with a great deal of proof reading, and much of the preparation of the great

SIR EDWARD COOK
with a volume of his *Ruskin*

index of 689 double-column pages and 150,000 entries. Cook and
he were fellow workers on the vast enterprise for nearly ten years,
and their relations were of the happiest—'never a jar', said Wedderburn. Mr. Roger Fulford was good enough to give me a story of
the index. 'The thirty-nine volumes were in the room in which
A. A. Brodribb[1] sat in *The Times* Office, and once when he saw me
consulting the index he said, "Ah, my dear sir, in Fleet Street
that volume is known as The Journalist's Friend because it can be
counted on to supply ideas for a leader".'

MATERIAL AND INDEX. How is the great size of the *Works*
to be accounted for? First, no doubt, by the enormous mass of
material. Apart from what was in Cook's hands he consulted ten
thousand volumes at the British Museum alone! As for what was
in print or in MS. by Ruskin, Cook believed with Engels that he
had 'never written anything worthless or unimportant'. Engels
might well have added or 'uninteresting'. To Mr. Fulford's anecdote may be added the experience of anyone who refers to the
index. The topics to which reference is offered are so interesting
and so wide in range that nothing but the physical labour involved
and lack of time hinder a reader turning to one volume after
another. Then Cook was pre-eminently a man who liked to do
well and finish well anything he undertook. He had satisfaction in
work and in method, and he could stick to his task. Further, he
had a true devotion to Ruskin and a full and judicious appreciation
of his service to the world, and he had closely studied every one
of the Master's books. Finally, much of the work done by Cook
before the volumes were published had the advantage of being
pressed forward when he suffered not only the death of his wife
but severance from the *Daily News* and the *Daily Chronicle*. No
labour could have more completely occupied his mind and heart.

After all, however, no more than 2,000 sets were printed, and
some, I believe, are still unsold. The financial arrangements in
respect of ten years' work were inadequate to Cook's and Wedderburn's labours. Cook had a slender reward, £1,500 I think, and
Wedderburn, I am told, got nothing; but neither regretted the
time they had spent and the labour they had given. If Ruskin,
in his fits of depression, could only have had the joy of knowing
of this great acknowledgment of the value of his life-work! The
publication of the volumes was in the hands of Ruskin's publisher,
George Allen, whose firm, after going into bankruptcy, was
absorbed by Allen & Unwin. The work, which bears the dates
1903–12, came out volume by volume. Cook's later *Life of John
Ruskin* in two volumes is dated 1911. As far back as 1890 Cook

---

[1] 'An experienced journalist and excellent scholar', says Mr. Stanley Morison
in the *History of 'The Times'*.

W

had written *Studies in Ruskin*, a quarto copy of which with his kind regards in it, I found on my desk one morning. There was also a small edition. His two-volume *Ruskin in Pictures* was published in 1902. I have heard that a plan for *Selections* from Ruskin's books, in a reasonable number of volumes, was considered by Cook but was found to be impracticable in War conditions. The account of Ruskin in the *Dictionary of National Biography* was his work.

THE TRUTH ABOUT RUSKIN AND HIS WIFE. The only complaint that can be justly made against the sacrificial labours of Cook and Wedderburn is, I think, that in one particular, they fell in with some notions of their time on what may and may not be said in telling the story of a great man's life. The right thing to do is, of course, to tell the truth. Unless biographers are prepared to tell the truth as far as they are able to ascertain it, what claim have they to undertake the task they have given themselves or other people have imposed upon them? Unhappily, as is known to so many biographers minded to do their duty, there are still plenty of relatives, friends and associates of the eminent, with the story of whose lives the world which honours them is rightly desirous of acquainting itself fully, who, in the name of a false propriety, destroy or secrete papers or cry 'Hush-hush'. Their offence is a form of snobbery, hypocrisy or social cowardice. If heed be given to them the result must be narratives which lack what is necessary for accurate and satisfying pictures of the men or women whose achievement, character and temperament are being presented. History is deprived of its dues, and mankind of profitable experience.[1]

Nor do such persons who, in their withholdings and suppressions, have so little faith in the impression made on the world by great service and high example, often succeed in the object they seek. Sooner or later, the facts which have been hidden come to light, as Sir George Lewis said, often in a curious way. The result is that greater attention is given to these details than they would have attracted had the truth been told in its proper relation at the proper time.

No instance of this has been more regrettable than what has happened with Ruskin. In their many volumes on the life and work of a great moralist, unquestionably one of the greatest of his era, and a man of courage conspicuous for his downright talk and writing, Cook and Wedderburn, because they and others of their day believed that certain things were not necessary, 'nice' or 'suitable', or were better kept out of sight, or not spoken about, chose to restrict their account of a married life of six years to—seventy-three words! About this unfortunate decision it is as well

---

[1] It has been noted that the Transcendental Club that met at Emerson's house 'completely neglected the sexual'. But they were not biographers.

to be plain. To suggest that a straightforward account of the married life of a great teacher of his generation is inessential to a fair and complete estimate of him is pernicious nonsense.

Our obligation to Ruskin the writer is vast. But why should we not be candid on matters in which Ruskin the man, constituted as he was, fell short? It is idle to cloak the fact that his wife suffered grievously, and that, if persons of wisdom had not intervened to prevent him marrying again, a second woman would have had a wretched time of it. Happily science, the development of our minds and hearts, and a new candour on things that matter will save many men and women from some of the sorrows of John Ruskin and Effie Gray.

The passage to which Cook and Wedderburn restricted themselves is as follows:

'This was a period in Ruskin's private fortunes to which only a brief reference may here be made. His wife left him in April 1845, returned to her parents, and immediately instituted a suit. Ruskin declined to put in any answer, and went abroad with his parents. The marriage (which in many respects had not been happy) was annulled on July 15, and a year later Millais was married to Euphemia Chalmers Gray.'

In his later *Life of Ruskin* (published in 1912) Cook does not go beyond this except to say that 'Ruskin's private affairs were much canvassed in literary and artistic circles', and to omit the statement that 'the marriage in many respects had not been happy'.

THE PREVENTED SECOND MARRIAGE. To Ruskin's later friendship with Rose la Touche several pages are given in the *Works*. We have some of the correspondence with her as a child and as a young girl; we learn of the proposal of marriage to Rose when she was eighteen by Ruskin aged forty-seven, of her postponement of a decision until she was twenty-one, of her death at twenty-seven and of Ruskin's depression. But Cook says 'men do not die of a broken heart'; Ruskin, though he carried a scrap of Rose's writing between gold plates in his pocketbook, found relief in work.

'Great wits are sure to madness near allied.' Ruskin's father and mother, judged by their own letters, were among the most curious parents of whom we have an honest record. One of his grandfathers committed suicide. Ruskin himself was repeatedly in mental confusion. Such a letter as one he wrote to me, of which the following is an extract, was among a number that showed that from time to time his mind was upset: 'Railroads are to me the loathsomest form of devilry now extant, destructive of all wise social habit and possible natural beauty, carriage of damned souls on the ridges of their own graves'. Yet the dear man, in his first-class compartment, rode thousands of miles.[1] Many of the letters he wrote when in possession of all his faculties are marked by what may be called a girlishness out of character in the writing of a normal man.

That excellent schoolmaster to whom so many young people have been indebted, Mr. Howard Whitehouse, the devoted student of Ruskin and collector of his work, once asked me, in company with Sir John Squire and Dr. Inge, to speak to his boys at Bembridge, and at a later date kindly invited me to the yearly luncheon he gives at the Dorchester Hotel in Ruskin's memory. I could not but note in the Dorchester speeches preceding mine a lack of downrightness regarding the book by a grandson of Effie Gray, Admiral Sir William James, G.C.B., which had just been published, *The Order of Release*. It reproduces correspondence of Effie Gray's and Ruskin's found below a loose floor-board at Brantwood and behind a wardrobe at the home of Effie Gray's parents in Scotland. The speakers at the luncheon took the line either that they had not read the book or that it was not the kind of book they would want to read. To say, as one speaker said, that such a book is 'painful' is surely beside the mark. So are lots of things that have to be faced. I asked why we should not take the sensible course of acknowledging frankly that, with all the service Ruskin rendered to the English-speaking world and to Italy, he was frequently out of or passing out of his wits; that, as indicated by his correspondence throughout his career—take some queer letters to Carlyle—he was at all times abnormal in one way or another; and that the tortured soul knew that he was? When he wrote so beautifully, 'What can you say about Carlyle but that he was born in the clouds and struck by lightning, not meant for happiness, but for other purposes?' might not we think that he had in his mind his own nature and life?

Mrs. Ruskin showed strength of character in not revealing, even to her parents, until her decision to seek an annulment, the distress she had suffered during the six years of an association that was not marriage. No person open to conviction can read what, on the eve of legal proceedings, she wrote to her father without feeling that she is telling the truth about Ruskin's refusal, first and last, to consummate the marriage; and that in all probability she is also reciting facts when she speaks of the measure of ill-treatment she suffered, when they were both in conditions of strain, from a man who was not at times rational.

THE BODLEIAN PAPERS AND THE PROCEEDINGS. *The Order of Release* was published by John Murray in 1947 and contains

---

[1] Ruskin later told one literalist among his correspondents to 'pray indeed for the destruction of railways but meanwhile use them.' Like Gandhi.

speaking photographs of Ruskin, his father and mother, his wife, her father and her sisters. During the years which have elapsed since the book came out the world has been told that it should suspend judgment until the period elapses for the publication of the Ruskin documents at the Bodleian. I find, however, that there is nothing to wait for. These documents are only copies of originals in the hands of Mr. Whitehouse. In his *Vindication of Ruskin*, published in 1950,[1] he furnishes the text and a photograph of a document which Ruskin drew up for his proctor when his wife initiated the annulment proceedings, and he entered no defence and left for the Continent with his parents. In it is the declaration, 'I can prove my virility at once', but no medical certificate is attached. There is in the statement Ruskin's criticism of his wife and his reasons for not desiring that the marriage should continue. Although he had been so deeply in love with Effie before marriage, as his letters to her witness, and a year after marriage wrote to her in one letter, 'I look forward to you next bridal night, to the time when I shall again draw your dress from your snowy shoulders and lean my cheek upon them as if you were still my betrothed only and I had never held you in my arms',[2] he excuses himself for non-consummation of his marriage because his wife's body was unpleasing to him, because she has ceased to love him, and because she is suffering from incipient insanity which makes it wrong to have children. Therefore, he admits, the marriage has never been consummated.

In a second paper Ruskin answers a series of questions sent to him by his proctor, evidently before a decision had been taken not to defend the suit. Morally, Ruskin says of his wife, 'the lady's conduct has been without reproach'. To the precise question whether she is 'at the moment a pure virgin' and 'is likely to stand the test of a medical and surgical examination' he replies 'I have no doubt'. The finding of the Court was in the following terms:

Therefore we John Haggard Doctor of Laws the Commissary aforesaid having heard counsel learned in the Law in this behalf on the part of the said Euphemia Chalmers Gray falsely called Ruskin DO PRONOUNCE DECREE AND DECLARE that he the said John Ruskin being then a Bachelor did at the time libellate contract a pretended Marriage with the said Euphemia Chalmers Gray then and still a Spinster but since falsely called Ruskin and we do also pronounce decree and declare according to the lawful proofs made in the said Cause as aforesaid that the said Marriage howsoever in fact had between the said John Ruskin and the said Euphemia

---

[1] Basil Blackwell.

[2] Two months later he replied to a letter from Effie in which she had said she would like to have a child: 'So should I, a little Effie at least. Only I wish they were not so small at first that one hardly knows what one has got hold of.'

Chalmers Gray falsely called Ruskin was had and celebrated whilst the said John Ruskin was incapable of consummating the same by reason of incurable impotency WHEREFORE and by reason of the premises WE DO pronounce decree and declare that such Marriage or rather show or effigy of Marriage so had and solemnised or rather profaned between the said John Ruskin and Euphemia Gray falsely called Ruskin was and is free from all Bond of Marriage with him the said John Ruskin by this our definitive sentence of final decree which we give and promulge by these presents.

With Dr. Haggard sat A. F. Bayford, a well-known lawyer whom I have heard in the courts, and Robert Phillimore, later a Judge of the High Court and a peer and the author of many legal works.[1]

It is only necessary to state that no one but Ruskin saw traces of mental disorder in Effie Gray, and that, when she married Millais, a year after the annulment proceedings, she had a happy normal life and became the mother of several children.[2]

---

[1] The ecclesiastical court sat in the Lady Chapel of St. Saviour's Church, Southwark. The case may have gone to a civil court for final decree.

[2] OTHER AVAILABLE INFORMATION. I am permitted to publish the two following letters to me, the first from Sir William James and the second from Mr. Wedderburn.

Admiral Sir William James, April 5, 1951: 'My grandmother's first marriage was never mentioned by her family, and, except for that one occasion when she broke her reserve after Mrs. La Touche had implored her to help her to save her daughter from the disastrous step she was contemplating, I do not think that the name of Ruskin ever passed her lips after the marriage was annulled. I did hear that my cousin Clare Stuart Wortley, was preparing the material for a book but when she died I thought that would end the matter. However, my cousin, Sir R. Millais, appeared here one day to ask my views on publishing the letters that would once and for all establish that our grandmother was in no way to blame. He brought with him some recently published books and a poster of an American film, and after examining these I expressed agreement to publishing. He was already in correspondence with a man who had written some books, and if I concurred, he intended to tell his friend to proceed. I told him that as the only grandson who had known all the principals, except Ruskin, he himself should undertake the work. He agreed and I was soon busy sorting out the large quantity of material. I included in my book every letter that had any bearing on the subject and when I had finished I thought that it would be the end.

Among the papers was a copy of Ruskin's statement to his proctor but I was not free to publish it, which I regretted, as by comparing it with the letters I could have shown that it was quite valueless. As the proctor put it in a pigeon-hole, where it remained for seventy years, I expect he was of opinion that it would not help his client's case. I did let Peter Quennell see it when he was writing his book, but he, too, evidently found there was nothing in it to alter the story that emerged from the letters written by Ruskin and by Effie before and during their marriage.

It is nonsense to suggest that Ruskin did not know that he was impotent when he sent that frivolous reply to his wife's letter in which she said she wished they could have a child. When he wrote those dreadful letters to Effie's parents suggesting that her illness was really incipient insanity Mrs. Gray wrote on the envelope 'Remarkable letter from J. Ruskin in which he artfully puts down his then so-called wife's unhappiness to everything but the real cause which he himself only knew'.

Mr. A. H. M. Wedderburn, March 26, 1951: 'Possibly to my shame, I was always aloof from my father's deep interest in Ruskinian affairs. I can only tell you that what I handed to Howard Whitehouse were the *originals* of Ruskin's statement to

There is something more to add: that in the words of Charles
Eliot Norton respecting Ruskin, 'No other master of literature in
our time endeavoured more earnestly and steadily to set forth
whatsoever things are true, honest, just, pure, lovely and of good
report, or in his own life', and when in his right mind, 'tried
more faithfully to practise the virtues which spring from the
contemplation of such things and from their adoption as the
rule of conduct.'

Having diverged so far as to write all this, because Cook's
handling of the Ruskin–Effie Gray case was a fact of some significance in his life and throws a trustworthy light on his temperament
and outlook, I may repeat what I have said, as a North Countryman, in *The Day Before Yesterday*,[1] 'I sometimes wonder whether,
a century hence, social historians may not be saying that, in the
sum of things, more may possibly have been done for us, in a
trying period of our national development, by the labours of
Ruskin of Coniston than by those of Wordsworth of Grasmere.
No one will undervalue Wordsworth's contribution to our aspirations, to our appreciation of Nature and to poetic beauty. But at a
time when industrialism was almost too much for us, Ruskin as
economist and social reformer grasped a nettle. How firmly he
did it was shown when, after he began to write for *Cornhill* and
Fraser, he was successively rejected from both.'

his proctor and answers to his proctor's questions, as published by Whitehouse,
and the facsimile reproduced at the end of the Whitehouse book shows these
documents were in Ruskin's own hand. These original documents were always in
my possession from my father's death in 1931 until 1949, when I handed them to
Whitehouse, in whose hands, so far as I know, they still are.'

[1] Methuen, 1951.

CHAPTER XXVII

THE BIOGRAPHIES OF FLORENCE NIGHTINGALE
AND DELANE

A TRUE ACCOUNT OF 'F.N.' If Cook had never edited Ruskin with such devotion and skill and on so commanding a scale and now depended for his literary standing on *The Life of Florence Nightingale*[1] and *Delane of 'The Times'* he would have an assured place among men of letters. The mass of material available for a true account of F.N., as he came in time to call her, approached in its extent and variety that which piled itself around Cook and was available all over the country when he entered on his labours with Ruskin. Florence Nightingale was a woman not of one but of several careers. She was a woman of action all her life, an unceasing writer, a most complex character, a personage with unending official relationships, and no gift for throwing anything away. Cook, by his pluck, persistence and technical competence, his cultivated talent for system, his human sympathies and his judicial quality overcame the difficulties and conquered the confusion. In a work of two large volumes of 538 and 483 pages (with a perfect index of twenty pages, two columns to the page), he placed before the world a convincing representation, at once fair and adequate, attractive and instructive, of an astonishing person. I find pencilled in my copy of the work, on my first reading of it nearly forty years ago: 'This work is interesting to me, first of all, for the picture it paints of its author. Here one realises his modesty, his industry, his fairness, his sincerity, his loyalty and his dislike of flamboyance, assertiveness and showing-off of any sort. His quality as a writer and his value as a publicist also come home. He had judgment, downrightness, honesty, skill, power in expression, and will. His *Ruskin* is his *magnum opus*, no doubt, and his other volumes have great merit, but I am inclined to think that this book successfully shows the man he was. Two volumes are not excessive. Florence Nightingale tops not a few men who call each other "statesmen". She was unquestionably one of the great personages of her time, and how poor the pretentions of "rank" and "station"—although much outmoded in our days—seem to be when we consider all she managed to do and the tremendous influence she exerted in so many fields and for so many years.'

The writing of the work began in October 1912, and it was

[1] Macmillan, 1913.

published—at thirty shillings—in November, 1913, quick work by both author and publisher.[1]

THE ARTS OF EDITING AND INDEXING. Two books which have given pleasure are Cook's *Literary Recreations* (1918) and *More Literary Recreations* (1919)[2], as I have said elsewhere 'supreme in their kind'. 'I always think they contain some of E.T.C's best work', Sir Harold Hartley writes to me. 'Much of them was written while he was waiting for stuff to come in at the Press Bureau.[3] They show his great literary memory, and what fun they are! He enlivens even the indexes.'

In one of the essays Cook decides judiciously that the pages of a biography 'may be rightly many and rightly few'. While he quotes Frederic Harrison's view that 'the conventional biography records what a person did while the true biography reveals what the person was', he agrees that a reasonable account of his achievement is essential. In *Florence Nightingale*, in which he says that a biography 'is worth nothing unless it is sincere', he states his aim to have been 'to tell the truth; I have done my work under no conscious temptation to suppress, exaggerate, extenuate or distort.'

In his wise essay on 'The Art of Editing' he does not help much in the journalistic field, for he is chiefly concerned with the editing of books. But he has the remark that the need of the editor of a newspaper, before all things, is 'rapidity of judgment', and he does say that 'the essential objects' of a good editor of a book or newspaper are 'to be interesting and helpful'. He has a paper on 'Literature and Journalism' in which he quotes that estimable message, 'Mr. Lowe will be very happy to write for *The Times* on any subject on which he possesses the requisite information'.[4] Cook points out, however, that if a newspaper were produced wholly by experts 'no one would read it'. He says truly that there are today more personalities in the papers because there are more papers, 'but the personalities are much less offensively personal than they were in former times'.[5]

---

[1] Shortly after the appearance of Lytton Strachey's deprecatory, harsh and, for all his skill, somewhat undiscerning account of Florence Nightingale, a relative of hers and friend of mine who knew her well, the widow of Vaughan Nash, a colleague in my *Daily Chronicle* days—the pair are remembered for their own successful activities in more than one department of public welfare—had in *The Times Literary Supplement* and in the *Nineteenth Century* some plain speaking about that author's misquotations and misstatements. See also Bertrand Russell.

[2] Macmillan.

[3] See end of this chapter.

[4] Robert Lowe, the Chancellor of the Exchequer of the proposed match tax (*ex luce lucellum*, out of light a little gain) of which Queen Victoria disapproved.

[5] 'When Mrs. Humphry Ward said to Gladstone that "more was made of scandals nowadays by the newspapers", the old man would not have it. "When I was a boy", he said—he left Eton in 1827—"there were two papers, the *Age* and the *Satirist*, which were worse than anything which exists now".'—*Faith and Works in Fleet Street*, J. W. Robertson Scott (Hodder & Stoughton, 1947).

A feature of these *Recreations,* as of every one of Cook's books, is that they are perfectly indexed. When so many indexes are scamped and not a few books by authors who ought to know better come out with no indexes at all, it is worth while recalling his view, as a man of particular experience in indexing, that 'in the category of general literature there is no book so good that it is not made better by an index, and no book so bad that it may not by this adjunct escape the worst condemnation'. Carlyle is quoted for the view that the publisher who issues an index-less book should be hanged, and the Roxburghe Club for the more moderate suggestion that the author of a book without an index should be deprived of copyright. As will be seen by reference to 'The Art of Indexing', Cook was clear that the right kind of index should enable one to find readily the place where the author has said a particular thing, and also what it is that he has said. In the indexes of his own books one seldom finds strings of figures after the fashion of the indexes which are no indexes. His indexes are of this satisfying type:

Goethe, his place as poet, 183–5; scientific studies, 88; on his commen-tators, 240; on the arts, 243.
Greenwood, Frederick, and *Cornhill,* 96, as journalist, 123.

Few of us have been sufficient for such things; but what a blessing it would be if every author—for, as Cook says, indexes should always be made by the authors themselves—could act upon the counsel! In the present volume I have walked some distance in Cook's footsteps, but the job took my secretary and myself three weeks, I dictating and she typing and afterwards cutting up the entries, arranging them and sticking them on sheets; and with the by no means encouraging thought all the time that the publisher might turn a baleful eye on the result of our labours and suggest that the index was eating up paper. Nevertheless the industrious author has the advantage of feeling, in Cook's words, that 'there is nothing like making an index for discovering inconsistencies and needless repetitions'. Alas, however, the finds are mostly made when the book is in page proof and omissions or adjustments must be difficult and costly, thus causing publishers to tear at their locks again. Cook praises the index to Morley's *Gladstone.* It is a page of index to thirty pages of text and is beaten by the index of Morley's own *Recollections,* one to ten. In Freeman's *Norman Conquest* the scale is one to fourteen, in Carlyle's *French Revolution* about one to thirty-six. But indexes, alas, must often be made against time.

THE BIOGRAPHY OF DELANE. Sir Harold Hartley who thinks, as most journalists do, that Cook's *Delane of 'The Times'*[1] is 'his most brilliant piece of writing', tells me that he has been in the

[1] Constable, 1915.

habit, on a change of editors of *The Times*, of sending the newcomer a passage from E.T.C. to remind him of the paper's tradition.[1] Cook discussed the relations of Delane with the Prime Ministers and Foreign Secretaries of his day, and was avid of details of the life and professional practice of an editor who, entering upon his duties at twenty-six, retained his chair for more than thirty-six years. In days and nights very different from ours, he 'dined out nearly every night, sometimes as often as a hundred nights in succession', and in the country 'stayed in nearly all the great houses, hunting with hosts and fellow guests, shooting with them, fishing with them and sometimes betting with them'. He went on horseback from Printing House Square down Fleet Street and the Strand to the West End, and a retainer of *The Times* once relished the sight of him riding down Pall Mall with a duke walking on either side of him! Few editors can have done more for their papers or kept a closer eye on them. He cared about even the 'spacing' and 'leading'.[2] He was at his desk from ten or eleven at night until four or five in the morning. An ex-leader writer, Dean Wace, states that Delane read his proofs carefully enough to be able to rate men who wrote that a marriage or a race had 'taken place' when they ought to have written that 'a marriage had been solemnised or a race had been run'. He once said that, within a certain period, there was not a proof which had not 'some of my handwriting on the margin'. He did not write leading articles himself, and when he was absent from the office he would send such messages as, 'Pray do not let Lowe write any more on personal questions; he is shooting his own arrows from behind our shield'. It has been told how Delane 'kept his beasts in separate cages' and, as a writer in the *D.N.B.* has related, 'if one of them met another in a passage or on the stairs it was not etiquette for them to speak'. He had the advantage of never being worried by his proprietor. He was also paid, in addition to a handsome salary, a half-yearly dividend on the paper's profits. 'Plenty of work and a dogged pleasure in doing it' was the entry in his diary when his mother died; he had tried to see her daily. He passed away as late as 1879 and the *Pall Mall* declared that 'as long as his mind retained its vigour he had not his equal in all Europe'. The Poet Laureate, Alfred Austin, is said to have written the pronouncement in the *Standard* in which Delane's work is described as having 'lifted journalism above the

[1] Cook had the advantage of being given for his single volume the freedom of the two large volumes of *John Thaddeus Delane, His Life and Correspondence* by the great editor's nephew, A. L. Dasent. (Constable, 1915.) Sir Harold Hartley is a director of *The Times*.

[2] For the novice it may be explained that 'spacing' is the arrangement of the white space between words, and 'leading' the way in which the beginning of an article may be made more conspicuous and more attractive to the eye by metal rules being placed between the lines.

enervating influences of political servility and the mechanical usages of party compliance'.

PRESS CENSOR AND *THE PRESS IN WAR TIME*.[1] Many journalists have still to make acquaintance with the last book Cook wrote, based on his experience as Press Censor with Sir Frank Swettenham, who afterwards spoke of his 'wisdom and industry— he always knew the right course'. The book is a valuable discussion of the complex question of the relations of a Free State with a Free Press in times of national emergency. The small volume is full of sidelights on the work of a newspaper in its editorial and news departments, and is particularly worth reading as the work of a journalist of distinction and acknowledged integrity. It is written with gravity, but, like so much of Cook's work, is light in hand. This is his account of how he spoke to the representative of an important American news agency who came to the Press Bureau to interview him and Sir Frank Swettenham. Cook said to their visitor that he must make one condition. The interviewer thought it was that he must submit his 'copy' to be censored. But what Cook said was: 'We never censor articles or telegrams criticising the Censorship. The condition I make is that you do not give us any flowers. It would really be a terrible blow if you did. The enterprising newspaper or news agency and an efficient Censorship are natural enemies.' Again: 'When the Press Bureau was closed and I was able to return to the country village from which I had been "dug out" four-and-a-half years before, a neighbour met me and suggested that now we might resume negotiations with the Post Office for giving us a telephone service. "Not just now", was my reply; "the holiday treat to which I have been looking forward is to be in a place where no telephone call can reach me".'

Cook had his anxieties at the Press Bureau. There were a number of occasions on which he felt he had committed what he calls a 'howler', and he lay awake at night over slips at an exacting task. It may be recalled, however, that Count Bernstorff complained that this country had a Press Bureau which in its efficiency and imaginative powers had never had its equal 'in the history of the world'.

[1] Macmillan, 1920.

CHAPTER XXVIII

'E.T.C.' BY LADY HARTLEY[1]

'A UNIQUE PERSON.' It is now more than thirty years since E.T.C. died, but he has left with me a memory so vivid that years seem unable to dim it. He was the gentlest, quietest and most self-effacing man I have ever known, and also the best, a unique person, a great man.

It was probably soon after he married that I first saw him. I was perched on a table and in my childish treble sang solemnly through 'The Bailiff's Daughter of Islington' followed by 'Barbara Allen'. All the time he smiled and nodded to me at intervals in encouragement. It was a grief to him and to Aunt Emmie that they had no children. My aunt was a slave as well as a captivating companion for any child. She was a wonderful story-teller, especially of gruesome ghost stories. She could quote poetry by the mile and even whole pages of gardening advice, incited by E.T.C., for whom this retentive memory was an unfailing pride and amusement. She knew her London well and loved it and was the best companion in the metropolis, for she was just as knowledgeable with places of historic interest as with flowers and nature. As a child I stayed with her and Uncle Teddy, as I have always called him, a great deal, and they were incredibly kind and good to me always. E.T.C's charming personality pervaded the house and however busy he was he seemed always ready to rise up in his brown velveteen jacket from behind his large, orderly desk and smile and stroke my head. I can see him now, rolling his bulky, untidy-looking cigarettes, for though his handwriting was so neat he was very clumsy, he always admitted, with his hands.

'HE LIKES TO SLEEP IN HIS COFFIN.' Many gifted and distinguished people drifted in and out and one day especially I remember Aunt Emmie saying to me, 'There is a very great man coming to tea today, but he is rather odd and he likes to sleep in his coffin, quite a comfortable one as it is made of wicker-work'. This was Samuel Butler and I thought he seemed strange and rather grubby. Years afterwards this incident had an amusing sequel. My husband and I with a friend were travelling in

---

[1] When Cook lost his wife he asked that Lady Hartley, then a girl in her teens and described by Mrs. Cook's aunt, Mrs. A. L. Smith (in her life of her husband, the Master of Balliol) as his 'favourite niece', should come to him.

Sicily. While I was sketching they went to hunt for possible accommodation in Calatafimi so that I should be able to continue painting at Segesta, that most exquisite of all Sicilian temples to which, on purpose to see it, Garibaldi made a detour on his historic march with his 'Thousand'. The two men presently returned triumphant saying, 'The inn is a bit rough, but it will do; it is the Albergo Samuel Butler'. In all my wanderings I have never been in any place so alive with every kind of biter!

I also remember meeting Hugh Thomson, a delightful Irishman whose brogue captivated me and who was at that time doing the illustrations to *Highways and Byways of London*, which Aunt Emmie and Uncle Teddy were writing together. This delightful book, with its felicitous pictures and description of horse buses, 'Arry and 'Arriets, and other bygone glories, gives me a better picture of the London one used to know than any other.

E.T.C. was extremely silent, in fact I really think I believed my aunt when she said to me one day, 'One of Gus's brothers (she always called him 'Gus') is coming to lunch today and you mustn't mind that he is even more speechless than Gus—quite dumb in fact'.

TRIPS ABROAD. I shall never forget my first trip abroad when I was about sixteen, as I was treated to it by these two darlings who were such a devoted and self-sufficing couple that it must have been sheer unselfishness that made them saddle themselves with a hobbledehoy schoolgirl. Aunt Emmie was a water-colour artist and I sat at her elbow trying to put on paper what I saw. Uncle Teddy meanwhile would be prowling about looking for fresh 'sketchable bits', as he called them, for us to proceed to—as well as spying out possibilities for their camera as they were keen photographers.

I had several lovely trips on the Continent with him, twice with my husband as well, when we went to places Uncle Teddy loved, Naples, Rome, Capri and Venice, and once when he and I alone followed the spring from the south of France, up over the Col du Tenda to Turin and so on to Chamonix and Zermatt. Together we revelled in mild mountaineering, finding the sweet little flowers which so bravely thrust fragile heads through the melting snow. He was the perfect travelling companion, for he enjoyed everything, and every moment, from delicious meals and drinks at clear mountain streams to exquisite moments in the flowery spring meadows.

I can remember so very well his beaming and happy face. No one could have called him an athletic person, but he was an indefatigable walker and sightseer. He wore the same clothes when we 'did' picture galleries together or climbed the mountain paths

round Zermatt and Chamonix. I think that his shoes must have
been unsuitable for such rough walks for I seem to remember a
good many glissades down steep mountain paths—one especially
when we both slithered together and he ended up clasping the
remains of what had once been an umbrella—snapped clean in
half.

'BE A NAUGHTY SCHOOLBOY.' When Aunt Emmie died he
was indeed stricken to the heart. But he did not let his loss break
him and he continued to do all the things they had done together
and to love as dearly as they both loved their little Rose Cottage.
From the time of my aunt's death until his own I was a great deal
with him. I think he was happy in my companionship and once or
twice I was so touched by his saying suddenly, 'You are so like Em'.
We liked the same things—books, flowers, pictures, lovely places
and children. When I married and my own children came he got
great pleasure from their company. The children always treated
him as if he was their age. I can hear my little girl calling out to
him, 'Uncle Teddy, be a naughty schoolboy and get stuck in that
bog', which he obediently did, never minding that perhaps he had
on his best suit and quite unsuitable shoes, while she skipped
lightly across the said bog in water-boots shrieking with delight
when he got stuck and muddy. He would play these foolish games
with the children by the hour, no matter how busy he was and
what book he was working on.

He was the most wonderfully quiet worker and his great books
on Ruskin, Florence Nightingale and the *Handbook to the National
Gallery* seemed to appear as if by magic. As I have said, his desk
was a model of neatness, and he could put his finger immediately
on anything and give an answer to any question on any subject
at a moment's notice. He always appeared serene and unruffled
no matter how busy he must have been.

From his dear Rose Cottage he used to like to scull me in a
cumbersome old double-sculler for many miles on the lovely
reaches of the Thames between Wallingford and Pangbourne,
getting out of the boat at times to tow it for a bit of a change.
He would garden, too, by the hour, but I do not think that his
good but somewhat autocratic gardener trusted him to do much
beyond removing 'deaders' or pulling up convolvulus, 'the devil'
as he called it.

I do not know how I could have borne those anxious and unhappy
years of the War, with a husband at the front and our home broken
up, without his loving sympathy and understanding. He was a
rock of strength in the nation's darkest days and always confident
of complete victory. He was very strict with himself about rations,
including the voluntary ones, and I thought his health suffered,

for he was not a strong man and had always been a small eater. He lived just to see the end of the War and those he loved safe—and for me there is the vivid, unchanging memory of a man all goodness, kindness and modesty, whose wise counsels and advice I find myself still trying to follow.

CHAPTER XXIX

A BOX OF LETTERS

'WE WERE NOT VERY WELL OFF.' During the months in which I have been writing the part of this book preceding the Chapter by Lady Hartley I have held myself back from looking into the box of letters she kindly entrusted to me. I looked forward to enjoying them towards the end of my agreeable task of discovering my respected editor to a new public. It may be suggested, perhaps, that I should have done better to go through the letters earlier and quilt bits from them into my narrative. There seemed three objections to this course. First, the letters put us on a new footing with Cook. The shy man of whom we have repeatedly heard opens out. Then they not infrequently deal with matters which have not presented themselves in the previous Chapters. Thirdly, it is agreeable to read all together extracts from a collection of letters which were almost all written to the same person.

I may note that for me the perusal of the letters was singularly easy, for the handwriting of Cook, before he got writer's cramp, is as clear and neat as it is individual. If I may be pardoned commending my wares of this Chapter and the next, I venture to propose them as good chit-chat for reading in bed.

The first letter, from 61 Russell Square, to 'My dear Gertrude', is of January 1903, thanking her for a drawing of his Rose Cottage, 'a most successful impression of summer, which I look at a lot'.[1] His wife is still alive, but in June comes a black-bordered letter sending with his love a little pearl chain and pendant which 'Aunt Emmie used to wear a great deal and I should so much like you to wear sometimes in memory of her'. 'When we were first married', he explains, 'we were not very well off. So I gave her the necklet one birthday and the pendant the next.'

There is mention of Aunty Dolly (Dorothea Baird, that is Dorothea Irving) rehearsing for J. M. Barrie's *Admirable Crichton*. Cook speaks of her boy, little Laurence Irving (Sir Henry's grandson and successful biographer) as 'very sweet and affectionate'. Later he has got for him a printing press 'which has been rather a success'. Cook has children with him. 'The Threlfall boys are up

[1] It was at Southstoke on the Thames, in Oxfordshire, across the water from Berkshire. Still rose-covered but now Panters, its original name.

x

at 5.30 fishing, Richie comes in at 10.30 p.m. after moth-hunting and Dick nurse-maids them excellently'. By one small person he is 'quite fascinated'.

TO THE SWEETHEARTS. Gertrude is 'a real comfort'. In August he is thanking her for a certain Balliol undergraduate (Harold Hartley) having found some Wordsworth quotation for the Ruskin. And here I include bits from a packet of letters from Cook to 'My dear Harold' beginning July 1904. In the first of a series of some as delightful letters as were ever written for two young people, he is inviting Hartley to stay over the weekend at Rose Cottage when Gertrude and two members of the family are coming: 'I suppose I must not say anything about a matter which is not declared. But I cannot refrain from letting you know how happy I should be to hear that Gertrude had chosen well and wisely, and how warmly I should congratulate the man who won her affections. She is the best and dearest of girls—but that I need not tell you—except to add that she is associated with many solemn memories to me, and that her affectionate sympathy brought me some help in great sorrow. Both on my own account, and because my wife was so fond of her, I long for her happiness—and rejoice that there is every reason to believe that she has secured it. Behind these stiff and halting words there is, believe me, a very warm sympathy for you both in the great happiness which is going to be yours.' In a further note he says 'how intensely pleased I am to hear that "smooth waters" have been reached, thanks to the loving patience of your navigation!' Within two months he and Hartley are at the British Museum together in quest of Ruskin papers.

'My dearest Gertrude' hears from him at the end of September 1904 to say how his wife would have understood, 'as I have seemed able to do, all the doubts and reluctances and backwaters and fightings against the stream, now all submerged, I feel sure, in the full tide of your happiness. It will grow, believe me, to more and more, and as years go by you will be more and more thankful that your heart has guided you aright. You are very dear to me and I cannot say how thankful I am that you have chosen a man who will make your life so bright and happy and useful—in whom you will find every day something more to attach you to him—and of whom all your relations and friends think so highly, and will think the more highly the better they know him. Perhaps you will find all these remarks a bore or an impertinence—they are the feeble expression of my very real sympathy with you in your happiness.'

In January of the new year, we hear that the greatest success of his present-giving was the electric torch to Laurence, who plays Peter Pan. The torch does for Tinker Bell's fairy flash in *The*

Admirable Crichton. On the eve of May he gives a reminder for later in the year, 'Strawberries by moonlight again'.

The marriage of Gertrude and Harold is coming on and he is glad that they are going to begin their new life in 'easy circumstances'. He adds a bit of autobiography: 'I started on borrowed money mostly, and even the pawnshop was not unknown in those days—but I don't think we much minded. However I was fairly lucky and soon got into fairly lucrative work'. He has been to Oxford to see the house for which Harold's father has provided 'all the furnishing; you will really start in great riches.'

The quarter-inch black border on Cook's letter paper and envelopes become an eighth, and finally the smallest possible edging.

GETTING OFF JURY SERVICE. 'Isn't it abominable? I've got to serve on a jury', one reads in a 1907 letter. And then comes a curious confession: 'I used to get off by favour in Coleridge's and Russell's time, but I don't know Alverstone. My only hope is that Darling may be my judge, as I should enjoy finding contrary to his directions.'[1]

January 1912 finds him 'very busy indeed auditing Winchester accounts, writing a report on them, running Victoria League conferences with Royal Colonial Institute, and sitting up every night with Florence N. till 1 or 2'. He is 'turning over the pages of my old favourite among Samuel Butler's books, *Alps and Sanctuaries of Piedmont and the Canton Ticino*'.

A question to Harold is about 'the Balliol system of requiring no poverty-test for scholarships and exhibitions, and of circularising parents afterwards and thereby getting emoluments returned in many instances. And who administers the eleemosynary fund formed out of returned emoluments?' The whole subject is being considered at Winchester and he is writing a memorandum on it.

A letter from Cook to his sister described 'dearest Gertrude's' wedding: 'Everything was so pretty, cordial and well arranged, and when things are well arranged it looks as if they arranged themselves, but they don't. Gertrude was perfectly delightful, so composed, natural and yet radiantly happy, and a dream of prettiness. How amiable the Duke [of Leinster] made himself, doing the honours of the presents like a professional.'

In February 1914 he joins the happy pair on a holiday in the Mediterranean,[2] bringing guide-books, Trevelyan, sketching blocks, metallic books and tubes. Later he says 'how sweet it was of you

---

[1] Was it not said of this facetious judge that he had all the disqualifications for being a judge but corruption?

[2] 'Passports?' writes Cook. 'Your bank will do it, 2s. 6d.' Things were as simple as that then.

to put up with me on your wedding journey. I must have been in the way'. But this was but paying back.[1]

Before this a letter brings out again his delight in children: 'Dinah very demure but jolly in her brown frock. Cubby a little fat red apple. Dinah full of her school, and the "naughty school-boyishness" of Michael.' Then in one note he speaks of visiting little Laurence in hospital where he has been having his tonsils out. 'Played endless noughts and crosses with him'.

TRICKS WITH THE KING. 'What fetches me most', Cook writes to Harold when his new nephew joins up, 'is your account of your first day, like, as you say, the first day at Balliol, or still more (in my experience) the first day at Winchester. How beastly it was! But how soon one tumbled to the new conditions! It's one thing, however, to do these things as a boy or a youth—and quite another, as a man. And I do admire your spirit, my dear Harold, very greatly; and it gave me quite "a ball in the throat" to see and hear Gertrude's pride in her Captain.'

It was at the beginning of December 1914 that Sir Stanley Buckmaster asked Asquith to appoint Cook to the Press Bureau. 'But hearing news a little sooner than other people is no novelty to an old editor. The dug-outs at the Bureau are by no means such old fossils as I had been led to expect. In fact I feel rather a humbug in being a sort of Court of Appeal for them.'

In reporting that that 'singularly attractive person', F. E. Smith, is back on four days' leave from the trenches, he says: 'Some of his little Gurkhas were put into trenches previously occupied by Guardsmen! He was amusingly cynical on the King's visit and the tricks resorted to in connection with it, in order to let H.M. imagine he was seeing the real thing.' Cook met Asquith at dinner and says: 'I certainly prefer Asquith plus Balfour to L. George and Northcliffe. The latter is said to be very keen on getting high office.' Meantime Robertson[2] is making things hum at the War Office.

I now come back to letters to Lady Hartley in 1906.

In a note on an invitation to the new house he says: 'I count on being made useful by helping with picture hanging—in which m'um, I shall do my best to please, and m'um, I can produce characters as to experience in the job.'

'I WENT A MUCKER.' There are references to 'Trilby' (Dorothea Baird) in America who, he hopes, 'will find comfort in the multitude of her counsellors and care-takers and checkers and counter-checkers'. Once he had 'found her baking bread in a house a mass of dress baskets and "properties" of all kinds'. He is

[1] See page 320.

[2] Field Marshal Sir W. R. Robertson, a cottager's son. See page 349.

'longing to hear that she has been carried as a suffragist in a policeman's arms to a magistrate and then to Holloway'.

He wants to take Gertrude and Harold to an exhibition of Ruskin drawings. 'I went a mucker and bought three little ones. And afterwards wished I hadn't as Mrs. Severn says she is going to present me with some.' Harold is to be his guest at the Colonial Premiers' dinner.

There is a reference to being shown at the National History Museum 'a huge pile of letters from Ruskin about the Museum minerals'. The letter goes on: 'I cannot say what I think of Christ Church now that its rebuilding of the village [Southstoke] in corrugated iron is in full swing. When the parson remonstrated, the College replied "Oh, we are going to paint the roofs red so that they will look like tiles!"[1] Such is Oxford culture.'[2]

'BORED INEXPRESSIBLY BY THE MOUNTAINS'. In August 1907 he gives a lecture in Oxford and is surprised to have an audience of a thousand. 'If I had had the least idea of what awaited me I should have been at the trouble to learn off the lecture (which is not really much trouble), for an (apparently) extempore one produces twice the effect of one obviously given from notes.' He tells a tale about some relative who on the Continent was 'bored inexpressibly with the mountains, and Venice she loathed even more, except only the shops in the Piazza'. The Hartleys are abroad in the autumn and in reference to Gertrude's account of mountains and a balcony he asks if there is 'anything nicer in the world than a balcony in lovely scenery?' Going back to his own 'memories of many golden days' he speaks of a pre-Gothard railway place 'where we had our balcony, and Lord Leighton the other, and he gave himself such airs and always went in from his when we came out from ours—as if everyone else was thinking only of getting a stare at *him* instead of at Monte Rosa.'

By February 1908 a baby has arrived for the Hartleys—'I am simply more delighted than I can express. But what will become of the poor child with a mother so badly up in the Prayer Book? A girl is only allowed one godfather. I want you to put the enclosed in a little P.O. Savings Bank for her—children like (at least we did) a little account of their own when they grow up, and by letting the deposit accumulate at compound interest, it mounts up a bit by the time they reach "years of discretion".' He mentions Irene Vanbrugh having sent the same christening present for a baby of Dorothea Baird's. The difficulty of wedding presents for relations recurs. 'What is one to give a millionairess almost?'

[1] As in New Zealand.
[2] Not now. The Oxford college which owns a farm building facing my house promises to renew the decayed roof in stone.

The gardener in him records in the June of 1909 that 'the briar hedging is a sight.' The next year he is sending a box of annuals. The Alpine pinks are 'from seeds I brought from Zermatt; they will want re-planting immediately.' Rose Cottage has won the Wallingford Horticultural Show firsts for nectarines and sweet peas but only a second for roses; 'a beastly swindle that it wasn't first; they allowed a professional grower to compete'. The garden was 'an awful sight before the show—old brollies over the roses, and newspapers to screen the peas'. He has had 'nearly five hours' of some energetic village resident's conversation and is 'worn out'.

At Zermatt he had seen a lot of J. M. Barrie and 'spotted a chalet in the most exquisite situation and made it a castle in Spain. Such a sketching ground!'

Towards the close of 1909 he speaks of giving a Ruskin lecture in London. In the summer of the next year he has to speak at 'the journalists' supper to Roosevelt'—another Teddy.

'A ROOFER.' When he has visitors his letters always contain the most precise particulars as to train times and the traps he has ordered. In one letter to Gertrude he asks, 'Could the pram go on the roof?' On one occasion he promises to pack into Rose Cottage half a dozen young girls and to find accommodation for Harold and Gertrude and four others at the Beetle and Wedge, a public-house name out of the ordinary.[1] At Christmas 1911 'my Christmas-sing'—he always sent lots of presents to lots of children—'will be extra difficult owing to my being likely to be 'rather broke in the future compared with what I have been in past years'. But for a special purpose, of helping somebody to a Continental holiday, he is going to draw on a 'special fund'. For a trip with some members of the family he did all the planning and ticket-buying. When he returned he wrote sixty-five letters. He seems always to have written a great many. The word for a bread and butter letter is a 'roofer'.

A June letter tells of trouble that authors with two dwelling places endure: 'I am always finding something I want to look up is at the Cottage and not here, and I suppose when I go down there I shall want things that are here'.

For *Homes and Haunts of Ruskin* he insists that Gertrude shall write some impressions of 'distinctly Ruskinian things' they saw when they were in Italy. When he thanks her for her notes he writes: 'Don't talk of yourself as "illiterate". The essence of literature is feeling and observation, and you have both.' In a later letter he urges more contributions and says there are blanks in his roughed-out MS. 'G. to add' or 'G's point about So and So'. Later he speaks

[1] I have heard it said that no fewer than four honeymoons were spent at Rose Cottage.

of congratulations on the *Haunts*; 'you will have to be shown them some day, for there is not much pleasure if one keeps one's pleasure to oneself. The three I have liked best (apart from relations) are a very nice one from the editor of *The Times*; one from my old office-boy at the *P.M.G.* 25 years ago; and one from an ex-upholsteress who used to do a lot of work for us at Tavistock Square.'

GARDENER AND GARRICK. He is 'looking forward to a quiet time with you all at the Cottage', for he is 'worn out with luncheon parties, dinner parties and tea parties, though I shirk as many as I decently can. Such a fussation at Winchester, I am commanded to tea with the King and Queen.' Lady Scott-Gatty had been telling him about her garden and a long row of white lilies in front of a yew hedge with a grass path in front; 'I could only reply, "You should see my delphiniums and sweet peas and my niece's weeping Dorothy" '. Later on he promises an account of a Windsor garden party. Harry Irving had taken him to 'a popular melodrama' at the Lyceum, *The Women of France*, 'the oddest mixture of guillotines, Marie Antoinette, hair-breadth escapes, sickly sentiment, pantomime "comic relief", very broad jokes, the Union Jack and the roast beef of Old England for ever. Then we went to the Garrick to supper and I didn't come home till 2 in the morning. A well-known actor talking stage scandals and a half-boozy Colonel fighting his battles in India and Africa over again and telling incredible tales about his devilish smart dodges in the Secret Intelligence Branch. A very little pleasantry goes a long way on such occasions, and when the Colonel retired I remarked, "Rather a strange person to employ on secret service", at which the party broke up in merriment.'

The next day he was 'sticking to the *Haunts* hard. Getting on with the tiresome chapters. Next I shall have to find mottoes for all the chapter headings. It is always a difficult job to find a quotation which suggests or covers the point of a whole chapter, but I have come on some good ones. For one chapter I think of Wordsworth's

> The silence that is in the starry sky
> The sleep that is among the lonely hills.

Kisses to Dia [that is the baby, Diana] and a loving pat for Ango' [Angus the Skye terrier, the 'Angel Face' of a later letter in which he says 'Love to Angel Face. Poor dear, with so many ill-tempered dogs around him!']

'KOON KAN' AND THE SECRET OF LIFE. An August letter begins with 'Plantagenista making much larger leaves. Tuberose— two buds in flower, the others look like bursting soon'. He has done 'an hour's work in the garden'. A 'sweet letter' from Gertrude has come 'but why address "Sir E.T.C" instead of the nicer "Sir Edward" as before? The Ruskin book is almost done and I have a beastly political article to do'. Then in a day or two: 'Revised the whole MS. [note, not typescript] and sent it off to the publishers. Some of it was rather nicer the last time of re-reading, especially our chapters. But at other times I thought much of it was dull. When you come to write a book all by yourself you will know how many times one changes one's own opinion of it. You know it already, I expect, in the case of sketches—which must be much the same. The rains have quite changed the look of the river. It is swirled with a very strong stream, completely conquering the wind.' He seems to have done a good deal of rowing.

The next letter mentions that some people who dined with him 'taught us all "Koon Kan", which they say is the latest rage in London. I had never heard the name before. Of course I thought it quite a good game as I won! But nothing will oust our Bez [bezique] from my affections—even though you do beat me so badly. The sort of thing people ask me to write, now that I am known to be unattached:

Dear Sir E., I should take it as a personal favour if you would write an article for me on: How to live our own life and get essential value out of it; how to be proficient in the fine art of living; or, to give the question a different form, What are the great things which want doing for ourselves and others? 1,000 words. 5 guineas.

The secret of life to be given away for 5 guineas! I would give 500 to anybody who would tell it to me. But everyone has to grope after it for himself or herself.'

The next letter is yet further evidence of his interest in children, however young: 'I *am* so sorry to hear about Diana and the wasps. Poor little dear!' He wants Gertrude to look at some of the letters written by Florence Nightingale as a girl and 'tell me what you think of them.' He is hard at work 'except for my constitutional in the afternoon'. But he also seems to have his Dulwich Gallery catalogue on hand, and is bothered about finding something to say about some of the pictures. 'For a meal-book I have taken up Tollemache's *Old and Odd Memories*. At dinner I found on every other page the most terrible sentiments, "Woman is born to superstition as the sparks fly upward", etc. I, as a loyal women's-righter, entirely disagree. For any "superstitious woman" I could certainly produce a "superstitious man".'

He has a 'real serious' offer from Gertrude about vegetables from Rose Cottage, and he replies: 'You shall have them at market price, which is nil. For where there is no market there can be no market price; there is no market at R.C.; therefore the price of the vegetables is o, as follows by all the rules of logic, Euclid and common-sense. But you shall pay the carriage if you want to.'

THE DOWNS AND DOMESTIC IDYLLS. He was taken to see *Bunty Pulls the Strings* and thought the play dragged, but 'I loved Bunty'. On visits he has paid to members of the family he says, 'I do like seeing little domestic idylls'. He goes for longish walks: 'I love the freshness and spaciousness of the downs, and the grass roads which have been the same for centuries. But solitude I do not love'. He is sometimes 'very solitary'. A neighbour, Sir Some-body, who is 'very rich, has mediums down from London who have persuaded him that they have messages from the Almighty for him. And the old boy sits in a watch-tower at the top of his big house receiving the said messages. The room is painted pink and green—to correspond with the "aura" of his particular spirit-friends.' Cook has taken grapes to a niece and sat beside her and her infant, which Dorothea describes as 'nicely finished off'.

While he is working away at *Florence Nightingale* he says that 'writing a book must be something like waiting for a baby to arrive —only in the case of a big book, the period of waiting is ever so much longer'. He says, 'I love the little evening scene you draw— the cosy fire, your reading aloud, and Harold brushing your hair. I always remember the story about John Philips, a Winchester poet who out of schooltime read Milton aloud while a "junior" combed his flowing locks. How the other boys abstained from cutting them I know not—perhaps he was sturdy, though a poet.'

ON BEING DISMAL. On Gertrude reporting being 'rather dismal' he says: 'When I feel dismal (which I fear is not seldom) I often turn to the *Letters of Sydney Smith*—a mine of gentle wisdom as of wit. At lunch to-day I found the following passage which must be meant for you: "If with a good husband, three children—that is D., plus the coming twins—a good house, many books and many friends who wish me well, I cannot be happy, I am etc., etc." As to Harold being away sometimes, here is what S.S. says to a Lady Grey who was "out of spirits" on account of her husband's absence: "You must rather thank Providence that you did not marry one of those stupid fellows who are never wanted on any occasion. Mr. A. never loses the society of Mrs. A. And Mr. B. lives always beside Mrs. B. And why? Because no one else ever wants them. Who would ever think of wanting them? What good could they be to any human being?" '

He speaks of being at a first night with Dorothea Irving when Harry 'had a tiny part which he does awfully well. These first nights are rather fun as the pit and gallery cheer all theatrical celebrities as they come in to the stalls. Irene Vanbrugh got the best reception. But the most conspicuous person in the audience was Mrs. Langtry (Lady de Bathe) in the centre of the swagger box, clad in very bright emerald green. Some people were unkind enough to wonder whether she felt at all uncomfortable at some passages in the play.' Regarding an actress in the play he says that Mrs. Aria, who was of the company along with Cook, stated that 'first she married a trick bicyclist and divorced him, and now she has married a music-hall comedian who etc. Dolly seized my arm at intervals during the play and said "Oh, how thankful I am not to be acting". In the next box was Hall Caine who leaned over between the acts and discoursed to me on the mistakes of the play in mixing up the Abstract with the Concrete.'

From his note after his visit to the Rose Show at the Horticultural Hall with Dorothea, I extract a sentence or two for rose-growers: 'Oh such roses! You positively must get Rayon d'Or, the yellowest rose out, much better, we thought, than Lady Hillingdon. Another very pretty one—"coppery reddish salmon"—is Lady Pirrie. But I really like the reds best—and here is my list of the reds I marked for approval: Richmond, Horace Vernet, Comte de Raimband, A. K. Williams, General McArthur, C. J. Grahame, Comm. F. Faure. But I don't know that any of these are better than Hugh Dickson and J. B. Clark.'

Then to Tottenham Court Road 'where Dolly bought and carried home various luxuries for Harry's dinner—the whole of which she was going to cook herself.'

Next day he 'pottered about the garden all the afternoon' discussing next year's plans. A new lavender hedge is to be 'white and mauve alternately'. I always go and look at your plantagenista first thing on coming down, to see if it needs watering'. He hopes there will be pieces of Alpines for her from the four spots they visited. And the letter ends with 'A kiss for my dear little Dia'.

'THE NECESSARY PRICE OF YOUR HAPPINESS.' 'You do well to count your mercies', he writes one day, 'and to remember the necessary price of your happiness. If you knew—which thank God you don't—the bitter grief and life-long disappointment which some women have to bear you would "count your mercies still more".' In going through and tidying up old correspondence he turns up 'boy friendship letters—letters recalling early loves too! And heaps of letters from Curzon in Oxford days.'

'Oh my dearest Gertrude', one letter begins, 'I am so sorry about the nasty, horrid boil.' Harold has been helping with the Dulwich Gallery notes: 'With my usual alertness to crib whenever I can (a journalist's habit) I shall bring him in my introduction.'

In the autumn he has been busy 'on a political article for one of the Reviews'—the Reviews got a capital letter then—'and as I am a bit out of practice in that particular kind of writing it took me much longer than it ought. Harold says civilly, "You can bring all your Florence N. papers". Can I indeed! they are contained in 20 tin boxes and 10 packing cases! I think I won't. But I will bring down some of the letters and diaries for you to advise on. And this afternoon I am going to Mudie's to see if I can get *The Romance of a Favourite* which, from the reviews, sounds amusing. Bez. cards I suppose you have, but I have been almost persuaded that Coon Can'—that is his spelling this time—'is better.'

Lawyers advised against a house the Irvings are taken by. 'But that is a way lawyers have', writes Cook; 'I advised that, though the price was certainly not cheap, neither was it extra-ordinarily dear, and I think they will take it'. He had been at a Winchester meeting. 'The Close and the College and the walls were all looking so beautiful with the sunshine playing on the autumn tints.'

On dreams he writes: 'I wish I could cultivate the faculty for "dreaming true" (*Peter Ibbetson*) but I cannot. Distressing dreams repeat in aggravated forms of horror the great sorrows of my life.' He likes the practical work of the Victoria League which organises 'a friendly handshake for new settlers in the Colonies. I have seen a good deal of Committees and Societies in my time but never one which is better run than the League—and all its officers and chairmen (except me) are women. Rather picked women, no doubt—the secretary is a woman of lively humour. Your friend Susan Buchan [afterwards Lady Tweedsmuir] for instance.' I knew her as a sound backer when I was chairman of the Oxfordshire County Council's Library Committee and we had branches in nearly 400 villages.

CHAPTER XXX

LUNCHEON AND DINNER GOSSIP

A CARSON ANECDOTE. Dining somewhere, a fellow guest was Sir West Ridgeway, formerly Under Secretary in Ireland, who told a story. 'When he was Balfour's right hand man he had ordered the prosecution of a Nationalist, and Sir Edward Carson had been retained as prosecuting counsel. In the middle of the trial a telegram from Dublin Castle was put in his hands saying that the Irish Government had decided to drop the prosecution. Most counsel would have obeyed. But Carson devised some pretext for getting the Court to make an adjournment, which he used to send an indignant telegram to Ridgeway, "Why the devil have you done this thing? It's giving away the whole show. Are you mad? etc." Ridgeway replied, "Have no idea what you mean. Have sent no instructions whatever". It came out that the Nationalists had got hold of the official cypher and forged the telegram.'

Mrs. Vaughan Nash, in charge of the Nightingale papers—she was a cousin of F.N.—is, he says, 'a brick', which is my recollection of her. He has been undoing 'another case of dust-begrimed old letters': 'I came upon a bundle of congratulations to Emmie on her engagement to me. Much the nicest of the lot was from your father [the Master of Balliol]. Your mother's was much more hesitating—she seemed to think I had "rushed" E. against her real inclination and doubted if I was "a kindred soul". For she knew nothing about me at the time, whereas your father had heard me well-spoken of by my friend Arnold Toynbee.'

NORTH VERSUS SOUTH. 'If it is another brilliant summer day', the letter proceeds, 'I ought to take one of my long walks. I cannot deny that the green softness of the South appeals to me more than the tree-less severity of Northumberland (Gertrude's native county). I felt it on that long railway journey the other day—felt that—somewhere about Nottingham was, I think, the dividing line—it was like passing from austerity to gentleness.' There is an apology for a reference to the food at some luncheon he has been at—'what a pig I am, always coming to the point of the eatables, and then pulling up—remembering that to your pure and simpler taste, chalk is as cheese. And you will live to be 90.' He had made a reference somewhere to his new housemaid, 'very superior in voice, manners, etc.', and had met with the rejoinder, 'Of course, she's a clergyman's daughter'. He has a reflection on 'a very young youth who preached a semi-jocose sermon which made the yokels titter'. Cook prefers 'the quiet old-fashioned ways to the slap-'em-on-the-back, poke-'em-in-the-ribs style which many young parsons imitate nowadays from the Bishop of London.' He speaks of a begging-letter man: 'I could not detect any sign of drink—no smell, no shaky hands—very sedate and shabby-genteel get-up. So, as he poured out his woes the half-sov. had to become a whole one. He may be a deserving case; but, in spite of my failure to catch him out, I rather doubted it. Begging seemed to come so very easily and naturally. It's horribly diff. to know what to do in such cases.'

EYE-ACHING PROOF READING. He has done 'a good day's work at Florence N., taking her up to 20. For a wonder, I fancy it comes not badly'. One night in the autumn he reports himself as 'sleepy, having spent hours over final revises [of the *Haunts*, no doubt] and there is nothing more eye-aching than proof-reading'.[1] A woman interviewing a prospective governess is reported as saying to her: 'I hope you are religious, for I am not very, and I want my little children to have every advantage'!

He has dined with the Vaughan Nashes to meet some other Nightingale relatives. 'I hope the whole family don't mean to invite me, for Florence N. had 126 cousins! But they will all be rather sick in the end, I feel sure; for I am resolved to make my book a Life of Florence N. herself and not a sort of *Pillars of the House*, one of hundreds of relations. Emmie used to laugh at it.' He is working at 59 Portman Mansions and 'taking my constitutional in the Parks'. Dorothea is reported as being 'very much snubbed and over-awed by her infant' who had said to her one day, 'I know you would like all the world to be little babies'. He speaks of the Castiglione, 'a person of extraordinary beauty', in a company of 'not very shockable ladies' in a drawingroom in Paris, when a point came up about a statue. 'Whereupon the Castiglione took off her shoes and stockings, raised her skirt and remarked, "Here is the Divine model against which there can be no appeal". There seems to be no doubt that the Castiglione was a person of extraordinary beauty, vogue and, well, notoriety.'

While in somebody's nursery 'playing with her "Bubbly"', he thought 'it would be nice if your "it" were a boy this time. Little boys can be very angelic (but so can little girls); though sometimes the sweetest and most seraphic boy-bodies turn out, in looks, a sad sell. Witness a relative—a sort of show Infant Samuel child,

---

[1] There are also the weeks on end that authors who have many allusions and references, spend on the preceding galley proofs, in which by far the more time-consuming (and expensive) corrections and deletions are made.

and now one of the plainest men that ever were or could be.'

Although he 'exercises', he has been 'plodding at F. Nightingale no end—10 hours a day often. Here's a remark of hers which shows how tastes differ. "What is it to be read aloud to? The most miserable exercise of the human intellect. It is like being on one's back with one's hand tied and having liquid poured down one's throat".'

'THE ONLY WAY TO DO ANYTHING.' He has had to go by request to the House of Commons to meet a Minister: 'I wish I had the happy knack which some people have of always thinking themselves well qualified for any work proposed to them—but I always feel precisely the opposite. Also the job would take up a lot of time and I am not well enough off to give very much of mine for nothing. On the other hand, having been given an "honour" by the Government I suppose I ought not to shirk doing what one of them says would help him. So you see I am in a state of wobble. I think I shall write my friend stating the *cons* and giving him every opportunity of backing out. And then if he still presses me, I shall have to say yes.'

He has been reviewing Queen Victoria's *Journals*, 'a steady grind'. A review means not only 'a lot of reading first, but a lot of trouble in thinking of some scheme on which to thread the points'. He has been at Cambridge 'speaking in defence of Sir Edward Grey's Persian policy', has had to do a *Quarterly* article on Samuel Butler and has been 'asked to stand for some hopeless constituencies'. 'Long ago I came to the conclusion that the only way to do anything was to sit tight at the chief work of the moment'. So he has been again hard at F.N., 'but it is slow work, in the sense of time-consuming. Has it ever struck you, as a woman's advocate of women, that literary work is often so spoken of in terms of the special functions of women? The difference between the conception of a literary work and the bringing of it to the birth, the labour of composition, the throes of authorship, and so on. Literature is full of such phrases. I suppose men have employed these metaphorical terms in order to suggest that even Man has some of the rough work of the world to do!'

He says of one letter that it is 'as long as one of Miss Nightingale's: if not more "readable" it will at any rate be more legible than her pencil scrawls which threaten to destroy my eyesight'. In November 1912 he speaks of 'slaving away' at the book. A quarter has been done; the remaining three-quarters will be 'more difficult and time-consuming'.

Gertrude has just got the advance copy of *Homes and Haunts*. He hopes she has 'noticed with pleasure' that the members of the Divorce Commission are agreed that 'a thing bad enough to divorce a wife from a husband should also be considered bad enough to

divorce a husband from a wife. A great step in advance; the movement of public opinion is very marked. I can remember that when
Stead—and I—preached the equality doctrine, no man hardly
agreed—and not all women, either!'

A BIOGRAPHER'S METHOD. Dorothea is reported to have—
such were the possibilities of that time—four servants, in addition
to some other help. 'As a thank offering for being quit of the
stage', she says, she is 'full of good works'. The Nightingale task
Cook finds 'quite exciting now that his heroine has gone to the
Crimea; the story is tangled but he is gradually getting it straight.
'I wish I had not so many outside things to distract—one loses so
much time in picking up threads'. As to his method, 'First one reads
endless letters and books and feels utterly muddled and hopeless—
not seeing how the mass of points can ever be made interesting or
intelligible or coherent. Then suddenly it flashes across one how
the thing can be nicely mapped out, and one feels as if one could
not write fast enough.' But what author engaged on biography
has not had the same despairs and, now and then, illuminations?
He is 'rather pleased because the First Part, tracing F.N.'s early
life as a Revolting Daughter has immensely pleased and interested
Mrs. Vaughan Nash, much the most intelligent of the huge
Nightingale group'.

He had had an amusing time at a Victoria League Settlers'
Welcome Committee at which the question arose as to the age at
which it should be unnecessary to give the young women voyagers
introductions to the captains of the vessels so 'that they could
chaperon'. The secretary whispered to Cook, 'It's all very well to
say the captains must chaperon them, but who are to chaperon
the captains?'

He is going to be interrupted by some young woman who is to see
the Bishop of London and wants 'to talk it all over with me afterwards. I suppose the Bishop will tell her that she will be damned if
she goes over to Rome, and she wants me to tell her that she won't.
But I shall urge the World against both Anglican Bishop and Rome!'

In some chat about Christmas he says that Lord Rosebery has
asked him 'to spend the dreary season' with him at Dalmeny, 'but
of course I refused that'. He had dined with Sir Thomas Barlow,
'the swell doctor'. 'The doctors say we all eat too much, but my
experience is that they do too. One dish was "a dream", as D.
would say, but what was nicer was that I sat next to my dear Mrs.
Prothero.' [Mrs. G. W. Prothero.] Then he had 'a tremendous
confab about Florence with Barlow, who used to be her doctor.
He is very proud, he said, of having attended the three greatest
women of the time, Queen Victoria, F.N. and Lady Burdett-Coutts.
He is a dear old boy; his link with me is that he is a great Ruskinian

—also that he spends every Saturday afternoon either at the British Museum or the National Gallery with my *Handbooks*.'

He tells of a Medici prints exhibition which it was proposed to hold in Melbourne. It was put off first because 'it included an Endymion and Venus, which would corrupt the morals of the Melbourne maidens and young men respectively, and also a Reynolds Holy Family to which the Protestants objected as encouraging Madonna worship, and the Catholics objected because it was painted by a Protestant'.

'I WISH I WERE NOT SO FOND OF CHILDREN.' At lunch somewhere he had met a colonel whom he presumed to be a descendant of the officer of the same name who in India, as he and his companions were being massacred, exclaimed, 'We are not the last of the English'. And he gets on to anecdotes of children. 'Oh, dear', he says, 'I wish I were not so fond of children. For one thing because all the while I am afraid of them.'

At an Alpine Club dinner, he continues, he had to speak extempore and told, with success, an experience at a Chamonix hotel when the host and hostess asked the party on arriving 'Do you prefer Mt. Blanc or a bath?' In the course of his remarks he excused his not climbing with the precept of Confucius, 'Respect the gods but keep them at a distance'. At 'a City gorge' Sir Robert Morant talked South Kensington to him—'it was he who suggested me for the Advisory Council job'.

JOHN MORLEY, POWER AND THE FUTURE. In December he stumbles from a motor bus, the first accident of his we have heard of. He is 'wiring into work till 11 at night, very early for me'. At the next dinner he attends he talked with Dorothy Stanley, 'the artist widow of the explorer and widow of someone else since, and we got on like anything, though she is a rabid Tory. She told me how she was driving John Morley home from a party and said, "Is it all worth while?" "Of course it is worth while", he replied. "Only if there is another life", she rejoined. "But there isn't", he said; "take my word for it and make the most of the life that now is, dear young lady". "Oh, but I *know* better", was her response, "and as you don't know better you deserve to be miserable". "Miserable", exclaimed he, "don't you know that the one thing worth living for is Power, and that I am on the crest of the wave?"'

He encloses a batch of reviews of *Haunts* and asks Gertrude to keep them, 'for, if a time ever comes when I have nothing to do, I shall perhaps continue the Cutting Book which Emmie began many years ago'.[1] He tells of someone saying to him that 'the

---

[1] I have read them. They couldn't have been more appreciative and were interesting to look through at this time of day; but they were never stuck in the Cuttings Book.

man who fell by the wayside was a blessing to the good Samaritan'. Some person had asked him 'to use my influence to get a title for her dear brother. I have no such influence, and, if I had, I should never use it in such a way'. Indefatigable as ever, he has been doing some 'picture and furniture arranging' for Dorothea.

He has spared time to give a lecture to a 'very attractive and appreciative Brotherhood, a pleasant Sunday afternoon, but it was rather trying to be introduced by a prayer in which the Almighty was asked to put the Words of Trewth into the speaker's mouth. The man who hooked me for the lecture used to be a humble compositor on one of my papers, and I was fairly astonished at finding that he had blossomed out into a great, fat, pompous-looking elder with an immaculate topper and a white inset to his waistcoat.'

At a dinner a member of the family is giving he will not have a chance 'because of the Retinue of Poets and Essayists'. At a party of Mrs. Aria's, 'a Christmas gorge', somebody knew the salaries of pantomime lions—'quite wicked, £450 a week, one of them'. [This is forty years ago.] Coon Can[1] was played, 'happily not for money or I should have been ruined'. A well known editor 'sat on a sofa holding Mrs. Aria's hand and in a loud cheery voice she declared that she was "never in a room with Will in which he didn't find some woman whose hand he could hold". "It will be my turn to reminisce next", he said.' In some connexion or other he states his opinion that 'Sargent's genius is essentially that of a satirist, who picks out and emphasises any weakness or ugliness'. While Canon and Mrs. Barnett sent him for Christmas 'a colour print of Watts's "Hope" with a good motto from Browning which I must try to take to heart,' another wellwisher's present was a Coon Can set.

'A RED LETTER YEAR'. He will 'always count 1912 a Red Letter year—not because of the Knighthood (though I don't pretend not to have been pleased with that too) but because—and he says several affectionate things about Gertrude—'the desire of your heart has come to you and you and Harold are now to be made happy, so soon now, by the arrival of the Twins'. With his 'bank book and yearly budget' he has 'had to "cook" accounts in order to make them come approximately right. For all my boasted care in such things, I fear accounts are great humbug.'

And then we go into 1913. He hopes that Gertrude is 'not getting more impatient than can be helped. Almost every bundle I untie from the Nightingale packing cases contains some letters or pamphlet about such affairs and I am beginning to feel quite an expert, and believe I could pass an examination! Well, you have

---

[1] Mr. Laurence Irving tells me it was a kind of Canasta.

Y

not much longer to wait now and you must keep as placid a you can.'

He has been to Newcastle-on-Tyne—'trains packed and hideously delayed'—where he gave some gathering 'a full hour, and al asked for more'. He stayed with 'a rather nice type of the simple studious German, a scientific chemist now retired and writing philosophy and studying Ruskin, a great book-lover, the big house full of books, and every volume elaborately bound by Zaensdorf— he must be rich. She is a Quakeress.' Back at home he has been playing with some child 'cutting out a Zoo'. The girl, to whom reference was made a page or two back has 'now definitely gone over to Rome and I only hope she will like it and stay there'. He is pegging away at F.N. and is kept away from 'a swagger At Home because he was 'in the middle of a chapter'.

'Oh dear', he says, 'what an expense a garden is! Geall is sad and sore over the comparative failure of his chrysans—so many infected with rust. So I have told him to make a bonfire and I am going to order a new set from a swell mum grower in Guernsey I am surrounded in the library with so-called Alpine primulas ir pots, but "Alpine" they are not—the colour all washed out, they are primulas and water.'

Of all his distractions 'dining out is the most tiring'. One 'very good dinner' was for his South Kensington Advisory Council a Pease's (Minister of Education). 'Then, upstairs, all the Heads of Departments of the Museum came in, and Pease introduced me to everyone of them till I could have dropped with fatigue at having to think of appropriate remarks on every branch of Arts and Craft in turn. Lastly Mrs. Pease came up briskly and said "Now perhap it's time to"—break up, I hoped; but no—"to go down to supper" Another big spread—more champagne, more talk. I was a wreck next morning.'

WELCOME TO THE BABE. 'But I hope, my dear, you will no have much longer to wait. Mind you give my love at an early opportunity to

Hubert-Miltiades-Leonardo-Leontes-Lionel
or
Juliet-Elizabeth-Hermione-Rosalind-Nausicaa-Artemis
or
to both.'

A post or two afterwards he writes, 'Oh my dearest Gertrude I am so glad in your happiness. I know you said you would no mind whether the newcomer was a boy or a girl; but I know al the same that you will be additionally happy in being the Mothe of a Son. It is lovely for you, and I congratulate very much. wonder what Dia will make of her prayers having been answered

by a Baby Brother instead of a Baby Sister. I shall look forward to
making his acquaintance: and meanwhile do let one of your kisses
come as from me. I send my best love for a nice, restful convales-
cence'. And he signs, 'Ever your very affectionate Uncle Teddy'.

The next note says that Dorothea would not agree that Christopher, Gertrude's baby, had 'a marked nose, but I am determined
that either he has or will have such. For somebody says that all
Great Men have marked noses and Christopher is going to be a
Great Man, as his very name implies. Therefore he must have a
nose—*quod erat demonstrandum*.'

JOWETT'S KINDNESS FOR FLORENCE NIGHTINGALE. But he
has to break off to answer a ten-page letter from the converted
correspondent, 'who sends me talk about mental tortures, Holy
Church, quiet waters, peace of mind, etc.' Though he has been
'wiring into the book for 10 or even 20 hours a day' he has 'endless
bothersome committees'. Florence is 'getting on, and so is Jowett.
He has reached the point of discovering that they must have
been brother and sister in a previous existence. Now she has become
one of the "Queens of the Earth" to him, his "Spring of Life", and
lots more. And she is writing his sermons for him! The other day
I was lunching with Mrs. A. Murray Smith, a daughter of the old
Dean of Westminster, and when she was a girl Jowett would often
stay with her people and he was always slipping out "to see a
friend". And they were quite determined to find out who the
mysterious friend was, and when they discovered they teased him—
and he rather liked it. But I shall have to be discreet or Harold
and the rest of Balliol will say I mustn't use his letters.'

Dorothea has been buying curtains for Rose Cottage—'Liberty,
I shall be broke. The old ones have lasted 11 years'. He likes
'Dolly' because of 'her keenness. By way of preparation for being
a Poor Law Guardian,[1] she is attending a course of lectures at the
School of Economics.'

There have been references to the practical jokes of a girl in
her 'teens. We now hear that she 'had got together a band with
whistles and pans and other beastly noises and invaded the Cottage.
I thought the time had come for striking—so I just locked myself
into the library, didn't look out of the window or take any notice
whatever. And now she will think I am a sulky old brute. At least
I hope she will—for I am rather sick of that young woman and her
antics.'

A February letter from his house in London says he 'must really
take some fresh air, but there are such mountains of F.N. still to
be surmounted and I feel in such a fever to get on with the job

---

[1] Since then Guardians of the Poor—I was one—have disappeared, and
'Workhouse' and 'Poor Law Institution' have gone too.

that I simply can't knock off. Jowett, confound him! gets more voluminous every year and his letters are not racy—they are a sort of soothing syrup and always the same ingredients.' In March Cook has 'to inspect some Winchester farms in the wilds of Wilts'.

The next month he mentions dining with the Benchers at the Temple at Wedderburn's invitation, 'and jolly well they do themselves, I can tell you'. He was taken in by a Lord Justice; 'taken in' is literal. 'It's the quaintest custom I ever saw. The guests, as if they were ladies, go in, each on the arm of an allotted Bencher.' He next has dinner with the City Saddlers Company, 'not so interesting'. 'Somebody has gardens of 11 acres, but I envy no one's palaces. I honestly prefer my cot.'

Regarding a dinner where there were many South Africans he mentions one dame 'with huge diamonds' who had taken a country house and on arriving in April asked, 'Why are these beds not full of bright flowers?'

'Congratulate me', he writes in May, 'I have finished the first stage of "Florence", i.e. to the end of her packing cases, and also, in a first draft, got the story all written. But there is still a lot of patching.' On June 1 he hopes all the MSS. will have gone to the publisher in a day or two.

CHAPTER XXXI

MORE STORIES

'VERY CAREFUL WEEDING WOULD BE NECESSARY'. At the Leo Maxses Cook was told of a peeress who, in a letter to the widow of a man who was being buried in the family vault, had written, 'You will of course arrange to take up as little room as possible'. Rhodes who heard the tale 'roared with laughter at the clear hint that it was her duty (1) to die at once, (2) to be cremated and packed up small'. A remark of his own about an invitation to dinner is, 'Why should I mind whether she is legally married or not?' After lunch with the G. W. Protheros he writes: 'I do like Mrs. Prothero very much. She is essentially *simpatico*. An old lady, a fellow guest, told stories of her success in bringing men and women together—it was everyone's duty to do so'. After seeing some girls he says, 'I do think well of Girton and Newnham'.

He has got the Nightingale family to agree to give most of the Jowett letters to Balliol—'I am to select them'. But he can't advise Mr. Bonham Carter how many to give without knowing if letters would be open freely to inspection in the library—very careful weeding by me would be necessary. Perhaps the best solution would be for the Nightingale family to retain most'. In the summer he is going to stay with Clough, one of the Nightingale executors.[1] 'Croquet all the afternoon between showers'. Lots of friends row up to Rose Cottage. At some dinner he sat next the wife of Mr. Herbert Samuel M.P. (now Lord Samuel) and 'liked her very much'. Some dinner party was so boring that 'I must give a little shriek to you'. In his host's 'voice or manner there is something which makes you feel as if you simply could not listen to him'. He has found someone besides himself who has not seen Arnold Bennett's *Milestones* and they are going to it together.

His *Homes and Haunts of Ruskin*, in the preface of which there are some personal details not in the *Life*, is dedicated to 'the dear memory of E.C.C., the partner of many travels in happy years' and to G.F.H. (Gertrude) 'in gratitude for kind companionship and help given in many ways and not least in the preparation of

[1] It was his son, I think, whom I found so successful in devising good-looking convenient, inexpensive cottages—for £150 or so—when I was writing *In Search of a £150 Cottage* and working at the arrangements for the Letchworth Cheap Cottages Exhibition.

this book'. He had said to Gertrude that he did not usually wear his heart on his sleeve, but he would like to have this reference.

At some dinner Cook 'never' heard so many Home Office secrets related.

He notes how Robert Barrington-Ward has 'got on to *The Times* straight off and indeed seems to be writing the greater part of the paper; to me, remembering my early struggles, it seems almost incredible'. While I have been making these extracts I have chanced to turn up one of several kind letters in which this lamented editor of *The Times* who died too soon helped me to references for one of my books.

At Rose Cottage Cook is planning not only a boathouse; 'the architect has sent his drawings for terraces, sun-dial, pond, arched bridge, yew hedges and I know not what; how he contrives to get so much into so little space is a wonder'. He agreed to the plan, but the 'garden', though he is well pleased with it, is 'chiefly paving stones'. Cook sent to Holland for his bulbs.

There is mention of a house at which he was 'the "guest" (i.e. the victim) of the evening'.

A METHOD IN ITALY. Writing of somebody's coming visit to Italy he says: 'The first time Emmie and I went to Rome she wanted to sketch in the Palatine, which was forbidden, and I asked the hotel landlord how to work it. He said, "You will go to the Ministry of the Interior and will ask to see Signor Somebody on private business. You will explain to him, apologising for troubling him, and make him a little present. And he will give you a *permesso* which will pass you everywhere". "Yes", said I, fearing that the little present might ruin me, "but how much?" "Oh, a 5 franc note will be quite enough". And it was. And I remember someone saying that 10 francs was quite enough to give the very greatest swell at the Venetian custom house in order to smuggle through important things. But all this refers to long ago.'

BOOKS, REVIEWERS AND PUBLISHERS. '*Florence Nightingale* comes out on Tuesday (Nov. 4) and I feel like Harry on a first night.' The day after he 'went out to buy a lot of papers. Of my old papers, the *Pall Mall*, the *Daily News* and the *Daily Chronicle* have played up handsomely. The *Westminster* alone has nothing, which is not very friendly of Alfred. Several of the papers goodish too. Still it is not the papers that make or mar books and plays.'[1] Later: *The Times* is 'tiresome'. 'Alfred Spender writes nicely in Saturday's *Westminster*, but the best was the *Morning Post*. There are swarms of them, and Macmillan writes cheerily.'

A few days afterwards: 'The begging-letter writers who used to plague F.N. are beginning at me. Will I send a widow a copy of

[1] See page 350.

the book? Will I send £15 to enable a Christian woman to print a volume of poems? I will not.' There is 'such a nice notice of my St. Paul's brother, à propos of his retirement, in the school magazine. Alfie is awfully self-effacing and would never dream of showing me such a thing himself.'

Referring to the almost finished Dulwich Gallery catalogue he says that Harold and he, 'when Yates Thompson returns, are going to explore the College and see if we can discover some of the pictures that have disappeared'. This plan was carried out with Yates Thompson.

Lloyd George had 'won over the Oxford Union; I knew he would—he is so artful and ingratiating'. At the Verneys at Claydon he saw a portrait of an ancestor 'who was a standard bearer at Edgehill. He was hacked to pieces—only his hand with his ring on it was found. The ring, with an enamelled portrait of Charles I, given by the King, is one of the treasures of the house. It was nice seeing "Florence Nightingale's room" which they religiously keep as it was in her time.' Then he has been dining with Yates Thompson, 'full of Dulwich as usual'.

On his housemaid at Portman Mansions giving notice two months before his lease runs out he says that he shall move down to Rose Cottage and at the flat do for himself—after all at Winchester 'I had to light fires and make beds'—and eat at a convenient restaurant two minutes off. He is having more oak bookcases made for the Rose Cottage library, but is once more 'weeding out' his books.

'George Allen and Co. have gone smash', and he will 'lose what might have been a substantial sum' in respect, not of the *Works* but of the *Life of Ruskin*. 'Fortunately I sold *Homes and Haunts* to them outright, and they had paid up'. At the Sydney Buxtons in Sussex 'everybody was full of F.N.' The book is now in its fourth edition, which is 'not so bad considering how expensive it is'—30s.!

AN EAST END AUDIENCE AND A CURE. He has been speaking at Cambridge and, Oxford man though he is, 'my opinion is confirmed that there is nothing at Oxford so pretty as the best parts of it'. In some connexion or other he says Violet Markham is 'about the cleverest woman I know'. He mentions that his wife 'used to have pupil teacher parties', that one of these pupils is 'mistress of a board school in a very slummy East End slum among the docks', and that he had been 'asked down to—of all things in the world—their "monthly Ruskin hour"'. He had to give an address as a man who had known Ruskin and written his *Life*, and 'then, to my amusement, the girls whisked off shoes and stockings and danced bare-legged—so up-to-date have even slummy Board schools become'. 'Two little girls—so pretty—were told off to see me to the station, and chattered without a bit of shyness'.

In contrast, he was for a week-end with the Rothschilds at Tring. 'Winston Churchill was there and I had some interesting talk with him. I always get on well with Lord Rothschild, and it's nice every now and again to eat and drink gorgeous dinners surrounded by masterpieces of Reynolds and Gainsborough. Both Lord and Lady R. were full of *F.N.*—Lady R. told me that before she married her great ambition was to be a nurse. With regard to the sons' wonderful museum of animals, birds and fleas, Lowther, the Speaker, made the remark, "What a nightmare you might have, Walter, if you imagined yourself shut in your museum and all the creatures suddenly became alive!" '

In April he is off to Naples to meet Gertrude and Harold. 'My recollections of Sicily are a mixture of great delight and of shivering over meagre fires in uncomfortable inns'. He is 'undergoing before starting a rigorous "cure" as a long bout of dining out has brought back symptoms of gout and I was beginning to hobble'. He asks if Harold has got a ticket as a 'Professor' to admit him free to all museums, etc.; 'they give such things in Italy.' He is 'coming back to an opinion, which for many years I gave up, that Switzerland beats Italy'.

Back in England he cuts off a piece of curl from one of the Hartley children, sends it to its mother on the Continent, and reports 'eight teeth'. It is mid-May and he writes, 'Let me tell you Italianisers that a fine May Day in England, when the fields are ablaze with buttercups and daisies and the air is sweet with the pink thorn and the white, requires a lot of beating'.[1] He copies out for Gertrude a closely written full page of Tennyson's poem on Virgil, 'one of his best pieces': 'Perfect in a literary way and hitting off Virgil's characteristics, and conveying so much of the charm of Italy. I cannot feel that the "bloody", "damn you" style of the New Poetry is an improvement on the old models, but perhaps that is because I am an old Fogey.' 'Tell Harold', he adds, 'that if he finds his bank account too low before the tour is over, I should gladly make a temporary advance.'

'VERY NICE BUT A BIT YEARNING.' The Dulwich catalogue is out and 'an amiable old gentleman writes that he is buying 100 *F.N.*s to present to 100 hospitals'. Cook has been attending a Conference on Town Planning and Care of Child Life 'pretty regularly, because at the last sitting I take the chair and sum up'. When his speech had to be made, 'I was rather in trepidation, but brought into it a nice quotation from Blake and Ruskin and the ruins of Imperial Rome, and that did the trick. Violet Markham wept and they cheered for a minute or two, and men and women

[1] Possible conjunction in the Thames valley.

came up to shake my hand! Lady Aberdeen was in the front row, looking very handsome.' At luncheon one day he sat next to Lady Jekyll—'how agreeable she is! She is a thorough Venetian and says June is the month for Venice.' A blind lady is 'very nice but a bit yearning'. As for art critics, 'the cocksure Mr. X invents new painters to suit his theories, and seems to assume that every painter always painted in exactly the same way'. On a member of a large family: 'I should not stay with her even if she did ask me; I always feel that we live in different worlds'. About someone else he is 'relenting just a little bit because she has sent me a delightful American wasp-killer'.

An editor I knew has had 'all the spirit killed in him' by his wife. A child story is of a youngster who used to watch A. when Mr. B. came to tea. '"What did you notice?" I asked. "Well", said the child quite poetically, "a sort of light came into her eyes and then she looked up, and then she looked down, and then she got red".'

There is a lawyer relative who has been made a Recorder, and does not 'a Recorder mean a full-bottomed wig and Court clothes?'

He enjoys himself when he makes a speech at the annual banquet of the Royal Academy. Has Harold a candidate for the Dulwich headmastership? 'If so I could drop a word into Yates Thompson's ear.'

Of Venetian and Florentine painters he writes: 'The Venetians give the pomp and colour of this world; in the Florentines there is the beauty of "other worldliness". But of course there are exceptions. Tintoretto is full of imaginative thought.'

THE WAR 'MAKES ONE SICK'. And then of the first Great War—'how sudden was the catastrophe!' Now 'there is a sort of iron screen round Southampton. All the bridges are guarded. The Government expect the War to be long and to be attended by many and heavy losses. All the moral forces are on our side. On the other hand in Germany the censorship has been very strict— the German people do not know the truth. I have been studying the Bluebook almost as carefully as if I were still an editor. I think Grey was splendid. The only criticism he is open to is that if he had taken a stronger and more definite line earlier he *might* have held Germany back. On the other hand, if Grey had done what the French and Russians wanted he would have lost moral force. His actual course united the nation behind him. It makes one sick to think what this European war, the biggest for a hundred years, will mean. But we may all tingle with pride when we think of the part that England is playing.'

He attends with Miss Markham a church at which the rector 'pitched bravely into members of his congregation who had selfishly been laying in stores. "You are all known and marked down", he said, "and if I hear of anything more of the kind I shall publish your names".' Cook thought the Archbishop's special Prayer 'rather namby-pamby'.

'All day cheap tickets are off. To people like me who have to live on savings the War will mean a great reduction of income. Big business men with whom I have talked calculate that the War will ultimately mean a loss of half one's capital. For the immediate moment it means more, for many companies are deciding to declare no dividend.' He adds, 'How ugly the £1 notes are'. An Admiral is 'in such a state of fuss—I wish the Admiralty would give him a job. Everyone seems bent on "organising" everybody else. No one is allowed out on the downs after sunset'. Hyde Park is 'now a multitude of drill grounds'. 'Balliol looks lively as recruiting is going on briskly there.' 'It may be two or three years before Germany is exhausted.'

He is meeting John Masefield, also Abercrombie and Drinkwater—'nice young men both of them'. 'I had to hold forth on Poetry to a conference of teachers.'

He has been foreman at a coroner's inquest 'on a trooper drowned just opposite here. The officer who jumped after him is in hospital.' A friend was condoling with George Wyndham's widow on her two sons going to the front. 'Oh no', she said, 'I feel that George will be with them, and I only pity the women who have no sons to give'. 'I wish the German plan prevailed of giving the wife the husband's title, for then I could address this to "Mrs. Captain Hartley".'

He has officers quartered on him. A tale one of them told was of the Boer War; 'He was then a Hussar and one day fell in with Strathcona's Horse, who were trotting along, laughing and singing, not spotting some Boers in the distance. So he said "I suppose you know those are Boers in front of you". "Oh, are they? Do you think we may shoot at them?" "Well, I certainly should if I were you, for if you don't they will jolly well fire at you." "Oh, what larks!" shouted the Canadians, galloping and firing a volley. Which seems to show that they are fine fellows but untrained.' 'A very rich Jew has been appointed to the regiment. He is bumptious and unnecessarily talkative, but I cannot help pitying him rather, for the others seem to be beastly to him and after all it is public-spirited of him, a very rich man, about 40 apparently, to join up.'

At the Press Bureau he has had to 'conquer my terror of the telephone. I now ring up the War Office or the Foreign Office with the utmost sangfroid. I was rather amused to find that Buckmaster shared my dread. I can't say I like my [Press Bureau] job—but in a way I am glad not to like it. I would rather be writing

Victoria League pamphlets. My three are known as Cook 1, Cook 2 and Cook 3 and have been or are being translated into French, German, Italian, Spanish, Norwegian, Swedish, Portuguese, Bulgarian, Arabic and Chinese.'

AN IMPRESSION OF KITCHENER. When the Zeppelins were at Yarmouth, 'everyone expected they would come to London. The Secretary of the War Office debated whether he should tell Kitchener or not. He decided not to as K. likes to go to bed at 11, he said.' And they didn't come. One day Cook 'nearly ran into Kitchener—what a magnificent creature he is!' At a conference at which Asquith was present Kitchener's ill-concealed impatience was amusing. In the middle he signalled to B, "Please fix another appointment for me at once".'

Cook had met at lunch the Prime Minister (L.G.). When he dined with a brother at the Athenaeum 'we had the huge club almost to ourselves'. 'It would be a good thing if the Dardanelles were forced, for it would bring down the price of bread, as the Russian corn-ships would then be able to leave the Black Sea.' Dorothea Irving's son is flying and his mother 'has cut up her sealskin as a lining for his coat which is the envy of other lieutenants.' A nephew has 'come back from China to join the Army— spirited of him isn't it?'

'The Government offered to pay for my work (at the Bureau) but I didn't like the idea of making a good thing out of the War; so I told McKenna that I would not be paid and, after some demur, they accepted me as a Volunteer Civil Servant and I have felt much more comfortable since, though the projected motor and other possible luxuries disappear! The luxury of serving gratis remains.' Later, he writes, (Sir John) Simon 'insisted on Sir Frank and me being paid from the time when Buckmaster left. As I have put in a good long spell unpaid, I don't feel so bad about it.'

'The poor Russians', another letter says, speaking of a necessitated retreat. 'But the end is not yet and the tables will be turned. The Russians won't give in.' He has been 'invited to go on a short visit to Sir John French's headquarters in order to have a look round and discuss censorship matters'. Later he reports: 'I was given an anti-frightfulness respirator and was taken, in deep mud, to the trenches in the front line. Had a peep through a periscope at the Boches, witnessed our stretcher parties at work and heard and saw the whizbangs and the evening hate.'

'KEEP A STOUT HEART.' He has met Sir W. Robertson and was 'much impressed by him'—'so keep a stout heart, my dear'— and has been 'reading Pliny's letters (with a crib)—how full the ancients are, like Shakespeare, of "quotations". And *Villette*, how good it is. There are times when to be busy is best—I simply can't

enjoy the garden a bit. I feel all the time I ought to be doing something else. I liked the picture of you and Harold reading Symonds
on the hill till the sun went down.'

At dinner with Lord Haldane he had sat next to Lady (Ian)
Hamilton 'who was full of various ointments, insect powders and
whisks, as her husband says flies and mosquitoes are the great
curse. Old Haldane was quite cheery and supposed we had heard
the latest charges against him, that his mother (Northumbrian)
was a German, and that he was really the illegitimate son of the
Kaiser!'

Cook had been in bed with a 'slight attack of pleurisy' and does
not like having a night nurse, 'who seems to be a service for pre-
venting the patient sleeping'. On returning to work he finds
himself in a railway carriage 'full of smoking, noisy, boozy
Tommies—poor dears—not at all bad sorts really, but not pleasant
company for an old fogey with a cough'. He is 'sick at the way the
papers and other people snarl and carp and grouse over Mesopo-
tamia. As if there were ever a long war without reverses and mis-
calculations and disappointments.' Quoting 'Ionica',

> Your chilly stars I can forgo,
> This warm kind earth is all I know,

he says Ruskin once asked him for a copy of the lines and said
they were 'very beautiful, but he had never thought of stars as
chilly'.

Speaking of complimentary reviews of his outstanding book on
Delane in the *Westminster Gazette* (by Spender) and in the *New
Statesman*, he repeats the view that 'reviews do not affect sales'.
Surely he was too sweeping? The public attention which books re-
ceive is surely not attracted exclusively by the restricted amount
of money their publishers are able to spend on advertisement space.

As 1916 opens we come to the last batch of the letters. Cook's
view is that 'commercialism needs scotching as well as militarism'.
Some men of business he meets he does not think much of. He sends
a nice story of a conscientious Colonel who was bent on getting
his men to send more money to their wives. With one man who
refused the Colonel pleaded that 'even another shilling a week
might make all the difference to her'. 'Very well, Sir, I will try,
but I already allow her £3,000 a year and the use of the motors!'

He has dined with Yates Thompson, 'a pro-German', he calls
him. 'He told me that he said to Lord Morley, "Don't you think
that Sir Edward Grey ought to be hanged?" and that Morley (he
had resigned from the Government over the War) had sardonically
replied, "I am against capital punishment".'

READING AND GARDENING. During the past year Cook's handwriting has become less clear, and now he begins to type, with all a beginner's troubles. But his machine is 'quite a nice toy, especially the red ink contrivance'. He soon improves in speed. May 12 is 'my birthday and Florence Nightingale's, and lamps are being sold in the streets for a women's fund'. Some friend in the Navy 'was at his fire control station when the ship was blown up; death must have been as instantaneous as glorious.' Of another, 'when last seen he was smiling and "passing cheery remarks to us" '.

'A rising barrister' came in to see him at the Press Bureau in the uniform of a private in the R.F.A. 'He said his first few days were awful till a sergeant-major spotted him and said he was to come and live with him. Now he seems to like it and says he shall not apply for a commission but try to become a sergeant-major.' Cook has been dining with Milner, back from a talk with Generals. They spoke of 'the awful responsibility'. In February 1917 (when he mentions that he has chilblains), he is interested in seeing Jellicoe —'he has a fine face, stronger than it looks in the photographs'.

He rejoices in his fields of potatoes and reports that his gardener has been appointed a food production inspector by the county council with charge of nine villages, the work to be done in the evenings. He writes: 'I do love to see the girl soldiers and drivers. The prettiest girl I have seen for some time gives out the tickets at Westminster Underground Station and looks like a Rossetti model.' At Rose Cottage 'we cannot get any oil or matches and butter only with difficulty'. In December it is so cold that 'my finger will hardly work this machine', so he did not fully learn the typing art.

By the summer of 1918 'my garden is a wreck and a wilderness, but there are lots of roses tumbling about'. He rejoices in Harold becoming a Colonel and then a General; 'apart from the honour and glory, which are the main things, the pay will not be unwelcome in these lean times'.

Among the novels he has last been reading in 1919 are *Humphrey Clinker* and *Wives and Daughters*. Rhoda Broughton had 'cracked up Mrs. Gaskell as far superior to George Eliot and said in particular that *Wives and Daughters* was a much better book than *Middlemarch*, but I don't think that'.

———

No two persons would have picked the same things from these letters. I have copied out what has interested me. I feel that the extracts, as I said when I began making them, get us to the man Cook really was. He shows himself a rarer, fuller man than I had known. How I wish I had taken more advantage as a young fellow of the opportunities I had of knowing him better! I am greatly obliged to Lady Hartley for giving me the privilege of reading and quoting freely from a worthy and affecting correspondence.

CHAPTER XXXII

THE END AND THE ESTIMATE

JOURNALISTS AND 'THE GROWING GOOD OF THE WORLD'. As Cook writes in his *Recreations*,[1] in expansion of what he once said in a speech, the journalist has his 'golden opportunities which make up for hours of obscure drudgery, opportunities to strike some blow for a cause he believes in, to help, rightly or wrongly, to form, not merely to follow, public opinion, to nerve, it may even be, a nation's purpose. He may have had on occasion, in Thomas Hardy's words, "the grin of delight" which William Morris assures us comes over the real artist, in letters or in any other form of art, at a close approximation, if not an exact achievement of his ideal. And did not George Eliot say that "the growing good of the world", the fact that things are not so ill with you and me as they might have been is half owing to the number who lived faithfully a hidden life and rest in unvisited tombs?'

I have reproduced practically nothing of Cook's leading articles. Journalists in their old age sometimes think sardonically of a lifetime's labours lost for ever in 'the files' on which Kipling rhymed. The veterans comfort themselves with the conviction that in Cook's words, 'the more effective a journalistic piece is for the immediate purpose of the day the less chance it has of permanent interest'. Then they feel that, working somewhat after the manner of the coral island insects and the creatures which, we used to be taught, gave us the chalk hills, their exertions played a part in the slow building up of national intelligence and character. Only a few men and women with special subjects on their minds look into the unwieldy volumes at Colindale and the Bodleian, in which are entombed the leading articles of the years of the *Gazettes* under Morley, Stead and Cook. But knowledge, ability and skill, political prescience and personal devotion went to the writing of them.

AT THE NATIONAL PORTRAIT GALLERY. Plaques are put on houses in which some men and women of eminence toiled. The National Portrait Gallery has no department, however, for Famous Editors. It is to be hoped that such a department may come into existence. I had some correspondence on the subject with the late Director, Sir Henry Hake. Last December, when I renewed the

---

[1] *Literary Recreations* and *More Literary Recreations*. (Macmillan, 1918 and 1919.)

subject with Mr. Kingsley Adams, the present Director, he kindly wrote to me:

We have two pencil sketches of W. T. Stead by Sydney P. Hall. These we were given before Miss Stead offered a painting of her father, and I think it was on account of the possession of these that the Trustees decided against accepting a painting of him. We have a painting of Delane which was given in 1911 by his nephew, Arthur Irwin Dasent. Barnes is portrayed in the large group of the House of Lords in 1820 by Sir George Hayter.[1] There are very few portraits of him. We had a detail photograph of the portrait made for *The Times*. I hope you will bequeath your portrait of Frederick Greenwood to the Gallery. [I had said I would. It is the only portrait of him.] I cannot say for certain that it would be accepted as the Trustees will not commit their successors. Our usual advice is that an alternative destination should be named in the will.

You ask about an Editors' Corner beginning, say, with Defoe. As you know, the collection is arranged chronologically and so we cannot group members of a profession except in the case of contemporaries and except on rare occasions for temporary exhibitions.'

When in a conspicuous place the other day I came on the statue of a man who was ranked as a statesman, and I failed to recall anything in his character or achievement that could be held to have contributed markedly to public advancement, there came to mind the service rendered by a dozen editors with an effectual calling and an effective pulpit. It was all in the day's work for such men to provide pabulum and a lead for Downing Street. It is well to offer the truth about some politicians if they have been plumed beyond their service. It is well also when the biographies of statesmen come to be written by editors, as for example in the case of Harcourt, 'C.B.', Chamberlain and, of course, Gladstone.

H. W. NEVINSON'S TRIBUTE. Of that sorry streak across the careers of some statesmen, personal ambition, hindering or soiling good work, I find no trace in Cook. This makes his contribution to his time the worthier and more memorable. No doubt he felt the urge of

> I too will something make
> And joy in the making,

but that is not the gross ambition which shows its ugly head so often in politics. I always attach value to the view taken of a public man by an old colleague of mine who had goodness and searching intelligence, H. W. Nevinson. He wrote in *Changes and Chances*:[2] 'Cook was one for whom, like everybody else, I had felt extraordinary respect ever since I had known him as President of the

---

[1] During the discussion of the Bill to dissolve the marriage of George IV. Among the spectators are two editors, those of *The Times* and the *Courier*.

[2] Nesbit, 1923.

Oxford Union. I met him occasionally while he edited the *Pall Mall*, the *Westminster* and the *Daily News*, and my respect always increased. He was a man of extraordinary knowledge, of sensitive judgment and capable of unusual generosity, which his natural shyness concealed under a frosty and even repellent manner.' As Nevinson took the opposite side from Cook on South Africa it is of particular interest to read his judgment on Cook's action on what happened there; 'So warm-hearted was the nature hidden behind that unemotional face and those chilling grey eyes that he allowed his feelings of friendship sometimes to influence his political sense, and even his sense of justice, as was seen in his unwavering support of Milner in the South Africa controversy. Yet not one has stated Milner's and Chamberlain's case with more judicial fairness and generous allowance for the passion of national freedom on the other side.'

Mrs. Edmund Garrett once said in a letter to me: 'Cook was reserved, even somewhat unresponsive perhaps, but real warmth and understanding showed in the way he spoke of others'.

LETTERS TO MISS VIOLET MARKHAM. Mrs. Carruthers, C.H. (Miss Violet Markham), who was cordially with Cook in the stand he made on South Africa, writes to me: 'I admired him enormously —his courage, his simplicity and his integrity. A very fine man whose friendship was valued by all who were privileged with it.' Cordial letters from him that Mrs. Carruthers kindly let me see include a note on the 'frightening' of so many people by 'George's Limehousing' and 'a Budget which did too much at one time'. Lloyd George 'must let off steam—and I don't know that it does much harm. There is always somebody of the kind—I hate the style of thing myself—but I suppose somebody must do the dirty work. It used to be Chamberlain; now it's L.G. And L.G., though more vulgar, is less bitter than Joe used to be. However, I look forward hopefully to the future'.

Referring to the recent death of Miss Markham's mother, Cook writes: 'Would that I could attain to the same surety of faith that shines through your words and must be so great a solace to you. Yet something of it I cling to and strive after—and there are moments, especially when sympathy of other souls in this present life comes home very vividly and everything falls into harmony.'

Writing on 'Official Press Bureau' paper, on April 5, 1915, on his correspondent's marriage, he is pleased to hear of 'the brilliant success of the great experiment—or, as I see you call it, the Tremendous Venture'. He relishes 'the picture of you surrounded by military Tories and longing to be up and at them, and just in time the Major saving the situation by a friendly wink'. He goes on: 'It is a way they have in the Army and Navy to be "no politicians" and to be "non-party men"—"but when it comes to such scoundrels as this Radical Government", etc., etc.'

During the War he still hopes that 'it may be possible to get through without conscription, which, however, is clearly the democratic thing. If it has to come, the State should be completely socialised *ad hoc*; every man enrolled, and told off to some service, whether military, operational, civil, or agricultural.' Of a deputation to Mr. Winston Churchill and Kitchener on the Press Bureau he says, 'I could not make up my mind whether Asquith or the Press talked the greater humbug'.[1]

'The worst of all the Cabinet appointments', he writes, 'is Winston to be Chancellor of the Duchy—no department to give him anything to do, so that he will be free to meddle everywhere. However, I suppose Asquith thought he would be less mischievous inside than out. Asquith, thank goodness, is of tough fibre.'

Returning to the impression Cook made upon his Press Bureau associates, Sir Frank Mitchell, formerly at Buckingham Palace, told me that he was 'beloved by all'.

AN ASSISTANT EDITOR'S EXPERIENCE. One of the best things J. A. Spender ever wrote was the article he had in the *Westminster* over the signature 'S' when Cook died. He said with feeling and conviction, 'Cook was unquestionably one of the small company who leave their mark on their time, and his unflagging industry enabled him to do as much in the forty years of his working life as would have taken other men half as long again.' He made this just comparison between Stead and Cook: 'Stead was the most talkative of men; Cook very nearly the most reticent. The one poured out his innermost thoughts to anyone whose face he happened to like; the other would nod his head, vertically or horizontally, rather than say "yes" or "no". From midday when the *Pall Mall* went to press till three or four in the afternoon Stead was in a whirl of callers and took a frantic lunch with a clattering company; Cook shut his door with a sigh of relief when the last proof was through and opened it again only to a strictly revised list of visitors by appointment.'

---

[1] Another 1915 letter from the Bureau is about stopping reports of air raids: 'I wrote a letter to the War Office and got Sir Stanley [Buckmaster] to sign it. The answer returned was that we were fussing about something which did not matter, and that the newspapers had better be left alone! The reply came from a very high authority, but we nagged on and ultimately got the Admiralty and War Office jointly to authorise us to issue restrictive notices. Unfortunately we are powerless to *enforce* them. The power of taking proceedings under the Defence of the Realm Act is vested solely in the military and naval authorities. Sir Stanley tried hard to get this altered, as long ago we wished action to be taken against certain important papers, but the Government declined to amend the Order in Council as we desired. I hope that the new Government will give the Bureau more power; but some of the Tories who are coming in have been among the noisiest opponents of the Censorship.

z

'In describing Cook as reticent', Spender continued: 'I should give an entirely wrong impression if this were taken to mean cold or intimidating. His silence was always benevolent and, when his reserve was broken, he talked to his intimates with rare point and humour. No one who had seen him at home could doubt that his affections were deeply rooted. In all his private relations he was generous, modest and unselfish. He deliberately chose the quieter path in life and some of the most thankless tasks. I remember him as the kindest and most considerate of chiefs.'

Speaking of the Ruskin connexion, Spender said the fact that 'the most copious and unrestrained of English writers should have had the coolest, most cautious and most critical of writers for his editor and biographer is one of the oddities of literary history but great good fortune for Ruskin'.

When one turns to the Spender *D.N.B.* article one finds him writing that Cook, 'to the end of his life acknowledged the debt he owed Stead and applied not a few of Stead's ideas to the papers he edited. But as a writer his methods were the opposite of Stead's; he relied rather on quiet, incisive argument than on emphatic assertion and remonstrance. He was in fact a most skilful debater with his pen and few people fell into controversy with him without discovering the variety of his weapons and the deadly accuracy of his memory for facts.'

'SYSTEM AND EFFICIENCY.' Sir Charles Oman, in his *Memories of Victorian Oxford*, calls Cook 'the greatest journalist in London'. R. C. K. Ensor in *England, 1870–1914*, describes him as a political journalist of great sobriety and sagacity, one of the last and greatest "writing editors" of the old school'.

Sir Harold Hartley spoke to me of a speech by 'Uncle Teddy' as 'a brilliant and most polished performance, so ready'. He was impressed by Cook's 'system and efficiency'. It explains 'his immense output and great economy of effort. Everything tidied up as he went along, no loose ends, and nothing escaped his eye. If only he had lived to write more Lives like his *Florence Nightingale*! You will remember that Lytton Strachey in *Eminent Victorians* quotes it as perfection. He got all his material from E.T.C. He picks a phrase here, a phrase there, puts them together and gets that over-emphasis which was the key to his technique.'

It was typical of Cook that, unlike so many people, he did not allow books to accumulate unnecessarily. Several times over I find notes in his diaries of a resolute weeding out. I asked Sir Harold what his recollection was of the number of books that finally stood on the shelves of Rose Cottage. He doubted whether there remained as many as three thousand. Lady Hartley has Cook's careful index of Ruskin's books which he began in 1883 before he entered upon the editing of the *Works*. I often wondered how in his leading articles and other writing he had always his Ruskin 'quotes' so pat, and this was the secret.

'COOKINE.' The author of a trenchant book, *The Free and Independent*, Mr. Hartley Kemball Cook, a nephew, told me that in his early *Saturday Review* and *Observer* days, he did get matter into the *Pall Mall* and *Westminster*, but his uncle had 'a morbid hatred of nepotism; all the advice I had from him was, "If you want to write, write you will. Study the papers." ' After a visit to Rose Cottage he remembered a family saying that 'when one had been with Uncle Teddy one reflected that one had done most of the talking and he had contributed either H'ms or Um'. 'He was not a forthcoming man and did not invite confidences. Perhaps he was at heart sentimental and so armed himself against sentiment. In the years that followed his wife's death I should doubt whether even his sisters or any of the Bairds penetrated deeply into his thoughts. Neither in Saxon Mills's book nor in Spender's appreciation in the *D.N.B.* did the writers get far beneath the surface. In my own branch of the family we had a word, "Cookine", for a cold and cynical outlook. As so many people have said, he was naturally shy, and life increased the tendency to shut himself up. Not really a very complex character, perhaps, but certainly no "mixer", and half priding himself on that, but secretly wishing that he was a "mixer" and despising himself for the wish.'

When Mr. Laurence Irving looked in on me he dwelt on the difficulty of picturing Cook's 'unworldliness, immense principle and marked *amour propre*', and that 'combination of adventurousness and extreme sedateness' seen on his holidays. When Cook and his brother, the Winchester master—they were much alike and greatly attached to one another—took out a boat from Rose Cottage there were collars and ties beneath both their jerseys. Something of Cook's rather old-fashioned formality may be illustrated by the fact, Mr. Irving thought, that he was probably one of the last people to provide a glass of sherry after a funeral. An example of Cook's inability to cope easily with some of the problems of life was when he failed to anticipate that there would be a crowd outside his house in Tavistock Square on the occasion of his sister-in-law, 'Trilby's' marriage. When the house was quite full and still beset, he wrote on a card for the front door: 'No further admittance', but failed to realise that as he had put the instruction on the back of one of the cards of invitation it would be reversed and bring in more admirers. The writing of the Ruskin tomes was done on a desk on which there was a reel of red tape in 'a room entirely Morris and de Morgan'.

DEATH OF MRS. COOK. Although so many people thought

Cook was an unemotional man, we have seen that he was full of emotion. His lifelong delight in fine scenery and in Ruskin; the domestic passages in the letters to Lady Hartley and his expressions to herself as a girl; the photographs I have seen of his gambolling with children—I think of one in which he is walking with a child on his shoulders; his attachment to Stead (which caused him to be blackballed at the Athenaeum)[1] and to Rosebery, Milner and Garrett; the distress he felt for years when he thought of his dead wife—there can be no doubt as to his emotional endowment. But he disliked the display of emotion and esteemed reticence.

The death of his warm-hearted and extremely able wife in 1903, the year in which the stately Ruskin came out, stunned him. Two passages in his diary show his mind and heart. The first is: 'To-day walked my usual round to Mongewell—very sunny and frosty. Sun went down on Streatley Hill as I came back. Full moon opposition. When the fire of love and gold of happiness die, there rises the cold orb of duty, with some faint rosy streaks around it from the sunken sun'. The second passage quotes 'But with the soul's December' and adds, 'How often we said or read the poem together!'[2]

MORLEY AND COOK ON JOURNALISM. His knighthood came in the summer of 1912, the K.B.E. five years afterwards. At the dinner given to him on his retirement, John Morley, who was in the chair, said he had 'dignified public discussion and brought into coarse affairs the spirit of cultivation and refinement; while he argues sincerely and firmly from his point of view, he does perfect justice to the arguments of other people'. He had shown untiring industry and perfect modesty. 'There are the men', Morley went on, 'who have a natural pleasure in wrath, and there are also the trim swordsmen. The worst of journalism is that it is so precarious and insecure. Journalism is a great profession in many ways or the greatest—excepting the profession of the Cabinet Minister!'

[1] This was shortly after 'The Maiden Tribute'. In 1916 there was no difficulty about the election of a man who might almost be said to have been made for the Athenaeum. He appreciated the fact that he was elected under Rule II.

[2] Mrs. Cook's *London and Environs* had 'chapters on the British Museum, the National Gallery and South Kensington by E.T.C.' The following paragraph about Westminster Abbey is an example of Mrs. Cook's non-guide-book-y style: 'It is perhaps not unnatural that the vergers should feel a certain satiety and that they should wish to hurry a visitor through the Chapels as quickly and perfunctorily as may be. In an unwashed and noisy crowd, which seems to imagine that the Tombs of the Kings are a species of wax-works, who can think, or enjoy, or remember? Moreover, when one is, so to speak, "in custody" one must always be very careful to do nothing which may draw down on oneself the suspicion of the custodian. For who does not remember the verger either in the Abbey or some other fane who found a visitor kneeling before an altar tomb. Reprimanded by the verger he urged that he was "only praying". "Oh," the verger said severely, "that can't be allowed. We can't let people pray about wherever they like: that would never do." '

Cook, in his reply, referred to his early contributions to *Truth* under Voules, whose advice he asked. The advice was 'There is only one golden rule: give it 'em straight'. He endeavoured to provide Voules with what he wanted and the first gentleman to whom he gave it underwent a period of enforced seclusion. He had edited three different papers in London, and he missed familiar faces. One was he whom they knew as 'dear old Stead'. Another was his dear friend, Edmund Garrett. The journalist was the middle-man between the expert and the complete ignoramus. The journalist was more or less evanescent, but he had opportunities for striking a blow for a cause in which he greatly believed, or at any rate of endeavouring to form and not merely to follow public opinion.

Milner also spoke. He said Cook's work had been done in so unobtrusive a manner that he had nothing like his meed of public appreciation.

Cook, in a letter to Mrs. Carruthers about the dinner, writes: 'Yes I did feel a little proud at such evidence of goodwill and esteem. "If I could have said all that was in my mind I could never have said it." The speech, I was relieved to find, did not fall flat at all, I think, even after Lord Morley's charming discourse. But really, what about my "modesty"? It was a gratification that the funeral feast held over me as a journalist should have shaped itself into a kind of celebration of the better aspects of journalism. But this is too much about myself.'

THE LAST BOOK AND LAST DAYS. Cook worked at *The Press in War Time* with difficulty and Sir Frank Swettenham had to finish it. The entries in the diary get briefer and briefer, and they are in smaller handwriting. I have had to use a magnifying glass, for the lines are sometimes half a dozen to the inch. Plainly, his health was not what it had been. There is an entry about 'brainfag symptoms and having a nurse'. A year before his death he had a stroke. On September 30, 1919, he died suddenly at his Rose Cottage, a true Rose Cottage with 'lovely roses'. He had had pleurisy and died during a third attack of pneumonia. He was only sixty-five.

No tribute pictured him more truly than H. A. L. Fisher's, 'For sheer unostentatious competence upon a very high level he had few equals in this country, and there was never a life more worthily or completely filled'. His career showed the energetic publicist and man of letters, the active social reformer and politician and the life-long student of art subsisting reasonably together. Outstanding among his fellows and constant in good works, blameless in his private life and loving to children, a man of 'quiet dignity and gentle bearing' controverted Froude's silly saying that the intellectual man does no fighting.

CHAPTER XXXIII

ENTER A 'SOUL' AND A MILLIONAIRE

'BY TRUEFITT OUT OF MADAME TUSSAUD.' What had been happening all this time to the old *Pall Mall*, the begetter of the *St. James's Gazette* and the *Westminster Gazette*? When Cook walked out of Northumberland Street and Henry John Cockayne Cust walked in, the paper kept up its reputation for personality in its conductors. Morley, as man and editor, had been of a different pattern from Greenwood. Stead did not resemble Morley. Cook was in a category by himself. Cust was conspicuously in contrast with all four.

For most of the facts of his editorship I have before me letters and papers which Mrs. Cust has kindly let me see. Some things about him I find in various books, chiefly in an able and inviting volume which, originally published in 1937, was reprinted thrice and then republished in a definitive edition in 1943. That it is no ordinary book may be judged from the fact that once, in mid-Atlantic, I saw an irate reader of it hurry up on deck and, with bad language, fling his copy into the sea. The author is Sir Ronald Storrs, K.C.M.G., the man of whom, in *The Seven Pillars of Wisdom*, Lawrence says that 'he was always first and the great man among us'. Storrs was Cust's affectionate and understanding nephew. His book is *Orientations*,[1] and it is like him to give me leave to take from his Cust chapter anything I need.

Cust's grandfather was a kind of parson of which there are few nowadays, Hon. as well as Rev. He became a Canon of St. George's, Windsor. His wife was a connection of a peer who was twice smuggled out of a debtor's prison in a coffin. Their son, a Hussar Captain, agent of his cousin Lord Brownlow, married a friend of Elizabeth Barrett Browning, a woman whom the poet describes as 'one of the most graceful, elegant creatures of the age, charming, fascinating, good and intelligent, sympathetical besides'. Cust was her son and Storrs is her grandson.

THE 'SOULS'. At Eton, Cust (born Oct. 10, 1861), Captain of

[1] Nicholson & Watson, 1943.

the Oppidans, 'with the profile of a Greek coin', presented with
marked distinction a sword of honour to 'Bobs'—that is, the public
memory is so short, Lord Roberts of Kandahar. Arthur Benson,
who was acquainted with Rosebery, Curzon and Cust at Eton,
told Storrs that he had predicted that, of the three, Cust would
be Prime Minister. An 'Apostle' at Trinity, Cambridge, he was
later of the 'Souls', 'the rarest and most brilliant of us all'.[1] It is
related that Balfour, Curzon, Wilfrid Scawen Blunt and Cust once
played tennis naked before breakfast. As for his wit, asked to
describe a rather too-good-looking peer—but Cust was almost too
good-looking himself—he said, 'By Truefitt[2] out of Madame
Tussaud'. In one political crisis he declared that he had nailed his
colours to the fence. When in an election row an enormous man
was advancing on him, fists up, he flung off his coat, squared up
and whispered to friends behind, 'Hold me back, hold me back'.

[1] The Group nicknamed the 'Souls' is described in Haldane's *Autobiography*
(Hodder & Stoughton, 1929). 'They sometimes took themselves too seriously and
it is doubtful whether their influence was, on balance, good. But they cared for
literature and art, and their social gifts were so high that people sought much to
be admitted into their circle. Among the men were Lord Pembroke, George
Curzon, Harry Cust, George Wyndham and Alfred Lyttelton. Among the women
were Lady Ribblesdale, Margot Tennant (afterwards Mrs. Asquith), Lady
Elcho, Lady Desborough and Lady Horner [and Violet Rutland]. Week-end
parties were given at Panshanger, Ashridge, Wilton, and Taplow. Among the
hostesses were Lady Cowper, Lady Brownlow and Lady Pembroke, older but
attractive women who were gratefully but irreverently called the "Aunts". One
or two outside men were welcomed frequently. Among them were John Morley,
Sir Alfred Lyall, Asquith and myself. We were not 'Souls' but they liked our
company and we liked theirs' because of its brilliance.'
   Lord Balfour went so far as to say that 'no history of our time will be complete
unless the influence of the "Souls" upon society is accurately and dispassionately
recorded'.
   Lady Violet Bonham Carter, in a wireless talk, said that Lord Charles Beresford
invented the name and that Balfour was 'the Soul of Souls'. 'They all indulged
with passionate zest in talk, in discussion on every kind of subject—politics, religion,
literature, art, scholarship, human relations, last night's play, or last Sunday's
sermon. They were intellectually ambitious, they were adventurous, unconven-
tional, tolerant of everything except stupidity. Their aim, if indeed they had a
conscious aim, was to be a kind of Third Programme in terms of social intercourse.
At the tables and in the houses of the "Souls" everyone met. By their daring disregard of all barriers and taboos, they performed a great act of rescue work to
Victorian society. Thanks to them it was no longer smart to be exclusive, or
fashionable to be dull. Above all they revived the art of conversation, which in
Victorian days had fallen into a decline. Their rather intellectual and literary
after-dinner games were their peculiar pride. Of these games the two I heard
most about were "Clumps" and "Styles". Clumps is just a more ambitious
variant of "Twenty Questions", but instead of trying to guess concrete objects
like "the Roast Beef of Old England" or "Noah's Ark" the "Souls" struggled to
guess elusive abstractions such as "A Lost Cause", "A Contract" or an "Interval".
In "Styles" each player was given half-an-hour in which to compose a poem or a
piece of prose in the style of, say, Browning, Carlyle or Meredith.' There is a full
report in the *Listener* of Oct. 30, 1947. In the *Letters of Sir Walter Raleigh* it is
noted that Cust had a new game 'Boring the Bore'. 'He does it by flat, long,
interminable reminiscences of his childhood until even the bore screams.'

[2] The West End hairdresser.

At election times, a local paper records, he 'revelled in interruptions; his repartee and rapier thrusts dismayed, but his utterance was so rapid as to be the despair of all but the most experienced reporters'. When he stood for Bermondsey, voters were brought up on costers' barrows bearing placards: 'Benn[1] and Bunkum. Vote for Cust and the Costers.' At a later election he was defeated because of his inability, he declared, to 'dam the flowing lie'. At a meeting at which Asquith had been assaulted by suffragettes, Cust, as secretary of the golf club on whose ground the gathering was being held, told the women that, whatever their dispute with the Prime Minister might be, they could not be allowed to walk on the grass as it was against the club rules.

WILLIAM WALDORF ASTOR. When, as we have seen in Chapter XXII, the dull efforts of the representatives of the undeclared purchaser of the *Pall Mall* failed to retain E. T. Cook in the editorship, as had evidently been counted on, it was plain to us in the office that the investor was at a loss. He turned out to be an American millionaire, William Waldorf Astor, son of John Jacob Astor and father of the present Lord Astor. The man he first put in Cook's chair (for a few weeks), a namesake with an 'e', Kinloch Cooke, plainly lacked weight.[2] Then Astor happened to meet Cust at luncheon, and, taken by his conversation, asked him right off to edit the *Pall Mall*.[3] Cust's entry into journalism was as easy as that. The combination of a proprietor and an editor equally ignorant of newspaper work promised entertainment. Yates Thompson gave the paper two years.

We knew nothing of Astor but his riches. One of the many stories, true and untrue, told about him was that he had come to England and acquired citizenship here—he was to become Baron Astor of Hever Castle—because in New York he disliked hearing his wife distinguished as 'Mrs. W. W. Astor' instead of 'Mrs. Astor'.

CUST'S WAYS. Cust, we understood, was a remarkable person. He had been called to the French Bar because, he said, it was more difficult and 'more fun' than the English Bar. He had made at twenty-nine a speech in the House of Commons—his forebears had included not only M.P.s but a Speaker—which was described as 'dashing'. Further, he was heir to the barony of Brownlow and resources which, it was asserted, were 'worth a million and a half'. As for the M.P.-ship, Cook wrote: 'He is attempting to do two

---

[1] The late Sir J. Williams Benn.

[2] He was the author of a memoir of the Duchess of Teck which extended to 862 pages.

[3] Cust was not the only member of the staff who had been suddenly engaged. Mr. G. S. Hussey, of the Railway Executive, tells me that his father found himself as unexpectedly appointed advertising manager. Later he went to the *Daily Chronicle*, on the staff of which he died in 1914.

incompatible things, sit in the House and edit the *Pall Mall*. Mr.
Morley tried it in circumstances much more favourable and found
it impossible. Mr. Cust will have to choose. If he has any journalistic
instinct in him he will not hesitate a moment as to which course
to pursue'.[1]

I was a witness of Cust's début at the *Pall Mall* because, curious
about him and about the development of a paper with which I
had been so closely linked, I could not forbear lending a hand
until the *Westminster* started. Was not the *Pall Mall* making another of its trial trips and now determinedly going gay? And,
strangely enough, there was a look sometimes in Cust's handsome
face which often reminded one, of all men, of Stead. And after
three years of Cook's lymphatic handshake, it was like old times
to get from Cust a grip as cordial as Stead gave. In general appearance Cust did not, of course, look in the least like Stead. For one
thing Stead did not care what he wore. Cust was almost a dandy.
He is seen to the life in the *Vanity Fair* cartoon. An attractive
accessory was his dog, Lo Ben (called after Lobengula, the blood-
thirsty Matabele chieftain). Further, there was some promise of
political independence for the paper. In fact Cust soon got into
trouble •with his proprietor for backing the Progressives in the
London County Council elections. He was evidently no Party hack.
He was a debonair, witty, friendly fellow whom one could not help
liking. We never knew what he might not do. A tale by J. P. Collins
is of his giving a Government messenger £5 because he brought
some publication to the *Pall Mall* first, and of hearing later from
the hall porter that the man had said to him as he went out, 'The
Pall Mall was nearest, so why shouldn't I call there first?' After
the first edition (that is the 'second edition') had been got to press
the editorial writers, led by the editor, had been known to sing
'Now the labourer's task is o'er'.

I pick up a copy of the paper under Cust's hand. The leader,
on Turkey, in what had been a rather sedate newspaper, is flippantly
headed, 'The Voice of the Turkey'. Another day when the fate
of the Chinese statesman, Li Hung Chang, was in the news, it was
'Li Chang—Hung?' Once, when Mr. Diggle was concerned in a
School Board controversy, the public read 'To Diggle I am not
able; to Beggle I am ashamed'. When, in France, Casimir Perier's
career was in question the heading was 'Casimir Joué?' Another
day, more prankishly, the line ran, 'Can't Think of a Title'; on
yet another day, soberly, 'The Leading Article'. The Occ. Notes
are as merry. The Occ. Verses, not infrequently by the editor,
scintillate. Among the articles is one, easy to read and forcible, by
the first editor of the *Pall Mall*, Frederick Greenwood. A sympathetic

[1] Page 791.

contribution on life in East London is headed, 'They Also Serve Who Only Stand and Wait'. Cust's first contents bill was 'Read the New *Pall Mall Gazette*'. The *Westminster* replied with 'Read the Old *Westminster*'. Later in the day the *P.M.G.* tried again: 'Older, but less Aged'. On a day when all the other papers' contents bills had a murder on them the *Pall Mall* in derision gave up its bill to 'Art Notes. Special.'

H. G. WELLS, R.L.S., KIPLING AND HENLEY. A procession of distinguished writers began to arrive at the office, in person or by post, among them R.L.S., Kipling, H. G. Wells, W. E. Henley, Sir F. Pollock and G. W. Steevens, who was to become so wonderful a war correspondent. The first home article he had published in London was 'The Other Side of Barnum', in the *Speaker*. 'It was his endeavour', Sidney Low writes in the *D.N.B.*, 'to present with all possible vividness, frankness and terseness what he saw, thought and felt'. As assistant editor, Iwan-Müller was with Cust throughout his editorship.[1] Marriott Watson, Balfour's tutor at Oxford, was also doing editorials. One he wrote in Chaucerian English attracted the expected attention. It was Iwan-Müller whom H. G. Wells consulted about giving up teaching. The counsel he got was that, on the strength of the contributions he had had accepted in Northumberland Street, he could safely devote himself to literature. The irrepressible Lincoln Springfield—the kind of man who could write a book entitled *Some Piquant People*—and Charlie Hands, the most insouciant of pressmen, arrived as reporters from the *Star* and rivalled the editor in their freakishness. Springfield was impressed by the number of letters of introduction he was given by Cust to eminent persons signed 'Your affectionate cousin'. Nicol Dunn, later editor of the *Morning Post* for seven years, was news editor. There was also a girl reporter who described her sham attempts to be, in turn, a ballet girl, a nurse probationer, a Salvation Army lass, and a hired guest from Whiteley's, the Universal Provider.

Geoffrey West quotes H. G. Wells as saying, 'The *Pall Mall Gazette* has seen fit to appreciate the pleasant vices of my style and I have some enjoyable times writing foolishness'. *The Stolen Bacillus* was an early production and something new. Lewis Hind has this passage in his *Authors and I*,[2] telling us something not only about Wells and Hind but about the atmosphere of Cust's *Pall Mall*:

Cust, when he was not involved in a crisis, would encourage me to be amusing. One day I said to him, 'I want a new friend, please.' A few hours later an office boy came to my room (I was then editor of the *Pall Mall Budget*) and said, 'Mr. Cust's compliments and 'es got a new friend for yer, sir.' I hastened to Mr. Cust's apartment (it was more than a room)

[1] He went from the *Pall Mall* to the *Daily Telegraph*.   [2] Lane, 1921.

and there a little figure was hunched up on the magnificent maple couch. It was H. G. Wells. He smiled, I smiled. His overcoat was not Poole's, but his face was like an electrified note of interrogation, questioning and absorbing everything.

Those amazing tales, 'the jolly art of making something very bright and moving', to quote his own words, came into the office in copperplate handwriting with regularity. His unresting, exploring mind, so curious and combative, is very orderly; so are his habits, meticulously so. His imaginative schemes, like his housekeeping books, are tabulated with the precision of an accountant. He once showed me a fixture of pigeonholes in his study; these contained the manuscripts of his next three books, neatly typewritten by Mrs. Wells, each labelled with the year in which it was to appear.

Wells had a turn on the paper as dramatic critic. He was qualified by having seen *Romeo and Juliet* and *The Private Secretary* only.

'THE WARES OF AUTOLYCUS.' Of Mrs. Meynell's 'Wares of Autolycus', E. V. Lucas writes in *Reading, Writing, and Remembering*:[1] 'In the midst of the riot of news and comment, rumours and sensation, turmoil and restlessness that make up an evening paper, came this silver rivulet, cool, limpid, and peaceful. Mrs. Meynell wrote the calmest prose of any, with every word weighed in the balance.' 'Bread and wine to me in my benighted youth', said Walter de la Mare at the Alice Meynell Centenary Exhibition. 'In a few years,' Max Beerbohm would have it, 'Mrs. Meynell will be a sort of substitute for the English Sabbath'. The *Pall Mall* ran her for Poet Laureate. Katharine Tynan, Mrs. Hubert Bland (E. Nesbit), Mrs. Marriott Watson and Mrs. Joseph Pennell also contributed to 'Autolycus'. Katharine Tynan wrote, besides, articles and Occ. Verse. One year she had fifty poems in the 'brilliant and whimsical' paper. 'There was no stated rate of pay; Cust paid as he was moved to do.'

In succession to F. Carruthers Gould, G. R. Halkett was House of Commons cartoonist in a fashion of his own. When G. W. Steevens was sent to the Press Gallery he wrote of the number of bald heads among the legislators. After a row in the House in which there were fisticuffs, Cust interviewed the participants. Kennedy Jones's attempt to picture the new *Pall Mall* régime was 'Stead's methods, refined'. For news of Gladstone's impending retirement, over which Fleet Street's mouth watered, Cust is alleged to have paid a servant £500. When the paper got to press, it is recorded somewhere that he would sometimes adjourn to a restaurant with such bright spirits as Aubrey Beardsley, George Wyndham, W. E. Henley, Will Rothenstein, Beerbohm Tree, George Alexander, and Lord Frederic Hamilton. Or one day he

[1] Methuen, 1932.

might lunch at Downing Street with Asquith, Kitchener, Balfour and Grey.

'THE SHAH OF SHAHS OF SUBLIME GLORY.' He is at Constantinople after the Armenian atrocities, writing, ever so vivaciously, articles headed and afterwards republished as *The Shadow of God and the 'P.M.G.'* In the most agreeable humour they rake fore and aft 'the Shah of Shahs of Sublime Glory and Eminently Majestic and several kinds of Pasha', a title neither claimed nor applied to the Sultans but reflecting Cust's genial interpretation and exaggeration of the environment in which he found himself. All did not go swimmingly, however, on this adventure. Iwan-Müller got into sore trouble. 'You have probably ruined everything mentioning me', wires his chief. 'Exceedingly vexed disappointed pray minimise everywhere if necessary disown telegram was purely private'. At a later date when in the *Westminster* William Watson was apostrophising the Sultan as 'Abdul the Damned', a rhyme of Cust's began:

> Dear Mr. Watson we have read with wonder
> Not altogether unmingled with regret
> The little penny blast of purple thunder
> You published in the *Westminster Gazette*.
> The editor describes it as a Sonnet,
> We wish to make a few remarks upon it.

I come on the MS. of the lovely verses of R. L. Stevenson's which were published in the *Pall Mall*:

> In the highlands, in the country places
> Where the old plain men have rosy faces
> And the young fair maidens quiet eyes.

'Maidens' is pencilled in instead of 'lassies'. The *Pall Mall* had also the familiar verses ending

> Hear above the graves of the martyrs the peewees crying
> And hear no more at all.

CUST WHEN THE HOUSE WAS ON FIRE. In *Years of Endeavour* by Sir George Leveson-Gower, from which I have already quoted,[1] there is this story:

Among the guests at a dinner given by Harry Cust in his house at Delahaye Street were Balfour, Alfred Lyttelton, F. E. Smith (afterwards Lord Birkenhead), Winston Churchill, H. G. Wells, myself and a few prominent Liberals. In the middle of dinner a servant announced: 'If you please, sir, the house is on fire.' 'We have not finished dinner,' remarked our imperturbable host, 'bring in the next course, and ring up the fire brigade.' When the brigade arrived they not unnaturally suggested that we should depart. 'What!' said Harry, 'send my guests away before

[1] Murray, 1942.

dinner is over! I never heard of such a thing! You get on with your job and we'll get on with ours. It's quite safe, we're on the ground floor, with a window opening on to the terrace.' Reluctantly the firemen withdrew and proceeded to cope with the flames. Soon the effect of their activities was disclosed by trickles from the ceiling which gradually increased in number and in size. Presently an enormous discharge of dirty water descended upon me, to Churchill's intense delight. I was soon revenged by an even larger and dirtier downpour upon his head. 'This is getting intolerable!' cried Harry, who rang the bell and ordered 'Foot baths and bath towels.' The foot baths were placed to catch the heaviest cascades, and the company continued their dinner swathed in bath towels.

The scene is reproduced by H. G. Wells in *The New Machiavelli*.

CHAPTER XXXIV

AN EDITOR'S LETTERS

AUTHORS' ASIDES. It is not always the most interesting Letters to the Editor that get published. Here is a Chapter of letters received by Cust.

Andrew Lang is willing to review more than one author but not Coventry Patmore. Leslie Stephen, 'more at liberty than I have been since my bondage to the *D.N.B.*', 'may earn a few pence at my old trade of journalism'. Archibald Forbes, the war correspondent, wants to write on salmon fishing.

Whistler seeks 'a pretty place in the paper' for a letter of the period about du Maurier, stating that ''tis a long stair that has no turning'. He, of all men, complains of 'madness for repartee'. He goes on: ' "I could not call myself his friend for thirty years past", says du Maurier, "and egad! now that you come to look at it, neither do I. We were intimate in the old days, but that is all." Exactly, and 'tis the deuce of it. That's what's the matter with Hannah.' A second note of Whistler's is about a lawsuit over the *Indiscretions of a Baronet*, with gossip about his opponent, Eden, and about George Moore. As for Moore he writes: 'I will try to please you by pursuing him no more. But he is utterly weak and unreliable, if not unscrupulous.' Whistler is pleased by an invitation of Cust's to meet 'two nice ladies'. From Paris comes a note: 'I was very much touched by your nice kind letter.' He adds:

A word in your ear: you might perhaps help me a little. If it be at all possible on the plea of coarseness or, in short, if in your character as editor you can keep out of the *Pall Mall* further gross and foolish attacks of the nature of the last I should really be grateful. For I am not at all now in the gayest of humours and I am greatly driven—not a moment to lose and I have other anxieties.

How far away it all seems!

Kipling wants to be sure of a proof of a contribution thirteen stanzas long; 'the editor saved space by omitting three.' Another piece, of a column and a half, the author has corrected beautifully. On a later occasion he regrets that, as he has a book going to press, 'my time is not my own, so I am unable to give you any.'

There are three letters from George Meredith. One asks for help for 'one of the women of activity'. She wants to establish county council scholarships for cooks, 'so making a further advance to civilize the country'. A second note bids Cust behold 'a harnessed fast-trotting donkey on my way to two markets—the *Pall Mall Magazine* and *Scribner's*. If I sing, imagine the sound, and if I turn aside to pasture see the gallop I go with the blows on my back.' He proposes as 'a bridge of peace at Box Hill, you, Haldane, Asquith, and F. Pollock, also your Bard, A. Austin—good at the table I should fancy!' The *Pall Mall* he finds 'generally very good'.

The Duke of Norfolk sends ten pages of particulars about a Pilgrimage to Rome from England.

WILDE, SWINBURNE AND HERBERT SPENCER. Oscar Wilde wants to contradict 'in the most emphatic manner, the suggestion that I am the author of *The Green Carnation*. I invented the magnificent flower, but with the middleclass and mediocre book that usurps its strangely beautiful name I have, I need hardly say, nothing whatever do to. The Flower is a work of art, the book is not.'

Swinburne, in rather schoolboyish handwriting, lets himself go about being 'accosted, without any sort of introduction, and solicited for some sort of contribution to the *Pall Mall*. The decision with which your proposal was declined would appear to mislead you as to the decision with which it was rejected.' He will not have his name connected with a paper which has printed an article, 'Mr. Theodore Watts as Critic?'

The Marquis of Lorne is among Cust's contributors on the basis of his Canadian Viceregal experience. His tall upright signature was surely the very thing for a Governor-General. W. E. H. Lecky, in one of several letters, gives three-quarters of a page to expressing his annoyance at being dubbed 'Professor'.

There is a batch of letters from Huxley. His working power 'requires economical expenditure'. He deals, however, with approval, with Pearson's *National Life and Character*. *Mesmerism* he knows too much about 'to touch with tongs'; *Esoteric Buddhism* he will 'return with all speed', but he proposes a couple of columns on Caird's *Evolution of Religion*. On a proposal to review Herbert Spencer: 'I put it to you as a fair-minded editor whether, fifteen centuries ago, you could have asked Arius to review Athanasius, or vice versa. There is nothing in common between our opinions, outside the belief in the fact of Evolution, and in respect of the foundations of ethical and political science we have long been utterly opposed'. To a request to Spencer himself to contribute there came his well-known lithographed circular of reproach. On the front he has dictated a note in which he says, 'You may judge of my condition from the fact that I have been able to write only 30 pages of print since 1st January.' It was then the fourteenth of March.

Many eminent persons, including Lord Acton, W. S. Lilly, Tyndall, Froude, Justin McCarthy, Admiral Mahan, Lord Wolseley, Walter Pater and James Bryce, intimate their inability to undertake reviewing. Acton, in a beautiful fine hand, says of 'bloated volumes sent to him, there is no scholarly person who could be pleased with them'. Tyndall reports that he has not even felt equal to writing a commemorative note on a friend with whom he had 'a bond of affection of forty-two years' standing'. Pater will do a Dante article. Goldwin Smith, whose temporary address is 'care of Judge Thomas Hughes', author of *Tom Brown's Schooldays*, reminds Cust that Lord Salisbury and he, who were originally together on the *Saturday Review*, 'meet again after many years as contributors to the *Pall Mall*'.

That amiable Liberal gossip, G. W. E. Russell, answers an invitation to dinner: 'It is rash of you not to keep the wolf from the door; but will have pleasure in consuming your substance and flirting with your Lioness'. H. M. Stanley is obliged for 'a generous cheque'. Stepniak wants to call, on the introduction of W. E. Henley.

Arthur Symons says he instructed his solicitor to ask for an apology for the *Pall Mall* review of his verses, *London Nights*, but he finds he has issued a writ, and 'I have no money whatever, and no matter how confident I may feel in the strength of my case I cannot possibly match Mr. Astor's wealth.'

J. L. Toole sends two guineas for some fund. J. M. Barrie is at Fowey, 'because one must be somewhere.' A letter from W. B. Richmond is addressed to 'My dear Cust and his charming wife'. Cunninghame Graham has two engagements or—the rest, as usual, is illegible. Rhoda Broughton's three notes to 'Dear Harry' are almost as difficult to read. Henry James writes of his Ibsen copy, 'God grant it be of about the proper length, for it hangs pretty damnably together'.

MORLEY, MILNER AND DR. W. G. GRACE. Mention has been made of contributions by Frederick Greenwood. Morley, his successor as editor of the *Pall Mall*, says: 'Your proposed feast has a ghostly feel about it and "in a little filthy room" too! Invite me to dine with you in some other circumstances. *Haec non meminisse juvet.*' He is 'your very cordial and obliged well-wisher'. Had he asked him to a meal at the *Pall Mall* office? A telegram on an earlier date from Margot Asquith invites Cust to lunch, for 'John Morley wishes to meet you'. Stead writes good-naturedly about an imputation that he is 'a filthy-minded swine'.

Three letters from 'The Board Room, Inland Revenue', also bring back the *Pall Mall* past. In the first, Milner is downright on money matters—Cust could be hard up. 'I suppose you are like

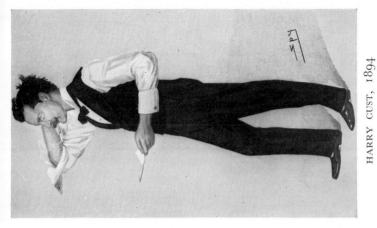

SIR EDWARD COOK, 1899

HARRY CUST, 1894

From the cartoons by 'Spy' in *Vanity Fair*

Stead and want to go to Holloway. Heaven forbid that I should stand in the way. I will only say that, as it is so easy to go to prison by breaking the law in various directions, I think it would have been nicer of you to choose some other Department to collide with, and some other official to make your executioner than me, an old friend. However, it is just possible that you may not be aware that you owe upwards of £40 Income Tax (for the year before last), that we have exhausted every conceivable method of persuasion without the smallest result, and that, as in the immediate future arrears of equal amount for last year will be included in our "schedule of defaults", we must either seize your goods or your person at an early date. It will bore me horribly and so perhaps on reflection you will let me off.'[1] At an earlier date (1894) Milner had sent twenty pages of urgent counsel on how to tackle an Egyptian crisis.

Cust was a cricketer, and I come on a two-feet long, foot-and-a-half wide questionnaire put in type by the *Pall Mall* printer for the elderly Dr. W. G. Grace and carefully filled up by that mighty performer. 'On good wickets he finds no difference' between half a dozen of the best bowlers whose names are mentioned. What kind of bowler does he prefer? 'I used to prefer fast, but now I am growing old, my muscles do not act quickly'. 'And', he adds, 'as it is midnight I must bid you good-bye'.

Lincoln Springfield has been to Lord Roberts to ask him for stories on returning to England after having spent only eighteen months at home out of twenty-seven years' service. The General remembered Cust's boyhood presentation of the sword of honour 'but adventures I have none to relate'. He offered his congratulations, however, 'on being the editor of such an important paper' and a week or two later there was an invitation to lunch 'with Lady Roberts and me'.

'MY DEAR OLD HARRY.' Curzon asks 'My dear old Harry' to accept his 'dearest thanks' for 'a lovely silver seal' he has brought him, evidently from Turkey. Sarah Bernhardt—is it generally known, as I learnt in my twenties in Holland, that she was a Dutchwoman?—makes an appointment.

Writing to the Duke of Rutland at the start of Cust's term in Northumberland Street, Lord Salisbury had pronounced the *Pall Mall* to be 'very well done', but, he added, 'it will be hard work to

---

[1] When Milner went from the *Pall Mall* to the Chancellor of the Exchequer, Goschen, he was described as 'tall, dignified, aloof and old beyond his years'. Such were Milner's abilities that Goschen treated him as a colleague and one notices that, later, Milner, in talking to Lady Goschen about her husband, spoke of 'George'. It was said that Goschen 'would be remembered because Milner had been his secretary'. When Milner went to Somerset House he spoke of men sent him from Whitehall who were 'labelled experienced but had fossil written on the other side'.

conduct an evening paper and to represent Stamford in Parliament at the same time'. Light on the political position taken up by the paper is afforded in a letter from Lord Salisbury in which, in replying to an invitation to contribute, the Conservative leader combines the attitude of an old journalist and party chief. 'Your independent position, which you are very wise to have adopted and to maintain firmly, makes it very difficult for me to enlist myself in your goodly fellowship of prophets. I have already declined an analogous proposal from one of the Conservative party organs and I should get into great disgrace if afterwards I appeared in your columns.' Eventually, however, he does send fourteen carefully corrected foolscap sheets. They had been preceded by a letter in which he said that he had earlier written 2,000 or 3,000 words, but 'it made me sick to read it and I tore it up'. A letter from Lady Salisbury, on notepaper which has the letters of the address curiously decorated, conveys an invitation 'for a few days to shoot'.

'Dear Harry' or 'My dear Harry' has a sheaf of letters from Balfour. A jocular note asks for the Party to be allowed to republish something or other without attribution to the *Pall Mall*. 'Their point of view is that the *Pall Mall* is a journal so discredited in public estimation that, on the rare occasions on which it produces anything good, the value of the said product would be wholly destroyed in the eyes of a discriminating public if any suspicion of its origin were permitted to get abroad. Are you prepared to sacrifice your petty vanities as an editor on the altar of patriotism?' But Balfour adds to his typed letter, 'Don't bother to answer'.

When Cust is no longer an M.P. a Balfour letter says that 'Middleton has not a single uncontested seat it would be worth your while to look at'; with the addition, 'I hope it may not be beyond the bounds of diplomacy to persuade A. [Astor of course] that it is not the end of the world if his Editor happens for a short while to be out of the House!' Another note asks Cust to a small dinner and adds 'I have asked Astor'.

One Balfour letter is about an article he has written. 'I have no doubt', he says, 'that it stands in dire need of minute revision. *You* may correct it if you like.' Reference has been made to the help Cust gave the Progressives in the London County Council election. Balfour writes: 'As you know, I do not read your degraded print. But it is worth your while thinking whether you are not violating the canon of policy laid down by Lord Salisbury, viz, that a Party paper should never show its independence (valuable as that quality may be) by hitting its own side in the crisis of any struggle the issue of which is doubtful and important.' Balfour sportingly adds that he hopes he has stopped any remonstrance going to Astor.

The Duke of Devonshire says he has never written anything for a newspaper, is afraid he would make a hash of it and that anyhow he has not the least idea of the length of an article of 4,000 words.

'A MOST FOOLISH PARAGRAPH'. Lord Randolph Churchill, in shaky handwriting—it is towards the end of his life—is aggressive: 'Sir', he writes, 'I shall be obliged if you will explain to me the meaning of this paragraph from this afternoon's *Pall Mall*':

Lord Randolph Churchill was at the Criterion Theatre last night and afterwards went behind the scenes. It was curious to observe a former Leader of the House, whose resignation made some stir, watching a representation of a not dissimilar course of events.

Two months afterwards Lord Randolph is invited to contribute something and says he won't. 'I look upon writing articles', he says, 'as a work of supererogation for a fairly busy member of Parliament. I want all my ideas for my speeches, which at any rate are more my *métier* than articles for which I never had qualification or training.' Six months later—the year is 1893—he is almost peevish:

Sir,—I draw your attention to a most foolish paragraph about myself, 'Lord Randolph has undertaken to write a pamphlet on the House of Lords.' You could not have used a more ridiculous word than 'pamphlet'. And there is no one outside the editorial circle of the *Pall Mall* who would use such a word. You make me look ridiculous. For this amiability I thank you. Who in his senses would write a pamphlet if he wanted circulation among the masses?

He says that, in response to a request of 'most active political heads', he is writing a 'leaflet' that occupies '$3\frac{1}{2}$ pages out of 4, printed in clear type. The Primrose League and National Union buy thousands for a very small expenditure, of not more than $\frac{1}{4}$ of a penny for each copy, and the circulation will be very large.' 'After this', the letter concludes, 'you will probably understand the difference between a "pamphlet" below which your high gifts could not descend and a little leaflet'. But the letter is of Lord Randolph's last days when he was not at his best.

'Your very faithful and obedient' W. E. Gladstone, writing from Biarritz, contrives to get ten lines on a post-card with half the card to spare, but time has made it difficult to make out what he says.

CUST TO HIS WIFE. One of the things Cust put his heart into was the *Pall Mall* Christmas tree for 4,000 East End children. One tree, from the family estate of Belton, was 50 feet high. He tells his future wife that he has also 'plunged for Penny Dinners' and is 'giving 800 a day' from funds supplied by readers. As for the paper—he is writing on New Year's Eve, 1892—he is full of the new offices, for dowdy, inconvenient Northumberland Street was to be abandoned for a new building in Charing Cross Road. 'I've no time or energy for any dash till the new presses, premises and staff are settled. It means never less than 12 hours a day and I'm rather run down. I shall try for a week's holiday before Parliament. I've seen nobody and read nothing, merely grubbed. I grieve that your father should grieve over my politics; but I think they're consistent with themselves, tho' not with those of either Party, and I believe other people will think more in accord with them before two years are over. Point out to Sir W. that they are also self-defensive politics.' Sir William Welby-Gregory was himself considered rather too 'progressive' by the real die-hards.

Mrs. Cust mentioned to me that she was never in the new *Pall Mall* office or the old. 'My husband', she wrote, 'was strongly averse to female influence in the office, and my only contact with its various members was in occasional hospitality at our house. I did a certain amount of reviewing but (as Editor's wife) received no pay.' Here I have a chance of mentioning a reminiscence of Mrs. Cust in one of Mrs. Courtney's notes to me: 'I knew her as a girl of great beauty and mystical charm. Her gift of silence and her green, unfathomable eyes set her apart in any society.'

'TO SHOW YOU MY DESPISE AGAINST YOU.' Cust kept some of the abusive letters he got. A Czech writes devastatingly: 'With trembling lips and shaky hand promising revenge, I take pen in order to show you my despise against you. Your opinion about Sergius Stepniak excited me on the highest degree and if I should say truth I must confess that I cried bitterly while I was reading that paragraph. I would kindly advise you to refuse your function of editorship and to accept some more suitable of which you are capable: to deliver coals, to sweep streets. Please take notice of this for it is very important for your future life and take example from a young man of 18 who cannot stand it.'

Looking on at such of Cust's editorial adventures as they read of in the *Pall Mall* or heard about, his associates of the Crabbet Club professed to be concerned at his 'cheating Fleet Street at its own games'. One of the Club rules was that anyone becoming a Minister or a Bishop ceased to be a member.

'THE SUSSEX BELLE.' Mr. J. B. Atkins, so long associated with the *Spectator* and *Manchester Guardian* and for a time editor of the now deceased ecclesiastical *Guardian*, began his journalistic career with an account in the *Pall Mall* of a collision at sea with a vessel on which he was a passenger. Feeling it to be 'a kind of public duty to send any odd bits of information to a biographer', he writes to me of an agreeable association with Cust whom he speaks of as 'a meteor in journalism, a brilliant but passing phenomenon'. 'He often spent a weekend of leisure at a wayside house called "The Sussex Belle", not far beyond Haslemere. It was an old inn turned into a private dwellinghouse. He was one of a small group who rented the house for holidays. Two others in the group were Leonard Whibley (Fellow of Pembroke College, Cambridge) and Iwan-Müller. I also remember there Charles Whibley (L.W's elder brother) and Charles Furse, the painter, who painted a charmingly fanciful portrait of "The Sussex Belle" which he said was to be the sign of the inn, though an inn no longer. There was a good cook there; she was the wife of a handyman, and together they ran the house and garden for the group. Cust used to insist on the cook coming into the dining room after dinner to be complimented on the meal. The name of the couple was Yeoman. Cust was delighted with this name and always called the couple the Yeomanry. He also drew out the horse-sense and rustic wit of Mrs. Yeoman whose personality delighted him. She might have been a clown or fool in a Tudor household, for she was more than equal to every encounter. Yeoman himself was without words and could never be enticed into giving us any sort of entertainment.

'I remember a talk at "The Sussex Belle" about articles in the *P.M.G.* With regard to headlines, Cust was fond of Latin for this purpose, disregarding the convention of the popular press that everything should be intelligible to the majority of readers. I remember in particular a heading for an article on riots in Constantinople—a nice hexameter, *Perturbabantur Constantinopolitani.* When he had many differences with the proprietor and was about to resign, he suggested that the heading of his last leading article should be *Quis Custodiat*? But this was fun; if it had been proposed seriously he would have shrunk from the vulgarity.'

Mr. John Connell, whose book about W. E. Henley is so serviceable, once said to me, 'Of all the people who knew and liked Henley I found Cust the most elusive'. His 'kindnesses to Henley and his wife were', as he adds, 'countless'. Mr. Connell records that, when Henley was afflicted by the death of his child, Cust 'provided a burial ground at Cockayne Hartley, a place which had belonged to the Custs for centuries'.

CHAPTER XXXV

PROPRIETOR AND EDITOR, A COMEDY

'INSTRUCTIONS AND DIRECTIONS' TO AN EDITOR. As we have seen, Cust knew nothing of journalism until, as editor of the *Pall Mall*, he picked up a few notions about it. If he had known anything he would never have signed the agreement which lies before me. The document calmly stipulates, as if it were providing for the starting of a coffee stall, that the Able Editor 'shall at all times be bound by *any instructions and directions* which may be given him by the proprietor, whose rights of *controlling the policy*[1] and management of the paper are hereby acknowledged'. (The agreement was for a year, from Nov. 12, 1892, with six months' notice afterwards, the salary £1,500, and £13,000 was put in the bank in Cust's name.)

To be sure, Cust, something of a flibbertigibbet, tried it on very soon. Two men who knew him well told me, one that the editorship was 'a Gilbert and Sullivan affair', the other that 'one's sympathies must be slightly with the vain old proprietor'. Astor was not without humour, as witness this card of Dec. 16, dated 7.15 a.m.: 'Dear Mr. Cust, I have decided to adopt your good suggestion that I should call "any morning at 7.30" at the *Gazette* office and see the busy morning's work commenced at that early hour. I intend to arrive then at 7.45 and shall wait ten minutes to see whoever is in charge. If no one of the staff can be found at 7.55 I shall leave this note. You always get the better of me on so many points that it makes me merry to score now and then. Wishing you a pleasant Xmas holiday, believe me, sincerely yours, W. W. Astor.'

Cust is in trouble in the spring because of that support of the Progressives on the London County Council to which reference has been made. I have run through a memorandum which he sent to Astor. The material sentences are as follows: 'Before taking charge of the *Pall Mall Gazette*, I felt it only right to consult with Lord Salisbury and Mr. Balfour as to the effects which entering journalism in such a position would be likely, in their eyes, to have upon my political career. I explained to them that I could not be a mere Party hack but that, while adhering to the main principles of Conservatism, I should seek to retain the right of independent criticism and speak freely my mind even when adverse to themselves

---

[1] The italics are Astor's.

WILLIAM WALDORF ASTOR

From the portrait by Sir Hubert Herkomer in the possession of
Viscount Astor

as regards their conduct of affairs. They both entirely agreed with the line I had marked out and both observed that the support of such a newspaper, in times of political crises, would be infinitely more valuable because of its recognised independence in ordinary affairs. Such papers as the *St. James's Gazette* or the *Standard* are, as Mr. Balfour observed, of no earthly value to the party in the way of making opinion, as their criticisms are a foregone conclusion.' In a covering note Cust says meekly, 'In all my conversations with the Party leaders I have always represented myself merely as your editor'.

'PAID TO DO MY WORK.' When the summer comes there is commotion over what the *Pall Mall* has been saying about Arnold Morley (of Cook's *Daily News*). 'The nature of the attacks on me in the *Pall Mall* make it impossible for me', Morley wrote, 'to hold personal communication with Mr. Cust. As he thought fit to introduce your name into the matter as proprietor I forward you a copy of his letter.' Astor replies: 'I deeply regret that the newspaper of which I am proprietor should be used against one to whom I am indebted for acts of kindness, and I beg you to receive my assurance of the personal regret with which I shall always remember the matter.'

A month later Cust has a letter from Astor about the necessity for the editorial and managerial departments 'not encroaching on one another'. A reporter has been discharged and the proprietor asks that the editor will allow the manager 'to conduct the business part of such discharge'. Astor goes on to stipulate that the paper is 'not to be used for attacks such as the cordite, Harness belt, or London Hospital affairs'. Further, Cust is to understand that 'everyone employed in the *Pall Mall* building is paid by me to do my work'. Therefore Astor is 'at liberty to talk with entire freedom to anyone'.

It is known that Astor had literary ambitions and it has been understood that Cust seldom appreciated the value of his writing, even sent most of it back. The truth, I have been assured, is that he sent it all back—and there was a fair amount of it. Now comes this Astorial regulation: 'In future I shall expect that anything I send—provided it is not obscene or inciting to a breach of the peace—to be immediately printed in either the *Gazette* or the *Budget*[1] as I may indicate, and without the slightest alteration.'

Exactly what happened after that I have no documents to establish. But from now onwards the prayers of Cust's fellow Editors might well have been requested for him. That he brought not a few of his troubles on himself seems clear. At an odd time, however,

[1] A weekly edition, originally confined mainly to 'lifting' the most attractive things from the daily.

the proprietor could praise. On one number of the *Budget* his commendation is as extravagant as his demands have been:

> I have never seen, in any country, so excellent a weekly publication, so interesting and so well executed. The most super-critical—even a proprietor who I am told is the most vexatious creature that Providence allows to exist—could find no fault whatever.

> It is not difficult to recognise your hand in this, and I feel very proud and happy at the vast improvement which has been given to the *Budget* in the last three months. It has been a *tour de force* of a character that must give our rivals food for reflection and should show them that the pace, if they mean to keep in the race with us, will be a stiff one.

> I intend to co-operate with you very vigorously through my supervision of the Managerial department and it looks as if the year 1895 should open very auspiciously for us and that we may come within sight of the greatest journalistic success ever accomplished in this country.

And there was an occasion, in the Astor offices on the Embankment, when Astor said to Cust: 'Now, Mr. Cust, you are a man of unerring taste, I want you to tell me what is the matter with this room. I feel that there is something wrong but I can't quite make out what it is.' To this Cust made answer: 'Well that's easy enough to see. You've got a cedar wood room, with ebony furniture, looking like blobs of ink all over the floor'. 'Of course, of course,' said Astor; 'I was quite sure that you would at once spot the defect.'

The next year the London County Council issue is raised again. Astor makes no bones about the matter. 'Will you kindly oblige me', he writes, 'by placing the *Gazette* distinctly and unequivocably on the side of the Moderates, and in a position of such antagonism to the Progressives as will show beyond peradventure where we stand. Our delay has been mischievous.' It is a case, he says, for 'a few leaders in the right direction'.

'ON THE FINANCIAL LINE INDICATED.' Astor has sent messages from time to time by his solicitor, Adams of the fine office of 'The Estate of John Jacob Astor' on the Embankment, the Adams who, with Dove Keighley, tried falls unsuccessfully with E. T. Cook. Now Adams writes to Cust—and I notice that, even as late as the year of this letter, 1895, it is not typed but written in copying ink and put through a press:

> At your last interview with Mr. Astor you stated that you found it difficult, if not impossible, to conduct the *Pall Mall Gazette* with a due regard to economical considerations, in the absence of precise and constant information as to the financial condition of the paper. Mr. Astor has come to the conclusion that your complaint is well founded and that you ought to be given the opportunity you seek of acquainting yourself with the details

of receipts and expenditure. He has therefore authorised me to carry into execution a proposal that I have made to him that you and say, Iwan-Müller, [Assistant Editor] should meet Mr. Leslie [Manager from Stead's and Cook's time] and myself here regularly every month to receive the report of the Auditors upon the result of the trading and to take that report into consideration. In Mr. Astor's view the time has arrived when the paper should be made a commercial success and he desires that all those who are connected with its conduct and management shall combine together to achieve this object.

Writing in the summer of 1895 from Kissingen during the General Election, a rich ex-American instructs Cust on English politics:

Sir William Harcourt's defeat is the significant fact, and I beg you to lay great stress upon it editorially as a reflection largely due to his bad financial policy which the common sense of the country, irrespective of party, long since condemned. The death duties and estate duties and the fallacy of graduated taxation should receive the heaviest broadsides you can deliver. I shall be profoundly disappointed if you do not accede to my wish and seize on this opportunity to direct the *Gazette* upon the financial line I have thus generally indicated.

But Astor finds, alas, that 'the *Gazette* performance is extremely feeble and limited; it has in no way entered upon a discussion of the reason why estate duties and graduated taxes are bad; this I hope you will do'.

A sentence is added: 'Will you oblige me by printing verbatim the enclosed trifle as an Occasional Note?' If we had only Cust's reply or a sight of the Note!

The letter closes: 'Lady Henry Somerset. For personal reasons I ask you to give her a heavy broadside. I hope you will put some more gunpowder in your cartridges.' Poor Lady Henry! I was well acquainted with her. If ever there was a good-hearted woman, this well-known temperance advocate was one; and she had her own woes.

RESIGNATION IN A WEEK. Now we come to 1896. I have before me Cust's memorandum of a conversation with his proprietor on Feb. 1, following an ordinary business discussion. There have been many accounts of interviews between editors and proprietors, but these notes stand by themselves:

Astor. Do you know real reason of interview?

B. (Cust). No.

A. American crisis very severe, my position very delicate. Conduct of paper of great importance to me.

B. On first news I telegraphed to you for instructions. You answered maintain judicious attitude. I hoped for further instructions or interview. Has the paper gone wrong?

A. Not at all, perfectly satisfied; moderate and judicious, but acute crisis requires new editorial arrangements. You and Iwan-Müller must go, and in a week. Salary paid, of course, in lieu of notice.

B. Why?

A. Well in such case prefer dictated policy week by week and day by day.

B. Why the devil didn't you do so?

A. Knew no use.

B. Why?

A. You wouldn't have followed my wishes.

B. Did you express them?

A. No.

B. How could I follow them?

A. Take case of letter from Kissingen on Death Duties.

B. Didn't we follow it?

A. Not so much as I wished.

B. Did you ever say so?

A. No.

B. At first interview afterwards didn't I explain our plan of meeting your wishes and didn't you quite agree?

A. Yes.

B. Then what's the trouble?

A. Take old case of library.

B. What's the matter with that?

A. Well, whatever I wish is never done.

B. Give an instance.

A. I've done so. You've always shown me that what I want is wrong.

B. Oughtn't we to lay our views before you?

A. Certainly, but I can't do what I want.

B. Why do you never send for me to come to office as you used to?

A. No good.

B. Why? Have I ever refused to meet either you or your wishes?

A. I do not wish to enter into details.

B. I do. Hasn't the paper been a success, in circulation, advertisement and position?

A. The greatest. Heartily congratulate you.

B. Well,

A. Well?

B. Pig.

Following this cheery talk Cust and Iwan-Müller have letters from Adams requiring their resignations in a week. They both refuse to send them. Cust says to Astor, 'I have endeavoured to follow your instructions whenever you have communicated them, and have given the best of my life to make your paper a success'. Then Adams sends a formal notice, signed by Astor, with the statement that there will be a cheque in lieu of a notice. Cust desired time for a talk with Balfour and other friends, so he communicated with Astor, asking for a day's delay. He had the following reply:

I have received your letter of the 2nd inst. proposing a delay of another day before any action is taken with reference to the change I have decided upon in the editorship of the *Pall Mall Gazette*. I regret that I cannot comply with your suggestion.

Leaving wholly out of this discussion the ability with which you have edited the *Gazette*, I have always found you unwilling to carry out my wishes as to the course of the paper, which I told you at the outset I desired to control. My requests were either disregarded, or were met with reasons why they must be set aside.

One of our first differences related to the sneers and disparaging comments upon America which I told you were in bad taste and extremely offensive to me.

In December 1893 and again in March 1894 I spoke to you very plainly of my dissatisfaction at your habitual disregard of my instructions, but with little avail.

In July last I wrote to you my wish that the *Gazette* should lay stress upon the Harcourt Budget as having been an important cause of the Radical defeat, and this you wholly neglected to do.

We are suddenly confronted by a dangerous controversy between England and the United States in which I am deeply interested. I cannot any longer be responsible for the utterances of a paper over which I exercise only a nominal control.

'FEE-FO-FUM.' Cust, in the course of his chaffing of the United States, had headed one leader "Fee Fo Fum" and another 'Drink to me Olney with Thine Eyes'—Olney was the name of the Secretary of State. For one Anglo-American article Astor had asked that Iwan-Müller should be dismissed and Cust had refused.[1]

At the time of the sale of the *Pall Mall*, E. T. Cook and Yates Thompson had set forth in the *Standard* their views of the facts of their separation. Cust and Iwan-Müller acted in the same way by reproducing in *The Times* the correspondence I have somewhat abbreviated. Cust had a note from Mr. Buckle, editor of *The Times*: 'Your letter was so discreet that there could be no objection to its

---

[1] The following on the circumstances in which the American Colonies were lost is by Astor: 'George III and his advisers, being without any due understanding of the forces their repressive policy had called into being, were unable to appreciate the character and motives of the men who were guiding the Colonies. It will not be contested that the course of the King and his Ministers, based upon the principle of arbitrary taxation and aggravated by local intolerance, has never since been attempted towards any British Colony. The American provinces were not conquered dependencies, and the first resort to arms cemented the settlements from Massachusetts to the Carolinas in a single purpose. There is no chapter in her history from which Great Britain takes less credit than from the struggle commenced with every deficiency of statecraft, and conducted through seven long years with every want of generalship. What wonder if, in after years, brooding upon the calamity his reign had brought upon the Anglo-Saxon race in its violent disruption into two nations, King George's mind should have given way beneath the consciousness that to him personally, more than to any other single man, it was due that England had lost her greatest possession!' [See next page.]

publication. Are you going to follow the precedent of previous evicted *P.M.G.* editors and set up a new evening *Gazette*?

The notice in the *Pall Mall* followed so closely the lines of Greenwood's farewell that Cust must have looked it up:[1]

NOTICE

TO THE READERS OF THE *PALL MALL GAZETTE*

MR. HENRY CUST, who has had the Editorial Direction of the *Pall Mall Gazette* since October, 1892, will not be responsible for any opinions that may appear in its pages after to-day.

Private letters should be addressed to Mr. Cust at the Carlton Club, Pall Mall.

When it was all over, Cust wrote to a contributor, 'The catastrophe is disgusting but saved by humour'. Before his departure the editor and staff joined in singing 'Nunc Dimittis'! Cust had always had

Autograph of Waldorf Astor, proprietor of the 'Pall Mall'

jolly relations with his printers and the readers, and the 'chapel' gave him an illuminated address in particularly cordial terms— note the assertion in the last sentence:

We desire to express our deep sense of gratitude at the kind treatment we have always received from you. From the moment when you entered the composing room at the old office in Northumberland Street, and in the most frank and manly way asked us to treat you as a friend, we have always felt the respect and confidence due to a thorough English gentleman. At our social gatherings you have shown affability and courtesy. You have been in touch with us in a way that no other editor has been.

Henry Leslie, the manager, was a quiet, inoffensive little man who smoked no end of cigarettes; a bit of an enigma. On Cust's departure he let himself go in his cramped handwriting, with the only reference to Pendennis's *Pall Mall* I remember in all the *P.M.G.* correspondence I have read:

I never realised until Saturday how much you have entwined yourself in my affections. My Dutch courage at the last moment oozed out com-

[1] See page 237, *The Story of the 'Pall Mall Gazette'*.

pletely. I am not ashamed to admit my feelings got the mastery of me, and I could not trust myself to take an official farewell of you. To me the whole of this wretched business has been unutterably painful, and in my reflective moments today the only pleasing recollection has been the fact that you succeeded during the all-too-brief years of our comradeship in touching my affections. No period of the *Pall Mall Gazette* ever realised more closely Thackeray's conception than your brilliant editorship. It cannot be farewell where memory cherishes these thoughts.

Leslie is reported to have said of Cust that he was 'the best editor the *Pall Mall* ever had'.

It is of historical interest that in the offices behind the Alhambra (now occupied by Messrs. Pitman, the publishers) the *Pall Mall* was, I believe, the first London daily paper to have its machinery driven by electricity.

Stead had learnt, and told Cook, that in 1894 the advertisements of the paper doubled and that by the end of 1895 ends would have met. So that it was not for financial reasons but for general incompatibility and dissatisfaction, a conflict in political and personal views the natural waywardness of Cust, that, in February 1896, he was dismissed.

CHAPTER XXXVI

THE CURTAIN COMES DOWN

CURZON'S PRAISE OF CUST. Cust died on April 9, 1917, at the early age of fifty-five. He had caught a cold at a meeting in Wales at which he was speaking as chairman of the wartime Central Committee for National Patriotic Organisations. A reference to his work by Mr. Asquith in the House of Commons was made with feeling.

An appreciation contributed to *The Times* by Lord Curzon began 'But Oh the heavy change now thou art gone'. An end had come, he said, to the career of 'a gifted and lovable man that once seemed gilded with the brightest promise, and had already in some respects transcended the ordinary in accomplishment'. Cust 'created a stir wherever he moved and lit in others the vital spark which his own nature so easily generated. Gifted with an astonishing quickness of intellect, a genuine love of reading and scholarship, a rich vocabulary, a fastidious literary sense and a wonderful memory, he was the unchallenged leader of the dinner table. Quip, retort, repartee, quotation, allusion, epigram, jest—all flashed with lightning-like speed from that active workshop his brain. An almost amazing audacity winged the arrow as it flew to his mark. As editor of a great evening newspaper, political wisdom was garnished with the most piquant of sauces. His generous nature appealed equally to heart and brain, but fate ever seemed to be stalking him with uplifted dagger. Was it the accident of circumstance, or ill-health, or the weakness of some link in the chain of his moral and intellectual being, or the buffets of fortune by which, at some periods, his career was assailed, that were responsible for the impression of arrested movement that was acknowledged, even by himself? Those who loved him, and whom he loved, recognise that a daring and dynamic force, a unique and captivating personality, has passed into the unseen, and cherish a memory which will be both tender and lasting'. 'Intellectual sympathy and happiness', Curzon added, 'adorned a home which, in the subtle refinement of its decoration was a miniature country house set in the heart of London'.

Another tribute in *Blackwood*, was in 'Musings without Method'[1] by Charles Whibley, who, with Iwan-Müller, was Cust's literary executor. He quoted the testimony of 'this gay and gracious spoilt

[1] Originally contributed by Frederick Greenwood.

child of Eton and Cambridge' to what he owed to the late Lord
Burnham's advice at the beginning of his editorial career, to take
counsel with W. E. Henley whose *National Observer* was unquestionably in many ways the precursor of Cust's *P.M.G.* Cust said
he found in Henley 'a friend for life, a master of difficulty and
emergency, a wise, if somewhat strenuous mentor and counsellor'.
Whibley speaks of the 'natural hilarity' with which the *Pall Mall*
was conducted. The real medium of Cust's genius, he said, was
talk; a dinner table and a fit audience were necessary to him.
'Cust was the best talker of his day. He was, as all good talkers
must be, a full man, a reader deep and wide. Not merely was he
a classical scholar, he knew the modern literature of many tongues.
In his talk he never insisted; he never laboured his point; a chance
word, and he was off eagerly upon another quest. So long as
anyone is left who saw and spoke with him "his pleasant voices,
his nightingales, will still be awake".'

In the *Daily Telegraph* T. P. O'Connor described Cust as 'one of
the most brilliant and one of the most attractive men of his epoch;
very handsome, very distinguished, very well-read, also very
wayward, and destined by his waywardness to spoil what might
have been a great life and a brilliant career. After a little frivolity,
he was making the *Pall Mall* a full and attractive paper and getting
himself back on the rails of a regular and useful life after a stormy
period of youthful unrest and adventure.' The *Daily Telegraph*
itself declared that 'among the English personalities of the closing
years of the nineteenth century and the beginning of the present
there must always be found a place for Harry Cust'.

The editor of the *Pall Mall Magazine*, Lewis Hind, remembered
the 'sunny, amused smile, wonderful laugh, companionable air,
easy gait of perhaps the most remarkable, the most fortunate and
the most charming man of his day'.

THE MIGHT-HAVE-BEEN. But is it well to write about Cust all
in one key? As I am trying to be straightforward about Astor's
temperament it is just that as honest a statement as possible should
be made about his editor. Margot Asquith speaks of him as 'a
faithful friend, fearless, reckless and unforgettable', but adds that
'someone who knew him well wrote truly, "He tossed off the cup
of life without fear of it containing any poison, but like many
wilful men he was deficient in will-power". With his youth, brains
and looks, he might have done anything in life, but he was fatally
self-indulgent.' 'He had the ball at his feet', an editor said to me.
Another view given me by a friend of Cust's was that 'he had energy
but not industry'; a third told me that 'he lost his seat in Parliament
because he neglected it'. A fourth, a well-known public man, a
member of the House of Lords, deplored what he called 'the falling

off in Cust's last years'. A fifth spoke of Cust as the most remarkable man he had ever met—and stopped. A sixth, with whom I had talked in past years about Cust, of whom he had close knowledge, wrote to me, 'Brains added to noble birth (with expectations) and personal beauty have their drawbacks. Cust was throughout his life consistently run after by women, and such was his temperament that they seldom had to run very far or very fast.' It has been said that you may recognise a woman's virtues without loving her. Conversely, the faults of a man may be recognised without his being disliked. The late Marquis of Crewe told me that he knew Cust 'very well and liked him very much'.

THE POEMS OF CUST AND HIS WIFE. The ashes of Cust were placed in a niche in an inner wall of the church at Belton; the memorial service at St. Margaret's, Westminster, was attended by, among other friends, the Duke and Duchess of Rutland, the Duchess of Marlborough, Lady Diana Manners, the Marquis of Crewe, the Marquis of Granby, Mr. Balfour and Mr. Asquith. The fine, appealing, recumbent marble figure in the church was the 'unceasing work' of Mrs. Cust, she once told me, during a period of seven years; in its original clay it had the place of honour at the Academy. It is the subject of the following lines, 'The Monument', in Mrs. Cust's moving book of poems, *Not all the Suns*:[1]

> In golden glory gleams and dreams
> The ancient silent place. . . .
> Gold from the glory fall the beams
> On an upturning face.
>
> On shuttered eyes the holy fire
> In stirless beauty stays. . . .
> O humble, O most glorious pyre,
> Lit by immortal rays.

In the copy of the book the author kindly gave me she has written the words of Lady Julian of Norwich: 'He said not, thou shalt not be tempested, thou shalt not be travailed, thou shalt not be afflicted; but he said thou shalt not be overcome.' There are other pieces in which the mind and heart of the poet are on her husband, 'One Voice, Yet must I wait', 'Enough, thou art dead', 'Till I Die', 'My Prayer', 'Awearied he is Resting', and, finally, 'A Thanksgiving':

> I who the watcher of your ways have been,
> I who the radiance of your days have seen,
>   Thank God.
>
> I who the fire of your mind have known,
> I who in the flame of your soul have grown,
>   Thank God.

[1] Nicholson & Watson, 1944.

PLASTER MODEL FOR THE MONUMENT OF CUST BY HIS WIFE, IN
BELTON CHURCH

I who to you owe each least thought,
I who by you am less than nought,
        Thank God.

I who in you found all life's stay,
I who for you lived all life's day,
        Thank God.

I who from you drew all life's light,
I who for you live through life's night,
        Thank God, Thank God.

Mrs. Cust's second book was *Echoes of a Larger Life*,[1] a selection from the correspondence of Victoria, Lady Welby, her mother, in which will be found letters from, among others, Max Müller, Frederic Myers, Professor Lloyd Morgan, Sir Francis Galton, Mrs. W. K. Clifford, Sir Oliver Lodge, Charles Voysey and the author of *John Inglesant*. Her first book was *Gentlemen Errant*, an account of the journeys and adventures of four noblemen during the fifteenth and sixteenth centuries, a scholarly work of 560 pages illustrated by maps.[2]

Nothing of Cust's is to be found in the Bodleian but there exists '*Suetonius, A History of Twelve Caesars*, translated into English by Philemon Holland, anno 1606, with an introduction by H. Cockayne Cust, 1898'. And in 1918 there was published in Jerusalem, when Sir Ronald Storrs was Governor, *Occasional Poems* by Henry Cust 'chosen by N.C. (Nina Cust) and R.S.' (Ronald Storrs). Owing to the circumstances of the book's production it is full of misprints, but the poems, most of which had appeared in the *Pall Mall*, exhibit the quality of the author. One poem was written at Eton, others while going round the world. 'Non Nobis Domine' is included anonymously in the *Oxford Book of Verse*. A few lines from this poem run:

        Not unto us, O Lord;
        To us Thou givest the scorn, the scourge, the scar,
        The ache of life, the loneliness of Death,
        The insufferable insufficiency of breath,
        And with Thy sword
        Thou piercest very far.

At the end of the book are these sentences of Cust's: 'Everywhere and every day there will be amongst the living the others of their generation—a fellowship of presences, some dim, some shining, but presences never to be wholly put away—plucking at their hearts, flooding sometimes their memories, seeming sometimes to touch their hands, masterful sometimes to govern and to save their souls. There will be a sort of national Golden Treasury, sacred and serene, into which men and women will enter at their need to find new faith, new courage, and unfathomed unexhausted consolation.'

[1] Cape, 1929.   [2] Murray, 1909.

CHAPTER XXXVII

'THE SOLITARY' AT HEVER CASTLE

THE PROPRIETOR WHO COULD NOT GET HIS WRITING PRINTED. Now of the man who felt that he had a well-founded grievance against Cust, the only editor I have heard of who had the temerity to return all his proprietor's manuscripts. It is impossible not to sympathise a little with Astor. To him what he wrote had merit, considerable merit, and in his view well deserved to be printed. In his proprietorship of the *Pall Mall* he was seeking not only social and political recognition but recognition as a writer. Mrs. Cust is sure that it was the steady rejection of his MSS. that had as much as anything to do with the dismissal of her husband and Iwan-Müller.

As a former member of the New York State legislature, Astor could use 'Hon.' and had had an agreeable time as American Minister in Italy for four years from 1882. He took out English naturalisation papers in 1899, became a Baron in 1916 and a Viscount the following year. The crest for the Astor arms is a falcon (not an American eagle) rising from a little green mound with three gold stars over its head. The falcon reappears as one of the charges on the shield, standing on a red-gloved right hand, cut off at the wrist. Above this are two fleur-de-lys. The present Lord Astor was a boy at school when his father and Cust parted, and he tells me that there is nothing in his father's papers about their relations, and neither he nor his sister remembers hearing anything. Similarly, Mr. J. E. Berridge, of the *Observer* in its early Astor period and now a director, while most obliging in several ways about the *Pall Mall*, can neither recall nor put his hand on anything of significance about its finances.

When the first Lord Astor ceased to be a citizen of the United States, London correspondents of the American papers felt at liberty to write freely about him. There was a tale in which Hever Castle figures as a 'Mystery House before which a formidable person, something between a gamekeeper and a family retainer parades to warn off intruders'. The account was headed 'Viscount Astor Goes into Seclusion. Former American bars all Callers'. A friend of mine who was acquainted with Hever Castle writes to me: 'Astor's desire for privacy caused considerable local comment. Hever Castle is so situated as to be invisible from any part of the highway, but this was not sufficient; lakes were dug and the earth turned into a hill, further obscuring a possible sight of it, and rings of fencing with barbed wire were erected for many miles to keep out possible intruders. A visitor to the Castle, even if duly authorised, was held up at the gatehouse and scrutinised through a peephole. If the appearance of the visitor satisfied the janitor he could then present his credentials which, if in order, enabled him to proceed, under escort, to the portcullis. I have been told that the portcullis was raised every evening, when all connection between the castle and the outside world ceased. All these things have now disappeared; the castle gates stand open.'[1]

Lewis Hind wrote in Astor's time[2]: 'Of the few who visit the purlieus of the Tudor village that Astor aimed to create around Hever Castle not five per cent knew that the tall Solitary, engrossed in reflections, indifferent to passers-by, very lonely, was Lord Astor. And perhaps not one per cent even knew that he was a man of letters—or would have been if he could. Writing was always his hobby. He always had some literary work on hand, usually stories, long and short. In his literary efforts his mind rolled back a few hundred or a few thousand years, and he produced literature garbed in what was known in the nineties as Wardour Street English. Lest his fellow-millionaires may think I am romancing, I cull from *Who's Who* a list of William Waldorf Astor's literary productions: *Valentino, a Story of Rome, Sforza, a Historical Romance of the Sixteenth Century in Italy, Pharaoh's Daughter and Other Stories.* Parts of the longer books I have read and some of the shorter stories. They do not carry me off my feet.'

It was said that Astor started the *Pall Mall Magazine* in order to get his own writing published and that the suggestion that he should found it for this purpose came from the contribution-afflicted Cust. If my memory serves me, there was a story by the proprietor in the first number. Lewis Hind relates that, in his capacity as editor of the monthly, he periodically paid 'a ceremonious visit' to his proprietor. The invitation was issued by Adams.

'A MILLIONAIRE'S TOY.' 'At the palatial and beautiful offices with due ceremony, handed on from grave factotum to grave factotum, the editor was conducted into the Presence, to be commended or

---

[1] In *Years of Endeavour* (Murray, 1942) by Sir George Leveson Gower, there is a letter he wrote from Cliveden in the Duke of Westminster's time in which he says: 'Cliveden was afterwards sold to Mr. W. Waldorf Astor, who proceeded to surround the whole property with a wall which gave rise to the joke that he was "Waldorf by name and walled-off by nature".' 'Not by nature, however,' one who knew him assured me.

[2] I have unfortunately not kept a note of which of Hind's thirty or more books contains this passage, *Napthali, Influences and Adventures while Earning a Living,* I think. (Bodley Head, 1926.)

chided, and to receive instructions.' Once, alarmed at the gigantic
nature of a journalistic scheme, Hind said to Astor: 'But that will
cost a vast deal of money, sir'. 'There was a pause; then I was
vouchsafed this answer, quite friendly, but scornful and final:
"Pray, sir, who pays the bill?" ' Which is a reminder of the lines
in a Gaiety piece, 'I spend a sum infernal, To support an evening
journal, But it's nothing to a mighty millionaire'. Mrs. Astor was
understood to be specially interested in the magazine, and although
when she died it was doing well, Astor said he could not bear to
run it after she had gone and summarily shut it down. Hind
concludes, 'If Lord Astor's books did not have the circulation of
Nat Gould's, at least he had the satisfaction of knowing that he
played a hand, dour, domineering and unprecedented in the
journalism of the nineties!'

The curious may turn up an amusing recital on the *Pall Mall*
by that witty after-dinner speaker and columnist, L. F. Austin,
in the *Speaker* of Feb. 15, 1896, entitled 'A Millionaire's Toy'. A
story that went the rounds was that in connexion with a dispute
over the possession of a visitors' book at Cliveden which contained
the autograph of Charles I, the *Pall Mall* was instructed to exclude
the name of the Duke of Westminster. The sub-editors found it
difficult to obey orders because the Duke's horses insisted on
winning races.

The best description we have of Astor is that by Higginbottom
in his *Vivid Life*:[1] 'For all his wealth he was a man of simple tastes.
As I sat awaiting an interview at Astor House one day I was
edified to see a stately butler bearing up to the study the great
man's luncheon. It consisted of one rosy apple and a glass of water.
In manner Mr. Astor was courteous, and he bore himself with an
old-fashioned dignity. There was nothing of the bustling American
and but the merest trace of an un-English pronunciation. He had
a quiet humour and a striking physiognomy, a high, square frontal
and rugged profile that denoted the determination and decision
that was his character. His second son, the Hon. J. J. Astor, is
very like him in appearance. He was never seen in the House of
Lords after the day on which he was introduced to a limited circle.
He died at the age of seventy-one, and only his family and a
few of those who had served him (of whom I was privileged to be
one) were present at the ceremony at St. George's, Hanover Square,
on Oct. 22, 1919.'

[1] Simpkin Marshall, 1934.

The Bearers at the Funeral

SIR DOUGLAS STRAIGHT, J. L. GARVIN, F. J. HIGGINBOTTOM AND DONALD M. SUTHERLAND[1]

CHAPTER XXXVIII

THE LAST NUMBER OF THE *PALL MALL GAZETTE*

SIR DOUGLAS STRAIGHT. Mrs. W. L. Courtney tells me that on the dismissal of Cust the editorship of the *Pall Mall Gazette* was offered to her husband. Mrs. Courtney, who had been Courtney's pupil at Oxford, was at the time of her marriage his reader on the *Fortnightly*. 'He declined the *Pall Mall*', she writes, 'because he had a family of seven and the *Daily Telegraph* offered a safer background and better pension prospects'. The editorship was then given to Sir Douglas Straight, who had been Lord Frederic Hamilton's colleague in charge of the *Pall Mall Magazine*. He satisfied Astor from 1896 to the spring of 1909. T. P. O'Connor tells us about Straight in two sentences in the *Daily Telegraph*: 'After a brilliant career at the Bar he had served as a Judge in India and was now back again in London, of which, with his lightheartedness, knowledge of the world in all its phases, a certain light cynicism and an eighteenth century hatred of all enthusiasms, he was a typical child. He conducted the paper on the lines which might have been expected from such a temperament; it was decorous, reasonable and also a little dull.' An illustrated sixteen-page article by the good Charles Morley in the *Pall Mall Magazine* has two portraits of Straight with his glossy top hat on the back of his head, his well-tailored, silk-lapelled, velvet-collared overcoat and his neatly rolled umbrella. There are also a dozen *Pall Mall* office interiors. Morley, writing in Straight's lifetime, feels that 'a soft heart was lurking under the smart coloured waistcoat of the man of many, many friends, the diner-out, the best of after-dinner speakers, the man who can cap story with story, the connoisseur of the *haute cuisine*, of the drama—ah! he has lived his life'. On Straight's character someone said he lived up to his name. In early days he had written children's stories for *Aunt Judy* at a few shillings apiece. He had also produced a drama, *The Fatal Brand*, at the old Grecian. A lively writer on the *Pall Mall*, J. P. Collins—he was

[1] With the editors after my time at the *P.M.G.* I must deal with more briefly.

once described to me as 'mighty witty but sound on his facts'—
said that on Straight's *Pall Mall* the correction of the revises of the
editorial page matter was 'done in common: one man read out
and the other followed proof in hand, like a class construing.
Then and not till then was the title of the leader decided.'

'THE BLENHEIM PUP.' A kind correspondent whose name I
regret to have mislaid informs me that the chief leader-writer of
the *Pall Mall* under Straight, Barnard, wrote a leader on one
of Winston Churchill's early Parliamentary exploits which was
headed 'The Blenheim Pup' and ended, 'The Blenheim pup must
be got rid of as he is dirty about the House'.

With the exception of *Old Pictures in a New Frame*, all Straight's
books one finds in the Bodleian bear the pseudonym 'Sidney Daryl'.
They begin with *Harrow Recollections* and include *Routledge's Handbook of Quoits and Bowls*.

'Straight', Sir Alfred Watson says, 'gave as little encouragement
to Astor's journalistic ambitions as we gave to Mond's on the
Westminster'.

F. J. HIGGINBOTTOM, 'UNDISTINGUISHED BUT WORKMANLIKE.'
Straight's successor was a good fellow I knew, an experienced
journeyman journalist and political correspondent, characterised
to me by a well-known editor as 'plodding and over-cautious',
F. J. Higginbottom. He had been on the *Pall Mall* when Cust
arrived, but Sir Douglas's 'old-fashioned Conservatism' led him
to the *Daily Chronicle* or *Morning Leader*, for which he did the Lobby
sketch. When Henry Leslie, owing to ill-health, retired from the
managership of the *Pall Mall* it was given to Higginbottom. He
was actually managing editor, for he wrote a good deal and took
charge during the absence of Straight. It was during the managing editorship of Higginbottom that the paper and its monthly,
the *Pall Mall Magazine*, which 'did not pay', moved on from
Charing Cross Road to still newer premises in Newton Street,
Holborn. The suggestion that he should become editor was made
to Astor by his business man, Adams. Higginbottom served from
the spring of 1909 to the end of 1911. A contemporary editor
said to me that his *Pall Mall* was 'undistinguished but workmanlike'. In Higginbottom's view, Astor's stories in the *Pall Mall
Magazine* were of 'outstanding merit', which may be one explanation
of why he got on with their author. But I do not know that he
printed anything of his in the *Gazette*.

It is of interest that, when Higginbottom became editor of the
Pall Mall, all its six previous editors were still alive. Frederick
Greenwood was a contributor under both Straight and Higginbottom, who was at his funeral. Higginbottom and a colleague
were indeed the only journalists in the small group which attended.

DONALD SUTHERLAND

SIR DOUGLAS STRAIGHT

F. J. HIGGINBOTTOM

The Last Three Editors of the *Pall Mall Gazette*

Higginbottom founded the London Press Exchange, and the admirable R. J. Sykes, who was associated with him, made it one of the leading advertising agencies in London. Sykes valued the *Countryman* and became one of my best friends in the advertising world.

Higginbottom relates[1] that, when he took the editorial chair of the *Pall Mall*, he called on John Morley and Stead. Morley said, 'Sincerity will always win you friends', Stead that 'You must not be afraid of mistakes; I never was'. The banker, Sir Horace Farquhar, wrote to him that, in view of the action of the paper in approving the payment of M.P.s, 'a policy neither gentlemanlike, honest or intelligent,' he had 'given orders that your paper shall never enter my house'! I once sat by Farquhar's side at dinner, and he was just that kind of man. When Higginbottom retired, on coming into a little money, I believe, Astor wrote that he had 'raised the prestige of the *Pall Mall* far above anything attained since Cust's time'.

THE WAYS OF 'THE GARVE'. One of Straight's associates had been a young man whom T. P. O'Connor described as 'a Newcastle-on-Tyne-cum-Irish journalist', J. L. Garvin. He brought to his editorship 'the Press experience which Straight lacked, something of the fervour, though of a different type than Stead's, and in short made it very readable'. Lord Astor tells me that his father bought the *Observer* from Northcliffe in order that Garvin, who was its editor, should also edit the *Pall Mall*.

Garvin was a labourer's son, and an account of his beginnings and of his Olympian performances in the *Observer* has been given in moving terms by his daughter.[2] I never met 'the Garve', as he was known in his family and in Fleet Street, but he was pleasingly appreciative of my *Countryman* which he bought and sent back to the office every year to be bound; '1000 congratulations on the *Countryman* and 1000 personal thanks for it' ran one of his notes. When he was still a boy he sent in letters to the *Eastern Morning News* of Hull which J. A. Spender printed. In the *Newcastle Chronicle* he became a proof-reader and a leader-writer. His reputation had been established in the North when he came to London. He spread himself in the *Daily Telegraph* before he gave himself his head in the *Observer*. He was not only one of the noteworthy editors of his time but one of its noteworthy talkers. Miss Garvin tells a story of Mr. Hugh Massingham's of her father standing in a restaurant, talking on one subject after another, 'blind to the hungry queue stretching out into the street'. As either his first or his second wife said, 'you could scrape off his faults with a penknife'. He was full of kindness.

[1] *The Vivid Life* (Simpkin Marshall, 1934).
[2] *J. L. Garvin*, Katharine Garvin (Heinemann, 1948).

A saying of his was, 'When you're bitter you're beat'. The two words he liked best were 'fortitude' and 'charity'.

Mrs. Courtney, in her *Making of an Editor*,[1] speaks of a discovery, within six months of her husband's accession to the editorship of the *Fortnightly Review*, 'which meant much to its success'. She found among proffered MSS. 'a surprisingly able article on "The Failure of Irish Politics" from the youthful Garvin in Newcastle-on-Tyne. My husband shared my enthusiasm and put the article at the head of the number, anonymously. It was widely quoted. Our contributor, in the twenties, wrote not only on home affairs but increasingly on European politics. He was always writing—what was there he couldn't write about? Pseudonyms had to be found for him, "Pollux", "Z", finally "Calchas", and some work appeared with no name at all, notably the chronique on "Foreign Affairs", contributed monthly for several years. He would write ten articles in six months.'

TWO EDITORS' TESTIMONIES. Garvin's home, Gregories in Buckinghamshire—there were books to the doors—had the associations of Burke's previous ownership. Mr. Wilson Harris once wrote in the *Spectator* of 'the life of the whole household centring round the *Observer* article, conceived on Tuesday, travailed with for three days and then despatched from Beaconsfield by Daimler or Rolls-Royce to Tudor Street, whence an office messenger duly brought the proof and waited for final corrections. Garvin installed a private line to the *Observer* and visited the office once a week only, for a Wednesday office-lunch, transacting all editorial business apart from that by telephone.'

A London editor is good enough to write to me: 'He was a journalist of the first order whom I admired and liked. Before he edited the *Pall Mall*, 1912–1915, he had controlled the *Observer* for four years under Northcliffe. He was then in the prime of his abounding strength. The weekly editorship, less arduous than it afterwards became, absorbed only a part of his energies. To the public he was known as a political writer of outstanding gifts. Journalists who worked with him in his *Pall Mall* days, before he was drawn into laborious tasks outside the world of newspapers, recognised that he was also a first-class editor, fertile in ideas, masterful, energising every part of the paper. Readers felt the new life that throbbed in its pages. But the range of its appeal was now too narrow. The vast new reading public gave its suffrages to a new type of evening paper that supplied more news, presented it in a lively form that made it entertainment as well as information, and filled columns every day with gossip that was "mainly about people". This was the road to the million circulation and it was

[1] Macmillan, 1930.

Gregories Beaconsfield (Bucks) 22/3/45

Dear Robertson Scott,

Alas, no! I never met Greenwood the Great. Just too late; for owing to my good resolve not to come to London until I was thirty, my arrival there was not until the end of 1899. Stead never talked about him to me. By that time he was more identified [?] the younger generation with the St. James's Gazette. But for 3½ years — 1912/5 — I sat on the Pall Mall Gazette in the very chair acquainted with Greenwood's & John Morley's trousers. How fine a subject he is for your portraiture. The Countryman is still tip-top. Best wishes

yours sincerely

J.L. Garvin

AUTOGRAPH OF J. L. GARVIN

Phrases from other letters of J. L. G.'s to me: 'Have no thought of retiring from grim cricket and hope for a second innings.' 'Sick, sick, sick to see the loss of character, moral depth and clear, intellectual resolution in politics and hardly know which party I most abhor. Green blessings on you.' 'How to do one's best taxes the soul.' 'There's no life without speaking out, and every human being is the better for raising a breeze.' 'How to enhance life infinitely more?'

not travelled by Garvin. But students of the history of the three years during which he directed it will find the *Pall Mall* of that period eminently worthy of their attention. As an editor Garvin disabled himself for many years by his acceptance of work which was enough for any man—the editorship of the *Encyclopaedia Britannica* for example. Later he wrote three volumes of the life of Joseph Chamberlain, leaving it unfinished. These other interests left the *Observer* with little attention, apart from his leader page article.'

The speeches at the dinner given to Garvin on the twenty-first anniversary of his coming to Fleet Street—Sir Evelyn Wrench presided—showed the appreciation in which he was held by London journalism.

STEAD'S 'APOSTOLIC SUCCESSOR.' I am indebted to Mr. Gordon Brett for some recollections of Garvin at the *Pall Mall*. On his table he had a large batch of well-sharpened pencils and wrote rapidly. His proofs were pulled on specially wide paper so that he could embroider freely. He had a constant interest in increasing the circulation of the paper, and would write many of the contents bills himself—one on Turkey's doings was 'The Turkey Trot'; a stock one which Newnes had used for *Tit-Bits*, was 'Everyone's Reading It'. By his reluctance to part with his proofs, however, he would miss trains. At the *Observer* Mrs. Garvin would 'phone, 'Send him home'.

I have it from Mr. J. E. Berridge, director and manager of the *Observer*, that Garvin raised its circulation from about 4,000 to over 240,000.

Before the end, however, a friend writes, 'he had divided the readers of the paper into two sets, one, the larger, welcoming all he gave them and the other disliking his loquacity and dogmatism. I often thought that his best writing was in some of his reviews. It was sad that his career ended as it did, in a mutual loss of confidence between proprietor and editor. But the most tolerant of proprietors could hardly be content with an editor who did so little editing.'

I must record the fact that Garvin once wrote to me: 'Stead called on me twice at the *Pall Mall*—the last time just before he sailed on the *Titanic*—and each time to say that I ought to be his "apostolic successor".'

Garvin's *Pall Mall* had one amusing experience. A former colleague of mine, the late W. L. Randell, wrote a sketch a character in which was called George Flanders. One would have thought it a safe enough invention. But it was not, for a George Flanders started an action on the ground that he had been 'injured in his credit and reputation, and brought into public odium and contempt'. Randell, needless to say, had never heard of this Flanders

'THE GARVE'

From the cartoon by Low

There is a cartoon, by Ritchie, of J. L. Garvin with a dozen half-smoked cigars on his floor

and the plaintiff admitted in cross-examination by F. E. Smith that he had no reason to believe that he had. The jury found for the *Pall Mall*, with costs for a special jury.

Garvin's last writing was in his old paper, the *Daily Telegraph*.

On the retirement of Garvin from the *Observer* Mr. Ivor Brown, so well known for his able *Words* books, became acting editor. He continued until David Astor, Lord Astor's second son, who has a special interest in overseas affairs, assumed the position. Ivor Brown remained as associate editor and is still with the paper in that capacity. In 1945 Lord Astor and David Astor agreed to create the *Observer* Trust.

LATER PROPRIETORSHIPS OF THE PALL MALL. When the *Pall Mall* was under the editorship of F. J. Higginbottom the paper had been given by Astor to his son, the present Lord Astor.[1] But the time came when the recipient was unwilling, he tells me, to 'go on indefinitely making a very heavy loss'. So he sold it (August 20, 1915), and 'got very little for it'. The purchaser was Sir Davison Dalzell, chairman of the Pullman Car Company, who, if my memory serves me, first introduced motor cabs into London. He disposed of the paper to a man of nearly the same name, Henry James Dalziel, of Dalziel's News Agency, one of Lloyd George's henchmen who became director, chairman and managing director of United Newspapers, proprietors of the *Daily Chronicle* and *Lloyd's*, an M.P. and a peer.[2] He got the paper, it has been asserted, for £10,000, and formed a £20,000 company in which the Dewar family took a share.

The *Pall Mall* under Dalzell or Dalziel had absorbed the *Globe*,[3] and was bought in 1921 by Sir John Leigh, a wealthy cotton trader. T. P. O'Connor speaks of the paper under the Leigh régime as 'independent, even aggressively so'. A statement made

[1] The *Observer* was also given to Lord Astor by his father.

[2] There is a spirited account of him by R. C. K. Ensor in the *Dictionary of National Biography*.

[3] The *Globe* had been bought from Sir Robert Donald, editor of the *Daily Chronicle*. He had started with Frank Lloyd an evening *Echo*, with the sub-title of the *London Evening Chronicle*, only ten years after the decease of Passmore Edwards's *Echo* (1868–1905). This second *Echo* began without advertisements, the idea being that the novelty, with a superabundance of space for news, would give it an advantage over its rivals. Besides, the *Echo* was a good name for the street-sellers. In six weeks, however, it was amalgamated with the *Star*. Mr. H. A. Taylor in his life of Donald (Stanley Paul) puts the loss at between £60,000 and £100,000. Another figure of interest in the book is the 32.7 per cent dividend of the *Daily Chronicle* and *Lloyds* early in the first Great War. After Donald left the *Chronicle* he bought the Conservative *Globe*, founded in 1803, which had the distinction in 1915 of being suspended for a fortnight under the censorship regulations. The price paid was £40,000 and Frank Dilnot was appointed editor (1919). Donald's notion was to execute a political curve to independency. The paper eventually came under the control of Hatry, the financier, and in February 1921 was absorbed in the *Pall Mall*. Donald, whom I knew well, was an able, canny, kindly fellow, a big man with an insistent and not wholly pleasant voice.

to me is that the paper was 'a constant drain on Sir John Leigh's
resources'—Bernard Falk asserts in his *Five Years Dead* that
£100,000 was sunk in it. At any rate, on October 25, 1920, it was
announced by the Press Association that 'Sir John Leigh has
amalgamated his interest in the *Pall Mall Gazette* with the *Evening
Standard* and will join the reorganised Board'. The leading proprietor
of the *Evening Standard* at that time was Lord Beaverbrook. For a
period the subsidiary title line was 'with which is incorporated the
Pall Mall Gazette' alone. Then it was

WITH WHICH IS INCORPORATED   THE PALL MALL GAZETTE & GLOBE.

No. 30,966.   LONDON, MONDAY, OCTOBER 29, 1923.   ONE PENNY.

THE LAST OF THE *PALL MALL GAZETTE*

'THIS GRAND OLD PAPER'S' LAST EDITOR. The *Pall Mall
Gazette* had existed for fifty-eight years, but its make-up had been
completely altered from the original form. Its last editor (1915–
1923) was Donald M. Sutherland, who died last December. His
name was David. A Scot from the far north, who had completed
half his course at Edinburgh University, he had a rough start in
London and made his way slowly. The kindly S. K. Ratcliffe (who
in journalism, as Sir Norman Angell has just acknowledged, 'has
always had real distinction') was of service to him, and ultimately
Sutherland became editor of the *Sheffield Telegraph*. Patrick Bray-
brooke asserts him to have been, as editor of the *Pall Mall Gazette*, 'a
brilliant journalist with a calm dispassionate outlook and a power of
making right judgments'. (He was for a time Secretary of the Anti-
Socialist Union.) The Marchioness Townshend tells me that she contributed several articles. Mr. Willson Disher quoted Sutherland in
The Times as saying, 'If I were a wealthy man I would finance this
grand old paper no matter what it cost'. In a farewell leading article
he said of the *P.M.G.*: 'It has a standard of ability, brilliancy and
sound professional technique which has deeply influenced the development of modern newspapers, and some tribute of remembrance
and respect is due from the London public to a famous tradition and
an old friend of their youth. It has been conducted by journalists who
were also statesmen. It always refused to take refuge in cant from
the ordeals of clear thinking and frank expression. It has applied,
by example, a wholesome stimulus to the whole body of the English
Press. Of its line of great editors it can truly be said that they were

the real leaders of their profession, and there is no publication in the country which does not bear in some degree the stamp of their influence.' A special tribute was paid to Stead, 'Nothing was too great or too trivial for his attention'.

Unfortunately at this point in the article the managerial side of the property seems to have got to work on the proof and the article went on: 'Readers have been spellbound by features which appeared in no other journal. The incorporation will perpetuate these fine features and add to them too.' As for the *Evening Standard* with which the *Pall Mall* was amalgamating, it had 'pursued a career which has dazzled the public. A newspaper development of such magnitude as the amalgamation has not been known.'

Happily, Frederick Greenwood was not alive to be distressed. Harold Gale, sporting editor of the *Observer*, worked with Sutherland to the last and relates that at a farewell dinner the staff burnt a copy of the final number, 'whether', as J. E. Berridge, the present manager of the *Observer* writes to me, 'to express their regret, indignation or relief does not appear'. Anyhow, they took away the ashes in pillboxes. On hearing about it Morley would have had the right classical quotation and Stead a biblical one, Cook would have said 'Um', Cust would have laughed, and Garvin—no, I cannot imagine what his ejaculation would have been.

YEARS OF SERVICE OF

EDITORS OF THE *PALL MALL GAZETTE*

John Morley, 1880–1883	*Sir Douglas Straight, 1896–1909*
W. T. Stead, 1883–1890	*F. J. Higginbottom, 1909–1911*
E. T. Cook, 1890–1892	*J. L. Garvin, 1911–1915*
H. C. Cust, 1892–1896	*D. M. Sutherland, 1915–1923*

INDEX